VISUAL LITERACY
A Spectrum of Visual Learning

VISUAL LITERACY

A Spectrum of Visual Learning

David M. (Mike) Moore
Virginia Polytechnic Institute and State University

Francis M. Dwyer
The Pennsylvania State University

EDITORS

Educational Technology Publications
Englewood Cliffs, New Jersey 07632

Library of Congress Cataloging-in-Publication Data

Visual literacy : a spectrum of visual learning / David M. (Mike)
Moore, Francis M. Dwyer, editors.
   p.   cm.
Includes bibliographical references (p.) and index.
ISBN 0-87778-264-4
  1. Visual literacy.   2. Visual education.   I. Moore, David M.
(David Mike) II. Dwyer, Francis M.
LB1068.V57 1994
370.15'23--dc20   93-2437
                                              CIP

Printed in the United States of America.

Library of Congress Catalog Card Number:
93-2437.

International Standard Book Number:
0-87778-264-4.

First Printing: January, 1994.

To Arline and Carol

Acknowledgments

We appreciate the generous assistance of the members of the International Visual Literacy Association who made suggestions concerning the content and scope of this book. We are grateful to the contributors for their carefully written manuscripts and the positive manner in which they accepted the editors' comments and suggestions. The editors also appreciate the many hours of assistance by Laurie Ruberg, Bob Myers, Jamie Little, Tom Hergert, Terry Stevers, and Kelly Kerns along with others who made valuable suggestions and gave encouragement.

Preface

The study of visuals is a broad and complex mixture of many disciplines, interests, and functions. Scholars interested in the way visuals transmit information, emotion, and data are not limited to any one discipline because of the universal nature of images. These scholars include professionals from many disciplines such as education, medicine, advertising, business, industry, and art. Producers of visual media such as books, computers, film, and television are also involved in visual learning.

By the very nature of this diverse subject, there is necessarily a wide variety of interests and perspectives on the topic. Therefore this will be a book with many perspectives. Realizing that all topics related to the use of visuals can not be presented in one collection, the editors attempted to include a cross-section of topics dealing with the visual medium. To initiate the process of selection, the editors contacted professors and instructors across the country who teach, or have taught, courses dealing with the design, development, and implementation of visualization to facilitate effective communication. Their recommendations and syllabi were studied to determine what this book should address. Fortunately, many of these scholars belong to a professional organization focused on visual communicating and learning—the *International Visual Literacy Association* (IVLA). The goals of IVLA are:

- to provide a multidisciplinary forum for exploration, presentation, and discussion of visual communication;
- to serve as an organizational base and communications bond for professionals interested in visual "literacy"; and
- to promote and evaluate projects intended to increase the use of visuals in education and communication.

Early contacts with scholars interested in the use of visuals in communication helped to determine that there was a need for a college level book that can be used in teaching a course on visual learning/literacy/communication. Although there are many similar courses now being taught in many colleges and universities, those who teach such courses agreed that there was not a book available that could serve as a primary source for the wide variety of the course content. Since visual learning is a broad, complex discipline, courses in visual learning have a variety of titles including visual learning, visual communication, and visual literacy. Thus, the topics included in this book were by agreement of scholars within the area for the specific purpose of providing the most relevant content for those teaching a visual learning course. Once the topics were selected, scholars were solicited to write about the topics in which they had the most knowledge and experience.

What is visual literacy? As this book will illustrate, there are many definitions and interpretations. *Visual literacy* as defined by the International Visual Literacy Association is "a group of vision competencies a human being can develop by seeing and at the same time having and integrating other sensory experiences. The development of these competencies is fundamental to normal human learning. When developed, they enable a visually literate person to discriminate and interpret the visual actions, objects, and/or symbols, natural or man-made, that are [encountered] in [the] environment. Through the creative use of these competencies, [we are] able to communicate with others. Through the appreciative use of these competencies, [we are] able to comprehend and enjoy the masterworks of visual communications" (Fransecky & Debes, 1972, p. 7). This particular definition identifies the thrust of this book. However, the reader will note that the authors of chapters in this collection use the term visual literacy, visual learning, and visual communication interchangeably.

While the primary purpose of this collection of topics is to serve as a textbook for visual learning courses, its appeal is much broader and includes all who have interest in and seek knowledge about the visual communication process. Some of the writings overlap others. However, since these concepts are presented from different points of view, the duplication reinforces the importance and extent of these ideas. Following is a brief synopsis of each section in the volume:

Section I. Perceptual, Historical, and Theoretical Foundations of Visual Learning.

The chapters in this section deal with the various foundational concepts of visual literacy, such as: perceptual theory, communication models, physiological aspects, imagery and memory, and historical development.

Section II. Visual Language.

This section deals with the definitions of visual literacy, perceptual aesthetics, and visual language.

Section III. Nonverbal Communication.

Section III focuses on the use of symbols in communication, action (body) language, and object language.

Section IV. Visual Design.

Graphics, design considerations for visuals, visual/verbal relationships, and the use of visuals on computers are discussed in this section.

Section V. Use of Visuals.

This section deals with the use of visuals in business, industry, and schools. Emphasis is also placed on using visualization to instigate creativity.

Section VI. Cultural, Social, Political, and Technological Aspects of Visuals.

Deconstruction, cultural and technological coding, mass media, semiotics, and poststructural thought and concepts are discussed this section.

Section VII. Ethical Considerations.

Moral and ethical issues as they relate to the use of visuals and films are reviewed in this section.

Section VIII. Use of Visuals and Research Implications.

This section presents a brief review of prior visual research, describes a model for systematic visual research, and summarizes relevant research findings.

Reference

Fransecky, R. B., & Debes, J. L. (1972). *Visual literacy: A way to learn—A way to teach*. Washington, DC: Association for Educational Communications and Technology.

TABLE OF CONTENTS

Preface ix

Section I: **Perceptual, Historical, and Theoretical Foundations of Visual Learning** 3

Chapter One 5

Theoretical Foundations of Visual Learning   John A. Hortin

Objectives

Debes and The Rochester School

A Confluence of Thought
    Linguistics
    Art
    Psychology
    Philosophy

Theoretical Foundations

Summary

References

Chapter Two 31

Perception and Its Role in Communication and Learning
Richard C. Stern and Rhonda S. Robinson

Objectives

Introduction

What Is Perception?
    Definition
    Differences in Perception

Stages of Perception
    Frames of Reference
        Characteristics
        Personal Assessment
    Selection Factors
        Physiological Factors
        Psychological Factors
        Past Experience
        Present Feelings
    Organizing Data
        Simplicity and Patterns
        Proximity
        Similarity
        Figure and Background
        Closure and Good Form
        Perceptual Constancy
    Interpreting Information
        Beliefs, Values, and Attitudes
        Recency–Primacy
        Present Feelings and Expectations
        Interaction of Stages

Self-Concept
    Formation of Self-Concept
        Self-Appraisal
        Reactions and Responses
        Roles
        Impact of Roles

Functions of Self-Concept
    Self-Concept Filters
    Self-Concept as a Predictor
        Self-Fulfilling Prophesy
    Self-Concept as Influence on Style
        Nonverbal Communication and Self-Concept

References

Chapter Three 53

Physiological and Cognitive Factors in the Study of Visual Images
Nikos Metallinos

Objectives

Introduction

Anatomy of the Human Information System
    Neurophysiciological Factors of the Eyes, Ears, and Brain
    Basic Anatomy of the Eyes
    Basic Anatomy of the Ear
    Basic Anatomy of the Brain's Visual and Auditory Centers
    Stimuli and the Perceptual Process

Visual Stimulation

Auditory Stimulation

Threefold Process of Stimulation

Model of Reception/Cognition

References

Chapter Four 65

Images and Imagery Theory   Helen B. Miller and John K.
Burton

Objectives

History

Cognitive Overview
    Development of the Cognitive System

Visual Cognition
    The Controversy Over Imaginal Storage
    Dual Coding

Potential Research Variables
    Developmental
    Detail of Visuals and Experience
    Visual Schema and "Priming"

The Problem with Images

References

Chapter Five 85

Communication Models Forrest G. Wisely

    Objectives

    Definition of Communication

    Development of Communication Studies

    Functions of Models

    Communication Models
        Laswell's Model
        Shannon and Weaver's Model
        Schramm's Models
        Berlo's Model

    Elements of Communication

    References

Section II: **Visual Language** 95

Chapter Six 97

Visual Literacy: The Definition Problem Barbara A. Seels

    Objectives

    Visual Literacy as a Concept
        Evolution of the Concept "Literacy"
        Need for Visual Literacy

    Visual Literacy as a Construct
        Visual/Visible Language
        Concept or Construct

    Visual Literacy, Thinking, Learning, and Communication
        Visual Literacy
        Relationship Between Constructs
        Visual Thinking
        Visual Learning
        Visual Communication

    Summary

Glossary

References

Chapter Seven 113

Perceptual Aesthetics and Visual Language
Ann Marie Seward Barry

Objectives

Introduction

Perceptual Aesthetics
  Aesthetics and the Search for the Constant

Gestalt Isomorphism..
  The Aesthetic of T.S. Eliot

Gestalt Principles
  Gestalt Perceptual Simplicity
    Shape, Omission, Closure
  Gestalt Perceptual Regularity
    Cohesion, Segregation, Figure, and Ground
  Gestalt Perceptual Symmetry
    Closure, Good Continuation, and Unity

Perceptual Aesthetics and Analysis
  Poe and the Limits of Mathematical Reasoning

Perceptual Aesthetics and Visual Art
  Cézanne, Hemingway, and the Aesthetic of Icebergs

Perceptual Aesthetics and Film
  Renais, Eisenstein, and Montage

Conclusion

References

Section III: **Nonverbal Communication** 133

Chapter Eight 135

Visual Symbols Edward H. Sewell, Jr.

Objectives

Introduction

Approaches to the Study of Symbols

Symbols as Communication

Symbols as Knowledge

Symbols as Expression

Symbols as Control

Symbols in Political Cartoons

Conclusions

References

Chapter Nine 145

Action and Object Language   David M. (Mike) Moore

Objectives

Introduction

Action (body) Language
    Reflexive Actions
    Conventional Signals
    Appearance
    Physical Attributes
    Gestures
    Roles
    Groups
    Space

Object Language
    Utility
    Command
    Objects as Symbols

Summary

Notes

References

Section IV: **Visual Design** 163

Chapter Ten 165

Design Considerations of Visuals Merton E. Thompson

   Objectives

   Introduction

   Design Elements
      Point
      Line
      Shape
      Form
      Space
      Texture
      Light
      Color
      Motion

   Design Principles
      Simplicity
      Clarity
      Balance
      Harmony
      Organization
      Emphasis
      Legibility
      Unity
      Perspective
      Point of View
      Framing

   Conclusion

   References

Chapter Eleven 183

Graphics and How They Communicate Ann C. Saunders

   Objectives

   Introduction

Graphics (Graphic Designs) as Represented Through Print
and Electronic Media
        Definitions

    How Graphics Function as Communication Tools

    Graphics as a Form of Visual Communication

    How We Communicate Through Graphics

    Conclusion

    References

Chapter Twelve 193

Visual Verbal Relationships   Roberts A. Braden

    Objectives

    Introduction

    Terms

    Types of Visuals

    Degree of Realism

    Degree of Visualization vs. Degree of Verbalization

    Wileman's Typology

    The Roles of the Visual in Text

    Graphics

    Visually Dominated Graphics

    Verbally Dominated Graphics

    The Printed Word

    Outline Graphics

    Conclusion

    References

Chapter Thirteen 209

Computers and Visual Learning Nancy Nelson Knupfer

    Objectives

    Introduction

    Structure of the Image
        The Image
        Screen Design

    Meaning of the Image
        Learning from the Image
        Computer Creation of Data Displays

    Power of the Image
        Realistic Data Display
        Tapping the Imagination with Artificial Reality

    Summary

    References

Section V: **Use of Visuals** 233

Chapter Fourteen 235

Use of Visuals in Schools (Curriculum and Instruction)
Barbara W. Fredette

    Objectives

    Introduction

    The Visual Environment of Schools

    The Visual Environment of Students

    Use of Visuals in Schools
        WHAT Types of Visual Media to Use
        WHEN to Use Visual Concept Acquisition
        WHY Use Visuals
        WAYS to Use Visuals
        WHO Will Use the Visuals
    Preference for Visuals
        WHERE to Use Visuals

A Systematic Approach to Reading Pictures
    Visuals as Objects vs. Visuals as Tools
    Background

Description of the Levels of the Systematic Approach to
'Reading Pictures'
    First Two Levels: Description and Analysis of Form
    Bottom Levels: Creative and Critical Interpretation

References

Chapter Fifteen 257

Use of Visuals: Business and Industry Robert E. Griffin

    Objectives

    Introduction

    How Important Are Visuals to Business Presentations?

    What Are the Most Common Types of Business Visuals?

    What Purpose Do Visuals Serve in the Presentation?

    What Are Computer Generated Business Graphics?

    How Do Business People Learn to Use Visuals?

    What Does the Future Hold?

    References

Chapter Sixteen 277

*Making Meaning From Visuals: Creative Thinking and
Interpretation of Visual Information* Richard A. Couch,
Edward J. Caropreso with Helen B. Miller

    Objectives

    Visual Media: The Common Denominator

    Decoding Visuals: Differentiation and Interpretation

    What Is Creativity ?

Two Models of Creative Thinking

Can Creative Thinking Be Taught?

What Can We Do to Enhance Creative Thinking?

Creative Visual Consumers

References

Section VI: **Cultural, Social, Political , and Technological Aspects of Visuals** 293

Chapter Seventeen 295

Representations: You, Me, and Them   Robert Muffoletto

Objectives

Introduction

Ideology and Discourse

Photographs as Ideological Representations

Producer, Text, and Reader

Codes and Meanings

Representations

Semiotics as a Model for Understanding Communication

Intertextuality

Postsemiotics

Summary

End Notes

References

Chapter Eighteen 311

Deconstruction and Visuals: Is This a ~~Telephone~~?   Andrew R. J.
Yeaman

    Objectives

    Introduction: Deconstruction in Perspective

    Thinking Otherwise: Critical Theory and Deconstruction

    The Department of Postmodern Languages

    Theory

    More Theory

    Deconstructing Communication as a Telephone Conversation

    A Deconstruction of Communication

    Postmodern Resistance *with* Media

    Memoirs of an *ERIC Digest*

    At What Temperature Do Computers Catch Fire?

    Memoirs of The *Post Post News*

    The *Post Post News*

    Deconstructing the Dominant Narrative

    Postpedagogy

    Between the Posts

    Resistance

    Postscript and Signature

    Exercises

    References

Chapter Nineteen 337

Cultural and Technological Coding of Mass Media Images
Gretchen Bisplinghoff

    Objectives

    Introduction

    Media Communication Model
        Structures Exist in Each Part of the System

    Encoding and Decoding

    Physical Factors and Processes

    Cultural Conditioning
        Western Perspective
        Cultural Pre- existence

    Media Selectivity
        Cultural Bias
        Social Context

    Cultural Coding Levels
        Historical Reference Codes
        Semic and Symbolic Codes

    Structural Coding
        Invisibility
        Continuity of Space
        Visual Time Cues
        Verisimilitude

    Technical Coding
        Composition
        Camera Shots

    References

Section VII: **Ethical Considerations** 353

Chapter Twenty 355

*Ethical Considerations of Visuals in the Classroom: African-
Americans and Hollywood Film* Ann DeVaney

Objectives

Introduction

Purpose: Non Stereotypic Images

Audience

Assumptions: Images as Teachers

Method: Inverting the Critical Model

Textual Analysis and African-American Narrative

The Limitations of Popular Culture

African-American Hollywood Films of the 1990's

Interpreting Film Characters

The Camera Lies

Clues from African Literature
      Opposition
      Humor

Black English

The Role of the Black Male

Summary

References

Chapter Twenty-One 369

Considering Morals and Visuals (Beyond School)   Randall G.
Nichols

Objectives

Why Ethics and Visuals

Media, Morals, and Ethics

Content and Purposes of Visuals
Visual Content
Visual Purposes

Ethical Traditions
How Ought We Live?
Western Theoretic Traditions

Additional Views of Good Living, Good Visuals
Objections and Irresoluteness

A Critical Sense?

A Case in Point: Television and Children

So What Are You Going to Do?

References

Section VIII: **Use of Visuals and Research Implications** 381

Chapter Twenty-Two 383

*One Dimension of Visual Research: A Paradigm and Its
Implementation* Francis M. Dwyer

Objectives

Introduction

Visualization as Rehearsal

Popularity of Visualization

An Experimental Rationale for Visual Research

Visual Testing

Instructional Consistency/Congruency

The Program of Systematic Evaluation (PSE)

Program of Systematic Evaluation—Phase 1

Program of Systematic Evaluation—Phase 2

Program of Systematic Evaluation—Phase 3

Future Research Recommendations

References

Epilogue 403

About the Contributors 405

Author Index 409

Subject Index 417

VISUAL LITERACY
A Spectrum of Visual Learning

SECTION I

Perceptual, Historical, and Theoretical Foundations of Visual Learning

Visual literacy is a concept that has many foundational roots. To fully appreciate this concept it is necessary to examine its roots from their historical beginnings. Visual literacy has developed from ideas borrowed from philosophy, art, linguistics, perceptual psychology, imagery theory, and, of course, communication research. All of these areas have influenced and contributed to the development of the "visual literacy" concept. The purpose of this section is to provide the reader an overview of the principles and eclectic nature of this diverse concept.

There are many different interpretations of the meaning of "visual literacy." Using philosophy, art, and linguistics as the theoretical foundations of visual literacy, John Hortin proposes a definition of visual literacy as "... the ability to understand (read) and use (write) images and to think and learn in terms of images." In developing his perspective, he reviews and interprets relevant literature from a number of different disciplines that provides a valuable resource for further inquiry. His chapter ends with an interesting statement: "Visual literacy is really training for visual thinking."

Perception, being an integral component of visual literacy, is a complex and ongoing process that influences the related activities of communication and learning. Perception consists of several basic steps: selection, organization, and interpretation of data. These stages are, in turn, affected by other factors, including the perceiver's frame of reference.

While this process may seem complex enough, a person's self-concept also has a significant impact on the process of perception. Although perception has an effect on the one who perceives, the perceiver also influences the process of perception. Because an individual cannot possibly attend to all the data present in a given situation, a filtering process takes place. Consequently, an individual's prior experience, which subsequently influences the nature of the filtering process, is a critical dimension in developing competency in understanding visual literacy.

Richard Stern and Rhonda Robinson develop the position that perception is a complicated, dynamic process which can be improved by developing an accurate assessment of one's own self-concept and by possessing a willingness to change and improve.

The organs of visual and auditory perception, the eyes, the ears, and the brain, constitute a complex information system. This network of stations receives selected signals from the environment either electromagnetically or mechanically, transforms them into organized bits of information or codes, and channels them by electrical impulses to the brain. These codes are then processed by the brain, where they are decoded, translated, recognized, and assume their proper meaning. Nikos Metallinos in this section provides an overview of (1) the neurophysiological factors of the information centers—the eyes, the ears, and brain, (2) the threefold perceptual process, and (3) the codification of visual and auditory information. Metallinos concludes by suggesting that the bases for visual learning depend on understanding the complex functions of the human information organs in transforming visual and auditory signals into cognitive, cohesive, and meaningful visual messages.

Helen Miller and John Burton in their chapter on imagery and imagery theory point out that reality is constructed from what we see, which is based upon our experience and background. These notions of imagery are the basis of the cognitivist position on the interpretation of visuals. As the authors trace the current views, they provide an overview of how the human memory system works. Using the information-processing approach, which focuses on how we acquire, encode, retrieve, and use information, Miller and Burton discuss the concept and role of the sensory register as it relates to short-term and long-term memory.

To answer the question, does visual information function differently than verbal information in processing, Miller and Burton present two basic positions concerning imagery and propositions. The pro-image and anti-image positions are discussed, including the distinctions between the codes used for visual and verbal information. The dual-code theories of Paivio and others are also discussed.

Forrest Wisely identifies the elements of the visual communication process from a number of different perspectives. Several communication models are presented to show the interrelatedness of the elements and to illustrate our increasing awareness of the complexity of the communication process. He contends that one generality that may be derived from most communication models is that for communication to be successful, messages must be carefully designed, developed, and transmitted to the intended learners.

Chapter One

Theoretical Foundations of Visual Learning

John A. Hortin

Objectives

After reading this chapter, you should be able to:

1. *Discuss the evolution of the concept of visual literacy.*

2. *Define visual literacy.*

3. *Discuss the model of theoretical foundations which has contributed to our knowledge and understanding of visual literacy.*

4. *Identify several authors/resources whose work has enhanced the field of visual literacy.*

5. *Summarize Turbayne's theory of metaphor.*

6. *Discuss the differences/similarities between verbal and visual language.*

Debes and The Rochester School

Images in our world today cannot be overstated. We are influenced, taught, and manipulated by all kinds of visual information including television, computers, signs, and symbols, advertisements, body language, and motion picture films. The process by which we receive and transmit visual meaning is a major concern in the study of visual literacy. Visual literacy "is based on the confluence of knowledge, theory, and technology in many areas" (Debes, 1968, p. 963). A few pioneers who have influenced thinking about the concept of visual literacy include John Debes, Clarence Williams, Colin Murray Turbayne, Rudolf Arnheim, and Robert McKim. The *Eastman Kodak Company* has also played a role. Researchers on the left- and right-brain hemispheres and perception theory as well as artists and educators have been important in the visual literacy field. Debes coined the term visual literacy (Fransecky & Debes, 1972) and along with Clarence Williams helped found the International Visual Literacy Association. The "Rochester School" of John L. Debes, Clarence Williams, and Colin Murray Turbayne molded the development of theoretical foundations of visual literacy (Hortin, 1980).

A Confluence of Thought

Jonassen and Fork (1975) wrote that "Visual literacy is eclectic in origin" (p. 7). It developed from a confluence of theories of many disciplines that include linguistics, art, psychology, and philosophy.

Linguistics

Charles Carpenter Fries (1952) in his book, *The Structure of English*, presented some new ideas "about how the English language accomplishes its communicative function—about the mechanism of utterances" (p. 7). Traditional grammarians analyzed sentences by knowing the meaning of the utterance before beginning any analysis (Fries, 1952, p. 54). Fries (1952) wrote about beginning with a preconceived meaning in grammatical analysis, "It is this kind of grammatical analysis, this starting with the total meaning, and the using of this meaning as the basis for the analysis—an analysis that makes no advance beyond the ascribing of certain technical terms to parts of the meaning already known—it is this kind of grammatical analysis that modern linguistic science discards as belonging to a prescientific era" (p. 55). Fries (1952) provided the alternative of starting with a description of the elements and structure of an utterance and arriving at meaning only after the analysis (pp. 56–57). Fries (1952) said, "The total linguistic meaning of any utterance consists of the lexical meanings of the separate words plus structural meanings" (p. 56). Fries (1952) showed that words could serve multiple roles depending on their placement in an utterance and the intent of the writer. The focus on the intent of the sender of the message is similar to Wendt's (1962) often quoted statement, "But the basic error to fail to realize that the meanings of pictures are not in the pictures, but rather in what we bring to them" (p. 183).

According to Barley (1971), Fries (1952) paved the way for analyzing meaning in verbal language. Researchers interested in visual literacy applied Fries' theory on verbal language to visual language, claiming that one could find meaning in visual language through the study of visual composition, syntax, and elements. Fries (1952) said, "One cannot speak or understand a language without 'knowing' its grammar" (p. 57). Researchers in visual literacy said that the same principle held true for visual language. Although Dondis (1973) differentiated between visual and verbal language, she also said, "we create a design out of many colors and shapes and textures and tones and relative proportions; we relate these elements interactively, we intend meaning" (p. 20). However, Dondis (1973) was careful to point out that linear structure of verbal language differs from that of visual language:

One thing is certain. Visual literacy cannot ever be a clearcut logical system similar to language. Languages are made-up systems constructed by man to encode, store, and decode information. Therefore, their structure has a logic that visual literacy is unable to parallel. (p. 12)

Noam Chomsky (1957, 1964, 1968, 1975), a transformational grammarian at M.I.T., also contributed to visual literacy theory. In his book, *Language and Mind*, Chomsky (1968) said that in all men there are certain "innate structures" of mind. He drew upon psychology, philosophy, and linguistics to support the view that there is a "universal grammar." Chomsky (1968) wrote:

The principles that determine the form of grammar and that select a grammar of the appropriate form on the basis of certain data constitute a subject that might, following a traditional usage, be termed 'universal grammar.' The study of universal grammar, so understood, is a study of the nature of human intellectual capacities. (p. 27)

Gozemba (1975) provided an explanation as to how visual literacy researchers used Chomsky's ideas to build a case for visual literacy.
Gozemba (1975) said:

Following Chomsky's reasoning, it is possible to build analogically a case for the significance of studying form in visuals as a key to the 'nature of human capacities.' If there is indeed something approaching a universal form of grammar for speech, it is possible to consider certain universals of form in visuals and other aesthetic objects. The most perplexing and overwhelming question that such analogical speculating brings one to is that of the relationship between form in speech, form in visuals, and form in writing. (pp. 12–13)

Feldman (1976) used Chomsky's ideas to suggest that the grammar of visual language is innate:

I infer from the work of Noam Chomsky that everyone possesses an innate grammar which makes linguistic behavior possible. To be sure, such personal grammars do not necessarily conform to the grammar employed in the official culture. Still, our innate grammars provide us with "rules" for dealing with plurals, tense, voice, inflection, gender, and ideas of place, action, manner, and state of being. In other words, we "know" a grammar of verbal language without having studied its rules in any formal sense.
    Visual communication also relies on an innate grammar of images. In some respects, this grammar resembles the syntax of verbal language since written letters and words originated in visual images. The earliest written symbols were not copies of sounds; they were pictures of objects—pictographs. Afterward, they evolved into pictures of ideas—ideograms. Phonic symbols—images of syllabic sounds—grew out of the connection of pictographs with the sounds of the words used to designate objects, ideas, or events. In learning to read phonic symbols—letters—it was and is necessary to *forget* what symbols look like and to remember only the sounds they stand for—sometimes only an initial consonantal sound. After we learn to read well, this forgetting

operation takes place at a subcortical level. So we deliberately unlearn or repress our visual grammar in the course of becoming proficient readers of writing. (pp. 196–197)

Harpole and Hanhardt (1973) reported on the influence of Chomsky in the study of cinema. They pointed out that the linguistic concepts of Chomsky (1957, 1964, 1975) have been extended to other fields. Harpole and Hanhardt (1973) said:

> Recently, however, the writings of Noam Chomsky and his followers have created a revolution in linguistic studies, have influenced other fields and perhaps necessitated new ones—like psycholinguistics, where the search for the universals of language extends to the neurological foundations. The effect of Chomskian linguistics on structuralism and semiology, as they pertain to cinema and other fields, is currently only tentative but is likely to reveal some of the more profound problems with earlier work. Chomsky's research questions whether structuralism and semiology should continue to evolve within, or break away from, linguistic guidelines which now serve as a master pattern for general sign and system study. (p. 53)

Jonassen and Fork (1975) likened visual literacy to linguistic study:

> Visual literacy is most frequently referred to as the structure or syntax of visual language. The verbal language analogue can be utilized effectively in attempting to understand the various components of visual literacy. The verbal language syntactic structures postulated by Chomsky suggests an a priori model for the further investigation of the visual language. (p. 7)

The influence of linguistics on visual literacy has been significant. Barley (1971) explained:

> Students' visual literacy experiences will encourage them to identify parallelisms between verbal and visual syntax and will give them tools for creating visual/verbal utterances. When students set out to make photographs, slide sequences, one-reel, single concept films and other, longer motion pictures, they will demonstrate practical and theoretical knowledge of verbal and visual syntax. (p. 5)

Linguistics provided visual literacy with the concepts necessary to establish some connections between verbal and visual language. Linguistics also paved the way for the theory that learning visual language may help in learning verbal language. Research substantiates that theory (e.g., Newhouse, 1977).

Art

Barley (1971) said, "Visual literacy draws heavily an the field of art" (p. 9). Scholars in art have enthusiastically supported the visual literacy concept. Philosophers such as Arnheim (1967, 1969) and Cassirer (1944, 1963) provided theories in art that are applicable to visual literacy. In fact, Arnheim's (1967, 1969) theory on visual thinking may be the most important aspect of the visual literacy concept. Art educators such as Nelsen (1975), Davis (1975), and others offered rationales for incorporating art into the school curriculum. Theall (1973), Nash (1963), Whyte (1961), and others have all contributed important concepts of perception, communication, and art to provide a base for a theoretical beginning of visual literacy. Art historians like Lewin (1968) suggested some historical background in art for visual literacy theory.

Other sources on art theory useful to visual literacy theory development were Binkley's (1974) "On the Truth and Probity of Metaphor," Buettner's (1975) "John Dewey and the Visual Arts in America," and Parsons' (1976) "A Suggestion Concerning the Development of Aesthetic Experience in Children." All of these sources dealt with the need for enjoying, interpreting, promoting, developing, or recognizing art as a basic need in the human experience, and helped to form the rationale for visual literacy from the discipline of art.

Ruesch and Kees (1956) provided a vocabulary for developing the concept of visual literacy in terms of elements in visual stimuli and the developmental stages of visual growth in the infant (Debes, 1972). They identified three kinds of nonverbal languages (pictorial, action, object) in their book, *Nonverbal Communication*. Visual literacy can provide the skills necessary to understand these communicative and metacommunicative messages.

Debes (1972) developed a theory on the visual growth of the child from Ruesch and Kees' (1956) three kinds of nonverbal languages. Debes (1972) "traced the development of the child from a tactile, kinesthetic being to one in whom vision is the dominant sense and who develops a visual vocabulary which is active and by which he communicates his feelings" (Hocking, 1978, p. 2). Debes (1978) said, "For instance, actions made by the youngster's mother in preparation for feeding can be well enough read by an infant so that, even though hungry and crying, he will stop crying" (p. 3). Debes (1978) said that these infants were reading only visual action but that, as the infant becomes more aware of his environment, he will become visually sophisticated enough to read the objects around him and finally, as he becomes older, the signs and symbols of visual language. Debes (1978) wrote, "although, an infant does not come into the world with a visual vocabulary, he soon acquires a small one, learns how to 'read it' and learns how to communicate with it" (p. 5). The move from the tactile, kinesthetic stage is an important concept in visual literacy. Many of the calls for more visual learning in the schools are based on the idea that school learning is primarily verbal while most children just entering school have been operating in a predominantly visual environment. Debes (1968) wrote that the visually literate person entering school is "faced with a necessity to talk when he has not talked and to learn to write when he is not sure that this has any power to do anything useful for him" (p. 964). Debes (1968) and others suggested a gradual approach to verbal learning, a strategy for experiences in both the visual and verbal modes. Regarding the young school child, Debes (1968) wrote that "we must begin by giving him opportunities to manipulate change, react to things he can see" (p. 964). About the success of visual learning Debes (1974) wrote:

> For instance, it says that one of the most important possible things we can do
> is make it easy for children themselves to use pictures of various kinds to

communicate. Such 'pictures' can be drawings, illustrations cut from
magazines or newspapers, cartoon sequences, photographs they can take
themselves, slide sequences, movies or video. (p. 7)

Barley (1971) wrote:

> If the theory is correct that a visual vocabulary precedes a verbal one, then it
> might be argued that strengthening the visual vocabulary would have the
> consequence of strengthening the chances of a proper development of a verbal
> vocabulary. One hypothesis is that strengthening the visual vocabulary
> increases the inclination of a child to talk and may loosen the tongue of those
> disinclined to talk at all. (p. 10)

Once again, as in the field of linguistics, writers expressed the belief that visual
language can help promote the learning of verbal language.
Johnson (1977) wrote:

> It is possible that television-induced passivity has created a lack of interest in
> reading, writing, and learning. Teaching critical viewing skills, as well as some
> of the production skills involved with electric media, may present ways for
> schools to counter that passivity. (p. 40)

In *Toward a Psychology of Art*, Arnheim (1967) wrote, "Artistic abstraction, then,
is not a selective reproduction as a rearrangement of the model-perfect but the
representation of some of its structural characteristics in organized form" (p. 37).
Applying this concept to visual literacy, one can say that visual literacy involves
a group of skills that enables an individual to interpret those structural elements.
Furthermore, visual stimuli do not necessarily have to represent a
rearrangement of the verbal idea but can be ideas of their own. Arnheim (1967,
1969) believed that man's thinking could be visual. Since his book in 1967, other
people like McKim (1972) and Edwards (1979) have supported the visual
thinking concept. In fact as early as 1945 Hadamard reported, "Albert Einstein
once described his thinking as a 'combination play' of 'certain signs and more or
less clear images' " (p. 142). After envisioning these signs and images, Einstein
laboriously translated them into words (Hadamard, 1945, p. 142).
The fact that Arnheim (1967) believed that "Reasoning is in no way limited to
the manipulation of words and numbers" was an important aspect, perhaps the
crux, of the visual literacy concept. Cassirer (1944, 1963), who was quoted in
several visual literacy articles, spoke of the need to deliver sensory experiences
from the interpretations of words (Arnheim, 1967, p. 142). Arnheim (1967)
lamented that some psychologists believe "there can be no thinking except in
words" (p. 142). Sapir (1949) typified this belief when he wrote in his book,
Language, "the feeling entertained by so many that they can think, or even reason,
without language is an illusion" (p. 15). Arnheim (1967) expressed the fear that
educators inhibited creative thinking by overemphasizing verbal language:

> If it is true that genuine creative thinking, which makes for progress in the
> sciences and other exercises of the intellect, consists in the handling of
> perceptually conceived objects and forces, much of our education from grade

school to graduate school may be doing an efficient job of interfering with the development of this most precious capacity of the human mind. By reducing the work of the growing brain as much as possible to words and numbers, we may be reducing the thinking of our pupils and students to the accumulation and reshuffling of formalized chips or 'bits,' as the communication engineers call them. Those engineers also tell us that computing machines cannot think. (p. 146)

An art educator, Harry S. Broudy (1977), described the importance of aesthetic education in our schools. Broudy's ideas are similar to those of visual literacy advocates:

We can demystify aesthetic instruction without destroying the mystique of art if we concentrate on the skills of aesthetic perception, namely, the skills of aesthetic expression and impression. We can improve the sensitivity of the learner (any educated learner) to the aesthetic properties of objects. In the earlier grades, this can be done in connection with manipulation of materials in the various media; later more demonstrations and analyses can be used. The important point is that it can be done systematically with subjects not endowed with unusual artistic talent. These skills will neither turn the pupil into an artist nor an enlightened critic, but it will give the confidence that one is seeing, hearing, and imagining somewhat as the artist does. Perhaps this is not all we would wish aesthetic education to accomplish, but anything less is probably not worth the resources we are seeking, and anything more depends on our doing at least this much—the basics—well. (p.141)

Psychology

Past discussions on visual learning centered mainly on the research by perceptionists such as Gibson (1954) and Taylor (1960) although researchers in communication (Ball & Byrnes, 1960) and developmental psychologists like Piaget (1951) also contributed to visual learning research. All of this research helped develop a theory and definition for visual literacy.

Other researchers include Hill (1978), who called for more cooperation between communications theorists and instructional technologists. Hill (1978) suggested the starting point for cooperation was to conduct more research in the area of visual literacy (p. 51). He said that an example of a good medium for research in visual literacy was the broadcast commercial:

If visual literacy is indeed important, and becoming more so, then television simply cannot be ignored. When television commercials are at their best, they have a serious effect on the way we look at the world and its issues, be they frivolous or relevant. (p. 53)

Writings of developmentalists such as Piaget (1951) were used to help define the parameters for visual literacy. Brainard (1976) wrote:

Piaget considers the levels of thinking as concerned with, first, sensorimotor; next, representation or symbolic; and lastly, abstractions or signs. To Piaget, symbolic representation means a form which closely resembles the real thing, and signs are abstract forms such as words or numbers. As children move invariantly from sensorimotor (0–2 yrs.) through preoperational (2–7 yrs.), concrete operational (7–11 yrs.), and formal operational (11–15 yrs.–adult) stages of thinking, they are predominately involved in one of the three levels of development.

Visual literacy, then, is closely allied with the middle stage of development which involves representational thinking. According to Piaget, it is only when the child has had wide experiences in each state—many sensorimotor experiences, many opportunities to manipulate concrete materials and translate these experiences into representational form—that the child is capable of abstract thinking. However, it is during the sensorimotor stage that the foundations for visual literacy are being developed. At first the child cannot distinguish between himself and his surroundings. He will reach for an object only if he can see both his hand and the object to be grasped. If the object then disappears the search ends, for the child has no understanding of object permanence until around 18 months of age. The sensorimotor stage, then, involves the gradual coordination of sight with the other senses and the environment; intelligence is totally sensorimotor. It is only as the child becomes capable of mental imagery that the level of thinking moves beyond sensorimotor actions toward logical thinking. It is mental imagery which leads to memory and reflective thought. We cannot remember our lives as babies because we had no mechanism which could record memories in retrievable form. Deferred imitation is the first indication that the child can refer to the past. The child can now imitate a past action or can use objects in imaginative, representational play (a stick becomes an airplane, a sea shell, a cup, etc.). Language, play, and dreams begin at this stage. (p. 18)

Some perception theorists like Gibson (1954) and Vernon (1952) claimed that experience is what is needed to develop perceptual skills. Perception, Gibson (1954) said, is the process by which a person "becomes aware of something" (p. 4). Gibson (1954) said:

Learning requires not only that we make the appropriate reactions but also that we be sensitive to the appropriate stimuli. An important aspect of education, or of any kind of special training, military, industrial, or professional, is an increasing ability to discriminate and identify things. (p. 4)

About the transfer of learning Gibson (1954) wrote:

The learner must ordinarily be given an acquaintance with objects, places, and events which he has never physically encountered. The expedient is to train the individual in artificially constructed situations and expect that his learning will transfer to the novel situation, and this is essentially what any teacher does. The artificial situation is the crux of the matter. (p. 5)

The concept of visual literacy was derived to a great extent from the perceptionists (Amey, 1976). According to Amey (1976), visual perception "equals seeing plus cognition" (p. 7). The emphasis on the elements and ways of seeing vary from one authority to another. For instance, in his work Gibson (1954) was concerned with the use of "surrogates" in teaching ideas. His theory involved the discussion of associations the learner would have to make when confronted with "replicative" or "conventional" surrogates and the comparison of pictures or words in transmission potential (pp. 11–13).

Unlike Gibson, Taylor (1960) was interested in the "transaction" theory. Transactionalists like Tach, MacLean, and Norberg did not concentrate on either the subject or the object in a communication, but took an overview of the visual communication and the elements involved (Amey, 1976, p. 14). For transactionalists, the perceptual behavior of the individual becomes a transaction in which neither the individual nor the environment is regarded as a separate entity. Perception itself for the transactionalists is a form of learning" (Amey, 1976, p. 14). Perception is "functional; that is, it exists in order to enable the perceiver to carry out his or her purposes" (Amey, 1976, p. 14). According to Amey (1976) transactionalists are like the "introverted" perceptionists in that they apply personal meaning and interpretations to the visual world but are also like the "extroverted" perceptionists in that they are affected by the visual world (p. 15). "It is the perceiver who constantly brings the situation together as a creative act" (Amey, 1976, p. 15). Amey (1976) pointed out a weakness in the transactional theorist viewpoint:

> It is one thing to present these kinds of messages on television or in film, but are they reinforced by what children perceive in the actual world around them? (p. 17)

The transactional theorist believes if visual information is presented with purposes that are relevant, learning will take place, but as Amey said, "This seems rather incomplete, with both the nature and importance of the 'transaction' and 'function' left unclear" (Amey, 1976, p. 17).

Franklin Fearing, George Mead, and Martin Buber espoused the importance of the "mind" in perception (Amey, 1976, p. 21). Amey (1976) stated:

> Thus "mind" is the ability of a human being to take the role of the other toward its own developing behavior. That is to say, the communicator of the stimulus always makes certain assumptions about the needs or feeling of those whose behavior he is trying to influence. (p. 20)

Amey (1976) suggested that "Communication had moved from I-it to I-thou" (p. 23). Amey explained Buber's position:

> Buber advises that communicators must above all put aside any attempt to objectify and reduce the communicative relationship between one person and another. Communication of the I-thou sort, or that which is analogous to Mead's concept of "mind," requires a deep social perspective of human interaction. Symbols, be they visual or otherwise, are exchanged between people as part of a broad environment and spiritual unity. (p. 22)

Visual literacy in Buber's perspective implied a holistic or total view of the environment, the message, the teacher, and the student. "Visual symbols cannot be conceived of as separate from the social perspective" (Amey, 1976, p. 23). Arnheim (1969) wrote, "Visual thinking calls, more broadly, for the ability to see visual shapes as images of the patterns of forces that underlie our existence—the functioning of minds, of bodies or machines, the structure of societies or ideas" (p. 315). "'Mind' is not achieved by formula, it requires a deep understanding of the subject matter, as well as a fundamental comprehension on the part of the producers of the true meaning of 'communication' " (Amey, 1976, p. 25). Visual literacy advocates believe that teaching how to understand and create visuals will provide the necessary understanding.

Flory (1978) listed four primary concepts that support the rationale for the visual literacy movement:

(1)   A visual language exists;
(2)   people can and do think visually;
(3)   people can and do learn visually;
(4)   people can and should express themselves visually (p. 4).

Turbayne (1970) presented a philosophical justification for visual language. Arnheim (1967, 1969) demonstrated that words and numbers are not the only basis for thinking. Flory (1978) wrote, "If we can accept the premise that a visual language exists, we can easily extend the notion that this language can be utilized for visual thinking" (p. 5).

Hutton (1978) asked an important question about the necessity of visual literacy training:

> What about visual skills, like seeing and understanding objects and events, interpreting photographs, and making drawings? Are these automatic, developmental processes which all individuals in a community will acquire, or do they need to be taught and learned? (p. 72)

Hutton (1978) said that visual literacy does indeed need to be taught because visual skills "are not inevitable developmental processes like standing and walking" (p. 72). Hutton (1978) wrote that "visual skills are not simple" (p. 72). For instance, people from different cultures will interpret pictures quite differently: "people from so-called 'primitive' tribes may see things in their visual environment that we would never notice, but may find it difficult or impossible to extract any meaning from a photograph or film without careful training" (Hutton, 1978, p. 72).

The need for training in visual literacy is important because of the possible manipulation of the viewer by the media (Fillion, 1973). This training is usually recommended for the early ages of development (Brainard, 1976). However, a difference arises between Piaget and Gagné on approaches to readiness, which should be considered by teachers of visual literacy. Newell (1970) presented these two views:

> Gagné views the development of readiness factors as falling within the control, at least in part, of the classroom teacher, and, because of the cumulative nature of learning, he views a particular type of learning and its development as limited primarily by the lack of necessary prerequisites. That makes the development of readiness factors external to the learner and manageable by the classroom teacher, within limits. Piaget, on the other hand, reflects a different viewpoint which states that in the logical and predictable

development not only of neurological and muscular skills, but also of intellectual skills, outside influences cannot seriously alter or affect this development. The classroom teacher, then, needs to operate within the constraints of the levels of intellectual functioning possessed by the child at a certain level of development. There has been some work that has focused on the accuracy of the chronological age designations of each of Piaget's stages. While chronological age is at best a crude measure, and regardless of whether or not some variations in the chronological ages associated with each stage of development are demonstrated, the basic argument still holds about the sequential development of skills. These two approaches to developmental readiness are in part theoretical and in part supported by research evidence. The development of any theoretical model is a long-term process, and the final results will not be available for many years. It is important that the reader recognize that these approaches represent two of the most important and viable analyses of developmental readiness, that there is some research data that supports each viewpoint, that additional research will probably necessitate modifications in both approaches, and that both will have a critical effect on curriculum development for the classroom. (pp. 129–130)

Philosophy

Colin Murray Turbayne, a Professor of Philosophy at the University of Rochester, had the most influence on the development of visual literacy theory. In his book, *The Myth of Metaphor*, Turbayne (1970) presented a defense for visual language. He began by examining the "metaphor" and said that man used the metaphor to try to illustrate his ideas, control the thoughts of others and induce certain types of behavior in his audience (p. 3). He wrote that the metaphor "involves the pretense that something is the case when it is not" (Turbayne, 1970, p. 3). Herein lies the reason for the title of his book, *The Myth of Metaphor*. He cited some examples to illustrate his point:

> Hobbes pretended that the state was a many-jointed monster or leviathan, Shakespeare that it was a hive of honey bees, 'Creatures that by a rule in nature teach the art of order to a peopled kingdom.' Plato, however, presented the obscure facts of human nature as if they were luminous facts about the state. Descartes pretended that the mind in its body was the pilot of a ship; Locke that it was a room, empty at birth but full of furniture later; and Hume that it was a theatre. (Turbayne, 1970, p. 1)

A problem arises when people begin to take metaphors literally. Turbayne (1970) wrote that in some cases after a metaphor has been used for some time it is hard to distinguish the metaphor from reality (p. 4). Turbayne (1970) elaborated on myth of metaphor:

> There is a difference between using a metaphor and taking it literally, between using a model and mistaking it for the thing modeled. The one is to make believe that something is the case; the other is to believe that it is. The one is to use a disguise or mask for illustrative or explanatory purposes; the other is to mistake the mask for the face. (p. 1)

Turbayne (1970) was concerned about the inappropriateness of the metaphor which "results from the use of sign in a sense different from the usual, which use I shall call 'sort-crossing'" (p. 11). Evers (1969) said:

> Turbayne wants us to realize that all explanations and representations of reality are metaphors and being metaphors they stress certain things and suppress other things. In literature this is demonstrated by the famous Shakespearean metaphor that sees the world as a stage. Once we accept the world as a stage, we then begin to explain it in stage terms. Death is no longer death; it is tragedy. People are not people; they are actors who play roles, have entrances and exits. They experience rising action and falling action, and they can be heroes or villains. Language is no longer language; it is dialog, monology, or soliloquy. All, a most convenient way of explaining or giving order to life through a comparison-representation. (p. 34)

Turbayne (1970) used Aristotle's definition of metaphor taken from the *Poetics* as his starting point:

> Metaphor (meta-phora) consists in giving the thing a name that belongs to something else; the transference (epi-phora) being either from genus to species, or from species to genus, or from species to species, or on the grounds of analogy. (p.11)

Then Turbayne (1970) expanded Aristotle's definition to include nonverbal metaphors, especially visual stimuli:

> The definition is still not wide enough. Some cases of metaphor may not be expressed in words. Again without stretching Aristotle's meaning unduly, I interpret his 'name' to mean a sign or a collection of signs. This will allow artists who 'speak' in paint or clay to 'speak' in metaphor. Michelangelo, for example', used the figure of Leda with the swan to illustrate being lost in the rapture of physical passion, and the same figure of Leda, only this time without the swan, to illustrate being lost in the agony of dying. It will also allow the concrete physical models of applied scientists, the blackboard diagrams of teachers, the toy blocks of children that may be used to represent the battle of Trafalgar, and the raised eyebrow of the actor that may illustrate the whole situation in the state of Denmark, to be classified as metaphor. (pp. 12–13)

Evers (1969) said:

> Movies, photographs, commercials, and even printed statements are representations of reality. They are metaphors, and therefore must be understood as metaphorical points of view. That is what mediacy is all about. (p. 34)

Turbayne (1970) said that the metaphor has its useful purposes if we understand its potential. "To assist our thinking, we make allegories, parallels, and metaphors; models, diagrams, and gestures; flags, emblems, counters, and coins" (Turbayne, 1970, p. 74). The key to understanding metaphors is to know that they are myths. Evers (1969) explained how Turbayne's theory applies to media:

> Any medium or combination of media is a metaphor and must be understood as such. What is stressed? What is hidden? What is compared? What is contrasted? And most of all, who constructed the metaphor? Not knowing the answers to these questions may mean that one is trapped in the metaphor. With contemporary media, people, especially the young, get trapped most by film. Many people believe that the camera is a mirror that reflects reality. (p. 34)

For visual literacy experts, the answers to these questions raised lie in visual literacy training. The ability to read visual images is an essential skill even for those who can read and write well in the verbal language. Feldman (1976) listed three implications that visual literacy has for education:

> The most important is that there is a language of images and that it can be learned. Second, much of what many persons know about the world has been learned through visual images without the benefit of formal instruction in how to read them. The fact that many semi-literate or illiterate persons can cope successfully with their environments reinforces our second point, namely, that they have learned to read nonverbal, essentially visual, languages. Third, the several disciplines that study art—history of art, iconology, art criticism, and aesthetics—constitute well- established ways of reading visual language. Still, it is a matter of regret that these disciplines have had little or no application in school curricula. As for higher education, the role of these art languages has been peripheral. The marginal and specialized character of fine arts studies in college and university education has complex causes. Here let me argue that the most influential cause has to do with the perception of fine arts study as an ornamental feature of the typical liberal arts curriculum. Among the humanities, history, literature, and philosophy seem more relevant to the business of living than the chronological examination of the monuments of art. The situation would be otherwise, however, if college and university students had developed some degree of visual literacy during their elementary and secondary schooling. It would then be possible at the college level to show the connections between the varieties of imagery generated by our culture and the abiding concerns of the people who live in and hope to change that culture. (p. 199)

Turbayne (1970) demonstrated the myths of metaphors by showing that the Euclidean explanation of reality breaks down when it is shown as a metaphor (Evers, 1969, p. 34). Turbayne (1970) exposed the mechanism theory of Descartes and Newton:

> These two great 'sort-crossers' of our modern epoch have so imposed their arbitrary allocation of the facts upon us that it has now entered the coenesthesis of the entire Western World. Together they have founded a church, more powerful than that founded by Peter and Paul, whose dogmas are now so entrenched that anyone who tries to re-allocate the facts is guilty of more than heresy; he is opposing scientific truth. For the accepted allocation is

now identified with science. All this is so in spite of the meager opposition
offered by the theologians, a few poets, and fewer philosophers, who, in
general, have been victimized by their own metaphors to the same degree as
their rivals. They have opposed one metaphysics, done without awareness, by
another. They have been operating on the wrong level. (p. 5)

After exposing the myths of the mechanical explanation of reality, Turbayne
(1970) replaced it with his own humanistic explanation. His explanation used the
language metaphor which he felt was more humanistic and meaningful.
Turbayne (1970) described his language metaphor:

> I try to show that the metaphysics of mechanism can be dispensed with. The
> best way to do this is to show that it is only a metaphor; and the best way to
> show this is to invent a new metaphor. I therefore treat the events in nature as
> if they compose a language, in the belief that the world may be treated just as
> well, if not better, by making believe that it is a universal language instead of
> a giant clockwork. But my purpose in presenting the language metaphor is not
> so much to build as to destroy, not so much to plant flowers as to pull up
> weeds. I present the generation to whom it is first told cannot possibly believe
> it, the next may, and the generations after. I present it in order to begin to
> show: first, that there is a remedy against the domination imposed, not by
> generals, statesmen, and men of action, whose power dissolves when they
> retire, but by the great sort-crossers, whose power increases when they die—
> the remedy provided by becoming aware of metaphor; and second, that the
> metaphysics that still dominates science and enthralls the minds of men is
> nothing but a metaphor, and a limited one. (pp. 4–5)

Turbayne (1970) also presented a theory on the two functions of language. The
first is what he called the "communicative" function:

> We use the words of our language to enable us to think of absent things. The
> things we think of are not present to thought, only the words and certain—
> images, and sometimes only the words. But we say that we think of these
> absent things. (pp. 92–93)

The second function was the "pragmatic function":

> Words are used to excite to, or deter from, action. Sometimes words are used
> to communicate ideas or thoughts. Often ideas are communicated although
> this is subservient to the author's purpose which is to put the auditor's mind
> in a certain disposition. Sometimes no thing that can properly be called a
> thought or an idea is communicated. (p. 93)

Turbayne (1970) organized a theory of vision through nine basic principles
listed below:

> I. The sounds or colors that become signs of a language are neither identical
> with, nor pictures of, nor necessarily connected with, the things they signify.

II. If the sounds or colors that become the signs of a language were identical with, or pictures of, or necessarily connected with the things they signify, then we could interpret them although none of them had been ostensibly defined for us.

III. The consequent of Rule II is false; that is, we could not interpret them unless at least some of them had been ostensibly defined for us.

IV. If some similar sounds or colors have been ostensibly defined for us, then we can interpret them, and we find it increasingly easy to interpret other sounds or colors that are new to us.

V. Our expectations or pre-notions regarding the size, shape, and situation of things condition the meanings we give to the words we see or hear.

VI.   (a) Words are often ambiguous, that is, they do not 'always suggest things in the same uniform way and have the same constant regular connection with matters of fact.'
     (b) Words are meaningful although they denote nothing.
     (c) The means whereby [we may avoid falling into error] is the context of these expressions, for a word used in one context or circumstances often has a different meaning when used in another context or circumstance.

VII. (a) We sometimes want to talk about a language as well as from within. When this is done it is customary to call the signs and the things they signify by some of the same names.
     (b) Since signs are little considered in themselves or for their own sake, we often overlook them and carry our attention immediately on to the things signified, where nearly all our interest lies.

VIII. But these common names do not name common natures or abstract ideas.

IX. But if the ostensive definitions of language are, as it were, sucked in with our milk so that we cannot remember having learned them; if this language is universal; and if in our native tongue we call its signs and the things signified by the same names; then we cannot avoid confounding the signs with the things signified, and we suppose an identity of nature. (pp. 107–119)

For visual literacy proponents, Turbayne's principles were significant. In elucidating his principles of vision, Turbayne (1970) provided a way for connecting visual data and physical objects through linguistics (Johnson, 1977, p. 27). Johnson (1977) wrote, " His theory would perhaps be inaccurate if all words did have literal referents and if there was no such thing as illusion; but the interpretation of signs, which includes words and images, allows for 'confounding the signs' with the things signified" (p. 27).

Finally Turbayne (1970) offered the analogy between verbal language and visual language:

Just as a large part of learning to understand words consists in learning how to respond to them, so is it the case in learning how to see. To see an object is to recognize it, to know roughly how far away it is, its size, shape, and position in relation to us. But this involves knowing how to do things with it, remembering how long it takes to reach it, and feeling incipient movements in our muscles. Only a fragment of all that is fused into the object seen is actually presented. The rest are remembered associations including remembering how we acted in similar cases. (p. 125)

Flory (1978) summarized Turbayne's views on the visual/verbal language analogy:

Turbayne advances the view that seeing is not a simple task and that it is far more than the mere transmittal of information from the environment to the brain. Rather, seeing is a complex conceptual process that depends on our having learned the relationships between our tactual definitions of physical objects and our visual perceptions of those same objects, much as we 'learn' to relate sounds to the originator of the sound and to relate verbal definitions to the referent. The primary elements of visual language are line, shape, form, size, color, and movement.

The human mind, especially aided by the memory, can interpret the visual elements, decode what they signify, and can 'see through' visual ambiguities (such as illusions). As with verbal language, the visual language is learned by comparison of the physical/tactual world with what is seen of the world. Turbayne cites the famous Molyneux problem (using blind people who are suddenly made able to see) to demonstrate that the relationship between the physical and visual world is not established without a learning process. (pp. 4–5)

The parallels of visual and verbal language developed by Turbayne (1970) and the kinds on nonverbal communication described by Ruesch and Kees (1956) helped Fransecky and Debes (1972) to delineate the analogy between visual/verbal language:

The 'spoken' form of visual languages is body language, body signs, body English—gestures, movements, postures we use deliberately or unconsciously, to communicate without or with accompanying words. ... It is supplemented by object language when objects are used deliberately to transmit meaning, or when physical or visual context is used to transmit meaning.

The 'written' form of visual language is recorded images on film, videotape, paper, or other visual image carriers. (p. 8)

Also, Fransecky and Debes (1972) defined some terms of the visual literacy movement:

Visual literacy is the attribute we would hope to find in every well-educated adult in our society. Visual communication is what the person is exposed to, or when appropriate uses himself. Visual technology is what makes 'written' visual communication possible, and changes in visual technology alter the character of visual communication. (p. 8)

Feldman (1976) summarized the importance of the visual/verbal analogy and visual literacy's role in society:

> My contention is that everyone must learn to read images because our culture is increasingly represented and perceived in visual terms.
>
> Today, written language steadily recedes; the ratio of printed words to printed images grows smaller; only spoken language holds its own, and even here the image of the speaker (as in television and films) is more vivid and often cognitively and affectively more significant than what he says. Words multiply as they lose their semantic value in a desperate effort to catch up with the electronic and printed images that carry them along like so much baggage. We have in effect a reversal of the time-honored relation between a text and its illustrations: unlike the medieval manuscript in which the illuminated letter was an adornment of a sacred utterance, our forms of communication feature images whose embellishments are a kind of verbal calligraphy. Words have become decorative accessories so far as the sharing of essential ideas is concerned. Perhaps the situation will reverse itself. But it is more likely that we are moving in the direction of a mandarin culture in which the ability to employ verbal language with precision is confined to a small, highly trained caste. This caste, indispensable for the operation of our legal, economic, and political institutions, will then take its place alongside the technocratic and media elites now competing for control of the life of our democracy. The development of visual literacy, it is hoped, represents a countervailing force. The art educator (and by this title I mean all those engaged in fine or 'creative' arts instruction) can play a major role here, one that addresses itself to serious problems having to do with the ability to read—hence to accept or reject meanings—in the increasingly intense struggle that goes on in post-industrial societies. I mean the struggle between those who wish to educate truly, that is, maximize the individual's capacity to choose among alternatives; and those who wish to govern mass behavior (for profit or power) by controlling the consumption of images—the tools with which we think. (p. 200)

Theoretical Foundations

Disciplines such as art, education, English, linguistics, philosophy, and psychology have all contributed to our knowledge and understanding of visual literacy (Barley, 1971; Debes, 1968, 1972). The theory about visual literacy comes from these disciplines as well. However, the theoretical foundations of visual literacy have not been clearly stated and are not strongly evident from the research, programs, and practices, and theories found in the literature. Almost all the major ideas and concepts of visual literacy can be traced to four areas of study: linguistics, art, psychology, and philosophy (see Figure l).

A link between theories from these four areas to theories in visual literacy has been attempted by the visual literacy proponents. An example would be in the area of linguistics. Fries (1952) suggested that the meaning in verbal language was derived from the study of verbal structure and elements. Fries' (1952) ideas became a rationale for visual literacy training. According to visual literacy advocates, the study of visual elements such as color, form, syntax, and composition, would enable an individual to find meaning in visual information. Understanding verbal elements to derive meaning was analogous to understanding visual elements to understand visual information, visual literacy proponents claimed, thus providing a rationale for visual literacy training. Linguistics also contributed to the building of visual literacy theory with the ideas of Chomsky (1957, 1964, 1968, 1975), who coined the term *universal grammar*. Proponents of visual literacy have suggested that if there are universals in verbal language, there are universals in visual language as well (Gozemba, 1975, pp. 12–13). If Fries (1952) provided the theory that meaning could be derived from the study of elements, Chomsky's ideas of a universal or innate language justified the teaching of certain universal elements in visual language. If such visual elements exist, the recognition of those elements is an important step toward being visually literate. As can be seen in Figure 1, both Fries and Chomsky provided the original theory for the justification of visual literacy training.

Art's primary contribution in the development of a theoretical foundation for visual literacy is Arnheim's (1969) theory on visual thinking. Arnheim (1969) wrote, "Visual thinking calls, more broadly, for the ability to see visual shapes as images of the patterns of forces that underlie our existence—the functioning of minds, of bodies, or machines, the structure of societies, or ideas" (p. 315). However, Arnheim (1969) warned his readers about trying "to establish an island of visual literacy in an ocean of blindness" (p. 307). Visual literacy is a means to visual thinking, which is as much a processing of information as it is a knowledge of visual elements. Arnheim (1969) said that the comprehension of images cannot be taken lightly, nor do visual aids necessarily provide conditions for visual thinking. A visually literate person should be able to process information visually as well as verbally, and the processing of information visually might be called visual thinking.

In the area of psychology, the research of the perceptionists has had a strong influence on visual literacy theory. Most of the literature has been in the philosophical sense rather than the empirical. There is, however, a connection between the eye and the mind that is the focal point of the perceptionists' theory. The transactionalists believe that perception itself "is a form of learning" (Amey, 1976, p. 14). Gibson (1954) stressed experience as necessary in the development of visual perception. Both Gibson (1954) and the transactionalists provide some link to visual literacy training.

Mead, Fearing, and Buber espoused the importance of "mind" in perception (Amey, 1976, p. 21). This belief has led some visual literacy proponents to the increasingly popular position of using left- and right-brain hemispheric research to support visual literacy ideas. However, an emphasis on just left- and right-brain hemispheric research should be avoided. Rather, a broader perspective is necessary, one that would result from more investigation in other areas of mind research including brain chemistry, psychobiology, unconscious intellect, visualization, biofeedback, and mind-body connection. Mental processing of information both verbal and visual needs to be studied further before a substantive theoretical foundation can be formulated. The future of visual literacy most likely lies with the research being conducted on the brain. In her book, *Supermind*, Brown (1980) suggests we have just begun to scratch the surface:

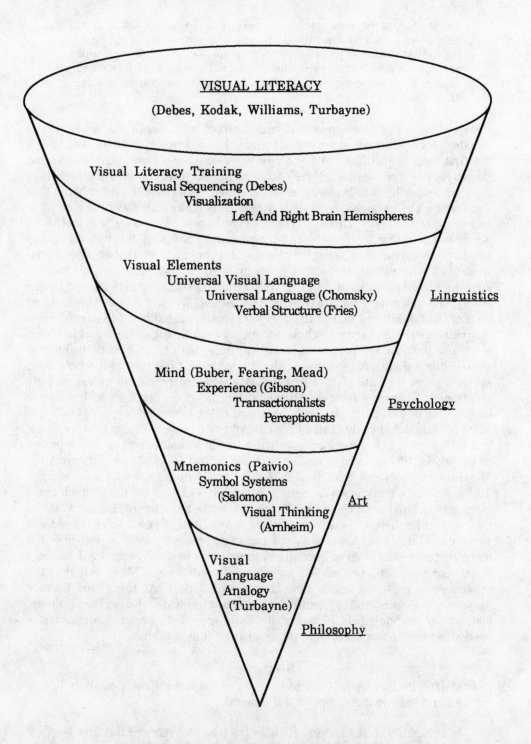

Figure 1. Model of the Theoretical Foundations of Visual Literacy.

The mystery of the mind is so gigantic that it renders even the best of minds helpless to absorb its magnitude, let alone set a proper course for exploring the endless reaches of its power. This, more than anything perhaps, explains why for centuries human beings have failed to be much more than passingly curious about the power and potential of their own mental apparatus. (pp. 1–2)

The philosopher Turbayne (1970) had the most influence on the development of a theoretical foundation for visual literacy. His defense of a visual language is the first step in justifying the analogy between visual language and verbal language. For most visual literacy advocates, once this analogy is established, the term visual literacy becomes relevant. However, it must be remembered that Turbayne's (1970) book, *The Myth of Metaphor*, is really a study of the metaphor and not visual literacy. Turbayne (1970) devotes most of the book to establishing a humanistic rather than mechanistic, explanation of reality through the use of language metaphor. Just what relationship his language-metaphor view of the world has with visual literacy remains unclear. Nevertheless, visual literacy advocates like Fransecky and Debes (1972), Flory (1978), Evers (1969), and Barley (1971) have selectively borrowed from Turbayne (1970) to theorize about visual literacy. It is significant that visual literacy proponents have had to borrow from many disciplines and several scholars to justify their theories. The trend has been to choose parts or segments of ideas and apply them in an eclectic fashion to visual literacy without examining the thoughts and theories as a whole. This appears to be the case with Turbayne as well as many of the others already mentioned. Turbayne's views on visual language are used as a descriptive explanation of visual literacy, without regard to the overall ideas of his book, *The Myth of Metaphor*. Besides these four disciplines of linguistics, art, psychology, and philosophy, two other elements had a strong influence on the development of the visual literacy movement and its theoretical foundations. First was the "Rochester school" of John L. Debes, Clarence Williams, and Colin Murray Turbayne; in the early years these men, especially Debes, were the visual literacy movement. Furthermore, without the financial backing of *Eastman Kodak Company* in Rochester, New York, the movement might never have started nor survived. Kodak's help was a mixed blessing, however, as it is probable that more credence would have been given to research in visual literacy if *Eastman Kodak Company* had not played such an influential role. Many felt that the movement was dominated by the commercial aspect. As the visual literacy movement stands today, more cooperation among the perceptionists, instructional technologists, philosophers, brain specialists, linguists, and artists is needed before the theoretical foundations can be fully established.

Summary

Postman (1971) referred back to the root of the term literacy to show how it evolved and grew to include print and nonprint:

In ancient Rome (literacy) referred to the letters of the alphabet and, by extension, to the epistles of earliest times. With the passage of the years, however, it came to be identified with literature and the increasingly crucial skills required in written communication. Little more than a decade ago, the term 'universal literacy' simply meant the hope that all men could have made available to them the skills of reading and writing. But the term continues to change as the means of communication change. Today literacy is the skills with which man manipulates the many media of mass communication. (p. 26)

Johnson (1977) wrote:

The writers and educators who have used terms like 'media literacy' and 'visual literacy' do so with that usage in mind. Both terms are, in a sense, analogies; they are used to say that an audiovisual learning experience can be like a reading experience. Clearly, 'literacy' has been stretched beyond the definition of reading and writing letters, not necessarily out of irreverence towards print but as a reaction to technological advancements in communication. Perhaps 'literacy' is the wrong word to associate with media and visual learning, but lament over the literal meaning of somewhat oxymoronic terms is too late. Visual literacy and media literacy have become established educational jargon. (p. 7)

Johnson (1977) was critical of the term *visual literacy* saying, "Where visual literacy has become bogged down with many definitions and has tried to include too many different theories, media literacy is simply meant as an analogy" (p. 141). However, a new definition is proposed that defines visual literacy as the "ability to understand (read) and use (write) images and to think and learn in terms of images." It is more than just "reading" visual images. If that were the case "reading" visual and audio messages might well be "media literacy" as Johnson (1977) suggested. Visual literacy does involve reading visuals and using and creating visuals, but most importantly, it is a method or process for thinking. Feldman (1976) made a distinction between reading or responding to visuals and really understanding visuals. The distinction is significant and draws attention to the need for the visual thinking principle in the proposed definition:

What really matters is whether the perception of visual images can be regarded as *critical understanding* rather than *programmed response*. In other words, does the reader of images have a literate as opposed to a reactive role?

At present, most persons (from children watching their television sets to adults looking at magazine acts) are visually literate in the sense that they are capable of receiving and acting on the signals sent out to them by electronic and printed pictures. They are not visually literate if by literacy we mean the ability to understand the rhetoric, the persuasive devices, employed in visual communication. Consider that the ephebes of Athens—the aristocratic youths being prepared for a life of enlightened citizenship and cultivated leisure—studied rhetoric as an instrument of governmental power. They needed to understand the combined ideas and images that control behavior. Merely lexical skills—the ability to read—have no more than an indirect connection to power. Ruling elites have always understood the political value of a language—spoken, written, or visual. For persons who are truly free, that is, capable of ruling themselves and others, language is an instrument of governance; for those who are unfree (by nature slaves, as Aristotle would have it), language is an instrument of obedience. If this classical conception of language is correct, then millions of people in the modern, self-governing societies of the West are unfree because they are merely half-literate. They are capable of reading only to the extent that they can obey the instructions implicit in certain linguistic codes: they can respond but they cannot initiate. Genuine literacy has to include an understanding of the ways language is used to govern behavior—how it enlarges or restrains the range of personal action. (pp. 195–196)

Dworkin (1970) noted that literacy provides us with a common meaning and forces us to take responsibility for meanings (p. 30). If verbal language or verbal literacy, i.e., to be literate, helps us to store information, provides us a means for transacting messages and gives us a method for problem solving and thinking, then visual language or visual literacy helps us to do the same. Visual literacy is really training for visual thinking.

(**Editors' note:** See Chapter Six, *Visual Literacy: The Definition Problem*, for more about definitions of the visual literacy concept.)

References

Amey, L. J. (1976). *Visual literacy: Implications for the production of children's television programs.* Halifax, Nova Scotia: Dalhousie University School of Library Service.

Arnheim, R. (1967). *Toward a psychology of art.* Berkeley, CA: University of California Press.

Arnheim, R. (1969). *Visual thinking.* Berkeley, CA: University of California Press.

Ball, J., & Byrnes, F. C. (Eds.). (1960). *Research, principles, and practices in visual communication.* Washington, DC: Department of Audiovisual Instruction.

Barley, S. D. (1971). *A new look at the loom of visual literacy.* Rochester, NY: Eastman Kodak Company. (ERIC Document Reproduction Service No. ED 057 585).

Binkley, T. (1974). On the truth and probity of metaphor. *The Journal of Aesthetics and Art Criticism, 33,* 171–180.

Brainard, H. L. (1976). Piaget and visual literacy. *AECT Research and Theory Newsletter, 5*(3), 17–18. Washington, DC: Association for Educational Communications and Technology. (ERIC Document Reproduction Service No. ED 126 822).

Broudy, H. S. (1977). How basic is aesthetic education? Or is it the fourth R? *Educational Leadership, 35*(2), 134–139, 141.

Brown, B. B. (1980). *Supermind, the ultimate energy.* New York: Harper & Row.

Buettner, S. (1975). John Dewey and the visual arts in America. *The Journal of Aesthetics and Art Criticism, 33,* 383–391.

Cassirer, E. (1944). *An essay on man.* New Haven, CT: Yale University Press.

Cassirer, E. (1963). *The individual and the cosmos in Renaissance philosophy.* New York: Barnes & Noble.

Chomsky, N. (1957). *Syntactic structures.* The Hague, Netherlands: Mouton.

Chomsky, N. (1964). *Current issues in linguistic theory.* The Hague, Netherlands: Mouton.

Chomsky, N. (1968). *Language and mind.* New York: Harcourt, Brace, Jovanovich.

Chomsky, N. (1975). *The logical structure of linguistic theory.* New York: Plenum Publishing.

Davis, B. J. (1975). Seeing together. *Science Teacher, 42*(2), 21.

Debes, J. L. (1968). Some foundations for visual literacy. *Audiovisual Instruction, 13,* 961–964.

Debes, J. L. (1972, March). *Some aspects of the reading of visual languages.* Paper presented at the National Conference on Visual Literacy, Cincinnati, OH. (ERIC Document Reproduction Service No. ED 079 974).

Debes, J. L. (1974). *Mind, languages, and literacy.* Paper presented at the meeting of the National Council of Teachers of English, New Orleans, LA. (ERIC Document Reproduction Service No. ED 108 659).

Debes, J. L. (1978). Introduction. In J. W. Armstrong (Ed.), *Proceedings of the tenth annual conference on visual literacy.* Bloomington, IN: International Visual Literacy Association.

Dondis, D. A. (1973). *A primer of visual literacy.* Cambridge, MA: The MIT Press.

Dworkin, M. S. (1970). Towards an image curriculum: Some questions and cautions. In C. M. Williams & J. L. Debes (Eds.), *Proceedings of the first national conference on visual literacy.* New York: Pitman Publishing Co.

Edwards, B. (1979). *Drawing on the right side of the brain.* Los Angeles: J. P. Tarcher.

Evers, J. L. (1969). Mediacy means understanding metaphor. *Audiovisual Instruction, 14*(8), 34–35.

Feldman, E. B. (1976). Visual literacy. *Journal of Aesthetic Education, 10*(3/4), 195–200.

Fillion, B. (1973). Visual literacy. *Clearing House, 47*(5), 308–311.

Flory, J. (1978, April). *Visual literacy: A vital skill in the process of rhetorical criticism.* Paper presented at the meeting of the Southern Speech Communication Association, Atlanta, GA. (ERIC Document Reproduction Service No. ED 155 772).

Fransecky, R. B., & Debes, J. L. (1972). *Visual literacy: A way to learn—A way to teach.* Washington, DC: Association for Educational Communications and Technology.

Fries, C. C. (1952). *The structure of English: An introduction to the construction of English sentences.* New York: Harcourt, Brace, and Co.

Gibson, J. J. (1954). A theory of pictorial perception. *Audio Visual Communication Review, 2,* 2–23.

Gozemba, P. A. (1975). The effects of rhetorical training in visual literacy on the writing skills of college freshman (Doctoral dissertation, Boston University). *Dissertation Abstracts International, 36,* 1269A. (University Microfilms No. 75–20,950).

Hadamard, J. S. (1945). *An essay on the psychology of invention in the mathematical field.* Princeton, NJ: Princeton University Press.

Harpole, C. H., & Hanhardt, J. G. (1973). Linguistics, structuralism, and seminology. *Film Comment, 9*(3), 52–59.

Hill, J. E. (1978). Communication research and instructional technology. *Educational Communications and Technology Journal, 26*(1), 47–54.

Hocking, F. O. (1978). *A nationwide study to determine visual literacy goals, constraints, and factors.* Unpublished doctoral dissertation, University of Colorado.

Hortin, J. (1980). Symbol systems and mental skills research: Their emphasis and future. *Media Adult Learning, 2*(2), 3–6.

Hutton, D. W. (1978). Seeing to learn. Using visual skills across the curriculum. In J. W. Armstrong (Ed.), *Proceedings of the tenth annual conference on visual literacy.* Bloomington, IN: International Visual Literacy Association.

Johnson, B. D. (1977). Visual literacy, media literacy, and mass communications for English instruction (Doctoral dissertation, Northwestern University). *Dissertation Abstract International, 38,* 6581A. (University Microfilms No. 78–5287).

Jonassen, D. H., & Fork, D. J. (1975, November). *Visual literacy: A bibliographic survey.* Paper presented at the Pennsylvania Learning Resource Association Annual Conference, Hershey, Pennsylvania. (ERIC Document Reproduction Service No. ED. 131 837).

Lewin, B. D. (1968). *The image and the past.* New York: International Universities Press.

McKim, R. H. (1972). *Experiences in visual thinking.* Monterey, CA: Brooks/Cole Publishing Co.

Nash, H. (1963). The role of metaphor in psychological theory. *Behavioral Science, 8,* 336–345.

Nelsen, R. (1975). Towards visual literacy. *Elementary English, 52,* 523–526.

Newell, J. M. (1970). *Student's guide to the conditions of learning.* New York: Holt, Rinehart, and Winston.

Newhouse, J. J. (1977). Study of two instructional approaches for the acquisition of a high level of visual literacy competency by undergraduate, preservice teacher trainees (Doctoral dissertation, Temple University). *Dissertation Abstracts International*, 1977, 37, 77–2A–7703A. (University Microfilms No. 77–13520).

Parsons, M. J. (1976). A suggestion concerning the development of aesthetic experience in children. *The Journal of Aesthetics and Art Criticism, 34*, 305–314.

Piaget, J. (1951). *The child's conception of physical causality.* New York: The Humanities Press.

Postman, N. (1971). The new literacy. *The Grade Teacher*, March, 26–27, 40.

Ruesch, J., & Kees, W. (1956). *Nonverbal communication.* Berkeley, CA: University of California Press.

Sapir, E. (1949). *Language.* New York: Harcourt.

Taylor, I. A. (1960). Perception and visual communication. In J. Ball & F. C. Byrnes (Eds.), *Research, principles, and practices in visual communication.* Washington, DC: Department of Audiovisual Instruction.

Theall, D. F. (1973, April). *The role of aesthetic theory in (mass) communications theory.* Paper presented at the meeting of the International Communication Association, Montreal, Canada. (ERIC Document Reproduction Service No. ED 077 047).

Turbayne, C. M. (1970). *The myth of metaphor.* New Haven, CT: Yale University Press.

Vernon, M. D. (1952). *A further study of visual perception.* London: Cambridge University Press.

Wendt, P. R. (1962). The language of pictures. In S. I. Hayakawa (Ed.), *The use and misuse of language.* Greenwich, CT: Fawcett Publications.

Whyte, L. (1961). *Aspects of form.* Bloomington, IN: Indiana University Press.

Chapter Two

Perception and Its Role in Communication and Learning

Richard C. Stern

Rhonda S. Robinson

Objectives

After reading this chapter, you should be able to:

1. *Define perception.*

2. *Explain each of the three stages of perception.*

3. *Explain how differences in perception affect the learning process.*

4. *Discuss sensitivity to one's own frame of reference as well as those of others as a factor in learning.*

5. *Define self-concept and the factors that influence change in self-concept.*

Introduction

Many processes are involved in the activity of learning; there are many ways we can learn. We can learn by means of our senses, through visual perception, the primary focus of this book. But we can also learn through the use of instruments that serve as extensions of our sensations and can allow us to learn what we could not learn through unaided, natural sensation. Language also is a learning tool that "makes learning explicit instead of tacit" (Gibson, 1986, p. 263). Pictures can also be vehicles of learning. The special interest of this chapter, however, is the relationship of learning and communication. Fundamental to both processes is perception. How does perception help or hinder the activity of learning? Consider this situation:

Two professors are talking quietly in their office, with the door open. An unfamiliar student walks in and interrupts them, asking for help. They ask the student to wait outside while they complete their discussion; in just a few moments they go out to the hallway to see how they can help. The student has disappeared, but reemerges from an office and stomps around them, saying "never mind, I'll figure it out for myself since no one will help me." The professors perceive the student as rude and irritating. The student perceives the professors as self-important and inattentive.

Can anything prevent this kind of situation? Can attention to some of the important elements of the learning process improve the chances of a constructive, productive learning environment? Certainly everyone will have an easier time in their role within a learning situation if they are attentive to the process of perception as it relates to learning. Misunderstandings or misperceptions like the one in the example can be prevented. As only one aspect of learning, perception nevertheless plays a pivotal role. A perceptive student or teacher could have avoided the above exchange.

How we perceive the world around us is a critical element in learning. Learning is a complex process, that is, several elements interrelate in any situation to create "learning." If you are aware of these elements and their interaction as the process occurs, you are more likely to be successful in understanding the process, in achieving desired objectives, and even in controlling the process to some degree.

The aspects of perception discussed in this chapter can work together to help you understand and participate efficiently and effectively in virtually any learning experience. Being more aware of the process of perception helps you to discover your learning style, and to evaluate learning situations more accurately. As you may have already observed, the processes of learning and communication are closely related, indeed, they overlap in many areas. As you increase understanding of these processes and intentionally try to control what variables may interfere with either learning or communication, you will become more alert to the elements of both processes and be in a position to be more sensitive to the learning environment and even to control them to your advantage.

What Is Perception?

Definition

All communication, including learning, is based on more than an individual's perceptions at the time that communication is taking place. Perception can be very subjective, and it is constantly changing. Perception is the gathering of information through our senses and the organizing of that information in order to create meaning. Perception, then, is a complex process by which we make sense out of our experiences. We rely on our senses to provide us with data; we rely on our experiences, thoughts, and values to organize, interpret, and explain what we see, hear, taste, touch, and smell.

From early infancy, even while in the womb, people experience the world through their senses. Sensation itself, however, is not a simple process; it is a system that is influenced by the one who senses. As we grow older, we learn to organize, categorize, and interpret the data or stimuli received through our eyes, ears, nose, skin, and taste buds. Yet even *what* we sense is affected by those same factors. There is a circularity to both sensation and perception. We interpret data collected by our senses. But what our senses collect is affected by values we bring to that moment (Gibson, 1985, p. 234). This is known as a hermeneutic or interpretive circle. We base sensation, organization, and interpretation on a variety of factors including experience and feelings, as well as present feelings.

The earliest research by psychologists into the nature of perception tried to separate discussions of the process of perception and the attribution of meaning. But Gibson and others concluded that the two were intertwined. Perception, meaning, and memory were linked under the larger umbrella of cognition, particularly with the information-processing approach to cognition and learning (Haber, 1985, p. 271). It was clear to these researchers that perception took place in a context, and that "the continuous act of perceiving necessarily involves the co-perceiving of the self" (Hagen, 1985, p. 233). Again, note the circular nature; we interpret the stimuli, but they also interpret us as we recognize what we sense and what we do not.

It is of interest to note that theories in both learning and communication as well as perception have tended to move away from seeing these dynamic processes as having discrete, isolatable, stimulus-response-type steps. Instead, the trend has been toward an understanding that views the processes as holistic or transactional. One might isolate certain aspects artificially for study or for descriptive reasons. The process itself, however, is a whole, a *Gestalt* in which steps are inter-related and mutually influential. To alter one element of the system is to alter the whole system. One cannot isolate an examination of the process of perception from an examination of the perceiver.

Differences in Perception

Perception, however, is not an absolute, objective or guaranteed process. There are various places in the process where variations in perception can occur, that is to say, perception is an analogic and not a digital process. The terms analog and digital are perhaps most familiar in the field of electronics, but they can describe and illustrate the process of *human* information processing as well. In electronics, you might encounter the terms either in audio and video recording or in discussions of computers. The terms describe how information—sounds and visual images—are recorded and how they are transformed or translated (encoded) for use is another medium. For example, an analog recording of a concert has to translate physical sound into electrical impulses so that it can be recorded onto magnetic audio tape that then reconverts the electricity back to physical sound through the stereo system's electronics and then out through the speakers. The same process applies to television—the need to make one type of signal work in another dissimilar medium.

An analog signal is fairly precise, otherwise, we would not recognize the music or voice or the picture on the tape. However, it is not absolutely accurate. There are many places for distortion to enter the recording process. The audio or videocassette is only an *analogy* of the original sounds or pictures; it is not an identical reproduction.

A digital signal, however, is far more precise, because the signal is converted into a binary computer code that virtually eliminates distortion. Instead of an analogy of sight and sound, there is almost a one-to-one transfer of information from the original to the recording, whether audio or video. Nothing is lost; nothing is added. The bits of information are discrete and are much, much smaller and more easily controlled.

While all this may sound rather technical and may not seem to apply to people trying to learn, the terms analog and digital can serve as an "analogy" for human communication. For example, in oral or written communication, one might employ an analogy to describe an unusual event or situation. The goal is to employ a familiar image to describe in a limited way the unfamiliar. Similes, metaphors, personification, and other figures of speech are types of analogies one can use to translate one idea into other terms for a person for whom that idea is unfamiliar. Analogies, however, are never perfect. They often break down if pushed too far. To suggest that a friend is behaving like a mule is probably limited only to a description of that person's stubbornness and nothing more. However, the recipient of such a remark may perceive the comment as having broader implications and take great, but uncalled for, offense. Let your imagination run with the possibilities.

Unfortunately, human forms of communication are analogic: particularly speech but also writing and fine arts. There is no way humans can communicate with one another ultimately without analogic communication. That is to say, human communication is limited, it depends on creating an image in the other of what it trying to be communicated. But the analogies are always limited and subject to various forms of distortion. Human communication requires interpretation.

The closest we can come to digital communication is by the use of precise, concrete, specific language that describes as comprehensively as possible, given the limitations and constraints of the particular situation, what it is the communicator is attempting to translate. The more general and abstract the language one uses, the more likely there is to be misunderstanding, misinterpretation and/or some other failure to reach shared meaning. The greater the level of detail, whether in oral or visual communication, the greater the likelihood that both parties—teacher and student, for example—will picture or create the same mental image, the same meaning.

Another very basic reason for differences in perception is that our perceptions are often limited by our experiences, as well as by the agenda we bring to a situation. We cannot pay attention to every sensory input in our environment. There is just too much going on as a rule. We learn to select those stimuli that are most important to us, whether they are the sound of traffic approaching, the telephone ringing, or the voice of a teacher speaking too softly. Learning the stages of perception helps us to attend to the important messages. When we improve our ability to perceive, we thereby develop the ability to evaluate which stimuli are more and less important to the activity of the moment.

Examples of differences in perception occur every day. These differences are created by individual uniqueness—the differences in people's backgrounds, experiences, roles, and feelings. The student in the earlier situation was frustrated and did not follow customary procedures; the professors were insensitive to the student's situation. Because of different perspectives on the event, miscommunication occurred, and time was lost. The individuals likely left that communication thinking that the "other" person had not understood their clear message; each person failed to recognize the perceptions of the other person.

Perception has several basic stages. These stages work together to create an image of the world. As with the communication model, the model of the perception process is really circular; the stages interact together to create communication.

Stages of Perception

Frames of Reference

Three basic steps have been identified in the process of perception: selection, organization, and interpretation of stimuli. Before addressing these three steps, however, it is important to identify an additional factor that is active in all three of these steps. This factor is frame of reference.

In the simplest terms, frame of reference is one's unique perspective, the way that one sees the world. Frame of reference is affected by a variety of demographic factors, including age, gender, race, cultural background, occupation, and education. Other psychographic factors include experience, future hopes and expectations, moods, and many other elements. For example, humor is strongly affected by culture. What is humorous in one culture may not be at all funny in another. Cultures also have different perceptions of time and timeliness. What is "ontime" in one culture may be inappropriately late (or early!) in another. Values of aesthetics also vary from culture to culture, as well as from person to person. The ramifications of these differences are important as more and more businesses become international in their scope. On a daily basis we are likely to encounter people of different cultures. Successful relationships with people of different cultures, different ages, genders, and all the other factors of frame of reference require a sensitivity to these differences. It requires that one try as much as possible to see the world, at least momentarily, from the perspective of the other person(s). Adapting this insight to the learning environment requires only a short step to recognize the importance for both teacher and student to recognize their own frames of reference as well as that of others to create a learning setting that is helpful for all involved.

The importance of frame of reference entails two considerations: analysis and adaptation. The first consideration, analysis, deals with developing a knowledge of one's own frame of reference as well as that of the person(s) with whom one is communicating. Every individual's frame of reference is a unique combination of many elements. Some of these are consciously chosen. Others, perhaps most, come as a result of unconscious choices. A few of the elements of one's frame of reference may even be unknown because they are not active parts of one's consciousness.

How frame of reference impacts visual learning may not be immediately obvious. Frame of reference, however, becomes very important in determining what we are used to seeing, what we expect to see, and what we want to see. All of these factors introduce a certain bias or subjectivity into the perception process that makes for a great deal of variation.

Characteristics

Frames of reference are active in all the steps of perception. For example, among the countless stimuli one constantly receives, it is impossible to select or pay attention to all of the stimuli. It would be very difficult, for example, to note in great detail what a fellow student is wearing while one is taking notes and also trying to recognize a song being played in the background. The selection process by which stimuli are actually attended to is based on many factors which will be explored later.

Even how stimuli are organized after they are selected is affected by one's frame of reference. For example, an international student who has never visited an American deli for a meal would have a great deal of difficulty. Often, patrons are asked what they want, and the lists of available breads, sandwich fillings, and side dishes are on boards. Unfortunately, the student is unfamiliar with rye bread, bagels, or hard rolls, and pastrami is a foreign word. No amount of selective perception can help; the individual needs further experience to help process this activity with success.

Finally, frames of reference affect the interpretation of what is selected and organized. A teacher or student may make a comment which two people will interpret in quite different ways. Even a smile can be interpreted in many ways depending on experience and the mood of the moment.

In a very real sense one's frame of reference serves as a filter in all communication-oriented activities. It affects all perception: what stimuli are selected, how they are organized, and finally how they are interpreted by the perceiver. As a person becomes more aware of her or his/her frame of reference, it becomes easier to understand why one responds to certain situations in particular ways, ways which may vary from time to time. Attempting to analyze the frame of reference of another person helps in accounting for their reactions, responses, and understandings as communication (including learning) takes place.

Personal Assessment

Assessing one's own frame of reference requires openness and honesty. Until one accurately assesses the elements contained within her or his/her frame of reference, it will be difficult to adapt to the frame of reference of another person. Yet that is a critical step in developing an awareness of the perception process.

Frame of reference is a key factor in all the steps of perception. Successful learning starts with participants understanding their frames of reference as well as the frames of reference of those others with whom they are involved. But understanding is not enough. Adapting one's frame of reference to that of another person is really at the heart of communication. Communication is at the heart of learning. Analysis and adaptation of frames of reference will result in the most accurate and trustworthy perceptions. Once these perceptions have been selected, organized, and interpreted, one can then choose the proper channels for learning based on the content of the course, the teaching style of the instructor, as well as the varying needs and learning styles of the students.

Selection Factors

From the discussion of frame of reference it should be obvious that learning is a very complex, fluid, and dynamic process. While the steps of selection, organization, and interpretation are isolated in this discussion for purposes of explanation, they are very interactive. Yet as they are identified and isolated, the steps can be held up for examination. This examination leads to increased understanding and the potential for greater control of the learning process. Learning can then become a more conscious activity, more in your control as the perceiver. Adjustments and conscious compensations can be made to account for inadequacies in the learning environment. You may need to do something as simple as moving to a different chair in order to see better. Or, the change can be as complex as the need for an entire industry to revise its approach to advertising because of changes in values, changes in market, adverse publicity, or other factors.

At every moment of every day a person is bombarded by stimuli, including sounds, sights, and smells. Because a person is unable to pay attention to these stimuli, a selection process takes place. Brighter colors stand out, as do louder sounds. People are more likely to perceive stimuli that are somewhat unusual, for example, an unusually tall or short person. On the other hand there is a tendency to become less sensitive to certain stimuli that are experienced repeatedly. For example, after living in a neighborhood with lots of traffic noise, you are likely to become less sensitive to the noises after time. A long-time resident may not even realize that the 5:05 commuter train has just gone by, though guests are overwhelmed by the racket.

Fleming and Levie (1978) listed over 50 principles and Winn (1993) noted more than 75 principles related to the process of perception. While intended for the instructional designer, the principles are also useful to the learner. The goal of these lists is to create better, more accurate perception, to avoid misperceptions, and help designers to create visuals that best represent the real world, for example, in a textbook. The learner who understands these general principles can be more critical in using textbooks, knowing the limits on goals that were used in creating the text.

Some of the basic principles include understanding perception as relative and not absolute. That is, we perceive not simply color or texture or brightness by itself but in relation to similar qualities which precede or follow. Second, perception is selective. We cannot be attentive to every stimulus available in the environment. Choices are made according to certain patterns. Third, perception is organized, as noted above, according to certain patterns. We may even try to create a pattern where there is none in order to organize data. Fourth, perception is affected by our expectations. Finally, perceptions may vary significantly from person to person (Fleming & Levie, 1978).

Physiological Factors

Selection is affected by a variety of factors including physiology, psychology, experience, and present feelings. Physiological factors are those factors dealing with the five senses. The sensitivity of human senses varies from person to person, depending on such factors as age, congenital variance, and environmental factors such as noise, smoky air, etc. Hearing acuity is limited from approximately 20 to 20,000 cycles per second. Continuous exposure to loud noise over time lessens one's overall sensitivity. As people get older their hearing often becomes less sensitive in higher frequencies.

Vision is also limited. Sight is limited to only a portion of the light spectrum. As people age, physiological changes often occur and people become far-sighted. Physical proximity to an event can affect perception. How close a person is to a conversation obviously affects how well it can be heard. How close one is to an automobile accident affects how well and what details of that event will be observed.

Psychological Factors

In addition to physiological factors are psychological factors which affect selection of stimuli. One psychological factor has to do with need. One is more likely to notice what *needs* to be noticed. For instance, instructors tend to focus on students and on the content of their teaching. Often, they are not as focused on the environment or the classroom, especially if they have seen it many times. Students, on the other hand, may let their attention wander enough to notice the faded carpeting or the torn drapes. Their need to observe all of their environment is greater than the instructor's need.

Related to need is the tendency not to notice what one does not want to see or hear. As you drive down the freeway, if you are a sports car enthusiast, you may notice all the sports cars. If you are interested in motorcycles, however, you may miss the sports cars but notice all the motorcycles. Occasionally this tendency becomes so strong that people may even distort the perception to the point that obvious details are deleted, or details may be added that did not occur, especially when the event is recalled later.

Past Experience

Past experience can also have a significant affect on one's perception. Perception is better for those objects or events for which one has been trained. An active football or basketball fan, for example, one who has played the game and studied its rules, would be much more likely to see a foul perpetrated than an inexperienced spectator.

Knowledge includes something as basic as language. Even the language we speak can affect our perception: what we perceive and how we perceive it. Different languages seem to be more sensitive to certain feelings, or certain experiences. The classic example of this is languages of Eskimo tribes which identify many different kinds of snow, each kind identified by a completely different term, not merely adjectives added to modify the basic word for snow. The Whorf-Sapir Hypothesis suggests that visual perception is significantly shaped by the language one speaks. The hypothesis contends that in large part

(1) thoughts are determined by language; (2) behavior is determined by language; (3) language is strongly related to the culture in which that language is spoken and reflects that culture's values; and (4) language serves as a filter for how one views the world. Language is an important element of the frame of reference (Faieta, 1983).

Language also includes jargon generated by a profession. The jargon reflects a very specialized perception which the layperson would likely not understand without experience and time spent learning the "language." Just knowing the words would not be as helpful as time spent in the culture of the profession learning the language much as an anthropologist spends time in a foreign culture. To those in the know, jargon reflects experience in perceiving data that the uninformed do not recognize as important or relevant. Their experience may not perceive certain data. Yet sometimes with brief education, the uninformed can learn to understand concepts that may be helpful in their financial affairs, for example, reading daily stock quotations, or understanding different methods for computing interest on a loan.

Present Feelings

In addition to past experience, present feelings affect one's perception. One may react to someone's sarcastic comment with anger on one occasion but with amusement on another depending on current emotional status. How responsive one is to another's needs can vary significantly if, for example, an employee has just been reprimanded by a superior or praised for excellence in customer relations, or, if someone a professor perceives as an excellent student hands in sub-standard work. Perceptions are different for one who has just learned of the death of a favorite relative or has been informed that they have won the lottery. Present feelings affect one's perception of the world. Even how well one person likes the way another person dresses can influence perceptions of that person.

Organizing Data

Once stimuli have been selected, the data will be organized according to a variety of principles. It is as though the perception must be placed in a file or it will soon be discarded as having no meaning, no place of belonging.

Simplicity and Patterns

Psychologists have identified several principles which are used to organize stimuli. These include simplicity and pattern, proximity, similarity, figure and background, closure and good form, and perceptual constancy.

The first principle is simplicity. Presented with a complex array of stimuli, individuals will typically try to simplify or categorize the information in some manner by finding a common characteristic that ties the stimuli together. We simply need to find some one to group impressions to make sense of our perceptions. If every stimulus were treated as absolutely unique and unrelated to every other stimulus, that would be an excellent definition for chaos.

Related to simplicity is the tendency to look for patterns in collections of stimuli. When confronted by a series of items, a search for common elements or qualities is conducted. The two series of numbers listed below illustrate the importance of patterns in perception. Which group of numbers would be easier to memorize?

1. 315194812131460929
2. 3-15-1948
    12,13,14
    60929

The second list is presumably easier to memorize because there are familiar patterns identifiable in the numbers. The first grouping looks like a date. The second is a simple series. The third number is a zip code. The patterns of the numbers in the second list help you to perceive and organize the numbers, even though the numbers are the same in the two lists.

Proximity

Proximity is another principle used to organize perceptions. Proximity is the tendency to group together those things that are located close to one another. If three people walk into a building at the same time, there is a tendency to believe that they are together, that, perhaps, they are returning from lunch. It may, however, be a mere coincidence that they walk in at the same time; they may have never met before that moment. Similarly, people may assume that when two people are talking and one smiles at the other that the two are friends.

Similarity

Similarity is a fourth principle for organizing perceptions. Similarity is the tendency to group elements because they seem to be alike in shape, color, size, sound, etc. This has been the source of a great deal of misunderstanding and miscommunication. Prejudice is an exaggerated use of similarity to organize perceptions, assuming all members of a gender, race, religion, or nationality are alike.

Figure and Background

A final example in the category of organizing principles is figure and background. Usually it is obvious what is the figure or object and what is the background, what is important and what is not. But it is not always the case as in the classic example in the following diagram. Is it a candleholder, or is it two people facing one another? In this instance it is difficult to tell which is the figure and which is the background. See Figure 1.

On an intellectual level, figure and background can also cause difficulties or variations in perception. For example one person may perceive something as a serious or annoying problem, while another may not notice it at all. If you cannot account for $5.00 at the end of the day you might be very upset; that was tomorrow's lunch money. If a major manufacturing firm cannot account for $5.00, it is hardly noticeable.

Closure and Good Form

Another type of organizing principle includes information that perceivers supply that may not actually be present in the original event. One example is

Figure 1. Figure and Background.

closure. Closure is the tendency to see as complete a figure or sentence which is not actually complete. The diagrams below illustrate this.

In creating closure the missing lines are supplied because it is more pleasing and easier to perceive and organize a figure that is complete. Triangles and squares are easier to perceive than sets of random lines. See Figure 2.

Similar to closure is good form. That which is incorrect or incomplete is perceived as proper. An example is the following sentence. "When entering the building it always necessary to punch the security code into the door keypad." The word "is" has been omitted from between "it" and "always." But many do not notice this because they have mentally supplied the missing word themselves. A similar occurrence happens in listening. Words are provided. Grammar is corrected. This happens so spontaneously that one is rarely aware of what has happened. The data is perceived as being correct, not corrected.

Perceptual Constancy

Perceptual constancy is the tendency to persist in perceiving something in a certain way even though that person or event has changed (Wakefield, 1976). First impressions of people fall in this category. It takes great effort to overcome first impressions, positive or negative.

One example of this is the way we perceive new acquaintances. If a new neighbor is initially perceived as rude, distant, sweet, or polite, it is likely that it will take a major incident to the contrary to change that perception. If a professor

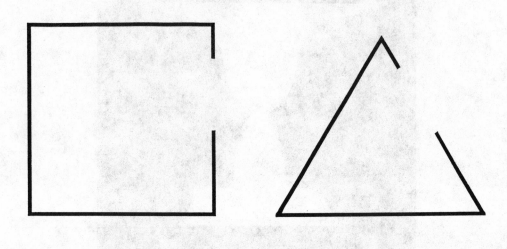

Figure 2. Closure and Good Form.

perceives a student as competent in one area, it is likely that he or she will perceive that student as competent in other areas as well. This is known as the "halo effect."

Another common example is the tendency to talk more loudly with someone who does not speak English well, as though a lack of familiarity with a language has affected their hearing. We surely know better, but we persist in responding in that manner.

Interpreting Information

After selecting stimuli and organizing the data, information is then interpreted. By interpreting information we give it meaning. The meaning attached to certain perceptions is based on a variety of principles. Differences in interpretation account for why two people may respond quite differently to the same situation. One may find a remark humorous while another does not understand it or finds it offensive. Mood may account for the differences in interpretation. Culture, age, and many of the elements of frame of reference may also account for differences in interpretation.

One important element which affects interpretation is made up of the interplay of beliefs, values, and attitudes. Beliefs, values, and attitudes are affected by the culture in which people are raised and in which they now live, by experience, and by expectations for the future. What one is taught or indirectly observes in parents and others of authority also plays an important part in the development of beliefs, values, and attitudes. Other factors include the recency–primacy effect, and present feelings.

Beliefs, Values, and Attitudes

Beliefs are those concepts which we assume to be true (Deetz & Stevenson, 1986). Individuals act on beliefs, not always testing them out before acting. Individuals write checks assuming the financial institution will process them properly. They do not check before every transaction. Beliefs are facts, what one trusts to be true.

Values are what one believes to be important, good, or valuable. Values also serve as a basis for perceptions and actions. Values are not true or false as with beliefs. However, they can be evaluated on whether they are helpful. "My classmates are basically honest." "All my classmates try to steal me blind." Which value is more likely to be truly helpful in living? Which is likely to result in a productive learning environment?

Attitudes are derived from beliefs and values. They are the manifestation of those beliefs and values. For example, people who believe that smoking is bad for health and who value good health may develop a positive attitude toward a referendum against smoking in public places. One may even initiate a petition to have designated smoking areas at work (Deetz & Stevenson, 1986).

One aspect of beliefs, attitudes, and values is past experience. As in the selection of data, past experience can also play a part in interpreting stimuli. Previous experience with types of people or situations may pre-condition one to act or think in certain ways. These habitual responses can be changed but only with effort and concentration. A bad experience with a supervisor may cause wariness the next time that supervisor is encountered. The supervisor may not behave in the apparently hostile manner, but one is more likely to notice hostile behaviors or interpret certain actions as hostile or threatening.

Recency–Primacy

Another example of past experiences is the recency/primacy effect. What happened recently has a significant impact on perception. When a manager writes performance evaluations, what a subordinate has done most recently may color how the manager fills out that evaluation. If the employee has done well overall, but recently made a mistake, the mistake may be given too much weight because it happened recently. It was fresh in the manager's mind. Similarly, the employee may have done well overall but made one serious error in judgment. The evaluation may be overly negative because of the primacy effect. One event is given disproportionate weight, regardless of when the event took place.

Present Feelings and Expectations

Present feelings are one last factor in the interpretation of data. Present feelings play a key role in shaping our expectations that, in turn, have significant impact not only on what we perceive but also on how we perceive it. The particular mood someone is in varies from one moment to the next, going from happy to sad to anxious to insecure to joy to anger. Obviously, mood can significantly affect how events are interpreted.

Interpretations are affected by "baggage" that is carried from the past and by present feelings, including expectations. For example, when several possible interpretations of an event exist, the one which fits with expectations is the one likely to be perceived. If employees expect the boss is not happy with their work, they are more likely to feel anxious when the boss calls them into the office. On the other hand, if they are expecting a promotion, that same call will cause joy (Adler & Rodman, 1985). Another type of expectation affecting perception is the self-fulfilling prophecy, when what is expected is unconsciously caused to happen.

An example of an expectation that is important for managers to be aware of is the halo effect mentioned earlier. If people know that a teller is competent in one area, an evaluator is likely to expect that the teller is competent in other areas (Hanna & Wilson, 1988). It may or may not be the case.

A variation of the halo effect is the tendency to view less critically the mistakes of those that are liked or who have been judged as competent. Conversely, there is a tendency to judge more harshly similar mistakes of those who have previously been judged to be less competent.

Similar to the halo effect is stereotyping. A stereotype is a generalization based on inadequate or incomplete information. Because one must select among available information about a person, place, or situation, there is no choice but to make judgments on incomplete or inadequate information. But it is easy to confuse that inadequate information with the complete story. This incomplete information is used to judge people or events that seem to fit with the original situation. A stereotype may be very individual or ingrained within an entire culture. Virtually everyone has formed stereotypes or fixed impressions about people, places, or situations. Even when they are partly true, they are never completely true (Hanna & Wilson, 1988). Stereotyping simplifies the process of perception, but overlooks legitimate differences that exist between people, places, and situations.

Interaction of Stages

As has been suggested, these three stages of perception—selection, organization, and interpretation—are not neatly segmented steps but are all happening constantly.

Perception is a cyclical process, as Figure 3 suggests. It is a never-ending process in which each step affects the other. Many of the principles detailed in selecting stimuli are similar to factors used to interpret stimuli. How one has interpreted past data will certainly affect how data is selected in the future and how that data will be organized. The steps have been separated only for ease of explanation. And, of course, one's frame of reference has impact on all of the stages.

Self-Concept

Another factor which is highly influential in the process of perception is self-concept. Self-concept is a "mental mirror" that reflects how we view ourselves. Self-concept includes both physical and emotional areas; how we see our appearance, intelligence, talents, likes and dislikes, and emotional states. Self-

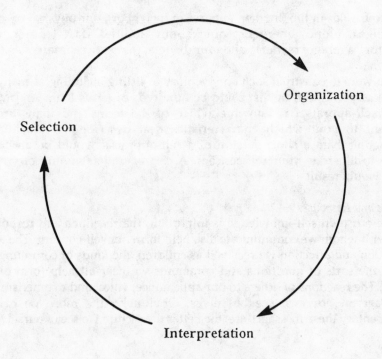

Figure 3. Interaction of Stages.

concept influences our frame of reference or understanding of ourselves. It individualizes and limits what we actually can perceive in any situation. It is what we consider unique about ourselves. The influence of self-concept becomes most noticeable at that point in the perception process when meaning is attributed to data which have been perceived by the senses.

Formation of Self-Concept

Self-concept is formed throughout our early lives and is virtually completely formed before we are adults. While self-concept can be altered and enhanced, it plays an important role in how we communicate and how we learn and in how well our communications are received. Self-concept is formed by self-appraisal, by the messages received from others through their reactions and responses, and by the roles we play in life. Because a significant degree of our self-concept is formed in early childhood, it serves as a powerful factor that a student brings to the learning environment. It may influence what topics a student is interested in, what topics a students feels incapable of learning, and whether one believes he or she has an ability to learn at all.

Self-Appraisal

Self-appraisal is our understanding of and definition of ourself. A self-appraisal might be a mental listing of terms that define our true self, such as daughter, mother, clever, bright, quiet, moody, sensitive, and fit. These terms include our roles in life (mother, supervisor, neighbor), our physical description (overweight, blond, energetic, quick), our abilities (fast learner, careful negotiator, average reader), and our beliefs (honest, religious, American, truthful).

If you were to construct such an inventory or listing including as many terms or items as you could, the list could be hundreds of terms long. An important part of self-appraisal is knowing which of the terms and items are most important to you; which characteristics best describe the essential self. Constructing even a short version of a self-appraisal would be an excellent exercise to illustrate your self-concept. A clearer understanding of your self-concept would result.

Reactions and Responses

While our own self-knowledge is important, the reactions and responses of others with whom we communicate also help form our self-concept. The amount of attention and affection we received as children, the kinds of compliments we receive, the sorts of questions and comments we hear all help form our self-concept. The reactions of others to our appearance, voice, and mannerisms make an impact on how we see ourselves. Obviously, the more positive and complimentary these messages are, the better the picture we see of ourselves.

Roles

The importance of self-concept in the process of perception in communication and learning is in how we identify ourselves. The various roles we play are a function of self-concept; the patterns of behavior that characterize how we act in a situation are the roles we play. These roles might be related to sex or race, to our position in the institution, or our place in society in general.

In the discussion of self-appraisal, it was suggested that an inventory of terms we use to define ourselves would be many items long. Think now just about the roles we play in our lives. The list includes parent, child, employee, supervisor, teller, friend, neighbor, spouse, church member, group member, and so on. Even if we limit the list to the workplace, there are several roles that apply. We may be at the same time an instructor, a student, an employee of an institution, someone's supervisor or boss, a provider of information, a withholder of services, a source of assistance, and a creator of problems. The list goes on. Obviously, the prominence of these roles varies with the occasion, but they are all influential.

How we view these roles ourselves has an impact on how others view us, and on how others communicate with and respond to us. If we are comfortable working with the public and feel good about helping others, then our self-concept in that role is a very positive one. If we are willing to learn and be corrected by our teachers or supervisors, then we respond appropriately to those people and respond well in that role. If others see us as a congenial and helpful classmate or co-worker, and come to us for help, then we feel successful. (**Editors' note**: See chapter on *Action and Object Language* for additional information.)

Impact of Roles

Our self-concept is affected by these various communications and by our awareness of and acceptance of our many roles. The feedback we receive, the rewards or punishment we receive in these roles influences self-concept and the perceptions of value of the many roles we fill. Self-concept affects the roles we play, the places we have in the world, either at work or in our private lives. Most of us are aware of the impact of some of these roles and the behaviors they cause. "Since I was the oldest, I was always given the most responsibility and the hardest jobs. I guess that helped me learn how to accept hard assignments and take charge in tough situations."

"I look much younger than I am, which has its advantages! However, I often get treated as if I were rather immature, or as if I might not be able to help someone with their situation. It really bothers me." These people are illustrating their knowledge of some of their roles, behaviors, and the causes for them.

But many of our roles and behaviors are not seen and appreciated by others. While you may have a clear perspective of yourself, others do not always share that perspective. For instance, a new teacher coming into the university may not recognize your abilities immediately, or be aware of your previous work in and out of the class. Consequently, a very capable and experienced student can be ignored or spoken "down" to by a teacher expecting someone else or someone new to take responsibility for some project.

While an individual may be perfectly capable and willing to assist another person, their age, sex, race, or other characteristics may influence the other's openness to receiving help. Becoming more aware of others' responses to you, of how others see you, makes you a more sensitive, and alert communicator. When you can see yourself the way others might, it helps facilitate better understanding between communicators. In the learning environment, it may mean being more assertive about informing an instructor about special needs and interests.

Functions of Self-Concept

The formation of self-concept, then, includes self-appraisal, the responses and reactions of others, and the roles one plays in life. Self-concept is formed by the interaction of these three. Self-concept as a filter of others' communications, as a predictor of behavior, and as an influence on communication style.

Self-Concept Filters

As a filter of perceptions, self-concept affects what we choose to hear and how well we receive the messages sent. If a student has a self-concept that includes a term like "poor listener," a formal classroom learning situation could be anxiety-producing and unpleasant. The student could allow self-concept filters to inhibit learning. If that student can obtain positive reactions to questions or comments, the self-concept may change enough to allow the learning to proceed more effectively. The student must be aware and believe that this change is possible, not allowing self-concept to filter out important messages to the contrary.

Self-concept's filters also affect how well we hear instructions, compliments, or questions. The more we are aware of this filtering possibility, the more we are watchful for problems that may arise from the filtering effects of self-concept. If we can carefully hear the messages given, and can combat the filtering effects of self-concept, we can actually change our self-concept and become a better communicator in the process.

For example, think of a situation when a group of friends have come to you for assistance with a problem. If you acted distracted or were very busy, the people might perceive that you had no intention or interest in being helpful. They could say something to you to indicate that they would like someone else to help them, which you could perceive as an insult. If your self-concept is already a low or negative one, you might really feel hurt or upset that they were displeased with your abilities. If you monitor your self-concept filters, you can selectively ignore your feelings of inadequacy, and think about the situation. If you apply your perception skills, you become aware that you were sending your "I'm busy" signals. Instead of acting angrily, you apologize for seeming preoccupied and make a special effort to help. In this case, you have overcome the effect of self-concept filters of reality; you have seen the situation from the friends' point of view, and you have saved the situation from becoming a problem. Perception and self-awareness are important parts of improving communication and shaping the environment in which constructive learning can take place.

The place of self-concept is also evident in the work of Gibson (1985). Gibson suggested that perception, particularly visual perception, was primarily the process of discriminating change from non-change. Changes in surface texture signal a change in object, for example. Changes in color would also alert one to a shift of some sort. The quality being perceived is not so much perceived for itself (color, size, texture, shading, etc.) but because some sort of change has occurred which creates a noticeable contrast. How carefully one perceives the change and the meaning one attributes to the change depend on what the change "affords" the one who perceives that change (Hagen, 1985, p. 248). The process of perception, then, is *not* objective or absolute; it is highly personal and contextual.

Self-Concept as a Predictor

Self-concept can also function as a predictor of behavior. If your analysis of yourself includes many positive terms, you have a high self-concept. If you have strong, positive feelings about yourself, you communicate those feelings to others. If the opposite is true, and you describe yourself in many negative terms, your interactions with others will likely reveal low self-concept and negative feelings about the world. These feelings predict or shade your behavior and reactions to daily encounters. If you expect not to be rewarded or promoted because you are "just not as good as the others," your behavior may actually reflect this attitude and prevent you from being promoted.

If, on the other hand, you feel positive about yourself, and give yourself credit for your abilities and efforts, the positive behaviors from that attitude may result in positive effects. Others may see you as positively as you see yourself, and the rewards may follow.

Self-Fulfilling Prophecy

The function of self-concept as a predictor of behavior is also termed a "self-fulfilling prophecy." Your self-concept predicts how you communicate and behave, and those communications and behaviors impact further your self-concept. You actually become what you think you will. Whether those are positive or negative predictions depends on your self-concept.

Another aspect of this prediction of behavior is that others see us as we see ourselves. If we project a positive self-image, others will respond with high opinions of our work or opinions. Usually, people work more quickly and better for professors or supervisors if they think that person already holds them in high esteem. Instinctively, we respond more positively to those who treat us with respect and regard for our abilities. It is important to note, however, that we can change behavior, and the cycle of the self-fulfilling prophecy can be turned into a positive direction.

For example, if we think positively, act with self-confidence, and reflect a positive self-concept, people will most likely respond positively to us, our suggestions, and our ideas. Having our ideas accepted helps other continue to see us positively, and gives us feedback which helps enhance our self-concept; it makes us feel better about ourselves. Making those first steps to positive self-concept, recognizing our roles, and the filters with which we may be operating, will all help us perform more effectively and communicate more clearly. Often right behavior results in right thinking. The opposite, however, can also be true.

Self-Concept as Influence on Style

The third function of self-concept involves our communication tone and style. The vocabulary we use, the tone of voice we select, and the nonverbal ways we communicate are all influenced by self-concept. An employee wants communications that are positive and effective; thus, vocabulary and tone must be carefully selected. Self-concept is reflected in our word choices and in the expressions we use. Constant self-deprecation (making fun of oneself) may be amusing from a television comedian, but it is not an effective communications tool. A whining or self-pitying tone also affects others negatively. The teacher or student who approaches others with a pleasant tone and positive expectations reflected in their words will be an effective communicator.

Nonverbal Communication and Self-Concept

In addition to vocabulary and tone, other nonverbal communications are affected by self-concept. The appropriateness of attire, cleanliness, neatness, posture, facial expressions, and gestures are all affected by self-concept. People who have a positive self-concept, and feel good about themselves, and their life, will appear eager, helpful, and competent in their communications style and tone. The nonverbal clues they send will be of confidence, capability, and courteousness. For example, their dress and appearance will be professional, their vocabulary will be clear and expressive, and their facial expression and gestures will reveal capability and interest in their work. The often trite "Have a good day" ending to a transaction may actually be meaningful if the employee uses a tone and style that makes the words seem genuine. Often the difference between opportunity and oppression in how we view a work-oriented task of a homework assignment is found in one's self-concept.

The formation of one's self-concept and the functions that self-concept serve in the communication/learning process are very individual and sometimes hard to recognize. Analyzing one's capabilities, roles, and values could help build self-awareness. A good communicator is one who reflects a positive self-concept, who is aware of nonverbal messages sent through appearance, gestures, and facial expressions, and who consistently strives to maintain a positive style and tone in communicating with others. This, in turn, influences our approach to the learning task and the process of perception. Self-concept is clearly an important factor of perception.

It is equally important to realize how our perception of ourselves affects the way we perceive events, ourselves, and our interactions with others. Improving perceptions can improve interpersonal communications. Understanding the complexity of perception helps prevent perceptual mistakes: assuming too much about perceptions without checking their accuracy, or forming hasty conclusions about people, places, and events.

References

Adler, R., & Rodman, G. (1985). *Understanding human communication* (2nd ed.). New York: Holt, Rinehart, and Winston.

Burke, K. (1969). *A rhetoric of motives.* Berkeley, CA: University of California Press.

Deetz, S., & Stevenson, S. (1986). *Managing interpersonal communication.* New York: Harper & Row.

Faieta, F. (1983). The P's and cues of perception. In Communication Research Associates (Eds.), *Communicate!* (3rd ed.). Dubuque, IA: Kendall/Hunt.

Fleming, M., & Levie, W. H. (1978). *Instructional message design: Principles from the behavioral sciences.* Englewood Cliffs, NJ: Educational Technology Publications.

Gibson, J. J. (1985). Conclusions from a century of research on sense perception. In S. Koch & D. E. Leary (Eds.), *A century of psychology as a science* (pp. 224–230). New York: McGraw-Hill.

Gibson, J. J. (1986). *The ecological approach to visual perception.* Hillsdale, NJ: Lawrence Erlbaum Associates.

Haber, R. N. (1985). Perception: A hundred year perspective. In S. Koch & D. E. Leary (Eds.), *A century of psychology as a science* (pp. 250–281). New York: McGraw-Hill.

Hagen, M. A. (1985). James J. Gibson's ecological approach to visual perception. In S. Koch & D. E. Leary (Eds.), *A century of psychology as a science* (pp. 231–249). New York: McGraw-Hill.

Hanna, M., & Wilson, G. (1988). *Communicating in business and professional settings.* New York: Random House.

Wakefield, B. (1976). *Perception and communication.* Urbana, IL: ERIC Clearinghouse on Reading and Communication Skills.

Winn, W. (1993). Perception principles. In M. Fleming & W. H. Levie (Eds.), *Instructional message design: Principles from the behavioral and cognitive sciences* (2nd ed.). Englewood Cliffs, NJ: Educational Technology Publications.

Chapter Three

Physiological and Cognitive Factors in the Study of Visual Images

Nikos Metallinos

Objectives

After reading this chapter, you should be able to:

1. *Define what is meant by cognition.*

2. *Identify the anatomy of the human information system.*

3. *Define visual stimulation.*

4. *Explain the threefold process of stimulation.*

Introduction

This chapter reviews the empirical data, examines the related theories, and underlines the pertinent principles of cognition as they relate to visual images. Whereas visual and auditory *perceptions* are processes by which sensoric information is depicted and codified by the eyes and ears and then processed to the brain, *cognition* is the process by which visual and oral inputs received by the brain are organized, decodified, and translated into meaningful holistic structures and messages.

Defined specifically as the "art or process of knowing in the broadest sense" (Webster's, 1971, p. 440), cognition here is synonymous to comprehension, interpretation, and understanding of visuals and sounds. Although studies of the visual and auditory perception processes are mostly dealt with in the fields of perceptual psychology, the processes of knowing, understanding, and interpreting such phenomena are principally dealt with in the fields of cognitive psychology. Neurophysiology is involved in both these domains. However, in perception our main concern is the physiology of the eyes and ears, whereas in cognition we concentrate on the neurophysiology and neurochemistry of the human brain (the anatomy of the brain), the processes involved in transferring sensoric data into cognitive structures (brain vs. mind), and the prerequisites for such transformations (recognition standards). This chapter deals primarily with the anatomy of the human information system and discusses specifically (1) the neurological factors of the ear, eye, and brain, (2) the stimuli and the perceptual processes, and (3) the codification of visual and auditory information.

Anatomy of the Human Information System

The organs of visual and auditory perception, the eyes and ears, constitute a complex information system, a network of stations which receive selected signals from the environment either electromagnetically or mechanically (by air vibration), transform them into organized bits of information or codes, and channel them by electrical impulses to the brain. In the brain these codes are processed to the appropriate part depending on their nature and particular characteristics where they are decoded, translated, recognized, and assume their meaning. Oversimplified, this is how perception and cognition work.

Neurophysiological Factors of the Eyes, Ears, and Brain

An understanding of how the complex human information networks work relies on a basic conceptualization of the anatomy of the eyes, ears, and brain. The discussion refers to the key stations of each of the three systems involved in the reception, organization, and recognition of visual and auditory signals. Of paramount importance to the students of visual literacy are three key factors which relate to the human information organs: *duplication, polarization*, and *interconnection* of the eyes, ears, and brain.

Like most other organs of the human body the eyes, ears, and brain are duplicated in the left and right side of a person's head. In our routine activity of receiving and processing images and sounds the fact that two identical, yet apart, eyes, ears, and brains are in operation seldom draws our attention. This duplication of the information organs, however, benefits us by (1) allowing a larger degree of reception of stimuli, (2) offering a greater flexibility to the delicate processes of perception and recognition, and (3) providing a *spare part* in case of a total loss or severe damage of one of these organs. In the structuring of visual and auditory images these factors must guide the process. They are fundamental to the study of visual literacy.

The polarization of the information organs is also of great significance and is beneficial to all humans. Our two eyes see the phenomena in front of us from two different positions. This is known as binocular disparity or stereopsis which allows us to see depth. Because of this polarization we perceive the world three-dimensionally. Equally, the perception of stereophonic or three-dimensional sounds is possible because of the polarization of our auditory organs in a left and a right ear apart from each other.

Lastly, the polarization of the incoming signals (half of which go to the left and half to the right hemisphere of the brain) creates the unique opportunity for the brain to recognize information entering from the left or the right sides, known as left or right visual or auditory fields. The polarization of the information organs is a factor of great value to the producers and viewers of visual and auditory messages, particularly televised ones, because among other things it indicates on or where the objects, subjects, or events should be staged to be readily perceived and easily recognized.

The third important factor regarding the human information network of great significance to students of visual literacy is that all three systems, the eyes, ears, and brain, are interconnected. The process of recognition, translation, or comprehension of visual and auditory information by the brain could not be achieved if all three systems were not interconnected. Such common phrases widely used by people as *'do you see what I mean? are you listening to me?,* etc., are examples of how interconnected, related, and dependent on each other the information organs are. Misinterpretations and misunderstandings of visuals or sounds are mainly prevented because the organs of perception and recognition are in close contact supporting and complementing each other. The degree of awareness and understanding of the situation, circumstances, and messages depends on the harmonious coexistence and correlation of the information organs.

Basic Anatomy of the Eyes

The most important factor regarding the anatomy of the human eyes is that each of its parts are extremely specialized structures, sensibly contrived, and harmonically related to the other organs of the information system.

The basic parts of the human eye principally related to the issues concerning this chapter are the *cornea,* the *aqueous humor,* the *iris,* the *pupil,* the *lens,* the *retina,* the *fovea,* the *vitreous humor,* and the *optic nerve.* See Figure 1. A plethora of smaller auxiliary organs are connected to the human eyes working harmoniously to receive and process visual stimuli to the appropriate hemisphere of the brain.

The cornea is the foremost external part of the human eye that receives the light that carries information about the shape, texture, and color of the object (Murch, 1973). The aqueous humor is the next external organ of the eye which receives the photon beam of the light and which is secreted and absorbed on an interval of four hours time (Gregory, 1966) regenerating its substance to allow a continuous and uniform reception of light. The internal part of the eye starts with the iris, an annular muscle which forms the pupil that regulates the amount of light allowed to pass through to the organ lying immediately behind, the lens. The lens then focuses the light through a semi-colorless viscus substance known as vitreous humor, for it to arrive at the sense cells of the retina which according to Gregory (1966), "... is a thin sheet of interconnected nerve cells, including the light sensitive rod and cone cells which convert light into electrical pulses" (pp. 44–45). These light sensitive cells of the retina are engaged in one of the most significant functions of the visual perception process described by Gregory (1966) as follows:

> The cones function in daylight conditions and give color vision. The rods function under low lumination and give vision only to shades of gray. Daylight is referred to as *photopic,* while the gray world given by the rods in dim light is called *scotopic.* (p. 48)

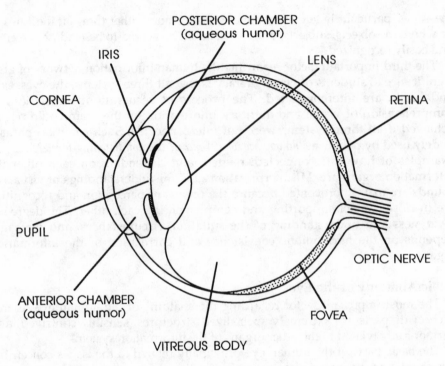

Figure 1. The Human Eye.

The cones occupy the central region of the retina. Exceedingly close together they form the fovea, the region of the retina which gives the best visual detail and color. The last organ of the eye to receive and process visual information is the optic nerve. Located at the back of the eye, slightly off the center of the eyeball, it receives light impulses from the eye and brings them to the *optic chiasm* located in the center of the brain. Here, for all practical purposes, the main task of the eyes to receive and process visual information to the brain actually ends and the brain takes over.

Basic Anatomy of the Ear

Two important factors regarding the human auditory system are its *intricacy* and *sensitivity*. This extremely fragile and delicate auditory system is a complex labyrinth which consists of a great number of chambers and auxiliary organs seemingly different, yet interconnected and related to each other.

The most crucial parts of the auditory system directly related to this discussion are (1) the organs of the exterior part such as the *external auditory meatus* and the *eardrum*, (2) the organs of the middle ear such as the *ossicles* (malleus, incus, and stapes), the *oral window*, and the *eustachian tube*, and (3) the inner ear or central hearing system consisting of three main organs, the *semicircular canals* which comprise the vestibular systems (unrelated to the acoustic system), the *cochlea* which furnishes the receptor apparatus of the *organ of Corti*, and the *auditory nerve* that transmits sound information to the brain. See Figure 2.

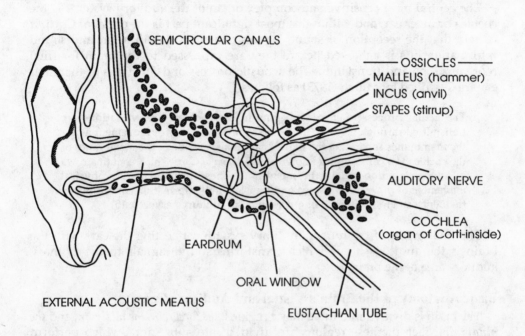

Figure 2. The Human Ear.

Extraneous auditory signals are funneled into the exterior ear known as the auditory meatus. At the end of the tunnel formed by the auditory meatus the sound signals resonated impinge on the eardrum. This membrane constitutes the gateway that connects the external ear with the middle ear. The resonated vibrations of the eardrum are then picked up by three small bones which form the ossicles called the malleus, incus, and stapes. The main function of the ossicles is to simplify the force exerted by the eardrum, to regulate, and to mechanically transmit the sound vibrations to yet another membrane of the middle ear, namely the oral window.

As its name indicates, the function assigned to the oral window is to close the opening end of the tube forming the central organ of the entire auditory system, the cochlea. The successful performance of all key organs of the middle ear, but primarily that of the ossicles is achieved because they are located in the air-filled cavity formed by the eustachian tube. Adjacent to the cochlea is the vestibular system, an information system which "... act as transducers for information about orientation with respect to gravity and angular acceleration of the head" (Boddy, 1978, p. 276). Because of the information provided by this vestibular system we are able to maintain a stable and constant visual world since the vestibular and visual human systems are in perfect correlation and harmony supporting each other in gathering, classifying, codifying, and processing information to its final destination, the brain.

The central most sensitive and complex organ of the auditory systems is the cochlea or inner ear, and within this most significant part is the organ of Corti. It is here that the reception of sound signals and their classification into sound information bits is achieved before they are processed to the brain for final reorganization and translation. The acoustic process and functions of the inner ear are described by Murch (1973) as follows:

> The actual process of hearing begins in the cochlea. The vibrations are transmitted through its three fluid-filled canals as a way of movement along the membranes separating the individual canals. On one of the membranes of the cochlea is a cell complex known as the *organ of Corti* which contains rows of hair cells embodied in the membrane. These respond to the physical movement of the traveling wave and translate into information concerning its frequency and intensity into impulses into the auditory nerve. (p. 15)

The final organ of the human auditory system connecting the ears with the brain is the auditory nerve which transforms sound signals to the primary auditory area of the brain.

Basic Anatomy of the Brain's Visual and Auditory Centers

The brain is divided into three major regions: *the forebrain, the midbrain,* and *the hindbrain*. Each of these regions are divided into subregions which perform specific functions that constitute the main purpose of the brain—to perceive, to memorize, and to think.

The forebrain is considered the highest intellectual area of the entire brain and includes the *cerebral cortex*. The two most important regions of the cerebral cortex bearing a direct connection to this chapter are the *occipital lobe* where the brain's center for vision is located and the *temporal lobe* which includes the brain's center for hearing. See Figure 3.

The midbrain is considered the relay station of all information coming in and going out of the forebrain. Specific structures within, monitor the incoming information and process it to the forebrain (Bloom, Lazerson, & Hofstader, 1985).

The hindbrain is known as the survival organ. The main functions of this organ are to transform information relating to the body and limb position and to regulate respiration and heart rhythms (Bloom *et al.*, 1985). According to Boddy (1978), "The hindbrain and midbrain are collectively referred to as the *brain stem* as even in the highest vertebrates they form a stem like structure which merges with the spinal cord and its lower end" (p. 46).

The largest, most complex part of the human brain is the cerebral cortex. The delicate occipital and temporal lobes of the cerebral cortex are significant to the study of visual and auditory cognitive processes.

The occipital lobe occupies the rear parts of the cerebral cortex. The two hemispheres of the occipital lobe form the visual region of the brain, also known as the primary visual area and linked to the optic chiasm which in turn is connected to the optic nerves. The *primary visual area* is where the visual stimuli is processed into the "image."

The temporal lobe of the cerebral cortex occupies the base of the brain and constitutes the *primary auditory area*. When auditory signals arrive at the auditory

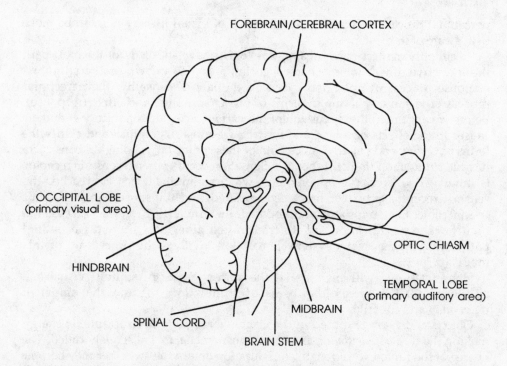

Figure 3. The Human Brain.

nerve and depending on their nature and scope (i.e., sound signals that need to be reproduced or regenerated as visuals or words), they pass through the primary auditory area occupying the temporal lobe of the cerebral cortex, which foremost enables comprehension of speech.

When we speak either a heard or written word, the pathways of sound signals, passing through the organs of the brain's auditory system, are altered.

This section provides basic information on the anatomy and broader functions of the three main information systems: the ears, eyes, and brain. Now that we have seen what these organs are and how they perform their broader functions, we will examine the role of stimulation in the perceptual process.

Stimuli and the Perceptual Process

This section discusses the role of stimulation in the perceptual process and examines the necessary conditions for the smooth and effective operation of the visual and auditory information process. Our interaction with the phenomena exposed in the environment and our mental processes of decoding, recognizing, and interpreting them is a continuous process that starts with birth and increases in complexity and sophistication as we grow older. We all engage in this process but few of us are aware or even concern ourselves with understanding how it works, how we can improve it, what the obstacles are that effect the smooth operation of the process, etc. Unquestionably, the neurophysiology of the perceptual process is complex. But students of visual literacy need to be more than aware of its existence.

To simplify matters perceptual psychologists have adopted, for the most part, the inductive, linear, or mechanical techniques also known as the stimulus-response process of operation based on the law of causality: the perceptual process of vision or hearing in terms of cause (stimulus) and effect (response). Before we engage in the discussion of the various visual and auditory stimuli as causes to the effects of seeing and hearing we must distinguish and clarify the terms *perception* and *sensation* since both of these crucial psychological constructs include stimulation in their functions. Sensation occurs when a sensoric receptor is stimulated whereas perception occurs when a stimulus which has reached the sensoric receptor is further processed, codified, and transported to the brain's special center to be translated or decodified. As Murch (1973) states: "A sensation occurs when neural impulses are transmitted along the afferent [incoming] pathways of the nervous system; perception involves the processing of this input" (p. 5).

Henceforth, we will examine (1) the various types of stimuli (visual and auditory), (2) the threefold process of stimulation, (3) and the model of perception and cognition.

Objects and events exposed in the visual world exert electromagnetic energy making them *potential stimuli*, as all such phenomena are collectively called. The degree of their intensity, strength, and duration determines whether they become *effective*, capable of reaching the receptors of vision or hearing or *ineffective stimuli*, unable to stimulate the sensoric organs of vision and hearing.

Scientists have tried to explain at what point potential stimuli become effective or remain ineffective by measuring their intensity, strength, and duration, examining the physical makeup of the organs of vision and hearing, and studying human behavior during the perceptual process. From the observations, hypotheses, and theories developed, scientists have come to the conclusion that the limitations are threefold: (1) insufficient intensity, strength, and duration, (2) physical/biological deficiency of the organs of perception, and (3) perceiver's degree of development, receptivity, awareness, etc.

The visual stimuli in regards to their nature, potential, and limitations are discussed hereunder.

Visual Stimulation

Visual stimuli are electromagnetic energy exerted by objects in the environment that strike the retina of the eyes. The light photons transform information of the particular shape, texture, and color of the object (Murch, 1973), and receive stimuli regarding the object's location, size, and whether it is stationary or not.

Stimuli that arrive at the retina are not the actual shapes, textures, colors, sizes, locations, and motions of a particular object of the environment but rather a collection of symbols of the various parts of the object (Frisby, 1980) such as corners, edges, lines, brightness, etc. When the symbols of a feature are put together and maintain the appropriate relationships in the input image they form structural descriptions of the particular feature (Frisby, 1980).

Frisby's (1980) theory of structural description of seeing coincides with Murch's (1973) spatial visual fixation in which a section of the visual field is fixated briefly and followed by another. Sequentially and topographically, bits of information or signals of shapes, borders, straight or curved lines, edges, etc., are received by the eyes and processed to the brain. Whereas in vision, "... separate inputs are defined primarily by their spatial relationship" (Murch, 1973, p. 105).

Therefore, we see here, that various visual stimuli are in reality various pieces of an object received individually and sequentially by the visual receptors which, in turn, assemble them into more complete structural units and process them to the higher centers of the visual system of the brain. However, only effective visual stimuli reach the brain where they are stored in either the short or the long-term memory. Furthermore, the effective visual stimulation process offers additional refinement to the reception of the signals.

Auditory Stimulation

Unlike the stimuli for vision which are electromagnetic energy that moves in an electromagnetic field to reach the retinas of the eyes, the stimulus for hearing "... is the physical change of a medium produced by a vibration of mechanical disturbance" (Murch, 1973, p. 12). The sounds produced by a source in the environment become either effective or ineffective stimuli depending on their intensity, strength, and duration. Those effective auditory stimuli that reach the receptors of hearing, unlike the visual ones, are organized by a temporal topographic order. This means that time frequency and temporal order rather than spatial order provide the bases for auditory stimulation. Experiments in sound stimulation and sensoric sound perception have shown that the afferent receptors of sensory information in audition are topographic (Erickson, 1968; Murch, 1973) and that each receptor receives only a narrow band of stimulus characteristics.

Effective auditory stimuli arriving mechanically into the hearing receptors are not the actual medium or event of the environment that exerts sounds. They are, rather, bits and pieces of air molecules and tones that stem from the original source. Like visual symbols, sound bits form temporal descriptions of the sound medium which are serially, topographically, and temporally organized and processed. According to Murch (1973): "In audition the nature of an effective stimulus is initially represented mechanically and then translated by topographic receptors into an electrical impulse. This information is then transmitted to the higher centers of auditory reception in the cortex" (p. 107).

Effective stimulation of auditory signals depends on the individual's ability to locate sounds in space. The perception of auditory space, known as sound localization, is an area of immediate concern to the students of verbo-visual literacy. Neuroscientists have suggested several factors which influence the perception of sound localization such as the restriction or reduction of free head movement, monaural listening, disuse or malfunctioning of the external ear, limited duration of sound vibration, distance of listeners and sound source, and sound frequency (Murch, 1973). In visual learning these factors must always be recognized and considered in studies relating to the effects of visual communication media.

Threefold Process of Stimulation

Now that we have defined the visual and auditory stimuli, discussed their nature, underlined their characteristics, and pointed out some of the conditions necessary for their effectiveness we turn to the analysis of the threefold process of auditory and visual stimulation: distal, proximal, and perceived.

1. *Distal Stimuli.*

All external objects or events are potential stimuli and because they are environmental are called distal stimuli. As stated earlier herein, in vision all distal stimuli are patterns of ambient light reflected from the various objects in the environment. In hearing, all distal stimuli are air molecules disturbed by some medium and travel in waves with a given frequency. The environment provides a continuous flow of countless potential or distal stimuli most of which go unnoticed and only a fraction of which become effective stimuli.

2. *Proximal Stimuli.*

Effective stimuli that reach the visual and auditory receptors cause a sensoric reaction that results in the assembling of the individual symbols, or bits of information, of particular objects or events into structural descriptions or representations are called proximal stimuli. The main task of the proximal stimuli is to assemble and codify all input and thus to assist in the building of the precepts which represent, to an extent, the initial distal stimuli.

3. *Perceived Stimuli.*

Proximal stimuli or precepts that reach the appropriate center of the brain and cause the decodification of the signals into cognitive structures are called perceived stimuli. The task of the perceived stimuli is to assist in the transformation of the proximal sounds into perceived, completed, and recognizable ones.

This threefold process of visual and auditory stimulation is actually an over simplification, a schematic presentation to explain how the human information system works and improves itself through continuous and systematic elimination and refinement. Furthermore, it helps us to recognize where in this process obstacles occur that need to be overcome and corrected so that the perceptual process can be improved. This is precisely the role of the perceptual model we provide and discuss next.

Model of Reception/Cognition

Models help to illustrate our thoughts, exemplify a theory, simplify a complex process. They are graphic explanations or illustrations of complex phenomena, events, or actions. Neuroscientists rely heavily on models to explain the complex process of stimulation, perception, and cognition for various reasons. Models help to clarify these processes, to intensify and focus on specific areas, and finally to interpret the functions of all parts involved as explained hereunder.

Objects and events that occur in the environment cause stimulation as distal or effective stimuli. This is clarification, the first step of the process. Subsequently, the eyes and ears receive distal effective stimuli in approximate, symbolic, or representative forms constituting the second step, intensification. Finally, the perceptual organs send the intensified and codified signals to the brain which perceives, decodifies, and recognizes them in the last step of the stimulative process, interpretation. See Figure 4.

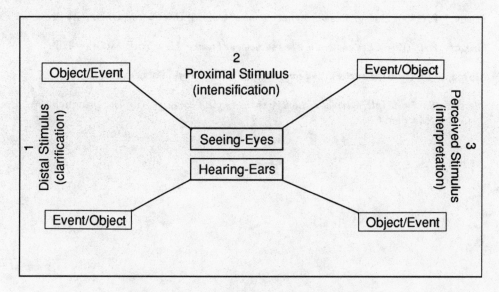

Figure 4. A Stimulus-Perception-Cognition Model.

We should not lose sight of the fact that: (1) this is only a model which helps us to explain a process; it is not the process itself, (2) the process itself is much more complex than described here and, as such, demands additional advanced models to exemplify it, (3) the steps of the provided process are either unknown or inexplicable and therefore a model that intends to illustrate and exemplify it is bound to be limited. Neuroscientists and neurophysiologists originally explained visual and auditory perceptual processes as such, but now suggest that perception starts even before stimulation and some even equate perception with cognition. We, in the field of visual communication media need to understand and exemplify various perceptual processes because the study of the visual media is in itself a complex undertaking. We analyze, simplify, and modelize complex phenomena and multilevel communication processes in order to study them closely and to learn how they effect the visual communication process.

Illustrations by Don Inman

References

Bloom, F. E., Lazerson, A., & Hofstader, L. (1985). *Brain, mind, and behavior*. New York: W. H. Freeman.

Boddy, J. (1978). *Brain systems and psychological concepts*. New York: John Wiley & Sons.

Erickson, R. P. (1968). Stimulus coding in topographic and non topographic afferent modalities. *Psychological Review, 75,* 447–65.

Frisby, J. P. (1980). *Seeing: Illusion, brain, and mind.* Oxford, UK: Oxford University Press.

Gregory, R. L. (1966). *Eye and brain: The psychology of seeing.* New York: McGraw-Hill.

Murch, G. M. (1973). *Visual and auditory perception.* New York: Bobbs-Merrill.

Webster's third new international dictionary of the English language. (1971). Springfield, MA: G. & C. Merriam Co.

Chapter Four

Images and Imagery Theory

Helen B. Miller

John K. Burton

Objectives

After reading this chapter, you should be able to:

1. *Define the Information Processing model's three main storage structures: sensory registers, short-term memory, and long-term memory.*

2. *Describe the process used to attend, decode, and encode a stimulus presented to a person.*

3. *Discuss how the ability to process information increases with age.*

4. *Describe Paivio's dual-code model of encoding visual and verbal information.*

5. *Describe the gender implications for presenting and designing instructional material for children.*

6. *Discuss the importance of research methodology in interpreting the development of the cognitive system.*

History

The colloquial notions of our "mind's eye" and that a "picture is worth a thousand words" reflect the popular belief in the value of pictures. These notions also allude to our ability to store pictures or images to be "viewed" later by our "third" or "inner eye." Popular self-help works encourage us to use images to help us remember and to rehearse mentally. For example, an athlete may visualize a successful high-jump or jump-shot before attempting either feat. Yet, the nature of image processing, storage, interpretation, and generation is not nearly as clear (nor as non-controversial) as we often assume.

The use of images to aid learning and recall is mentioned in Greek scrolls that date as early as 500 B.C. Greek orators, who were almost always illiterate (Plato apparently was pejoratively referred to as the "philosopher who writes" to indicate that he did not have the mental powers to adequately remember), tied topic sentences to the images of statues in a familiar garden. Thus, the speech was an imagined "walk" through the garden with each statue, in turn, cuing the next paragraph.

A few hundred years later, Simonodes related his use of an image to recreate the seating arrangement at a feast he was attending. The building in which the feast was being held had collapsed during an earthquake, and he was asked to help identify the bodies. (Simonodes apparently had stepped outside just prior to the tragedy.) The power of the mind to "see" is exemplified, for example, by authors such as St. Augustine (1952) (who refers to inner sight or insight) and Descartes (1958)[who believed that the mind/soul could wander (attached by a silver cord) and both see and hear during its "travels"]. In addition, people who report "out-of-body" experiences universally mention "seeing" themselves.

Not only is the notion of the mind as a seeing organ ancient, but constructivism, one of the central tenants of cognitive psychology, is nearly as old. The ancient Greeks first wrote of an interpreted reality over 2000 years ago. Plato (1961), and in a much more radical manner, Aristotle (1952), placed reality within the individual. In other words, reality is *constructed* from what we sense based on our experience, emotional condition, beliefs, and so forth. These ancient notions of imagery and constructivism are at the heart of the cognitivist position of images and imagery. To understand the current views of these historical concepts, however, it is necessary to take a position on how the human memory system works. For simplicity's sake, and to make comparisons between stimulus modalities easier, we have selected the model that began the current rise of cognitive psychology: Information Processing.

Cognitive Overview

The information processing approach to human cognition relies on the computer as the metaphor on which models are based. Gardner (1985) states that cognitive science was "officially" recognized at the Symposium on Information Theory held at MIT in 1956. While Broadbent (1958) published the first model, it was Neisser, in his 1967 book, *Cognitive Psychology*, who synthesized the earlier attempts to apply information theory and computer analogies to human learning (see, e.g., Bartlett, 1958; Broadbent, 1958; Miller, 1953; Posner, 1964).

The information processing approach focuses on how the human memory system acquires, transforms, compacts, elaborates, encodes, retrieves, and uses information. The memory system is divided into three main storage structures: sensory registers, short-term memory (STM), and long-term memory (LTM). Each structure is synonymous with a type of processing.

The first stage of processing is registering the stimulus presented to the memory system. The sensory registers briefly hold the information introduced by one of the senses until the stimulus is recognized or lost. Pattern recognition is the matching of stimulus information with previously acquired knowledge. Klatzky (1980) referred to this complex recognition process as assigning meaning to a stimulus. Unlike the sensory registers, STM does not hold information in its raw sensory form, (e.g., visual—"icon," auditory—"echo") but in its recognized form. For example, the letter "A" is recognized as a letter rather than as just a group of lines. STM can maintain the information longer than the sensory registers through a holding process known as maintenance rehearsal, which recycles material over and over as the system works on it. Without the rehearsal, the information would decay and be lost from STM.

Another characteristic of STM is its limited capacity for information. Miller (1956) determined that STM has room for about seven items (chunks) of information. Klatzky (1980) defined STM as a "work space" in which information may be rehearsed, elaborated, used for decision making, lost, or stored in the third memory structure: long-term memory. LTM is a complex and permanent storehouse for an individual's knowledge about the world and his/her experiences in it. LTM processes information to the two other memory structures and in turn receives information from the sensory registers and STM. First, the stimulus is recognized in the sensory registers through comparison with information in LTM. Second, information manipulated in STM can be permanently stored in LTM. See Figure 1.

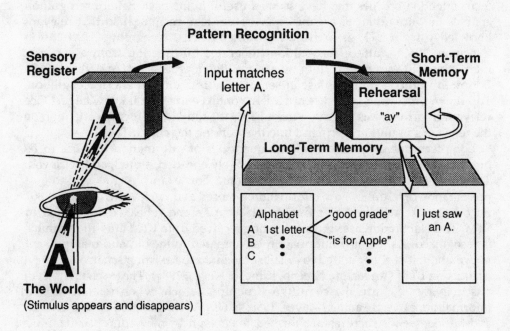

Figure 1. The Human Memory System.
(Adapted from Klatzky, 1980.)

According to Cleveland and McGill (1984), researchers should select a model, based on a scientific foundation for the use of visuals in presentations. Potentially, the information processing model provides a metaphor for the process by which graphic representations are decoded and encoded. Yet, in order to use cognitive models, researchers must demonstrate that these models are appropriate:

1. The models are appropriately descriptive of the phenomena.
2. The models of mental processes adequately account for or explain how the organization and coordination of mental operations can specify the cognitive processes that perform the experimental tasks (Cochran, Younghouse, Sorflaten, & Morlek, 1980).

To understand how an individual is able to interpret information, the researcher must first focus on the decisions made at each memory storage structure. Within the Information Processing Model, attention and pattern recognition determine the environmental factors that are processed. A large amount of information impinges on the sensory registers, but is quickly lost if not attended to. Attention, therefore, plays an important role in selecting sensory information. Attention is conceived of as being a very limited mental resource (Anderson, 1985). It is difficult to perform two demanding tasks, such as talking and writing, at the same time. While all information is registered by the sensory registers, only information attended to and processed to a more permanent form is retained. Bruner, Goodnow, and Austin (1967) stated that a person tends to focus attention on cues that have seemed useful in the past. Pattern recognition enables the individual to organize perceptual features (cues) so that relevant knowledge from LTM is activated. In other words, recognition *is* attention (Norman, 1969). Pattern recognition integrates information from a complex interaction that uses both bottom-up and top-down processing (Anderson, 1985). Bottom-up processing is the use of sensory information in pattern recognition. Top-down processing is the use of pattern context and general knowledge. Once relevant information is activated from LTM, the individual focuses attention on the relevant stimulus and brings it into the working memory (STM).

Long-term memory contains large quantities of information that has to be organized efficiently so that it can be effectively encoded, stored, and retrieved. These three processes are interdependent. For example, the method of presentation determines how information is stored and retrieved (Klatzky, 1980). Encoding is related to the amount of elaboration and rehearsal conducted in STM. This elaboration uses the information received from LTM after the stimulus is recognized. As the new information is compared to the old and manipulated information, it is either added to or subsumed into the existing schema and then encoded in LTM (Anderson, Greeno, Kline, & Neves, 1981). These schema "set of past experiences" are the cognitive structures which, when related to new information, cause meaning (Mayer, 1983, p. 68). As information is restructured and added, new structures are formed that result in new conceptualizations (Magliaro, 1988). These knowledge structures combine information in an organized manner. Evidence for memory storage indicates that representations can be both meaning-based and perception-based. Retrieval of information is also an active process. Information is accessed by a search of the memory structures.

The speed and accuracy of retrieval is directly dependent upon how the information was encoded and the attention being given to the stimulus. To be recalled from LTM, information must be activated. The level of activation seems to depend on the associative strength of the path. The strength of the activation increases with practice and with the associative properties (Anderson, 1985).

Using various graphic formats in an experimental task where people are asked to perform mental operations may provide evidence about the way that cognitive processes operate. Larkin and Simon (1987) proposed that a graphic representation may be more effective than a sentential (text) representation due to the reduction in search and computation of elements in the graphic representation. Their premise was that if two representations are informationally equivalent, the computational efficiency of each would depend on the information processing operators that are in operation. While a diagram and text may hold the same information, the individual may recognize features readily and efficiently in a diagram because the information is organized by location and, therefore, requires less search and computation time to solve the problem. Larkin and Simon proposed that the cost of computation must be included in any judgment of the relative efficiency of two representations. To empirically test their views, the researchers used a diagrammatic and a sentential representation of a physics problem with identical information. The data structure for the diagram was indexed by location in a plane where many elements shared the same location and each element was adjacent to any number of other elements. The data structure for the sentential representation was indexed by a position in a list, with each element "adjacent" only to the next element in the list. Their conclusions specified that the diagram was more efficient for making inferences. Yet, the point was made that some people are not able to use diagrams effectively. The researchers concluded that a diagram, to be useful, must be constructed correctly to take advantage of certain features and, secondly, that the failure to use the pertinent features of diagrams seems to be a reason why certain people cannot make effective use of them. People may have to be trained (experienced) to use diagrams effectively.

Development of the Cognitive System

The study of cognitive development examines the processes and products of the developing human mind. Cognitive development study is motivated by both scientific curiosity and a desire for practical applications. The traditional view of cognition recognizes such "intellectual" entities as knowledge, consciousness, intelligence, strategies, thinking, creating, imagining, reasoning, inferring, problem solving, conceptualizing, classifying, symbolizing, and dreaming. A contemporary view of cognition would also include the following processes as an integral part of cognition: social cognition (human versus non-human objects), organized motor movements, perception, imagery, memory, attention, and learning (Flavell, 1985). Cognition, so defined, includes all human psychological processes and activities. Given such an inclusive definition, Flavell explained the complexity of cognition by stating that "...the psychological events and processes that go into making up what we call 'thinking,' 'perceiving,' 'remembering,' and the rest are in fact complexly interwoven with one another in the tapestry of actual, real-time cognitive functioning" (1985, p. 3). Each process is involved in the development and operation of the other processes, affecting them and being affected by them. Human cognition is a complex, organized system of interacting components.

In the Information Processing Model, the structure of the memory system is complete by about age four years and remains invariant over a person's life span (Kail, 1979; Klahr, 1980). The further development of the child's cognition is explained by the child's increasing familiarity of cognitive structures and the ability to use processes more efficiently (Gross, 1985). Children are viewed as able to transform rules and acquire strategies that allow them to assimilate knowledge and propel themselves into a higher stage of development.

Both Piagetian and Information Processing Models offer explanations of how the human cognitive system develops, but from different perspectives. Piaget (1952, 1954; Phillips, 1969) emphasized the progressive development of both the structure and processing elements of an individual's cognitive system, but focused primarily on the structure. Information Processing Models focuses on the progressive development of the processing ability of the individual, theorizing that the structure remains stable after the stage of infancy. Due to their differing emphases, the theories more often are viewed as complementary rather than as adversarial.

Both the Information Processing approach and the Piagetian approach agree that the ability to use memory efficiently increases with age. The Information Processing Model proposes that the improvement of memory reflects the child's ability to use effective operative processes within the structure of the cognitive system. With this in mind, we return to our model.

The sensory registers are the points at which information is received from the external world. Studies examining the iconic (visual) and echoic (auditory) registers generally have generally found that the speed at which a stimulus is processed increases as the child grows older (Cowan, Soumi, & Morse, 1982; Lasky & Spiro, 1980; Welsandt & Meyer, 1974). Young children have difficulty processing information quickly. Sheingold (1973) concluded that decay of information is prevalent in young children due to their inability to process information quickly. Observations of adults interacting with children reflect the intuitiveness of this concept, for adults tend to use a slow, deliberate rate of presentation of both speech and visual stimuli when interacting with children (Gross, 1985). For example, adults tend to turn the pages of a picture book slowly when reading to a small child.

Why children do not process as quickly as adults is not entirely clear. Gross (1985) suggested that the problem may be with stimulus and task familiarity and not with the structure of the sensory registers. In processing sensory information, people need to attend to a number of dimensions. Young children may have difficulty concentrating on more than one dimension. Visually, one may have to attend to identification and spatial positioning. Finkle (1973) presented dot patterns to kindergarteners, third graders, sixth graders, and college students. Following tachistoscopic presentation of the dots, the students had to reconstruct the patterns. Although older students did better than younger ones, students from all age levels correctly recalled more positions as more dots were added to the pattern. In a second experiment by Finkle, the introduction of one bit of identity information into an array (a substitution of a dot by another geometric form) produced a decline in the younger children's recall of position information. It seems likely that young children have difficulty in simultaneously processing identity and position. Yet, Eimas and Miller (1980) suggested that, at least with acoustical information (place of articulation, stress, intonation, and pitch), even young infants are capable of simultaneously processing more than one acoustical feature.

A review of the development of selective auditory attention reveals a progressive improvement in children's ability to listen selectively (Geffen & Sexton, 1978; Hiscock & Kinsbourne, 1980). Broadbent (1958) proposed that selective attention occurs through the selective filtering of information. Lane and Presson (1982) indicated that with age, one becomes more adept at focusing on the central task itself. Doyle (1973) concluded that young children are distracted by competing auditory messages. When children listen to lists of simultaneously presented word pairs and repeat the words on only one list, older children recognize more words. Gross (1985) suggested that the issue is one of faulty methodology. Listening to words presented to both ears is not a natural task for children, while watching TV probably is. For example, young children demonstrated the ability to shift their attention appropriately between sources of information while watching a television.

Generally, the literature suggests that young children tend to possess less skill than adults in processing information stored in the sensory registers. Several possible reasons are suggested for this inadequacy, including developmental changes, lack of facilitating strategies, and the type of (unrealistic) tasks in the experimental design.

Short-term memory (STM) receives information that has been recognized in the sensory registers and retained. It is estimated that duration of information for children and adults in STM is very short (approximately 20 to 30 seconds) without some active attempt to retain it. Researchers (Peterson & Peterson, 1959; Rosner & Lindsay, 1974) have concluded that children have greater difficulty retaining information in STM than adults.

The amount of information that can be retained in STM is referred to as "capacity." Adults again are estimated to have a greater capacity for information than young children (Liben, 1979; Mandler, 1967; Miller, 1956). As children approach the upper elementary grades, there is little difference between them and adults in their capacity to hold information (Belmont, 1972; Farnham-Diggory, 1972; Liben, 1979). Case (1978) reasoned that children's apparent growth of STM capacity is the result of simple strategies becoming more automatic through use, and then being modified into more powerful strategies that allow for chunking of information held in STM.

A typical test of capacity for working memory is the digit span test. In general, digit span ability (string of digits recalled) increases with age. Piaget (1952) proposed that adults have structurally larger working memories than children. Case (1978), on the other hand, concluded that adults do not have larger capacities, but have developed better strategies. To resolve the controversy, Chi (1978) gave tests of digit recall and tests of recall of chess pieces to a group of children and adults. As expected, the adults were able to recall more digits, but the children were able to recall more chess pieces. The children, whose average age was 10.5, were knowledgeable about chess, while the adults were not. The results cast doubt on the concept that the structure of working memory increases with age. Chi suggested that the participants' experience with techniques for grouping items would explain the results. To an adult, a set of two or three numbers may be held as a single unit, while a chess player may group several chess configurations as a single unit.

Visual Cognition

The use of visual materials by educators to enhance the learning process is an accepted instructional technique. Dale's Cone of Experience theory (1946) described an instructional continuum with concrete experience at one end and written and spoken language at the other end. Within this framework, visual material becomes a necessary component for helping the inexperienced learner bridge the gap between concrete experiences and symbolic representations of real-world phenomena. Dwyer (1978), one of the most prolific researchers on the use of visuals in learning, stated that visuals (television, pictures, slide presentations, diagrams, graphs) are effective in teaching facts, concepts, and procedures. Levie (1987) suggested that visuals can be useful in analogical reasoning by making abstract information more concrete and imaginable.

Perceptual research focuses on the question of how mental representations are recognized, manipulated, encoded, and retrieved. Do visual and verbal information function differently in processing? Visual images may be represented by both perception-based and meaning-based knowledge (Anderson, 1985). Spatial images retain information about the positions of objects in space. The memory of the visual image can also be a meaningful representation. For example, the memory of a chess board would generate not only the positions of the pieces, but also the significance of the pieces in a chess game.

Posner's (1969) research with letter matching experiments supported two ideas:

1. Visual information can persist in STM after the stimulus is no longer available.
2. Visual information can be retrieved from LTM.

Kosslyn, Ball, and Reiser (1978) suggested that people are able to scan mental images of a map and make judgments similar to what would be expected if they were looking at an external map. The visual image seems to represent the stimulus item. Kosslyn (1975) and Baddeley, Grant, White, and Thomson (1975) interpreted visual images as having limited capacity in STM. This processing limitation was reflected by a similar limitation of acoustic codes.

The Controversy Over Imaginal Storage

How are mental representations encoded in long-term memory? Our common sense tells us that they are stored as pictures because we "see" them in our mind. The classic task of counting the number of windows in the house in which we grew up causes us to call up a picture of that house and "walk" around it, counting as we go. Simple. Yet, cognitive psychologists continue to debate two basic positions: imagery and propositions. Imagery depicts mental images as internally coded in a spatial structure of items. Propositions suggest that mental images are encoded in terms of linear orderings that sequence the items. Both positions support a hierarchical organization in which subimages or sublists can occur as elements in larger images or lists (Anderson, 1985). The pro-image group (Kosslyn & Pomerantz, 1977; Paivio, 1971, 1986; Shepard, 1967) argues that visual images are encoded by properties that are spatial and modality specific. The anti-image group (Anderson & Bower, 1973; Pylyshyn, 1981) argue that imagery is encoded as abstract propositions that serve as a neutral, meaning-based format for both pictorial and verbal information.

Although far from over, the differences at the applied level perhaps become moot. Even the most rabid pro-image researchers now concede that images are probably not very exact in terms of detail or real analog distance, and even the most dedicated anti-image people accept that humans experience "image like" events. Both arguments give strength to the position that visuals such as charts, graphs, and diagrams are useful in communication and instruction. With that in mind, we will focus on the pro-image position.

The basic assumptions of the pro-image group as interpreted by Kosslyn and Pomerantz (1977) are:

1. An image is a spatial representation like that underlying the experience of seeing an object during visual perception.
2. Only a finite processing capacity is available for constructing and representing images. This capacity will tend to limit the amount of detail that may be activated at any one time.
3. Images, once formed, are wholes that may be compared to percepts in a template-like manner.
4. The same structures that represent spatial information extracted during vision also support images.
5. Many of the same operators (excluding peripheral functions) that are used in analyzing percepts are also applied to images.

Dual Coding

The imagery theorists obviously make a distinction between the codes used for visual versus verbal information. Paivio (1971, 1986) developed the dual-code model which stated that the two types of information (verbal and visual) are encoded by separate subsystems, one specialized for visual images and the other specialized for verbal language. The two systems are assumed to be structurally and functionally distinct. Paivio (1986) defined structure as the difference in the nature of representational units and the way in which these units are organized into higher order systems. Structure, therefore, refers to LTM operations which correlate to perceptually identifiable verbal or visual objects and activities (Paivio). Functionally, the two subsystems are independent, meaning that either can operate without the other or both can work parallel to each other. Even though independent of one another, these two subsystems are interconnected so that a concept represented as an image in the visual system can also be converted to a verbal label in the other system, or vice versa (Klatzky, 1980). Paivio is very explicit, however, about the power of pictures: while words that can be imaged *may* be, pictures that can be translated *will* be, automatically. Paivio argues that this is why visual pictures are often remembered better than verbal information (Pressley & Miller, 1987). Graphs, charts, and diagrams can serve as visual aids to learning because they can display usually certain information that will be stored as both visual and verbal information. See Figure 2.

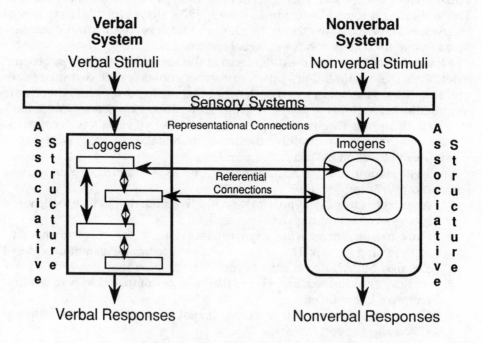

Figure 2. Verbal and Nonverbal Systems.
(Adapted from Paivio, 1986, p. 67.)

Dual-code theorists accept that mental images are not exact copies of pictures, but instead contain information that was encoded from a visual after perceptual analysis and pattern recognition (Klatzky, 1980). It is thought that the images are organized into subpictures at the time of perception (Anderson, 1978). Paivio (1986) further explained that mental representations have their developmental beginnings in perceptual, motor, and affective experience and are able to retain these characteristics when being encoded so that the structures and the processes are modality specific rather than a model. For example, a concrete object such as the ocean would be recognized by more than one modality—by its appearance, sound, smell, and taste. Therefore, a continuity between perception and memory as well as behavioral skills and cognitive skills is implied (Paivio). This theory also states that the visual system is simultaneously or synchronously organized. For example, on a perceptual level, a face is seen as the sum of all of its parts. On a cognitive level, mental images can be processed simultaneously so that one can see, and possibly scan, an entire complex scene, such as a graph or diagram.

There are, however, the same limits on visual processing that we see throughout the Information Processing Model. The concept of limited space was demonstrated by Kosslyn (1975), who asked students to visualize two named objects and then to answer questions about one of the objects. Students were slower to find parts that were next to an elephant than to find those next to a fly. STM for visuals appeared to have a processing limitation. Large objects like elephants (or even *very large* flies), "fill up" the system and slow it down. Retrieval of visually coded material also differs from other forms of internal representation. As previously stated, information is available simultaneously rather than by a sequential search and can be located by template or by an unlimited-capacity parallel search (Anderson, 1978).

Dual-coding theory can account for our personal impression of having images. The theory is often supported by research studies that conclude that individuals have a continuous and analog ability to judge space from images, in at least some cases (Kosslyn, 1975) and finally for studies which indicate strong visual memory abilities. Paivio's theory is also able to effectively support the recurrent finding that memory for pictures is better than memory for words (Shepard, 1967), otherwise known as the "pictorial superiority effect" (Levie, 1987). Imagery theories have been used by researchers to construct and test hypotheses on learning from graphics (Winn, 1987) and seem a fruitful heuristic source for visual research in the future.

Potential Research Variables

Developmental

Studies indicate that information is represented in STM in a variety of modalities, such as auditory-verbally, visually, and semantically. Studies with adults reveal the tendency for adults to talk to themselves as they do mental work, indicating encoding in an auditory-verbal mode (Atkinson & Shiffrin, 1968). Studies with pre-schoolers indicated that they tend to think with pictorial representations (Cramer, 1976; Hayes & Rosner, 1975). For example, Brown (1977) found that kindergartners made more errors in recalling visually similar letters sets in comparison to auditorally similar ones. Research completed with "real world" phenomena (TV watching) indicates that while visual information may be the preferred mode of encoding, children do not have difficulty encoding auditorally. Several researchers have suggested that perhaps the auditory messages may serve as attentional devices, directing children's attention to important aspects of a program (Calvert, Huston, Watkins, & Wright, 1982).

If the structure of STM is developmentally the same for adults and children as the Information Processing Model suggests, then why are there differences in memory ability between children and adults and differences in middle childhood and adolescence? One aspect that has already been discussed was the attention capacity of the different age levels. Another area for discussion is the use of cognitive processes such as rehearsal, chunking, and imagery, collectively known as cognitive strategies.

Rehearsal is generally categorized as either maintenance or elaborative in nature. Maintenance rehearsal is the repeating of information over and over in order to maintain it in STM. Flavell, Beach, and Chinsky (1966) demonstrated an increase with age in the spontaneous use of verbal rehearsal. In their study, seven pictures of common objects were displayed to children of ages 5, 7, and 10. The children understood that their task was to recall three of the pictures in a certain order. In observing the twenty children in each age group (n = 60), verbal rehearsal of the names of the pictures was evident for two 5-year-olds, twelve 7-year-olds, and seventeen 10-year-olds. In an extension of this study, Keeney, Cannizzo, and Flavell (1967) used the same procedure with a group of first graders. Because first grade is considered a transitional stage, some first graders would be expected to rehearse, and others would not. There were four major findings. First, children who spontaneously rehearsed remembered more pictures. Second, nonrehearsers could learn to rehearse with minimal instruction, and third, when they did, they obtained scores that matched those who spontaneously rehearsed. Fourth, when given the option on later trials of rehearsing or not rehearsing, more than half of the new recruits to rehearsal abandoned the strategy. In view of these findings, Flavell (1970) defined a production deficiency and a mediation deficiency. Production deficiency for a specific strategy means that the child does not produce or reproduce the strategy, even though he or she has the ability and skill to enact it. Mediational deficiency is the inability of the children to improve recall even if they try to use a specific strategy. Overall, rehearsal is responsible for extending the amount of time that information can be maintained in STM.

Chunking is thought to maximize the limited capacity of STM. Chunking involves grouping information together to form larger units. In a study involving first, fifth, and ninth graders, Rosner (1971) instructed children to learn a series of pictures by either rehearsing the items or by chunking the pictures together. The first graders failed to make use of either strategy, while the older students were able to use both strategies effectively.

Several studies have demonstrated that words that elicit high *imagery* are easier to remember than words that elicit low imagery. For example, the words "ice cream" elicit high imagery, while the word "noble" does not. When older children and adults are instructed to use visual images, memory for these items is enhanced (Kosslyn & Pomerantz, 1977). Young children who appear to have better factual knowledge of information when it is presented visually do not profit from imagery instructions as much as older children and adults (Reese, 1970; Rohwer, 1970). Studies of children from second to twelfth grades have shown that athletic, spatial, and mechanical skills are viewed as masculine, while verbal, artistic, and social skills are considered feminine. Elementary children do not tend to consistently stereotype math and science, but, by high-school age, students tend to think of these subjects as strictly masculine (Boswell, 1979; Stein, 1971). These differences have been well documented. Girls perceive math as more difficult than boys, and have a lower expectancy of success, even if actual performance is the same (Brush, 1979). This phenomena may help explain the tendency for boys to pick advanced math and science courses more often than girls (Steel & Wise, 1979). These choices could result in males receiving more training in visual-spatial tasks.

Maccoby and Jacklin (1974) suggested that while males are superior in spatial and mathematical skills, females are superior in verbal skills. Although differences in math do not appear until high-school level, gender differences in visual-spatial tasks begin to appear in middle childhood with the boys performing better than the girls (Thomas & Jamison, 1975). A likely candidate as the cause for these differences is social stereotyping.

Detail of Visuals and Experience

In terms of simple recognition, visual detail does not seem to be important. Nelson, Metzler, and Reed (1974), for example, varied visual representations of the same scene from non-detailed drawings to photographs and compared recognition for the visuals versus text descriptions. As we would expect, pictures were superior in recognition tests, but there were no differences among the detail levels used. For recall, however, detail is important in at least two ways. Mandler and Parker (1976) showed that the location of detail elements are best recalled if they are organized in a meaningful way. Thus, for example, graphic elements of classroom items that are placed in their "usual" locations are superior to the same elements when they are not organized in a meaningful manner. Obviously, "meaningful" reflects prior knowledge, including culture. In a related way, specific expertise impacts memory for visuals. Egan and Schwartz (1979) demonstrated that skilled electronics technicians showed superior recall for circuit diagrams relative to novices *as long as* the diagrams made "sense," that is, were organized in a meaningful manner.

Visual Schema and "Priming"

Visuals can also be used to organize incoming information. The classic demonstration of this use of visuals to "make sense" of subsequent textual information is Bransford and Johnson's (1972) *Balloons* passage. In their study, people found text without the visuals (or the visual following the text) to be difficult to comprehend and remember relative to the same text following an organizing visual. A related effect, "priming" (see, e.g., Neely, 1977; Posner & Snyder, 1975), has been demonstrated with text. Basically, a categorical prime, such as a bird, facilitated access to a specific bird, such as a robin. Conversely, an incorrect categorical prime inhibits access. A visual representative of the category should produce a similar effect.

The Problem with Images

Theory, basic research, and (as you will see in later chapters) applied research predict and support the efficacy of images (and instructions to image) in learning and memory. Yet, images are prone to the same processes (and problems) that affect all aspects of the human system: distortions from "reality." We assume that human sensation is about the same for all of us. When confronted with a visual stimulus, we assume that our nods, cues, nerves, and so forth react about the same. Perceptually, however, we do not *see* the same things. We extract (and create) meaning from visual stimuli just as we do from text. Therefore, our prior experience, inferences, expectations, beliefs, physical state, and other factors determine what we see as surely as the stimulus before us. A similar process operates when we recall an image from memory: we reconstruct from our constructed images. Naturally, like memory for text, we forget details.

Finally, where there are gaps, we unconsciously fill them. As you will see in later chapters, images are effective for connecting items to be remembered and, if the level of detail is correct, for learning new facts and relationships. However, these tasks are rather low level and rote. In general, unless images are entrained to the point of pattern recognition, we can assume that the human memory system deals with images as it deals with text: generally or prototypically. The system is great at "gist" or meaning and poor at specifics. Thus, images may work "better" than text in many applications, but they probably do not work differently.

References

Anderson, J. R. (1978). Arguments concerning representations for mental imagery. *Psychological Review, 85,* 249–277.

Anderson, J. R. (1985). *Cognitive psychology and its implications.* New York: W. H. Freeman.

Anderson, J. R., & Bower, G. H. (1973). *Human associative memory.* Washington, DC: Winston.

Anderson, R. C., Greeno, J. G., Kline, P. J., & Neves, D. M. (1981). Acquisition of problem solving skill. In J. R. Anderson (Ed.), *Cognitive skills and their acquisition.* Hillsdale, NJ: Lawrence Erlbaum Associates.

Aristotle. (1952). In *great books of the western world* (R. M. Hutchins, Ed.). Chicago: Encyclopaedia Britannica .

Atkinson, R. C., & Shiffrin, R. M. (1968). Human memory: A proposed system and its control processes. In K. W. Spence & J. T. Spence (Eds.), *The psychology of learning and motivation: Advances in research theory* (Vol. 2). New York: Academic Press.

Baddeley, A. D., Grant, S., White, E., & Thomson, N. (1975). Imagery and visual memory. In P. M. Rabbitt & S. Dornic (Eds.), *Attention and performance* (Vol. 5). New York: Academic Press.

Bartlett, F. C. (1958). *Thinking.* New York: Basic Books.

Belmont, J. M. (1972). Relations of age and intelligence to short-term color memory. *Child Development, 43,* 19–29.

Boswell, S. L. (1979). *Sex roles, attitudes, and achievement in mathematics: A study of elementary school children and Ph.D.'s.* Paper presented as part of a Symposium on Gender Differences in Participation in Mathematics at the annual meeting of the Society for Research in Child Development, San Francisco.

Bransford, J. D., & Johnson, M. K. (1972). Contextual prerequisites for understanding: Some investigations of comprehension and recall. *Journal of Verbal Learning and Verbal Behavior, 11,* 717–726.

Broadbent, D. E. (1958). *Perception and communication.* New York: Pergamon.

Brown, R. M. (1977). An examination of visual and verbal coding processes in preschool children. *Child Development, 48,* 38–45.

Bruner, J. S., Goodnow, J. J., & Austin, G. A. (1967). *A study of thinking.* New York: John Wiley & Sons.

Brush, L. R. (1979). *Why women avoid the study of mathematics: A longitudinal study.* Report to the National Institute of Education, ABT Associates, Inc., Cambridge, MA.

Calvert, S. L., Huston, A. C., Watkins, B. A., & Wright, J. C. (1982). The relation between selective attention to televisions forms and children's comprehension of content. *Child Development, 53,* 601–610.

Case, R. (1978). Intellectual development from birth to adulthood: A neo-Piagetian approach. In R. S. Siegler (Ed.), *Children's thinking: What develops?* Hillsdale, NJ: Lawrence Erlbaum Associates.

Chi, M. T. H. (1978). Knowledge structures and memory development. In R. S. Siegler (Ed.), *Children's thinking: What develops?* Hillsdale, NJ: Lawrence Erlbaum Associates.

Cleveland, W. S., & McGill, R. (1984). Graphical perception: Theory, experimentation, and application to the development of graphical methods. *Journal of the American Statistical Association, 79,* 531–554.

Cochran, L. M., Younghouse, P., Sorflaten, J., & Morlek, R. (1980). Exploring approaches to researching visual literacy. *Educational Communications and Technology Journal, 28,* 243–266.

Cowan, N., Soumi, K., & Morse, P. A. (1982). Echoic and storage in infant perception. *Child Development, 53,* 984–990.

Cramer, P. (1976). Changes from visual memory organization as a function of age. *Journal of Experimental Child Psychology, 22,* 50–57.

Dale, E. (1946). *Audiovisual methods in teaching.* New York: Holt, Rinehart, and Winston.

Descartes, R. (1958). *Philosophical writings* (N. Kemp-Smith, trans.). New York: Modern Library.

Doyle, A. (1973). Listening to distraction: A developmental study of selective attention. *Journal of Experimental Child Psychology, 15,* 100–115.

Dwyer, F M. (1978). *Strategies for improving visual learning.* State College, PA: Learning Services.

Egan, D. E., & Schwartz, B. J. (1979). Chunking in recall of symbolic drawings. *Memory & Cognition, 7*, 149–158.

Eimas, P. D., & Miller, J. L. (1980). Discrimination of information for manner of articulation. *Infant Behavior and Development, 3*, 367–385.

Farnham-Diggory, S. (1972). *Information processing in children.* New York: Academic Press.

Finkle, D. L. (1973). A development comparison of the processing of two types of visual information. *Journal of Experimental Child Psychology, 16*, 250–266.

Flavell, J. H. (1970). Developmental studies of mediated memory. In H. W. Reese & L. P. Lipsitt (Eds.), *Advances in child development and behavior* (Vol. 5). New York: Academic Press.

Flavell, J. H. (1985). *Cognitive development.* Englewood Cliffs, NJ: Prentice-Hall.

Flavell, J. H., Beach, D. R., & Chinsky, J. M. (1966). Spontaneous verbal rehearsal in memory tasks as a function of age. *Child Development, 37*, 283–289.

Gardner, H. (1985). *The mind's new science: A history of the cognitive revolution.* New York: Basic Books.

Geffen, G., & Sexton, M. A. (1978). The development of auditory strategies of attention. *Development Psychology, 14*, 11–17.

Gross, T. F. (1985). *Cognitive development.* Monterey, CA: Brooks/Cole Publishing Co.

Hayes, D. S., & Rosner, S. R. (1975). The phonetic effect in preschool children: The influence of overt rehearsal and verbal instructions. *Journal of Experimental Child Psychology, 20*, 391–399.

Hiscock, M., & Kinsbourne, M. (1980). Asymmetries of selective listening and attention switching in children. *Developmental Psychology, 16*, 70–82.

Kail, R. (1979). *The development of memory in children.* San Francisco: W. H. Freeman.

Keeney, T. J., Cannizzo, S. R., & Flavell, J. H. (1967). Spontaneous and induced verbal rehearsal in a recall task. *Child Development, 38*, 953–966.

Klahr, D. (1980). Information-processing models of intellectual development. In R. H. Kluwe & H. Spada (Eds.), *Developmental models of thinking.* New York: Academic Press.

Klatzky, R. L. (1980). *Human memory: Structures and processes.* New York: W. H. Freeman.

Kosslyn, S. M. (1975). Information representation in visual images. *Cognitive Psychology, 7*, 341–370.

Kosslyn, S. M., Ball, T. M., & Reiser, B. J. (1978). Visual images preserve metric spatial information: Evidence from studies of image scanning. *Journal of Experimental Psychology: Human Perception and Performance, 4*, 47–60.

Kosslyn, S. M., & Pomerantz, J. R. (1977). Imagery, propositions, and the form of internal representations. *Cognitive Psychology, 9*, 52–76.

Lane, D. M., & Presson, D. A. (1982). The development of selective attention. *Merrill-Palmer Quarterly, 28*, 317–337.

Larkin, J. H., & Simon, H. A. (1987). Why a diagram is (sometimes) worth ten thousand words. *Cognitive Science, 11*, 65–99.

Lasky, R. E., & Spiro, D. (1980). The processing of tachistoscopically presented visual stimuli by five-month-old infants. *Child Development, 51*, 1292–1294.

Levie, W. H. (1987). Research on pictures: A guide to the literature. In D. M. Willows & H. A. Houghton (Eds.), *The psychology of illustration: Basic research* (Vol. 1). New York: Springer-Verlag.

Liben, L. S. (1979). Free recall by deaf and hearing children: Semantic clustering and recall in trained and untrained persons. *Journal of Experimental Psychology, 27*, 105–119.

Maccoby, E. E., & Jacklin, C. N. (1974). *The psychology of sex differences*. Stanford, CA: Stanford University Press.

Magliaro, S. (1988). Expertise in problem identification: A descriptive analysis of the cue selection and hypothesis generation of reading diagnosticians. Unpublished doctoral dissertation, Virginia Polytechnic Institute & State University.

Mandler, G. (1967). Organization and memory. In K. W. Spence & J. T. Spence (Eds.), *Psychology of learning and motivation* (Vol. 1). New York: Academic Press.

Mandler, J. M., & Parker, R. E. (1976). Memory for descriptive and spatial information in complex pictures. *Journal of Experimental Psychology: Human Learning and Memory, 2*, 38–48.

Mayer, R. E. (1983). *Thinking, problem solving, and cognition*. New York: W. H. Freeman.

Miller, G. A. (1953). What is information measurement? *American Psychologist, 17*, 748–762.

Miller, G. A. (1956). The magical number seven, plus or minus two: Some limits on our capacity for processing information. *Psychological Review, 63*, 81–97.

Neely, J. H. (1977). Semantic priming and retrieval from lexical memory: Roles of inhibitionless spreading activation and limited-capacity attention. *Journal of Experimental Psychology: General, 106*, 226–254.

Neisser, U. (1967). *Cognitive psychology*. New York: Appleton-Century-Crofts.

Nelson, T. O., Metzler, J., & Reed, D. A. (1974). Role of details in the long-term recognition of pictures and verbal descriptions. *Journal of Experimental Psychology, 102*, 184–186.

Norman, D. A. (1969). *Memory and attention*. New York: John Wiley & Sons.

Paivio, A. (1971). *Imagery and verbal processes*. New York: Holt, Rinehart, and Winston.

Paivio, A. (1986). *Mental representations: A dual coding approach.* New York: Oxford University Press.

Peterson, C. R., & Peterson, M. J. (1959). Short-term retention of individual verbal items. *Journal of Experimental Psychology, 58,* 193–198.

Phillips, J. L. (1969). *The origins of intellect: Piaget's theory.* San Francisco: W. H. Freeman.

Piaget, J. (1952). *The origins of intelligence in children* (M. Cook, Trans.). New York: International Universities Press. (Original work published 1936.)

Piaget, J. (1954). *Construction of reality in the child* (M. Cook, Trans.). New York: Basic Books. (Original work published 1937.)

Plato. (1961). *The collected dialogues including the letters* (E. Hamilton & H. Chairns, Eds.). Princeton, NJ: Princeton University Press.

Posner, M. I., & Snyder, C. R. R. (1975). Facilitation and inhibition in the processing of signals. In P. M. A. Rabbitt & S. Dornic (Eds.), *Attention and performance* (Vol. 5). New York: Academic Press.

Posner, M. I. (1964). Information reduction in the analysis of sequential tasks. *Psychology Review, 71,* 491–504.

Posner, M. I. (1969). Abstraction and the process of recognition. In J. T. Spence & G. H. Bower (Eds.), *Advances in learning and motivation* (Vol. 3). New York: Academic Press.

Pressley, M., & Miller, G. (1987). Effects of illustrations on children's listening comprehension and oral prose memory. In D. M. Willows & H. A. Houghton (Eds.), *The psychology of illustration: Basic research* (Vol. 1). New York: Springer-Verlag.

Pylyshyn, Z. (1981). The imagery debate: Analogue media versus tacit knowledge. *Psychological Review, 88,* 16–45.

Reese, H. W. (1970). Imagery and contextual meaning. *Psychological Bulletin, 73,* 404–414.

Rohwer, W. D., Jr. (1970). Images and pictures in children's learning: Research results and educational implications. *Psychological Bulletin, 73,* 393–403.

Rosner, S. R. (1971). The effect of rehearsal and chunking instructions on children's multi-trial free recall. *Journal of Experimental Child Psychology, 11,* 93–105.

Rosner, S. R., & Lindsay, D. T. (1974). The effects of retention interval on preschool children's short-term memory of verbal items. *Journal of Experimental Child Psychology, 18,* 72–80.

Saint Augustine. (1952). In *great books of the western world* (R. M. Hutchins, Ed.). Chicago: Encyclopaedia Britannica.

Sheingold, K. (1973). Developmental differences in intake and storage of visual information. *Journal of Experimental Child Psychology, 16,* 1–11.

Shepard, R. N. (1967). Recognition memory for words, sentences, and pictures. *Journal of Verbal Learning and Verbal Behavior, 6,* 156–163.

Stein, A. H. (1971). The effects of sex-role standards for achievement and sex role preference on three determinants of achievement motivation. *Developmental Psychology, 4,* 219–231.

Steel, L. , & Wise, L. L. (1979). *Origins of sex differences in high school mathematics achievement and participation.* Paper presented at the annual meeting of the American Educational Research Association, San Francisco.

Thomas, H., & Jamison, W. (1975). On the acquisition of understanding that still water is horizontal. *Merrill-Palmer Quarterly, 21,* 31–44.

Welsandt, R. F., & Meyer, P. A. (1974). Visual masking, mental age, and retardation. *Journal of Experimental Child Psychology, 18,* 512–519.

Winn, B. (1987). Charts, graphs, and diagrams in educational materials. In D. M. Willows & H. A. Houghton (Eds.), *The psychology of illustration: Basic research* (Vol. 1). New York: Springer-Verlag.

Chapter Five

Communication Models

Forrest G. Wisely

Objectives

After reading this chapter, you should be able to:

1. *Define communication from different perspectives.*

2. *Discuss the development of communication as a field of study.*

3. *List and define the elements of the communication process.*

4. *Identify variables which affect communication.*

5. *Explain what is meant by key models of communication.*

Definition of Communication

Communication. It is something we are all involved with in one way or another. Audience research studies suggest the average working person may spend 70 percent or more of his or her time in some form of communication (Rankin, 1952). Students probably spend a larger percentage of their time communicating—reading and writing, listening and speaking, and viewing and imaging.

Some researchers are also interested in animal communication. The wolf defines its territory, and other wolves honor or challenge it. The honey bee shares the location of a newly found source of nectar with other bees in its hive through an intricate dance. This area of animal communication is not of particular interest here. The focus of this chapter is on learned human communication.

For an activity so widely practiced by living creatures, it should be an easy task to identify a simple, universally accepted definition of communication. It is not. Ruben (1984) lists seven factors that make it difficult to define communication. He states these factors as:

(1) the use of the same term to refer both to a discipline and the activity within it; (2) the methods of study drawing on traditions of sciences, on the one hand, and of the arts and humanities on the other; (3) the interdisciplinary heritage of communication study; (4) the use of a single term to refer both to natural and purposeful activities; (5) the association of the word with everyday activities that require no special training, as well as with techniques that demand professional expertise; (6) the blurring distinction between *communication* (discipline or process) and *communications* (technology or messages); and (7) the popularity of the field. (Ruben, 1984, p. 11)

A person may say in the same breath she is "studying communications" at school to enable her "to communicate" more effectively as a photojournalist in "mass communication." In one sentence communication has been used in three different ways: a field of study, an act, and an industry.

The information-based society in which we live today and the advances in technologies to deal with the creation, collection, manipulation, storage, retrieval, and dissemination of information have increased interest in the study of communication. Ruben defines communication as any "information related behavior" (Ruben, 1984). Edgar Dale (1969) defined communication as "the sharing of ideas and feelings in a mood of mutuality "(p. 10).

These two definitions focus on communication as an act or process of transmitting information. Other definitions focus on different aspects of communication. The definitions of particular interest here are those which deal with communication as a human activity or behavior. These definitions focus on communication as a deliberate act that uses various learned symbol systems.

One such definition of communication is "The transmission of information, ideas, emotions, skills etc., by the use of symbols—words, figures, graphs, etc. It is the act or process of transmission that is usually called communication" (Berelson & Steiner, 1964, p. 527). A similar definition comes from Theodorson and Theodorson (1969), who define communication as "the transmission of information, ideas, attitudes, or emotion from one person or group to another (or others) primarily through symbols" (pp. 13–14).

These two definitions add the element of how messages are transmitted to the process. These definitions also help us begin to separate human communication from animal communication. Symbolic human communication is not instinctive as animal communication but requires both formal learning and informal learning. Through the use of symbol systems humans are able to record, store, retrieve, manipulate, disseminate, and use information in an efficient and deliberate manner. This allows each new generation to build on previous generations' work and not have to "re-invent the wheel" each time.

Development of Communication Studies

Various factors and concepts of communication have been studied for centuries. Aristotle may have developed the first model of communication. It was primarily a linear, one-way relationship with three elements: speaker, message, and listener. See Figure 1.

The date for the formal study of communication as a discipline is difficult to determine. The early roots are usually placed in the 1920's in various fields of the

Figure 1. Aristotle's Model of Communication.

social sciences. Political scientists contributed greatly to the early development as well as specialists in philosophy, sociology, anthropology, and psychology. Their studies included communication as part of the broader studies of the many diverse dimensions of society. The formal beginning of communication as a new field of study is usually placed in the late 1940's with the development of the first communication models.

Functions of Models

In the pursuit of knowledge about an act or process, humans often build models. A model is not an exact replica of the thing itself but (1) simplifies the reality of the thing, (2) selects elements relevant to the focus of what is being studied, and (3) illustrates the relationships among the elements. The elements are then represented in some symbolic form. The representations may range from a mathematical formula to lines and boxes to computer simulations. The selection and representation of the various elements are based on the desired outcomes of the study and will probably evolve and change as the study progresses.

Karl W. Deutsch, a political scientist, first published his book, *The Nerves of Government: Models of Political Communication and Control* in 1963. His first chapter, "Tools for Thinking: The General Nature of Theory and Models," is a classic. He presents an excellent explanation of the process we use in choosing and using models in the quest to understand a topic being studied.

Deutsch (1963) presents four function models that serve in the pursuit of knowledge. They are:

—the organizing function;
—the heuristic function;
—the predictive function; and
—the mensurative function.

The organizing function of a model refers to its ability to help us take the data we have collected and place them in some order or pattern and to connect them to other data. Deutsch states this organizing of data may help us store them in our memory and to recall them when needed at a later date.

The heuristic function of a model refers to its ability to assist in making both general and specific predictions. Even if the techniques do not exist at the time to verify the predictions, a model may lead to new facts and methods.

The predictive function of a model refers to its ability to help us look at data patterns and by extending them into the future or other space not yet encountered. The researcher may be able to infer new or future facts that may or may not be confirmed later.

The mensurative (measurement) function of a model refers to its ability to help us answer such questions as when something will happen or how much. When a model helps obtain data of an understood process, the data will be a measure of the thing being modeled (Deutsch, 1963).

Communication Models

Since the late 1940's many models of communication have been developed. Some have attempted to model the general process of communication. Other models have been developed to focus on specific elements in the communication process like audience or channels. Still other models have been developed to focus on the form or an area of communication like interpersonal or organizational.

A discussion of a few models of communication will illustrate the evolution and range of communication models as well as their value in terms of the four functions listed earlier. It will also present the basic elements of communication and how they are emphasized in different models.

Laswell's Model

The basic elements of communication were presented in a model by political scientist, Harold D. Laswell (1948). His famous sentence states, "Who says what in which channel to whom with what effect?" (p. 117). This sentence structures the communication process and illustrates that the communicator has a clear intent to influence the receiver. The basic elements of communication, i.e., sender, message, channel, receiver, are all present in his model. See Figure 2.

Laswell also used his previously quoted sentence (formula, as it is sometimes called) to describe the different kinds of communication research. Studies of the "who" engage in "control analysis." "Content analysis" is the focus of studies in the "says what" or message area. The studies concerning "in which channel" are dealing with "media analysis." "Audience analysis" is the focus of studies in the "to whom" area, and the "with what effect" studies are studying "impact" or effect analysis on the audience (Laswell, 1948).

Shannon and Weaver's Model

Claude Shannon and his colleague, Warren Weaver, introduced their influential mathematical model of communication in 1949. Their model was concerned with information theory and focused on the transmission of messages in the field of telecommunication. Although this is a technical approach to communication, the Shannon-Weaver model's influence can be identified in many later models of communication.

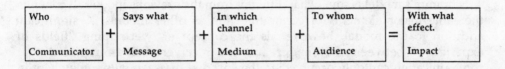

Figure 2. Laswell's Model of Communication.

Shannon and Weaver (1949) defined communication as a one way (linear) process. Their model is primarily directed at the channels of communication between the sender and the receiver. The first part of their model is the "information source" which produces the "messages." A "transmitter" then changes the message into a "signal" to be sent over a "channel" to a "receiver." The role of the "receiver" is to change the "signal" back to the "message" before it reaches it "destination."

The "noise source" in the Shannon-Weaver model may alter the signal which may mean that the message arriving at the destination is not the exact one sent from the information source. Noise is one reason communication fails (Shannon & Weaver, 1949). See Figure 3.

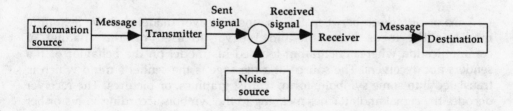

Figure 3. Shannon and Weaver's Model of Communication.

Schramm's Models

Wilbur Schramm (1954) is credited by many for making communication a legitimate field of study. He established the Institute for Communication Research at the University of Illinois and a similar one at Stanford University. Schramm was also a prolific writer who wrote many books and articles focusing on a wide range of communication research.

Schramm's model is somewhat different from the previous models. It contains the same major elements of communication as other models. A significant addition to the model, however, is the concept of overlapping "fields of experience" between the sender and the receiver. Schramm noted that communication can only occur when the encoded message falls somewhere in the overlapping fields of experience (Schramm, 1954). See Figure 4.

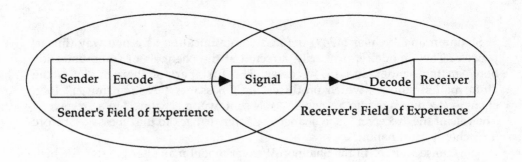

Figure 4. Schramm's Model of Communication.

A major difference between the Shannon-Weaver model and the Schramm model is the focus. Shannon and Weaver focused on the channel of communication whereas Schramm focused his model on the behavior of the senders and receivers. The source of a message is the sender's mind which is translated into some symbolic form, words, graphics, or pictures. The receiver decodes the signal and attaches meaning to the symbols according to his or her field of experience. The destination is the receiver's mind.

Schramm (1954) believed communication was endless, not something that began in one place and ended in another. Another Schramm model, in collaboration with C. E. Osgood, broke with the traditional linear models. A sender encodes a message which is sent to a receiver who decodes and interprets it. The receiver then encodes some kind of response to the message which is then sent as a new message to the original sender who becomes a receiver of the response message which is decoded and interpreted. This circular or cybernetic approach to communication increases the possibility of understanding the intent of the message.

Schramm was also responsible for other models to explain different forms of communication. His model of mass communication presents the concept of inferential feedback from mass audiences. See Figure 5.

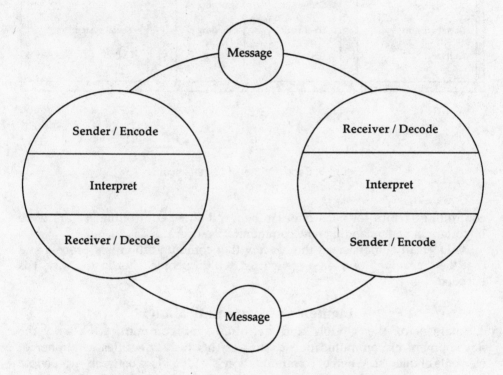

Figure 5. Schramm's Later Model of Communication.

Berlo's Model

David Berlo (1960) introduced a different kind of model whose function was to identify the variables which he considered important in the process of communication. He called his model, "a model of the ingredients in communication" (pp. 23–24). The focus of the Berlo model was on the characteristics of the sender and the receiver as they interact through various elements of the message and channel. See Figure 6.

Berlo's model is often referred to as the SMCR model. These four letters represent the four column headings in a table often used to represent the model. Berlo's model is linear like many of the early models and contains the same basic elements. The basic elements were explained in more detail by listing the

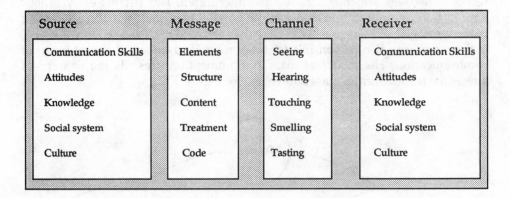

Source	Message	Channel	Receiver
Communication Skills	Elements	Seeing	Communication Skills
Attitudes	Structure	Hearing	Attitudes
Knowledge	Content	Touching	Knowledge
Social system	Treatment	Smelling	Social system
Culture	Code	Tasting	Culture

Figure 6. Berlo's Model of Communication.

controlling factors for each one. He believed these controlling factors were important in understanding how communication operates.

Berlo greatly emphasized the concept that communication is a process and that the "meaning" of a message existed within people—not in the way it is encoded.

Elements of Communication

Analysis of the models and definitions of communication and the development of communication as an area of study identifies a number of elements of interest. Whether communication is taking place between two people or among many people, all these elements must be considered.

The form and source of the information to be communicated, the symbol system in which the information is encoded, the medium on which it is fixed, the channel which delivers it to the intended receiver, the fields of experience shared by the sender and the receiver, the environment in which the communication is taking place, and the form of feedback possibilities are some of the elements which determine the success or failure of communication. It is easy to see that a message must be carefully planned, designed, produced, and delivered to increase the probability for successful communication.

References

Berelson, B., & Steiner, G. A. (1964). *Human behavior: An inventory of scientific findings.* New York: Harcourt, Brace, and World.

Berlo, D. (1960). *The process of communication: An introduction to theory and practice.* New York: Holt, Rinehart, and Winston.

Dale, E. (1969). *Audiovisual methods in teaching* (3rd ed.). New York: Holt, Rinehart, and Winston.

Deutsch, K. W. (1963). *The nerves of government: Models of political communication and control.* New York: The Free Press.

Laswell, H. D. (1948). The structure and function of communication in society. In L. Bryson, (Ed.), *The communication of ideas.* New York: Harper.

Rankin, R. T. (1952).The measurement of the ability to understand spoken language. *Dissertation Abstracts International, 12,* 847–848.

Ruben, B. D. (1984). *Communication and human behavior.* New York: Macmillan Publishing Co.

Schramm, W. (1954). How communication works. In W. Schramm (Ed.), *The process and effects of mass communication.* Urbana, IL: University of Illinois Press.

Shannon, C. E., & Weaver, W. (1949). *The mathematical theory of communication.* Urbana, IL: University of Illinois Press.

Theodorson, S. A., & Theodorson, A. G. (1969). *A modern dictionary of sociology.* New York: Cassell Education Limited.

SECTION II

Visual Language

In Chapter One, John Hortin indicated that there is considerable discussion related to the definition of "visual literacy." In this section, Barbara Seels continues to trace the evolutionary development of several of the these definitions as well as such related terms such as "visual learning" and "visual thinking." She also traces the concept of "visual language" and the verbal language metaphor. Seels discusses visual literacy as a construct item in a field of study having a variety of operational definitions. Major authors and events that have been influential in promoting the visual literacy concept are identified. Figures are provided throughout the chapter to show relationships between visual literacy and related concepts.

In discussing the work of Köhler, Koffka, and others, Ann Marie Barry introduces the reader to the concept of "Perceptual Aesthetics." Perceptual Aesthetics pursues an isomorphic understanding of the intersecting point where science, life, and art meet. T. S. Eliot articulated this isomorphism: "When a poet's mind is perfectly equipped for its work, it is constantly amalgamating disparate experience; the ordinary man's experience is chaotic, irregular, fragmentary ... in the mind of the poet these experiences are always forming new wholes" (Bate, 1952, p. 532).

Barry explores this concept in both film and literature through the work of artists and critics such as Edgar Allan Poe, William James, T. S. Eliot, Ernest Hemingway, Sergei Eisenstein, and Alain Renais. Gestalt perceptual theory is seen as a means of understanding not only how man perceives his environment, but also how he creates and perceives beauty as well—transforming perceptual theory into aesthetic theory. The goal of this approach is to come to an understanding of how it is that all great art, as T. S. Eliot observed, has "the same essential quality of transmuting ideas into sensations, and of transforming an observation into a state of mind" (Bate, 1952, p. 533). Ultimately, Barry suggests that the aesthetic genius of the artist may indeed by perceptually based.

Reference

Bate, W. J. (Ed.). (1952). *Criticism: The major texts.* New York: Harcourt, Brace, Jovanovich.

Chapter Six

Visual Literacy:
The Definition Problem

Barbara A. Seels

Objectives

After reading this chapter, you should be able to:

1. *Define visual thinking, learning, communication, and literacy.*

2. *Discuss the evolution of the concept "literacy."*

3. *Describe the relationship among visual thinking, learning, communication, and literacy.*

4. *Explain why "visual literacy" is needed.*

5. *Explain issues related to "visual literacy" as a construct.*

Visual Literacy as a Concept

It wasn't until the 1950's and 1960's, when television seemed to be influencing behavior and knowledge, that the concept of visual literacy caught the attention of educators. This interest was dispersed among leaders in many areas of education. As a movement, visual literacy has had relatively little impact on schools because, as with any new field, it has been building a theoretical and political base. Because the future of the movement depends on the clarity and acceptance of its terminology, the question of what "visual literacy" means is an important one.

> If the invention of moveable type created a mandate for universal verbal literacy, surely the invention of the camera and all its collateral and

continually developing forms makes the achievement of universal visual literacy as an educational necessity long overdue. (Dondis, 1973, p. ix)

Evolution of the Concept "Literacy"

The meaning of literacy has changed throughout history as communications and language have become more complex. In Colonial times in the USA, a literate person could read and write. This is still one meaning of the word. But there is another meaning. A literate person today is an educated person, a person who has learned the fundamentals needed to function as a responsible citizen. This can mean being able to vote intelligently, use computers efficiently, and parent effectively. Thus, we are urged to develop verbal literacy (Hall, 1987; Holdaway, 1984), media literacy (Salomon, 1982; Johnson, 1977), visual literacy (Platt, 1975; Dondis, 1973), computer literacy (Provenzo, 1986), technological literacy (Tuman, 1992a, b; LaConte, 1982), aesthetic literacy (Kaelin, 1989), and environmental literacy (Roth, 1992). Gavriel Salomon (1982) raised the question of whether transfer from one literacy to another occurs. Do the inference-making skills developed through televiewing help to develop reading and writing skills and vice versa? Some scholars argue that because too much time is spent on print literacy, "visual illiteracy" has serious consequences (DeSousa & Medhurst, 1982). Others counter that visual and verbal literacy are inseparable and thus part of a greater literacy. Howard Gardner (1983) of Harvard University, author of *Frames of Mind*, believes that aesthetic literacy is unique and needs to be developed for itself (H. Gardner, Personal Communication, October 10, 1988). He is among those who argue that visual languages are so unique they must be treated separately.

The position taken in this chapter is that today literacy is a broad concept that requires more than reading and writing. Even functional literacy, meaning basic literacy, includes computation along with reading and writing. Today, literacy encompasses verbal and visual literacy. Edgar Dale (1973) described this new literacy eloquently:

> What do I mean by the term "literacy" and the "new" literacy? I mean by literacy the ability to communicate through the three modes: reading and writing, speaking, and listening, visualizing and observing—print, audio, and visual literacy. This literacy, broadly speaking, can be at two levels. First, is at the level of training, initiative reaction. Here we communicate the simple, literal meaning of what is written, said or visualized ...
>
> Or second, we can have creative interaction, can read between the lines, draw inferences, understand the implications of what was written, said or spoken. We thus learn what the speaker, writer or visualizer "meant to say" which requires a greater degree of literacy. And finally, we learn to read beyond the lines, to evaluate, and apply the material to new situations. We use the message in our own varied ways.
>
> I would also classify responses as uncritical or accepting, or as critical and evaluating. The new literacy involves critical reading, critical listening, and critical observing. It is disciplined thinking about what is read, heard, and visualized. (pp. 92–93)

Need for Visual Literacy

Cassidy and Knowlton (1983) claim that visual literacy is the normal human condition because basic visual tasks, such as recognizing objects, are not difficult. Anthropologists have questioned the viability of the "visual literacy" concept because people are born with the capacity to develop vision and visual abilities. Children born in rural villages, for example, learn to deal with their environment visually. No intervention is needed to promote visual literacy. Gordon Hewes (1978) traces the evolutionary development of the visual system and its relationship to other sensory systems and concludes it is essential for learning, thinking, and communication. As Hewes explains, for most of us, our visual outputs are not naturally comparable to our reading and writing skills because we do not have artistic or drawing talent. This equation changes with the development of photography because photography empowers people visually. With computer graphics, digitized photography, and interactive video, we have tools that raise the ability to visualize to new planes. Using today's technology, researchers can electronically unwrap 3,000-year-old mummies, and consumers can turn their *Macs* and *PCs* into electronic darkrooms using Photo CD images. Hewes (1978) grants that people of normal vision who experience the concrete world develop similar visual abilities, but he argues that this fact does not make visual literacy superfluous. The "visual literacy is a general human condition" position is not sufficient because there are cross-cultural and technological phenomena that need to be taken into account. Cross-cultural differences in construction of meaning is a well-demonstrated phenomenon. Researchers have found some innate visual abilities, but at the same time research and practice have shown that visual abilities can be taught (Sless, 1984). The same argument has been made regarding the learning of verbal language. Linguist Noam Chomsky (1957, 1975, 1980) believes some kind of "innate acquisition desire " is necessary to explain how language is acquired. Even if this is also true of visual language learning, the corollary is not necessarily that visual literacy is superfluous. Deborah Curtiss (1987) believes that:

> With visual literacy—the ability to both understand and make visual statements—we become sensitized to the world around us, the relationships and systems of which we are a part. Visual literacy integrates personal experience, knowledge, and imagination with social experience, technology, and esthetics. (p. 238)

When artists and scientists are creative, visual literacy is essential. Visual knowledge and thinking are extensively reported as essential to creativity and problem-solving. It is impossible to do higher order thinking without using imagery (Paivio, 1978). Psychologist Rudolph Arnheim (1969) believes that visual perception is the basis for concept formation because thinking requires and depends on images.

Many strategies recommended for teaching verbal literacy are equally relevant to visual literacy (McGee & Richgels, 1990). But reaching the goal of visual literacy has been difficult for many reasons. Jack Debes (1968) believed visual literacy would only be possible after the development of special knowledge and technologies. It has taken 30 years of research on television's effects to build a body of knowledge that can be used to help parents and teachers (Comstock & Piak, 1987). In 1973 Donis A. Dondis, a pioneer in the area of visual literacy, wrote:

> Judgments of what is workable, appropriate, effective in visual communication have been abandoned to whim, some formless definition of taste or to the subjective, self-reflective evaluation of the sender or receiver with little or no attempt to realize, at the least, some of the prescribed levels we expect of what we call literacy in the verbal mode. This is probably not so much from bias as from a firm conviction that no methodology, no means for achieving visual literacy, is possible. However, the demand for media study has outstripped the capabilities of our schools and colleges. Facing the challenge of visual literacy may no longer be easy to ignore. (p. 11)

Jerome Bruner (1966), who postulated that knowledge is represented in three ways: enactive, iconic, and symbolic, said, "I do not think we have begun to scratch the surface of training in visualization, whether related to the arts, to science, or simply to the pleasures of viewing our environments more richly" (p. 34). In 1982, LaConte elaborated on this need for visual literacy:

> The flow of messages in the information age is no longer predominately down a chain of command but increasingly lateral. The modern communication process is also task specific, faster-paced, more graphic, and less verbal, and more technologically directed. These changes have rendered our definitions of communication skills and our school curriculum obsolete. Among the skills neglected in the typical curriculum are message comprehension, decoding, and interpreting condensed messages, kinesics, synthesizing information, visual literacy, rapid analysis, and evaluation of message validity. (p. 1)

Visual Literacy as a Construct

One of the problems the visual literacy movement has faced is the difficulty of communicating with unfamiliar terminology. Another problem has been the usefulness of the concept "visual literacy" for researchers and theorists. The issues and concerns related to these problems are discussed under the topics: "Visual/Visible Language" and "Concept or Construct."

Visual/Visible Language

The catalyst for the organization of the visual literacy movement was Jack Debes, who worked for *Kodak Corporation* in Rochester, New York. During the 1950's and 1960's he spent much time, energy, and imagination in developing programs that helped children develop skills in visualization. One of the programs used photographs to change the self-concept of inner-city teenagers in Washington, DC. Debes observed that the program not only succeeded in increasing self-esteem, but also it changed environmental awareness and attitudes toward society. He also organized a very successful program in photography skills for the 4H Club. Realizing he was observing important effects in the 1960's, he started searching the literature on visual language and literature and on structural linguistics (Debes, 1969). By the end of the 1960's he, with others, decided to call for a pre-conference in Rochester. This was held in August

1968 and led to the first national conference on visual literacy that was convened in March of 1969 by several co-sponsors (Williams & Debes, 1970).

Twenty-five conferences have followed in Canada, the United States, Sweden, and England. The International Visual Literacy Association was formed and became an affiliate of the Association for Educational Communications and Technology. Publications were promoted through books, articles, provocative papers, special issues, a journal, proceedings, and a newsletter. A National Center for Visual Literacy was established at Gallaudet College and an archives at Arizona State University.

It was Debes who started from the point-of-view that visual literacy is concerned with teaching visual languaging. The literature of that period, the 1960's and 1970's, is confusing because visual languages (sign language, body language), visual languaging (shots, composition), and visible languages (pictographic languages) are used as is the term visual/verbal languaging. In fact, the first name of the *Journal of Visual Literacy* was *Journal of Visual/Verbal Languaging*, which was intended to convey the inseparability of visual and verbal languaging. Needless to say, the literature of that period was very confusing and often not understood outside the movement. Jack Debes' and Clarence Williams' editorial statement for the Fall, 1982 *Journal of Visual/Verbal Languaging* read: "... It is most especially the Journal for the study of visual languaging and visual literacies, and of their interrelationships with verbal manifestations of man's languaging propensities" (p. 5).

One important issue tackled in the literature during this period was the characteristics of visual language. The literacy metaphor led to many parallels being made with verbal language, perhaps too many. Much time was spent relating the concept to linguistics (Braden & Hortin, 1982). There was much written about special effects, such as dissolves, being similar to punctuation in film, and shots and scenes being similar to paragraphs. The author of this chapter confesses to having written such an article herself (Seels, 1966). Others believed the characteristics of visual language did not parallel those of print language (Dondis, 1973; Arnheim, 1969). The search for the grammar of film did, however, lead to some fruitful analyses of the mental skills needed to learn from media (Peters, 1961). The pursuit of the question was worthwhile because it eventually illuminated the very different nature of visual language. The philosopher Susanne Langer (1951), said it best—verbal languages are sequential in nature, visual language is simultaneous in nature. She called these two forms discursive (verbal) and presentational (visual). The former is a tool for denotation and the latter for connotation. Because linear experience requires a lapse of time for perception and imaginative recreation, critical evaluation of verbal experiences is expected. On the other hand, there is a tendency with simultaneous experience to expect immediate recognition and reaction without time for reflection and critical judgment (Platt, 1975). Others distinguish between visual and verbal symbol systems by the reactions we have to each.

At least one theorist, Calvin Pryluck (1973), believes that context works differently for visual or pictorial signs than it does for verbal ones, that it leads us to generalize the pictorial stimulus but to particularize the verbal one. Thus he concludes that visual communication is 'structurally inductive,' whereas

language is 'structurally deductive.' Pryluck (1973) also makes the point that
sequencing and juxtaposition—contextual factors—are especially important in
pictorial communication because we do not have conventional relational
devices as we have for languages. 'The conceptual relationship between
images is indirect and inferential.' [p. 131] (Becker, 1978, p. 56)

Of course, a reader uses context to construct meaning in verbal language too.
The novice in verbal language needs the whole context to identify signs and cues
that enable him to link content and form (McGee & Richgels, 1990). However, the
way we search for patterns differs with visual language. With verbal language
one searches for rules, with visual language one searches for relationships of a
temporal, spatial, or salient nature. Dondis (1973) concluded that, "Visual literacy
could never be a clear-cut logical system similar to language. Languages are
made-up systems, constructed by man to encode, store, and decode information.
Therefore, their structure has a logic that visual literacy is unable to parallel"
(p. 12).

Concept or Construct

The existence of a visual literacy movement is beyond question. The answers
to the question of whether there is a visual literacy field, profession or discipline
is also clear. There is no field, profession or discipline of visual literacy. There is
an area of study. A discipline adds to its own knowledge. A profession has a
knowledge base and is characterized by the services it renders. This is not to
dispute the research and theory generated in the area of visual literacy over the
last 20 years. But a discipline needs to develop its own way of studying and
organizing (Beauchamp, 1975). Methods are still evolving in the area of visual
literacy. Past and current theoretical contributions have come from many other
disciplines and are still being synthesized. The practice of visual literacy takes
place through roles in other professions; therefore, visual literacy is not a
profession. The area of visual literacy does not at present comfortably encompass
both theory and practice; therefore, it is not a field. Yet for a relatively young area
of study and movement much progress has been made (Braden & Walker, 1980).
It is not surprising that the concepts are still vague and difficult to apply in
research situations.

Is visual literacy a concept or a construct? It is not a construct with operational
specificity. Thus, while appropriate for the pre-scientific development of this
investigation, it cannot lead to empirical research and theory construction (Marx,
1967). It is a concept that has captured the imagination of a movement. Things
can be classified as related to or characteristic of visual literacy. There have been
hierarchies of visual literacy skills (Fransecky & Debes, 1972; Debes, 1969;
Williams & Debes, 1970) and identification of elements and strategies (Dondis,
1973). Even as a concept the essential characteristics are under discussion. For
example, when is the ability to sequence a visual literacy characteristic, and when
is it a verbal literacy characteristic? Does visual thinking include all sensory
imagery as Arnheim (1969) proposes ?

What visual literacy may be is a theoretical construct rather than a construct
with operational specificity (Beauchamp, 1975). A construct is a specific kind of
concept. A concept that "refers to relationships among things or events, and their

various properties" is called a construct (Marx, 1963, p. 10). As such it is more theoretical than operational and is a psychological construct similar to motivation. "Visual literacy" has too many meanings currently to be operational, but it is still a construct like "justice," "school spirit" or "friendship." What is the point of making this distinction? The distinction reveals why "visual literacy" research and theory building have not been more fruitful. Synthesis is difficult because terms are not well-defined. Consequently it is difficult to identify research problems related to visual literacy. It is difficult to measure or observe that which you can't define. Herring (1980) distinguishes between elucidatory and evaluative inquiry. Elucidatory inquiry can establish cause-effect relationships. Evaluative inquiry can determine effects not causes. Most of the research on visual literacy has been evaluation of programs. The result has been a lack of methodology for basic research and lack of basic research on visual literacy. In order for research and synthesis to occur, visual literacy, the theoretical construct, will have to be related to more operational constructs.

Visual Literacy, Thinking, Learning, and Communication

Visual Literacy

According to Herring (1980), the concept of visual literacy is so ill-defined as to be uninteresting as a basis of research. This is because visual literacy is often defined as a set of competencies (Debes, 1969; Fransecky & Debes, 1972) that is culturally biased. As an alternative, Herring proposes visual literacy be defined as the relationship of visual skills to instructional tasks. For example, visual literacy would be defined as strategies to aid memorization. This does not contrast with the view that visual literacy is a range or hierarchy of competencies as much as he infers. Competencies would simply be tied to learning tasks more specifically.

Let's trace the evolution of the definition of visual literacy from the skills definition of the early 1970's to the present, keeping in mind Dondis' (1973) admonition that "the major pitfall in developing an approach to visual literacy is trying to overdefine it" (p. 9). By reviewing the major definitions we can identify similarities that will justify the selection and defense of a current definition. In 1975 Joan Platt reviewed research and theory about visual literacy for the National Education Association. The definition she used was: "the ability both to understand—and to express themselves in terms of visual material, to enable them to relate visual images to meanings beyond the images themselves" (p. 5). This is similar to the definition presented by Braden and Walker (1980) at the 12th Annual Conference on Visual Literacy. They based their definition on a historical overview of definitions: "to be visually literate is to be able to gain meaning from what we see and to be able to communicate meaning to others through the images we create" (p. 1). Wileman (1980) gave a similar definition: the ability to "read" and understand that which is seen and the ability to generate materials that have to be seen to be understood" (p. 13). Two definitions were significant in 1982: by Heinich, Molenda, and Russell, and by Braden and Hortin. In the first edition of their landmark text, *Instructional Media and the New Technologies of Instruction*, Heinich, Molenda, and Russell (1982) describe the concept as: "visual literacy is the learned ability to interpret visual messages accurately and to create such messages" (p. 62).

Braden and Hortin (1982) wrote a review which presented a definition consistent with the meaning proposed in this chapter. This definition is similar to the definitions that preceded it. "Visual literacy is the ability to understand and use images, including the ability to think, learn, and express oneself in terms of images" (p. 41). In 1987 Curtiss offered a variation:

> Visual literacy is the ability to understand the communication of a visual statement in any medium and the ability to express oneself with at least one visual discipline. It entails the ability to: understand the subject matter and meaning within the context of the culture that produced the work, analyze the syntax—compositional and stylistic principles of the work, evaluate the disciplinary and aesthetic merits of the work, and grasp intuitively the Gestalt, the interactive and synergistic quality of the work. (p. 3)

Relationship Between Constructs

The problem with constructing an operational definition of visual literacy is that the term refers to a product not a process, to a condition not a cause, to a state not an action. Even if operational definitions are derived, such as the ability to understand and the ability to create, they are too vague to reflect the literature related to the concept. Bikkar S. Randhawa (1978) suggests visual literacy be operationalized in terms of visual learning, thinking, and communication. These constructs provide a way to organize more specific terminology. If we accept visual literacy as a theoretical super construct then visual thinking, learning, and communication become "sub-concepts" that yield operational constructs. This relationship is shown in Figure 1—Relationship of Areas of Study in Visual Literacy.

A more holistic way of conceptualizing the relationship is shown in Figure 2—The Visual Literacy Cube.

It is more important to realize that these processes differ in the extent to which they are focused internally and externally. This focus is shown in Figure 3—The Visual Literacy Continuum.

Note that visual learning has both an internal and external focus. Similarly, if we compare these constructs in terms of direction, visual learning has a dual direction to self and others while the other two terms are unidirectional. This is illustrated in Figure 4—Directionality of Visual Literacy Components.

Each of these operational constructs is defined and discussed in the concluding sections of this chapter.

Visual Thinking

Visual thinking is the internal reaction stage. It involves more manipulation of mental imagery and more sensory and emotional association than other stages. Arnheim (1969) describes visual thinking as preconscious, metaphorical thought. He describes it as the unity of perception and conception which calls for the ability to see visual shapes as images (pictures, signs, and symbols). Wileman (1980) defines visual thinking "as organizing mental images around shapes, lines,

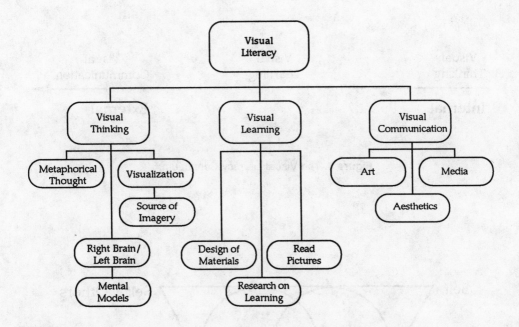

Figure 1. Relationship of Areas of Study in Visual Literacy.

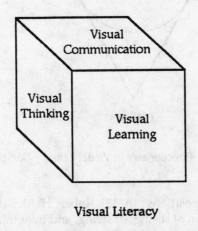

Figure 2. The Visual Literacy Cube.

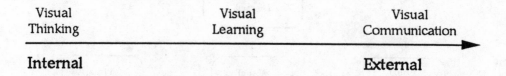

Figure 3. The Visual Literacy Continuum.

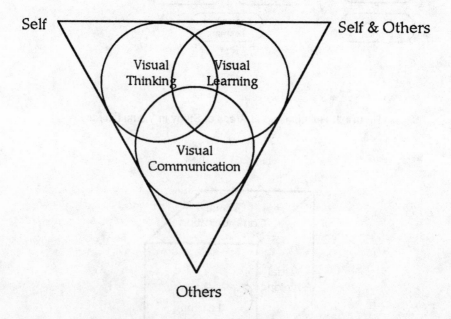

Figure 4. Directionality of Visual Literacy Components.

color, textures, and compositions" (p. 13). Robert H. McKim (1980) defines visual thinking as the interaction of seeing, drawing, and imagining.

Visual thinking refers to visualization through images. Images are mental pictures of sensory experiences, perceptions or conceptions. Visual thinking in its simplest form is manipulating symbols representing elements of the internal or external environment by using imagery (Ruch & Zimbardo, 1971).

Sources of imagery are an important part of visual thinking processes. Mike and Nancy Samuels (1975) illustrate the many sources of imagery necessary for visualization. Similarly, Deborah Curtiss (1987) discusses our heritage and environment as sources of imagery which influence visual thinking and literacy. Samples (1976) also reviews sources of metaphor in his book, *The Metaphoric Mind.*

Visual Learning

Visual learning is the most complex of the theoretical constructs because it refers to both learning from visuals and research on designing visuals for instruction. Both uses of the term have been in the literature for many years.

Visual learning, meaning learning from pictures and media, was the title of a television workshop and pamphlet series produced by the New York State Education Department in 1976. "Visual learning," meaning research on the design of visuals for instruction, was used by Dwyer (1972, 1978). Fleming and Levie (1978, 1993) compiled and published principles for the design of instructional visuals. Randhawa, Bach, and Myers (1977) used the term to refer to research on the design of visuals as did Jonassen and Fork in 1978.

The use of the term "visual learning" to refer to research related to the effect of visual stimuli on specific learning objectives was replaced first by the term "message design," then by the term "instructional design." These terms are currently in use to refer to research on the design of visuals for learning.

In the past the terms "reading pictures" or "learning from pictures" were used to refer to a student's visual learning. Heinich, Molenda, and Russell's first edition (1982) included a chart on the levels of learning from visuals. In that chart the stages of learning from visuals were described as differentiation and integration. Today, visual learning refers to the acquisition and construction of knowledge as a result of interaction with visual phenomenon.

Perhaps one way to understand the idea of levels of visual learning is to look at the work of someone who has mastered visual learning, D. W. Meinig (1992), who considers himself a historical, humanistic geographer. He has "paid particular attention to symbolic landscapes as representations of American values and generally tried to use the landscape as a kind of archive full of clues about cultural character and historical changes that one can learn to read with ever greater understanding. At the same time landscape is always more than a set of data; it is itself an integration, a composition, and one tries to develop an ever keener appreciation of that" (Meinig, p. 16). Meinig spent a lifetime developing skill in learning from visuals. When Meinig describes how he functions as a geographer, he is describing a high level of visual learning, one in which a great deal of meaning is derived from visual information, and visual information is used in conjunction with other information.

> Geography is a point of view, a way of looking at things. If one focuses on how all kinds of things exist together spatially, in areas, with a special emphasis on context and coherence, one is working as a geographer. The ultimate purpose is more synthetic than analytic. (p. 18)

Visual Communication

Wileman (1980) defines visual communication as "the attempt by human beings to use pictorial and graphic symbols to express ideas and to teach people in and out of the school setting"(p. 13). There are many models and definitions of communication. Most define communication as an interactive or transactional process. Components of the process are usually sender, message, channel, and receiver (Ball & Brynes, 1960). If one accepts these components as characteristics, it is not sufficient to express oneself visually. For visual communication to occur there also has to be an exchange of meaning.

The learning process is a form of communication. McFee (1969) believes that for learning to occur both the content and form of the message must be understood. We must learn to read symbols for both content and form, i.e., for concrete and metaphoric meaning. Visual communication, therefore, is using visual symbols to express ideas and convey meaning.

The ability to interact critically with the symbols of mass media is perhaps the most important aspect of visual literacy today. As part of the documentary series *The Public Mind* (1989), Bill Moyers produced a discussion on "Consuming Images." In it he explores image and reality in America—how public opinion is formed through the minglings of fact and fiction in a society saturated with images. On the program, Moyers interviews Mark Miller, a professor from Johns Hopkins University, who says:

> I think very early on students need to be educated into the idea that images speak, that images say certain kinds of things and that there are values and priorities and meaning embedded in images and that they need to learn something about the vocabulary and grammar of images to be critical. I think what's valuable about that—making visual literacy a basic part of education—is it will take materials which are primarily currently directed at the emotions and the senses and it will reposition them within the framework of critical reasoning and thought. All we see is the erotic, the allure, the aesthetic side when in fact what those images are doing is evoking the kind of consumer behavior which perpetuates an economy predicated on waste. So what is really necessary is that people take a close, critical historically informed look at images, not just knee jerk criticism. What I do in my classes is to encourage multiple meanings over longer historical periods. People have to be taught how to use their own individual minds, their own consciousness, as a way to negotiate the images and gain some kind of control over this oppressive atmosphere. (Moyers, 1989)

Summary

"Visual literacy" as a movement has experienced problems with communication and research because the phrase is a concept, not a construct. Three theoretical constructs, visual thinking, learning, and communication, help define the phrase. For research to proceed these terms need to be associated with more specific constructs which are defined operationally.

Glossary

Visual literacy "the ability to understand, and use images, including the ability to think, learn, and express oneself in terms of images" (Braden & Hortin, 1982).

Visual thinking "organizing mental images around shapes, lines, colors, textures, and compositions" (Wileman, 1980).

Visual learning learning from visuals and research on designing visuals for instruction.

Visual communication using visual symbols to express ideas and convey meaning.

References

Arnheim, R. (1969). *Visual thinking*. Berkeley, CA: University of California Press.

Ball, J., & Brynes, F. C. (1960). *Research, principles, and practices in visual communication*. Department of Audiovisual Instruction.

Becker, S. L. (1978). Visual stimuli and the construction of meaning. In B. S. Randhawa & W. E. Coffman (Eds.), *Visual learning, thinking, and communication* (pp. 39–60). New York: Academic Press.

Beauchamp, G. A. (1975). *Curriculum theory*. Wilmette, IL: Kagg Press.

Braden, R. A., & Hortin, J. A. (1982). Identifying the theoretical foundations of visual literacy. *Journal of Visual/Verbal Languaging, 2*, 37–42.

Braden, R. A., & Walker, A. D. (1980, November). *Reigning catachreses and dogmas related to visual literacy*. Paper presented at Annual Conference of the International Visual Literacy Association, College Park, MD. (ERIC Document Reproduction No. ED212 294).

Bruner, J. S. (1966). *Toward a theory of instruction*. New York: William Norton.

Cassidy, M. F., & Knowlton, J. Q. (1983). Visual literacy: A failed metaphor. *Educational Communications and Technology Journal, 31*, 67–90.

Comstock, G., & Piak, H.-J. (1987). Television and children: A review of recent research. (IR–71). Syracuse, New York: ERIC Clearinghouse on Information Resources.

Chomsky, N. (1957). *Syntactic structures*. The Hague, the Netherlands: Mouton.

Chomsky, N. (1975). *Reflections on language*. New York: Pantheon.

Chomsky, N. (1980). *Rules and representation*. New York: Columbia University Press.

Curtiss, D. C. (1987). *Introduction to visual literacy*. Englewood Cliffs, NJ: Prentice-Hall, Inc.

Dale, E. (1973). Things to come: The new literacy. In I. K. Tyler & C. M. McWilliams (Eds.), *Educational communication in a revolutionary age* (pp. 84–100). Worthington, OH: Charles A. Jones.

Debes, J. L. (1968, March). Visual literacy. Paper presented at the meeting of the Department of Audio-Visual Instruction of the National Education Association, Houston, TX.

Debes, J. L. (1969). The loom of visual literacy. *Audiovisual Instruction, 14* (8), 25–27.

DeSousa, M. A., & Medhurst, M. J. (1982). The editorial cartoon as visual rhetoric: Rethinking Boss Tweed. *Journal of Visual Verbal Languaging, 2,* Fall, 17–36.

Dondis, D. (1973). *A primer of visual literacy*. Cambridge, MA: The MIT Press.

Dwyer, F. M. (1972). *A guide for improving visualized instruction*. State College, PA: Learning Services.

Dwyer, F. M. (1978). *Strategies for improving visual learning*. State College, PA: Learning Services.

Fleming, M., & Levie, W. H. (1978). *Instructional message design: Principles from behavioral sciences*. Englewood Cliffs, NJ: Educational Technology Publications.

Fleming, M., & Levie, W. H. (Eds.) (1993). *Instructional message design: Principles from the behavioral and cognitive sciences* (2nd ed.). Englewood Cliffs, NJ: Educational Technology Publications.

Fransecky, R. B., & Debes, J. L. (1972). *Visual literacy: A way to learn—A way to teach*. Washington, DC: Association for Educational Communications and Technology.

Gardner, H. (1983). *Frames of mind: The theory of multiple intelligences*. New York: Basic Books.

Hall, N. (1987). *The emergence of literacy*. Portsmouth, NH: Heinemann Educational Books.

Heinich, R., Molenda, M., & Russell, J. (1982). *Instructional media and the new technologies of instruction*. New York: John Wiley & Sons.

Herring, R. D. (1980, June). *Visual strategies in problem solving: An aspect of visual literacy* (IR 009 371). Syracuse, New York: ERIC Clearinghouse on Information Resources. (ERIC Document Reproduction Service No. ED 202490).

Hewes, G. (1978). Visual learning, thinking, and communication in human biosocial evaluation. In B. S. Randhawa & W. E. Coffman (Eds.), *Visual learning, thinking, and communication* (pp. 39–60). New York: Academic Press.

Holdaway, D. (1984). *Stability and change in literacy learning*. Portsmouth, NH: Heinemann Educational Books.

Johnson, B. D. (1977). Visual literacy, media literacy, and mass communications for English instruction. (Doctoral dissertation, Northwestern University, 1977). Dissertation Abstracts International, 38, 78–6581a. (University Microfilms No. 78–5287).

Jonassen, D., & Fork, D. J. (1978). A constructive view of visual learning. In D. Fork & J. J. Newhouse (Eds.), *Exploration and interpretation: Theoretical approaches to the study of visual literacy and visual learning.* Philadelphia, PA: International Visual Literacy Association.

Kaelin, E. F. (1989). *An aesthetics for art educators.* New York: Teachers College Press.

LaConte, R. T. (1982). Teaching basic communication skills for an information society. Paper presented at the meeting of the World Future Society Conference, Washington, DC. (ERIC Document Reproduction Service No. ED219832).

Langer, S. (1951). *Philosophy in a new key.* New York: Mentor Books.

Marx, M. (Ed.). (1963). *Theories in contemporary psychology.* New York: Macmillan Publishing Co.

McFee, J. K. (1969). Visual communication. In R. V. Wiman & W. C. Meierhenry (Eds.), *Educational media: Theory into practice* (pp. 195–218). Columbus, OH: Charles E. Merrill.

McGee, L. M., & Richgels, D. J. (1990). *Literacy's beginnings.* New York: Macmillan Publishing Co.

McKim, R. H. (1980). *Experiences in visual thinking.* Monterey, CA: Brooks/Cole Publishing Co.

Meinig, D. W. (1992). *A life of learning.* (ACLS Occasional Paper No. 19). Washington, DC: American Council of Learned Societies.

Moyers, B. (Producer) (1989). *Consuming images* (#1403 of *The Public Mind* series) (Videotape). New York: PBS Video.

Paivio, A. (1978). On exploring visual knowledge. In B. S. Randhawa & W. E. Coffman (Eds.), *Visual learning, thinking, and communication* (pp. 113–131). New York: Academic Press.

Peters, J. M. L. (1961). *Teaching about the film.* New York: International Documents Service, Columbia University Press.

Platt, J. (1975). *Visual literacy (what research says to the teacher).* Washington, DC: National Education Association.

Provenzo, F. F. Jr. (1986). *Beyond the Gutenberg galaxy: Microcomputers and the emergence of post-typographic culture.* New York: Teachers College Press.

Pryluck, C. (1973). Sources of meaning in motion pictures and television. Unpublished doctoral dissertation, University of Iowa.

Randhawa, B. S. (1978). Visual trinity: An overview. In B. S. Randhawa & W. E. Coffman (Eds.), *Visual learning, thinking, and communication* (pp. 191–211). New York: Academic Press.

Randhawa, B. S., Bach, K. T., & Myers, P. J. (1977, April). Visual learning. Paper presented at the annual meeting of the Association for Educational Communications and Technology, Miami Beach, FL. (ERIC Document Reproduction Service No. ED 143319).

Roth, C. (1992). Environmental literacy: Its roots, evolution, and direction in the 1990's. Columbus, OH: ERIC Clearinghouse on Science, Mathematics, and Environmental Education.

Ruch, F. L., & Zimbardo, P. G. (1971). *Psychology and life.* Glenview, IL: Scott Foresman.

Salomon, G. (1982). Television literacy vs. literacy. *Journal of Visual/Verbal Languaging, 2,* Fall, 7–16.

Samples, B. (1976). *The metaphoric mind.* Reading, MA: Addison-Wesley.

Samuels, M., & Samuels, N. (1975). *Seeing with the mind's eye: The history, techniques, and uses of visualization.* New York: Random House.

Seels, B. (1966). How can students be good actors? *Educational Screen & AV Guide, 45,* July, 33.

Sless, D. (1984). Visual literacy: A failed opportunity. *Educational Communications and Technology Journal, 32,* Winter, 224–228.

Tuman, M. C. (Ed.). (1992a). *Literacy on-line: The promise (and peril) of reading and writing with computers.* Pittsburgh, PA: University of Pittsburgh Press.

Tuman, M. C. (1992b). *Word perfect: Literacy in the computer age.* Pittsburgh, PA: University of Pittsburgh Press.

Wileman, R. E. (1980). *Exercises in visual thinking.* New York: Hastings House.

Williams, C. W., & Debes, J. L. (Eds.). (1970). *Proceedings of the first national conference on visual literacy.* New York: Pitman Publishing Co.

Chapter Seven

Perceptual Aesthetics and Visual Language

Ann Marie Seward Barry

Objectives

After reading this chapter, you should be able to:

1. *Define aesthetics.*

2. *Explain how perceptual process serves as a link among art, music, literature, and film.*

3. *Explain the difference between linear logic and Gestalt logic.*

4. *Discuss the significance of the "whole" and relationship in Gestalt psychology.*

5. *Define the term "Perceptual Aesthetics" as it uses Gestalt psychology to build aesthetic theory.*

6. *Discuss the term "objective correlative" in relation to "Perceptual Aesthetics."*

Introduction

At the turn of the seventeenth century, German astronomer and mathematician Johannes Kepler (1571–1630) described the eye as an ingenious optical device, somewhat like a passive camera, which merely records the image of what it sees. A generation later, René Descartes (1596–1650) tried to prove the theory by direct observation when he took the eye of an ox, placed it in a window shutter, and looking at its back surface, saw an inverted image of the scene outside the window. As Ulric Neisser (1971, p. 4) notes, however, "Although this theory encounters insurmountable difficulties as soon as it is seriously considered, it has dominated philosophy and psychology for many years." In "The Processes of Vision," he tells us:

> the fact is that one does not see the retinal image; one sees with the aid of the retinal image. The incoming pattern of light provides information that the nervous system is well adapted to pick up. This information is used by the perceiver ... to construct the internal representations of objects and space called 'conscious experience.' These internal representations are not, however, at all like the corresponding optical images on the back of the eye. (Neisser, 1971, p. 4)

What we ultimately "see" is really a combination of the eye and brain working together to produce a coherent sense of where and how we are related to our environment. French philosopher Maurice Merleau-Ponty (1964) puts it more poetically: " ... our eyes are already much more than receptors for light rays, colors, and lines.... They are computers of the world, which have the gift of the visible as it was once said that the inspired man had the gift of tongues" (p. 164).

Roughly eighty percent of perception is visual: In *Understanding Video*, Jarice Hansen (1987) notes that 75 percent of information entering the brain is from the eyes, and 38 percent of the fibers entering or leaving the central nervous system are located in the optic nerve. Although there are five million channels to the brain from the retina, the eyes themselves have 100 million sensors in the retina.

Perception, which includes the 'gift of the visible' that comes to us primarily through the optic nerve, may be defined as the process by which we derive meaning from what we see, hear, feel, taste, and smell. Both a physiological and mental process, perception uses all of our past experience, values, attitudes, and needs to select relevant information and interpret the world around us; the eyes, the most active of all the sense organs, continually inspect the environment, scanning it for meaning, turning sensory stimuli into meaningful experience.

In the brain, information from the eye is further processed: the left hemisphere focuses on detail and thinks sequentially, analytically, and logically, while the right hemisphere recognizes larger patterns and "is primarily responsible for our orientation in space, artistic endeavor, crafts, body image, recognition of faces" (Ornstein, 1972, p. 51). This is why our current understanding of perception focuses on the eye *and* mind's active creation of meaning through innate patterns of organization—patterns which have evolved over the history of humankind to enabled us to survive within a variety of dangerous environments.

This creative organization of sense information and the patterns which govern it, primarily those associated with the right side of the brain, may also provide the key to an understanding of Aesthetics, a branch of the arts which focuses on the concrete creation and abstract apprehension of the beautiful in all of its forms. When viewed through perceptual principles, Aesthetics—which may be narrowly defined as the appreciation and creation of beauty—may be seen as a natural extension of the way we make sense of our surroundings and also give value to various shapes and forms.

The following discussion explores the theory of "Perceptual Aesthetics" as it allows us to understand how innate perceptual patterns suggest the creative workings of the eye and mind not only in everyday perception, but also in the appreciation and creation of art and literature, the highest expressions of our humanity.

Perceptual Aesthetics

Aesthetics and the Search for the Constant

Aesthetics—which we have broadly defined as an appreciation of the beautiful, and more narrowly defined as a philosophy of art, its creative sources, forms, and effects—implies a hierarchical judgment in which elements of any given composition and their organization are considered more or less appealing to the senses by virtue of their ability to call up a higher emotional, intellectual or moral appreciation in us. For example, Immanuel Kant, eighteenth century philosopher whose *Critique of Judgment* is one of the most influential works in aesthetic theory, defined aesthetic apprehension as "taste," an a priori judgment separate from cognition and morality. Philosophically he defended the validity of a "subjective universality" as a "universal voice" of the imagination through which beauty became known (Kant, 1790/1951).

All aesthetic theories seek or deny an immutable standard on which to base the judgment of beauty; aesthetic criticism implies a judgment which utilizes analysis, synthesis, evaluation, and feeling in the understanding of beauty. In the classical tradition, for example, Aristotle (384 B.C.–322 B.C.) defined art as a unified imitation of nature which expresses universal meaning "according to the law of probability or necessity" and which produces a profound positive psychological effect—catharsis—in those viewing it. Using the drama of his age as a point of departure and differentiation, he defined the proper aim of art as well as its appropriate form in terms of: length; sequence, arrangement of, and motivation for, incidents within the work; types of characters; and desirable emotional involvement of the audience. Aristotle believed that art should imitate nature, and he developed a system of principles to govern exactly how to imitate the ordered and harmonious universe, a universe which itself operated according to an organic, unified, and logical process. Since Aristotle's time, but especially during the Renaissance and the early eighteenth century, Aristotle's *Poetics* has provided the basis for major aesthetic criticism.

Perceptual Aesthetics, unlike classical tradition, seeks meaning through adherence to nature and the process of becoming or developing according to nature through perceptual dynamics. In *Art and Visual Perception*, for example, Rudolph Arnheim, twentieth century gestalt-oriented art theorist and critic, suggests that "In great works of art the deepest significance is transmitted to the eye with powerful directness by the perceptual characteristics of the compositional pattern" (Arnheim, 1954, p. 458). "Our senses," he tells us, "are not self-contained recording devices operating for their own sake. They have been developed by the organism as an aid in reacting to the environment, and the organism is primarily interested in the forces active around it—their place, strength, direction" (p. 455).

Rather than a specific school of thought, then, the concept of Perceptual Aesthetics gives us a unified approach to art which reveals a cross-pollination of perceptual and aesthetic insights in the form and content of creative works.

Based on common patterns inherent in perceptual process, a perceptually based approach to art provides a simpler, more basic, and truly more "natural" system of aesthetic judgment than do approaches based on notions of morality, contemporary manners, taste or style. By approaching creative works as metaphors of the perceptual process, Perceptual Aesthetics allows us to see connections between different artistic mediums and meaningful organization within specific works through an understanding of perceptual process and creative response, particularly of the eye itself. Arnheim (1954) explains: " ... the poetical habit of uniting practically disparate objects by metaphor is not a sophisticated invention of artists, but derives from and relies on the universal and spontaneous ways of approaching world experience" (p. 454). In other words, an understanding of how and why we see is also a means for creating and appreciating art as well.

Unlike Aristotelean aesthetics, the approach which we are calling "Perceptual Aesthetics" is based on Gestalt Psychology and its understanding of the perceptual process, and seeks to understand how art may be structured, within the limitations of its own medium and in accordance with the innate and unified psychological laws of perception. Although it is presaged much earlier in the work of various artists and critics who showed profound insights into perceptual process and used these insights to structure both the form and content of their works, a study of Perceptual Aesthetics must properly begin in the twentieth century with the work of the Gestalt psychologists Max Wertheimer, Wolfgang Köhler, and Kurt Koffka.

In early perceptual experiments with light, at Frankfort-on-Main, dating about the time of World War I, Wertheimer, using two slits in a screen illuminated a fraction of a second apart, was able to produce the effect of movement without the actuality of it (Koffka, 1929/1963, p. 53). Calling the effect the "phi phenomenon," Wertheimer, together with Köhler and Koffka, who observed the experiments, began to evolve a revolutionary theory that the key to perception lay in *relationship*—and together they formed the theory of the *gestalt*, an entity which could be understood *only* as a whole, something quite different from separate sensations or the combined sum of those sensations; and they focused their work on the nature of the spontaneous forces which formed gestalts out of separate sensations. The German word "gestalt" has no direct English translation, but rather embodies a sense of natural unity in which combining elements complement each other so strongly that they become something different. As Wertheimer suggested, "It cannot matter [of] what material the particles of the universe consist, what matters is the kind of whole, the significance of the whole" (Koffka, 1929/1963, p. 65).

Prior perceptual theories had treated perception as a sum of sensations combined with experience, but the gestalt psychologists analyzed relationships in order to understand how the mind organizes optical information into meaning—i.e., transformed quantity (external stimuli) into quality (meaningfulness, and by extension, aesthetic appeal). According to Koffka, they understood both the practical and aesthetic implications of their work and were attempting to "lay the foundations of a system of knowledge that will contain the behavior of a single atom as well as ... a human being, with all the latter's curious activities which we call social conduct, music and art, literature, and drama" (Koffka, 1929/1963, p. 23).

Gestalt Isomorphism

The Aesthetic of T.S. Eliot

Because they sought and theorized nothing less than an isomorphic understanding of the point where science and life meet, the work of these Gestaltists in perception had profound implications for the creation and understanding of art. T.S. Eliot (1888–1965) is the first modern critic to fully articulate this isomorphism: "When a poet's mind is perfectly equipped for its work," Eliot says in his 1921 essay on "The Metaphysical Poets," "it is constantly amalgamating disparate experience; the ordinary man's experience is chaotic, irregular, fragmentary ... in the mind of the poet these experiences are always forming new wholes" (Bate, 1952, p. 532).

The role of the artist, Eliot believed, is to transform his own perceptions into a series of sensations which will form a cohesive pattern. In his 1919 essay on "Hamlet," Eliot (1920/1969) outlines how the process of coalescence, which originates in the artist, can be made to evoke a similar state of mind in the reader: "The only way of expressing emotion in the form of art is by finding an 'objective correlative'; in other words, a set of objects, a situation, a chain of events which shall be the formula of that particular emotion; such that when the external facts, which must terminate in sensory experience, are given, the emotion is immediately evoked" (p. 100). The "objective correlative" represents a gestalt planned with care and accuracy to reproduce the artist's experience or emotion within the reader. Eliot saw in his formula for the objective correlative a dynamic principle to be manipulated by the artist "whose mind," claims Eliot in "Tradition and the Individual Talent" (1919), "is in fact a receptacle for seizing and storing up numberless feelings, phrases, images, which remain there until all the particles which can unite to form a new compound are present together ..." (Bate, 1952, p. 528).

The artist becomes catalyst to the creative process within him and subsequently within the reader as well. This, Eliot says, is also true of the relation of each work of art to all others:

> No poet, no artist of any art, has his complete meaning alone ... What happens when a new work of art is created is something that happens to all the works of art which preceded it. The existing monuments form an ideal order among themselves, which is modified by the introduction of the new (the really new) work of art among them ... The past [is] altered by the present as much as the present is directed by the past. (Bate, 1952, p. 526)

Perceptual psychologist Köhler explains in *Physical Gesaltën* (written 1922) how this explains the difference between a gestalt—which is spontaneous and whose elements are mutually transformative—and a sum—where each element keeps its own identity apart from all the others: "An aggregate of 'parts' or 'pieces' is a genuine 'sum,'" he says, "only when its constituents may be added together one after another without thereby causing any alteration in any of them; and conversely, a summation is that kind of togetherness from which any one or more units may be removed without any effect either on the ones remaining or the ones removed" (Köhler, 1938, p. 25).

In perceptual process, each part in turn affects each other part. But it is not simply a matter of interrelational synergy. In Eliot's poetry, for example, time is fractured and space collides with other space and time. Events not only do not occur in sequential, cause/effect order in relation to other events, as Aristotle insisted, they really don't "occur" at all in the usual sense of the term. We have instead the impression of simply "being in" separate moments that exist simultaneously in relation to one another as parts in a gestalt, not as 'and-summation pieces' in a linear narrative. In *Eye and Mind*, Merleau-Ponty (1964), Gestalt aestheticist, phrases it this way: "each creation changes, alters, enlightens, deepens, confirms, exalts, re-creates, or creates in advance all the others" (p.190).

In his *Four Quartets*, for example, Eliot observes " ... Only by form, the pattern,/Can words or music reach/The stillness, as a Chinese jar still/Moves perpetually in its stillness./Not the stillness of the violin, while the note lasts,/Not that only, but the co-existence/Or say that the end precedes the beginning,/ And the end and the beginning were always there/Before the beginning and after the end./ And all is always now." (*Four Quartets*, "Burnt Norton") This sense of the timelessness and interconnectedness of all art, an extension of the recognition that all parts of what we perceive are interdependent and spontaneously reforming new wholes with the addition of new stimuli, moves from sensation to meaning along a continuum always present in the perceptual process.

In order to understand more fully the implication of the application of perceptual principles to the comprehension of art, it is well to briefly examine the basic concepts of gestalt perceptual theory, and then to look specifically at how these principles are manifested in the work of some outstanding modern artists working within different mediums.

Gestalt Principles

Perceptual meaning in Gestalt theory is the result of an unconscious and automatic reduction of elements and organization to their simplest, most efficient form to reveal meaning through invariant patterns. According to the "Law of Prägnanz," the first principle upon which all others are based, a "psychological organization will always be as 'good' [i.e., simple, regular, symmetrical] as the prevailing conditions will allow"(Koffka, 1929/1963, p. 110). This simplicity, regularity, and symmetry provides the foundation from which to judge the effectiveness of composition in art.

Gestalt Perceptual Simplicity
Shape, Omission, Closure

Efficiency begins with simplicity. In perception, for example, we see a near-circle as a circle because the internal stresses of a simpler figure are less. Likewise, an open lined figure, even a series of dots, will be seen as a single triangle, a circle, and a square if, when adding "missing" lines or dots, the resultant mental figures approximate those basic shapes. See Figure 1. For the

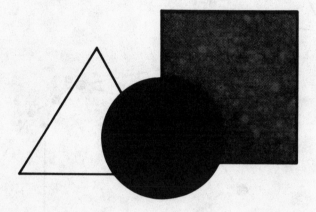

Figure 1. A near-circle will be perceived as a circle because the internal stresses of a simpler figure are less, just as a partial triangle and square will be perceived as complete figures which are obstructed rather than as partial shapes.

average person, the process is never even noticeable: the eye/brain simply, naturally groups elements and "fills in" space in the same way astronomers perceive constellations in the night sky. See Figure 2.

For the artist in the creative process, this means that the selection and combination of elements is crucial, necessitating the ability to consciously analyze the forces at work within a given medium; to find the extraneous word or add the necessary brushstroke; to place plot occurrence, descriptive detail or line so as to subtly suggest the shape of an idea. The schools of Impressionism and Pointillism in painting illustrate well how the eye will create familiar shapes out of simple dots and strokes on the canvas. In literature, the interaction of words and mental images is the result of similarly intricate design and of a seemingly infinite number of exacting choices to produce exactly the right effect in the perceiver.

As an aspiring novelist, Ernest Hemingway, whose writing style is noted for its simplicity, commented that Gertrude Stein had just such a gift of sensing the "rightness" of the form and organization of elements within the artistic whole: "As for Gertrude Stein … She's the best head I know. Never wrong … she can pick them—painters etc. When nobody else can see it. Never picked a loser. Can always tell you what's wrong with your stuff when you don't know but only that it aint right … " (Hemingway, unpublished letter to William Smith, 1925). For the

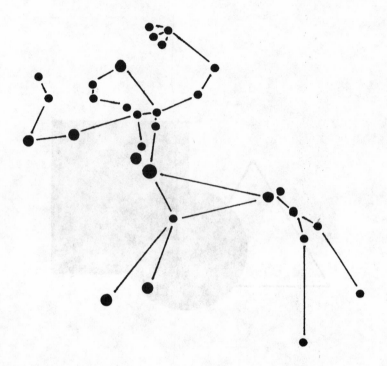

Figure 2. The eye/brain simply naturally "fills in" space according to lines of good continuation. Ancient Greeks saw the figure of a centaur in this star constellation.

perceptive artist, simplicity implies judiciously including material suggestive enough for the reader or viewer to complete the whole, and discarding material which detracts from or misleads the shape of the whole.

Gestalt Perceptual Regularity
Cohesion, Segregation, Figure, and Ground

Beginning with the observation that a system, left to itself, will lose its asymmetries and become more regular as it approaches a time-independent state, the Gestalt theorists noted that perception is organized by forces of cohesion and segregation (Koffka, 1929/1963, p. 109). Equality of stimulation produces cohesion or unification; inequality, segregation. For example, lines placed closer together and similar colors or shapes tend to form a single figure and segregate themselves from a background which appears to recede from the shape. This is why a red apple seen against a white tablecloth is perceived as an independent entity; a red apple against a red tablecloth tends to blend into the background. See Figure 3. The emergent shape is a result of the forces which segregate the figure from its field and hold it in equilibrium with it, much the same as a drop of oil will assume its most cohesive, simple shape in a body of water (Koffka, 1929/1963, p. 126).

A classic example of the phenomenon of figure/ground formation is the drawing of reversible goblet introduced by Edgar Rubin in 1915 where two faces

Figure 3. A red apple seen against a white tablecloth is perceived as an independent entity; if the tablecloth were also red, the apple would blend into the background.

in profile are transformed into a goblet, depending on which we see as figure and which ground. When the forces for segregation and cohesion are equivalent, ambiguity results: figure and ground alternate as each asserts itself to become the dominant figure.

The goblet/faces illustration is ambiguous because it vacillates between two interpretations which cannot be resolved definitively into one or the other. T.S. Eliot's poem "The Love Song of J. Alfred Prufrock" utilizes this device metaphorically: structured according to specific tensions or forces which fight for cohesion and segregation simultaneously throughout: in it, the external world, the poem's "universe," acts as "field" against which we perceive the "figure" of Prufrock. In this figure/ground differentiation, Eliot creates a persistent ambiguity between the tensions of decision and indecision, precise and imprecise feeling, meaning, and misunderstanding—with the result that Prufrock, like "the yellow fog that rubs its back upon the windowpanes," quite deliberately never clearly emerges as a cohesive figure.

Since ambiguity is Eliot's theme—expressed as "the overwhelming question" of the poem—the character of Prufrock is given no ego separation from the "ground" of sordidness and empty social convention, and no cohesion to assert himself as the dominant "figure." The field of "streets that follow like a tedious argument" and the room where "women come and go/Talking of Michelangelo" are filled with monotony, homogeneous figures, and conversations which blend into greyness; buildings are shrouded in fog and smoke; lonely men smoke pipes; dusk is falling; "the evening is spread out against the sky/like a patient etherized upon a table." Not daring to "disturb the universe," not able to "presume," Prufrock vacillates throughout the poem. With no precise boundaries separating him from his environment, Prufrock finally emerges only as a symbol of modern man's lack of identity and spiritual unity.

Gestalt Perceptual Symmetry
Closure, Good Continuation, and Unity

Because closed areas seem more stable and self-sustaining, we close off shapes according to their 'best' and most symmetrical forms. The closer and more like the parts, the greater the attraction among them; the greater the distance and inequality, the less stability, and the less the pull toward unification. See Figure 4. We also tend to extend any suggested continuing pattern along the direction previously established, since this also lends stability.

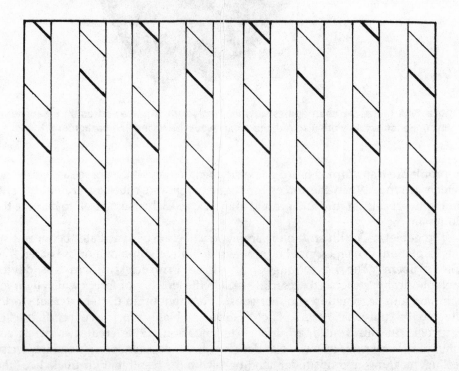

Figure 4. The more parts are alike, the greater the attraction among them. Even though horizontal lines are not connected, we tend to see them as stable, related and behind solid vertical bars.

A curve, for example, "will proceed in its own natural way, a circle as a circle, an ellipse as an ellipse, and so forth" (Koffka, 1929/1963, p. 153). The suggestion of a shape continues that shape until it is complete, just as the suggestion of a pattern implies its continuance. See Figures 1 and 2. First advanced by Wertheimer in 1923, this "Law of Good Continuation," suggests how we close and continue symmetrical patterns, which in turn become more stable the longer they are maintained.

Lest this begin to look like a mechanical formula to be mastered, however, it should be stressed that Gestalt perceptual principles, far from suggesting a *mechanical* formula for perception, in fact imply the reverse. Christian von Ehrenfels, who introduced the term "gestalt" into psychology, made this observation in relation to music, concluding that perception and appreciation of music are intrinsically related (Stansfeld & Stafford, 1965, p. 132). The melody, von Ehrenfels concluded, must be a function of *relationship*, since when it was transposed into another key, where all of the notes were subsequently different, it was still perfectly recognizable as the same melody as before. Erich von Hornbostel in his 1927 essay, "The Unity of the Senses," also concludes that in art "what is essential … is not that which separates the senses from one another, but that which unites them … It is the same organizing principle which calls forth organism from mere substance, and which binds the stream of happening into wholes, which makes the line a melody which we can follow, and the melody a figure which we can see in one glance … the unity of the senses is given from the very beginning. And together with this the unity of the arts" (Ellis, 1938, pp. 214, 216).

This unity of the arts—especially of poetry and music—is also suggested by T.S. Eliot and Edgar Allan Poe: "I know that a poem, or a passage of a poem," Eliot (1953) states, "may tend to realize itself first as a particular rhythm before it reaches expression in words, and that this rhythm may bring to birth the idea and the image; and I do not believe that this is an experience peculiar to myself" (p. 60). In his "Poetic Principle," Poe (1975) tells us that "An immortal instinct, deep within the spirit of man, is … a sense of the Beautiful … It is in Music, perhaps, that the soul most nearly attains the great end for which, when inspired by the Poetic Sentiment, it struggles—the creation of supernal Beauty …" (pp. 893–894).

Perceptual Aesthetics and Analysis

Poe and the Limits of Mathematical Reasoning

"Art," Cézanne suggested, "addresses itself only to an excessively limited number of individuals" (Wadley, p. 106). If the average person grasps gestalts as a natural part of perception without consciously realizing either the process or its implications, it may be said that within the artist the process is heightened not simply to awareness but to a transcendent aesthetic sensitivity. The difference is in degree rather than in kind—for the artist appears to have a genius for perceiving and creating relationships which deceptively seem to rise spontaneously from the material itself, while the observer of art may perceive only the unified effect of the artist's work. Once the gestalt is created, it is held together by its own internal forces and defies the systematic analysis applicable to quantifiable entities. Anti-linear, anti-formulaic in their thinking, the Gestalt psychologists insist on the integrity of the whole, and of grasping that whole to achieve meaning. The scientific method of classification and dissection, of rational logic and linear connection, they believe, miss the gestalt, and therefore the whole point of scientific inquiry. Art especially defies dissection and classification.

This becomes especially clear in Poe's detective fiction, where he pits the transcendent genius of his detective M. Auguste Dupin against the mundane, linear, and formulaic mind of the prefect of Police. Where the Prefect is mechanistically logical within a single consistent pattern, Dupin reasons dynamically and creatively, remaining open to new possibilities. The difference between them exemplifies the difference between scientific functionalism, as in the case of the machine, and the spontaneous generation of the gestalt, as in creation of art. Köhler, writing in 1922, for example, explains that the gestalt is never fixed or mechanical, but rather arises from "processes which are *determined by the forces within the system itself.* ... The more completely a system is governed by constraints, the more adequately does it exemplify a machine. The more freely the inner dynamics of a system are left to regulate themselves, the farther the system is from being a machine" (Ellis, 1938, p. 61).

Although the gestalt is not derived from externally applied, hardened linear, and formulaic rules, it is knowable through an analysis of the internal forces at work and the fluid principles underlying immediate conditions. This is why in "The Purloined Letter," Dupin tells us of his nemesis Minister D— that "As poet *and* mathematician he would reason well; as mere mathematician he could not have reasoned at all, and thus would have been at the mercy of the Prefect" (Poe, 1975, p. 217). Minister D— and Dupin represent poetic gestalt thinking, while the Prefect represents the inferior thinking of the mathematician.

Like the machine which can do only as it is programmed, the Prefect's constrained reasoning can solve only those crimes which have occurred before and are thus programmed into his scientific methodology. Dupin's creative perceptual ability, however, enables him to solve crimes which have never before been committed. In "Murders in the Rue Morgue" he tells the narrator: "In investigations such as we are now pursuing, it should not be so much asked 'what has occurred,' as 'what has occurred that has never occurred before.' In fact the facility with which I shall arrive, or have arrived, at the solution of this mystery, is in the direct ratio of its apparent insolubility in the eyes of the police" (Poe, 1975, p. 154).

The German philosopher and aestheticist Immanuel Kant (1724–1804) saw such genius as Dupin represents as "the talent (or natural gift) which gives the rule to art." It is, Kant explains, "a talent for producing that for which no definite rule can be given; it is not a mere aptitude for what can be learned by a rule." Kant (1951) believed that in genius, "*originality* must be its first property ... its products must be models. i.e., *exemplary*, and they consequently ought not to spring from imitation but must serve as a standard of judgment for others. ... It cannot describe scientifically how it brings about its products, but it gives the rule just as nature does" (pp. 150–151).

In "The Purloined Letter," Prefect G—, who reflects the thinking of his contemporary world, systematically examines "the rungs of every chair in the hotel, and indeed, the jointings of every description of furniture, by the aid of a most powerful microscope," and explores the entire house of the Minister by dividing "its entire surface into compartments ... numbered so that none might be missed," then does exactly the same with the two adjoining houses (Poe, 1975, p. 212). He examines minutely all the books in the library, the floorboards beneath the carpets, even the paper on the walls. Everything comes under the scrutiny of the microscope. Yet he misses the purloined letter nonetheless.

In contrast, Wertheimer explains a different type of scrutiny, one characteristic of Dupin's examination: "Closer scrutiny," Wertheimer says, "frequently discloses how an apparently unrelated aggregate of elements may really be a united, organized whole ... 'Pieces' almost always appear 'as parts' in whole processes. ... Thus the comprehension of whole properties and whole conditions *must* precede consideration of the real significance of 'parts'" (Ellis, 1938, pp. 14–15).

Although Edgar Allan Poe describes a separate purpose for each form of his writing—for his detective stories, the pursuit of truth; for his horror tales, the singularity of emotional effect; and for his poetry, the purely beautiful—nevertheless, all have at their center the concept of the unified gestalt, governed by coherence and inner necessity. In his seminal critical "Review of Hawthorne's *Twice Told Tales*," Poe explains how the gestalt may become the basis for a literary aesthetic:

> A skillful literary artist has constructed a tale. If wise, he has not fashioned his thoughts to accommodate his incidents; but having conceived, with deliberate care, a certain unique or single *effect* to be wrought out, he then invents such incidents—he then combines such events as may best aid him in establishing this preconceived effect. If his very initial sentence tend not to the outbringing of this effect, then he has failed in his first step. In the whole composition there should be no word written, of which the tendency, direct or indirect, is not to the one pre-established design. (Miller, 1962, p. 467)

Contemporary researcher Michael Gazzaniga (1985), in *The Social Brain* also describes the mind itself as a gestalt of separate parts unified to a common purpose. He visualizes the brain as consisting of perhaps a hundred or more separate modules which he calls "programs." The "mind," he believes, is itself a program, which he calls "the interpreter," which gives us a "strong subjective sense that we are a single, unified, conscious agent controlling life's events with a singular, integrated purpose," and whose function is to act as an explainer for decisions already made elsewhere in the brain by other cognitive variables (p.189).

In *The Mind's Sky*, Timothy Ferris (1992) extends Gazzaniga's theory to include mystical experience, proposing that "enlightenment occurs when introspection succeeds in breaking through the level of language to confront the mental module—call it the "integration program"—that is responsible for presenting the multipartite functions of the brain to the conscious mind as a unified whole" (p. 96). He explains that "because enlightenment means penetrating past words and reasoning to reach the realm of the program that unifies human thought, one must abandon language and logic to get there ... The enlightened individual does not regard language and logic as *necessarily* deceptive, but distrusts these faculties because he has seen how readily they can blind us to the truth" (pp. 96–97). "The mystical doctrine of cosmic unity," he tells us, "has more to do with the internal architecture of the brain than with the phenomena of the outer universe ... the doctrine of cosmic unity arises from the very mechanism that makes a unified mind out of the disparate parts of the human brain" (p. 95).

Perceptual Aesthetics and Visual Art

Cézanne, Hemingway, and the Aesthetic of Icebergs

One of the outstanding prose stylists of the twentieth century, Hemingway's prose reflects perhaps more clearly than any other writer in this century how the principles underlying gestalt psychology can be made to serve aesthetic sense.

Writing with a Spartan discipline reflecting gestalt simplicity, regularity and symmetry, Hemingway worked conscientiously to eliminate excess and involve the reader through closure and good continuation. Initially a journalist, he claimed to have first learned the power of simplicity and reduction through writing news stories. His later literary style retained this lean spareness and enriched it with an athletic rhythm, and as he developed as a writer, he continually acknowledged the power of the visual in developing his literary aesthetic. In a letter to Gertrude Stein, for example, Hemingway writes, "I have finished two long short stories ... before I went to Spain where I am trying to do the country like Cézanne and having a hell of a time ..." (Hemingway, 1924, unpublished letter, Item 274). In the end, he told Lillian Ross that he felt he had succeeded in his literary quest to write the way Cézanne painted, and that he was pretty sure that "if Paul was around, he would like the way I make them [landscapes] and be happy that I learned it from him" (Ross, 1950/1961, p. 60).

What Hemingway believed both Cézanne and he had succeeded in doing was breaking down the pictorial scene into its basic shapes—as Gestalt psychologists have suggested we do visually in order to get meaningful information from our environment—and then using these to imply patterns of a code of living parallel to what the Gestalt psychologist termed "good continuation" in perceptual process. In his essay/story "On Writing" cut from "Big Two-Hearted River," for example, Hemingway uses the experience of Nick fishing as both as a metaphor for living life and for the process of writing:

> He, Nick, wanted to write about country as it would be there like Cézanne had done it in painting. You had to do it from inside yourself. There wasn't any trick. Nobody had ever written about country like that. He felt almost holy about it. It was deadly serious. You could do it if you would fight it out. If you lived right with your eyes. ... [Then] seeing how Cézanne would do the stretch of river and the swamp, he stood up and stepped down into the stream. The water was cold and actual. He waded across the stream, moving in the picture. (Hemingway, 1972, p. 239)

This apparently simple theory of 'living right with your eyes' links perceptual process and creative process in several significant ways: it originates from direct contact with nature; its organization and content utilize the concept of maximum efficiency through simplicity, regularity, and good continuation; and it implies an organization of experience which begins in sensation and ends with meaning and value. Koffka's description of Gestalt psychology as a "thoroughly dynamic theory in which the processes organize themselves under the prevailing dynamic and constraining conditions" (Koffka, 1929/1963, p. 105) is in many ways a fairly satisfactory definition of Hemingway's "Code" of "grace under pressure." Hemingway's perceptual acuity was especially keen and well-integrated. Writing of Hemingway in 1966, John Dos Passos commented, for example, "Hemingway had uncommonly good eyesight, the hunter's cold acuity. ... He had the same shrewd eye for painting. ... He would take in excellence of color and design at a glance" (Dos Passos, 1966, pp. 143–144).

Cézanne himself consciously worked to reduce the objects on his canvas to basic shapes emerging from a ground. Writing to Émile Bernard in 1905, he comments: " ... I am able to reassess for you, undoubtedly rather too much, the obstinacy with which I pursue that part of nature, which, coming into our line of vision, gives the picture ... we must render the image of what we see, forgetting everything that existed before us ..." (Wadley, n.d., p. 110). For Hemingway, the pursuit which Cézanne describes took the form of direct observation of nature and the "true sentence": "All you have to do," he thought, "is to write one true sentence. ...Write the truest sentence you know" (Hemingway, 1964, p. 12). With direct observation such as Dupin's, avoiding the formulaic conceptions of Poe's Prefect, both Cézanne and Hemingway found the "true" shape of things and rendered them in their work with studied simplicity.

Hemingway also actively utilized the concept of Gestalt "good continuation" by paring back the storyline and detail to the point where they implicitly suggested the shape of things developed outside of the scene or beyond the time frame of the story. This aesthetic device, described by Hemingway as an 'iceberg' approach—i.e., with only one-eighth of the story made visible to the reader—at once relies upon and directly involves the reader through the natural perceptual tendency of continuing the shape of things to their "natural" conclusions.

In "Death in the Afternoon," for example, Hemingway insists that prose, like architecture, is not interior decoration; that the baroque period is over, and that what is now needed is a style whose restraint and dignity is governed by the art of implication and the aesthetic of omission. In *A Moveable Feast* Hemingway (1964) comments that he had learned that in a story "you could omit anything if you knew that you omitted, and the omitted part would strengthen the story and make people feel more than they understood" (p. 75). Writing in 1959, in an unpublished article titled "The Art of the Short Story," Hemingway comments, "A few things I have found to be true. If you leave out important things or events that you know about, the story is strengthened. If you leave out or skip something because you do not know it, the story will be worthless. The test of any story is how very good the stuff is that you, not your editors, omit" (Hemingway, 1959, unpublished manuscript, Item 251). "The dignity of movement of an iceberg," Hemingway (1932) insisted, "is due to only one-eighth of it being above water" (pp. 191–192).

In discussing "Big Two-Hearted River" in 1959, he explains that because those who had been in the war had had too much of it and "could not suffer that it be mentioned in their presence," "the war, all mention of the war, anything about the war, is omitted." Yet omitted elements are present nonetheless, through implication: "there were many Indians in the story, just as the war was in the story, and none of the Indians nor the war appeared. As you see, it is very simple and easy to explain. In a story called "A Sea Change," everything is left out. I had seen the couple in the Bar Basque in St. Jean de Luz and I knew the story too well ... so I left the story out. But it is all there. It is not visible but it is there" (Hemingway, 1959, unpublished manuscript, Item 251).

Of his short story "Out of Season," Hemingway said, "it was a very simple story," where he had "omitted the real end of it which was that the old man hanged himself" (Hemingway, 1959, unpublished manuscript, Item 251). A parallel in painting is Cézanne's "The House of the Hanged Man," in which, as in Hemingway's "Out of Season" ending, Cézanne lets its stark geometric landscape and buildings imply the inner tragedy of the anonymous man whose presence is felt but not seen. In both compositions we are expected to read the implications of the mystery of the man's suicide. Both works tax the perceptual concept of omission and good continuation to their limits.

Another example of the effective use of omission can be seen in Henry James' famous "ghost" story *Turn of the Screw*, where James fully develops what he called the art of "ambiguity." In the story which involves a governess attempting to save two children from what she perceives to be evil forces, James involves the reader's own perception in order to further the plot and theme of evil. In his Preface to *The Aspern Papers*, he explains that any objective depiction of evil in the story would lose power and trivialize the intensity he wished to capture. "Only make the reader's general vision of evil intense enough," James (1934) writes, "and his own experience, his own imagination, his own sympathy ... and horror ... will supply him quite sufficiently with all the particulars. Make him *think* the evil, make him think it for himself, and you are released from weak specifications" (p. 176). By using the power of the reader's perception to fill in the part omitted along the lines of the point of view established, James is able to complete his story in the mind of the reader rather than on the page itself.

Perceptual Aesthetics and Film

Renais, Eisenstein, and Montage

In film, this use of perceptual principles to evoke horror and make real the experience can be seen vividly in Alain Renais' powerfully moving *Night and Fog* (1955), a retrospective film on the horrors of Nazi concentration camps. In it, Renais, like Eliot, works effectively with tension between time present and time past; juxtaposes long, slow pan shots of apparent emptiness with flashes so quick that we can't quite grasp the shot content; and contrasts the tranquillity of nature in muted pastels with captured black and white Nazi film footage of the camps in the 1930's and 1940's.

To evoke the true horror of the camps, Renais, aware as T.S. Eliot commented in *The Four Quartets* that "human kind cannot bear very much reality," uses the same method of omission to conjure evil as James in *Turn of the Screw*. One particularly effective "empty" shot, for example, scans a roughly lined and apparently innocuous ceiling for a moment before we are told that what we are seeing is the scarring made by human fingers as poison gas victims clawed desperately to get out. Who could not turn away if shown the actuality? Like James, Renais knew how much more powerful and lingering the impact would be to have viewers create the scene in their own imaginations. Like Hemingway, he supplies the one-eighth visible surface and we complete the whole. Renais' subsequent classic films *Hiroshima, Mon Amour* (1959), and *Last Year at Marienbad* (1961) are similar experiments in the relativity of time and perception, of beauty and horror, and of the human capacity for love and cruelty.

This contrapuntal thematic development was undoubtedly influenced at least in part by the earlier work of Sergei Eisenstein, Soviet film director and perhaps the most influential film theorist of the twentieth century. Like the Gestalt psychologists, Eisenstein (1968) theorized that the meaning of the whole lay in the relationship between the shots, and extended political ideology into film aesthetics through the art of editing—"montage"—and deliberately avoided the narrative continuity characteristic of Aristotelian aesthetics in favor of unresolved tension between images in time, space, shape, and rhythm.

Eisenstein, reasoning that a collision of images would force the viewer to resolve the conflict and to derive a meaning not implicit in the content of any of the separate frames, perfected a dialectical method of shooting and editing which was both derived from and parallel to Marxist-Leninist thought, and which required the viewer to be an active participant in creating the meaning of the events shown on the screen. Inspired by the Japanese language and the Kabuki Theatre which performed in Moscow and Leningrad in 1928, Eisenstein saw in the principle of the Japanese ideogram the same perceptual principle which Wertheimer, Köhler, and Koffka identified as a gestalt: Eisenstein (1929) wrote in "The Cinematographic Principle and the Ideogram," that the combination "of two hieroglyphs of the simplest series is to be regarded not as their sum, but as their product, i.e., as a value of another dimension, another degree; each, separately, corresponds to an *object*, to a fact, but their combination corresponds to a *concept*.. .... It is exactly what we do in the cinema, combining shots that are *depictive*, single in meaning, neutral in content—into *intellectual* contexts and series" (Eisenstein, 1929/1949, pp. 29–30).

While other filmmakers continued to make films based on narrative continuity in the Aristotelian tradition, Eisenstein manipulated a synthesis of dialectical images into socialist thought by utilizing the principle of perceptual closure within the viewer. Eisenstein (1938/1942) believed that in watching a dialectically composed film, " ... the spectator is compelled to proceed along that selfsame road that the author traveled in creating the image. ... The spectator not only sees the represented elements of the finished work, but also experiences the dynamic process of the emergence and assembly of the image just as it was experienced by the author ..." (p. 32).

In this way Eisenstein aligned film aesthetics with the ideological spirit of the Soviet revolution. The method becomes clear in his 1925 film, *The Battleship Potemkin*. In its best known sequence, the slaughter on the Odessa Steps, we see a succession of horizontal lines which move downward on the screen. With only soldiers' boots to fill the frame, both the feet and the steps themselves seem to crush the people below. The soldiers—whose faces are deliberately omitted from the frames—become an impersonal czarist force which massacres men, women, and children as it descends the stairs. Only the soldiers' hands, bayonets, and boots are used in the oppressively horizontal sequence, while the faces of the victims are seen in close-up. Shadow is likewise emphasized to evoke fear and to reinforce horizontal planes, and stark contrasts in light and dark areas, and geometric planes achieve dynamic conflict.

Eisenstein also set the sequence antithetically to the previous one, where the dignity of the masses and the revolutionary cause are emphasized by bright light and the vertical lines of the Odessa columns, the sails of the boats joining the battleship, the pillars of the Odessa bridge, and even the top-mast of the revolutionary *Potemkin* herself. The movement of water and people, architectural arches, curvilinear queues of mourners: all these create an organic fluidity of humanity and warmth, against which the hardness of the steps and the mechanical movement of the soldiers appear in dramatic contrast.

At the same time, psychological tension is produced through conflicting geometric planes—triangles, circles, diagonals, and through a quickening montage rhythm as shots focusing on individuals are cross-cut with long shots of the fleeing masses. The complementary opposite of Eliot's figure/ground ambiguity in "Prufrock," Eisenstein's dialectical technique utilized spatial, temporal, and linear discontinuity as impactful rhetorical devices to argue the ideological concept of socialism and the inevitability of the 1917 Revolution. Stephen David Ross argues forcefully in *A Theory of Art: Inexhaustibility by Contrast*, that such conflict is at the very essence of all art, observing that "intensity is attained where the opposition is stronger or where the unification is exceptional. The most important feature of contrast is its capacity to produce level upon level" of complex meaning (Ross, 1982, p. 5).

Conclusion

Gestalt perceptual theory provides an intelligible bridge between psychology and aesthetics, sensation, and appreciation of art. The application of its principles within the arts becomes a means of understanding not only how man perceives his environment, but also how he creates and perceives beauty as well, transforming perceptual theory into aesthetic theory. "The gestalt concept," Koffka tells us, "cuts across this division of realms of existence [nature, life, and mind], being applicable in each of them. Köhler's demonstration of physical gestalten laid the foundation for a new unification of nature and life ... it [not only] gives definite directions to physiological hypotheses, ... but at the same time has implications of great philosophical significance ..." (Koffka, 1929/1963, p. 684).

Beginning with 'the unity of the senses' the process of perception thereby also implies an inherent 'unity of the arts' as von Hornbostel suggested. Perceptual Aesthetics, based on an assumption of this unity, finds meaning in relationships, and combines analysis, synthesis, evaluation, and feeling to explain how art may be created and appreciated. In this way, Perceptual Aesthetics seeks to know how it is that all great art, as T.S. Eliot stated, has "the same essential quality of transmuting ideas into sensations, of transforming an observation into a state of mind" (Bate, 1952, p. 533). Ultimately, it suggests that the aesthetic genius of the artist may indeed be perceptually based.

It is perhaps just this relation which Joseph Conrad expressed in his preface to *The Nigger of the Narcissus* when he defined his role as artist: "My task which I am trying to achieve is, by the power of the written word, to make you hear, to make you feel—it is, before all, to make you *see*" (1959).

References

Arnheim, R. (1954). *Art and visual perception.* Berkeley, CA: University of California Press.

Bate, W. J. (Ed.). (1952). *Criticism: The major texts.* New York: Harcourt, Brace, Jovanovich.

Conrad, J. (1959). *The nigger of the Narcissus.* New York: Doubleday & Co.

Dos Passos, J. (1966). *The best times.* New York: New American Library.

Eisenstein, S. (1968). *Film essays and a lecture.* (Jay Leyda, Ed.). Princeton, NJ: Princeton University Press. (Original work published 1926/1946.)

Eisenstein, S. (1949). *Film form.* (Jay Leyda, Trans. & Ed.). New York: Harcourt, Brace, Jovanovich. (Original work published 1928/1945.)

Eisenstein, S. (1942). *The film sense.* (rev. ed.) (Jay Leyda, Trans. & Ed.). New York: Harcourt, Brace, Jovanovich. (Original work published 1938/1942.)

Eliot, T. S. (1969). *The sacred wood* (4th ed.). London: Methuen. (Original work published 1920).

Eliot, T. S. (1953). *Selected prose.* London: Penguin Books.

Eliot, T. S . (1971). *The complete poems & plays 1909–1950.* New York: Harcourt, Brace, & World.

Ellis, W. D. (Ed.). (1938). *Source book of Gestalt psychology.* New York: Harcourt, Brace, & World.

Ferris, T. (1992). *The mind's sky.* New York: Bantam Books.

Gazzaniga, M. (1985). *The social brain.* New York: Basic Books.

Hansen, J. (1987). *Understanding video.* Newbury Park, CA: Sage Publications.

Hemingway, E. (1932). *Death in the afternoon.* New York: Charles Scribner's Sons.

Hemingway, E. (1925/1959). Unpublished Correspondence, "Hem 2" folder, Ernest Hemingway Collection, John F. Kennedy Library, Boston, MA.

Hemingway, E. (1964). *A moveable feast.* New York: Charles Scribner's Sons.

Hemingway, E. (1972). *The Nick Adams stories.* New York: Charles Scribner's Sons.

James, H. (1934). *The art of the novel.* New York: Charles Scribner's Sons.

Kant, I. (1951). *Critique of judgment.* (J. H. Bernard, Trans.). New York: Hafner. (Original work published 1790.)

Koffka, K. (1963). *Principles of Gestalt psychology.* New York: Harcourt, Brace, & World. (Original work published 1929.)

Köhler, W. (1938). Physical gestalten. In W. D. Ellis (Ed.), *Source book of Gestalt psychology.* New York: Harcourt, Brace, & World.

Merleau-Ponty, M. (1964). *Eye and mind: The primacy of perception.* (C. Dallery, Trans., J. Edie, Ed.). Evanston, IL: Northwestern University Press.

Miller, P. (Ed.). (1962). *Major writers of America* (Vol. 1). New York: Harcourt, Brace, & World.

Neisser, U. (1971). The processes of vision. In *Image, object, and illusion.* San Francisco, CA: W. H. Freeman.

Ornstein, R. (1972). *The psychology of consciousness.* San Francisco, CA: W. H. Freeman.

Poe, E. A. (1975). *Complete tales and poems.* New York: Vintage/Random House.

Ross, L. (1961). *Portrait of Hemingway.* New York: Simon & Schuster. (Originally published as "How do you like it now, gentlemen?" *The New Yorker;* May 13, 1950.)

Ross, S. D. (1982). *A theory of art: Inexhaustibility by contrast.* Albany, NY: SUNY Press.

Stansfeld, S. S., & Stafford K. R. (1965). *Basic teachings of the great psychologists.* New York: Dolphin Books.

Wadley, N. (n.d.). *Cézanne and his art.* New York: Galahad Books.

SECTION III

Nonverbal Communication

Symbolism is the foundation of effective communication. However, there is considerable controversy about the definition of a symbol. Edward Sewell, in discussing the persuasiveness of symbolism in society, reviews the literature related to symbol definitions and classification systems while highlighting the similarity and diversity of opinion. He discusses Firth's dichromatization of symbols into four instrumental areas (symbols as instruments of expression, communication, knowledge, and control). Using political cartoons as a case study, Sewell applies these concepts in an attempt to improve our understanding of the nature of symbols.

Mike Moore in his chapter contends that nonverbal communication plays a major role in the communications process as it helps determine our interpersonal relationships and provides information that is not always available from verbal communication alone. Some body (action) language appears to be universally understood, while at the same time other action language is culturally specific. The context of events and knowledge of the culture must be known to accurately understand the communication process in a nonverbal setting. Body (action) language can be better understood by studying its several categories including reflexive actions, conventional signals, personal appearance, physical attributes, gestures, interpersonal roles, groups, and personal space.

A third type of nonverbal communication, object language, is also discussed. Moore notes that objects can by their arrangement, location, etc., convey information and instruction. The ability of people to "read" object codes is extremely important, for often they set the stage for communication in a broader sense. However, object language must be learned and understood, for in some situations verbal and even body languages may not be present or available. He suggests that object language can be studied and understood by looking at the utility, command, and symbolic functions of objects.

Chapter Eight

Visual Symbols

Edward H. Sewell, Jr.

Objectives

After reading this chapter, you should be able to:

1. *Define symbol.*

2. *Explain how symbols influence communication.*

3. *Discuss the origin of three different symbol systems.*

4. *Define and give an example of a pictorial, graphic, and verbal symbol.*

5. *List authors whose writings have contributed significantly to the knowledge base of symbolism in visual communication.*

6. *Define and indicate the symbolic importance of political cartoons.*

Introduction

We are surrounded by visual symbols, but we usually take them for granted. About 35,000 years ago, the introduction of symbolic artifacts in the form of bone and stone ornaments and etching on bone appeared in Europe (White, 1989). Before that time, stone and bone tools were used, but never with any evident purpose other than utilitarian applications. It is the introduction of symbols that gives us our first glimpse into the cognitive development of our species, and it is not until some 5000 years ago that the first records of written language were left in the form of clay tablets in Mesopotamia.

We do not know the precise use made of the symbols developed by our early ancestors, but there is evidence that symbolic ornamentation representing animals was used to imbue the wearer with the characteristics of the animal being depicted in the symbol. Other early symbolic forms, however, have no clear function, including series of dots and outlines of the human hand.

It is from the Greek civilization that the linguistic roots for our word "symbol" come. The Greek word *symballein,* the source of our word, meant "to bring together" in the sense of reconstructing a past event from some concrete form of evident. Originally the word referred to a situation where a person would break an object into pieces, keep one piece, and give the other piece to another person. When the two met at a later date and place, the broken pieces, called *symbola,* would be joined together and serve as a sign of recognition and acceptance. It was a concrete form of expressing an abstract relationship that had developed in the past.

While the practice of using symbols has changed, the basic premises for their use remains rather similar. A symbol is a concrete expression of some abstract event or idea.

Approaches to the Study of Symbols

There has been little common agreement among scholars about the nature and meaning of symbols. Paul Ricoeur notes that in the study of symbols, the boundaries between meanings and definitions are blurred because in the symbol different realities meet but not with a sense of uniformity (Ricoeur, 1976). Rather than understanding symbols, we find ourselves caught in the web of the symbol, much as the fly who is attracted to and attempts to explore the spider web finds itself victim of its own curiosity.

There have been several major approaches to the study of symbols and symbolic behavior which have crossed disciplinary boundaries and generated the majority of productive thinking about symbols. These approaches include scholars who see symbols as "natural" in their origin, those who see symbols as "arbitrary" in their origin, and those who see symbols as "functional" in their origins.

A number of philosophers have focused on "natural symbols" that have their roots deep within the human psyche. Ernst Cassirer (1944, 1953) argued that the use of symbols is an essential function of human consciousness and culture. He distinguished between an *expressive function* of symbols (myth and language) and an *intuitive function* of symbols (mathematics and science). Cassirer believed that between the symbol and culture was a dialectic tendency of stability versus disintegration of symbolic relations. Carl Jung (1964) believed the natural symbol was deeply imbedded in the human psyche. It was created because of the human search for stability and wholeness, and it was expressed in symbols such as the cross and the mandala. According to Jung, symbols reach down into the depth of our primitive unconscious. Mary Douglas (1970) also believed symbols were an outgrowth of our psyche as it attempts to find a balance between the body or physical personality of the user and the external world expressed in terms of breath, blood, orifices, and excretions.

Most philosophers, however, have focused on symbols as "arbitrary" or "conventional" in origin. It is cultural conditions rather than the psyche that creates symbolic expression. Charles Morris (1945) used the term "sign" as a general term and "symbol" as a specific form of sign. Morris defined a symbol as a sign that is produced by its interpreter and acts as a substitute for some other sign with which it is synonymous. All signs that are not symbols are signals, and the same object or image can function as both signal and symbol. A red flag in the middle of a road can be a signal that danger is ahead while in the hands of people marching in Red Square it was a symbol of Soviet Communism.

C. S. Peirce (1958), who pioneered the study of semiotics or the science of signs, distinguished between three categories of sign: the index, the icon, and the symbol. An *index* bears a clear direct relationship between object and what it means, such as the relationship between smoke and fire. An *icon* has a physical resemblance relationship between an object and its meaning, such as a photograph of a person. A *symbol*, quite unlike the index and icon, has no inherent relationship between the object and its meaning, but derives all meaning from cultural convention. Thus, if we were to see the tracks of a lion in the sand, we would have an index sign; if we see a photograph of the lion, we have an iconic sign; but if we say someone is "brave as a lion," we have a symbolic sign based on the conventional or arbitrary relationship between lions and bravery. Thus while there is no causal (index) or image (icon) relationship between lion and bravery, we may invent and propagate conventional meaning by symbols. Approaching symbols from a "functional" or "instrumental" perspective, graphic designer Ralph Wileman (1980) defines a symbol as the representation of one object by another where the character of the "object" ranges from physical to abstract. Symbols are classified into a three-tiered hierarchy along a concrete to abstract continuum as *pictorial symbols* that include 3-D models, photographs, and illustration drawings, *graphic symbols* that include image-related graphics, concept-related graphics, and arbitrary graphics, and *verbal symbols* that are the most abstract since they have no graphic resemblance with the object to which they refer.

Another functional theorist, Raymond Firth (1973), acknowledging the diversity of opinions about what constitutes a symbol, emphasizes the instrumental role of symbols in four areas. First, symbols are instruments of *expression*, as in religious and political symbols such as flags, crests, dress, anthems, and art. Second, symbols are instruments of *communication* allowing people to share ideas and concepts as tangible as coins with images and mottoes on them or as abstract as an essay on the meaning of democracy. Third, symbols are instruments of *knowledge* that may reveal elements of "reality" that even the symbol user may not recognize as might be the case with mystics who use symbols to describe inexpressible knowledge. Finally, symbols are instruments of *control* or power as in the use of symbolic images or phrases to test the ideological orthodoxy or political correctness of events and ideas.

For the person whose primary interest is in visual literacy, the instrumental or functional approach to the study of symbols is most inviting. Using Firth's basic classification, let's explore symbols as expression, knowledge, communication, and control.

Symbols as Communication

At the most basic level, symbols are the foundation for all significant communication. Without symbols, communication is not possible as either spoken language or written language. We use symbols to communicate simple ideas such as "where is the nearest restaurant" or "where do I pick up my luggage." Even the smile, gesture, nod of the head, and handshake are communicative symbols.

In the development of symbolic communication, the symbol must begin as some arbitrary construction that is imbued with meaning. There is no inherent reason for the symbol-formation "DOG" to mean the four-legged canine that brings in the newspaper each morning and waits at the front window until I come home from work. Indeed, it is clear that initially a symbol may have a broad generic meaning, pictographic in content. With the addition of new elements, however, the meaning changes. We can all visualize a generic pictographic symbol for bird, but with only minor changes, to be discussed in the next sections, the pictograph for a bird takes on special characteristics that require knowledge and creative expression before an interpretation can be made about the meaning of the pictographic image.

We are most familiar with the use of symbols as communication in the numerous sets of signs that have developed to provide simple and direct information to the traveler, no matter what language is spoken. Go to any airport in the world and you can find the restroom, restaurant, baggage claim, or money exchange. The basic communicative function is possible because of the visual similarity between the object and the idea so that we visually see a fork and understand that it refers to eating, or a male or female silhouette and understand that it refers to the men's or ladies' room.

Symbols as Knowledge

As we move up the ladder of symbolic abstraction, the stop after communication is the use of symbols as knowledge. At this level of symbol use, the relationship between the object and idea is less obvious, since there is less correspondence between the object and the symbol. Take the pictographic symbol for a bird referred to in the last section. Add a simple olive branch and the meaning changes to "peace" because of the reference to the Biblical flood and the story of Noah and the ark. Even people who may not be familiar with the origin of the symbol understand its meaning. Add a halo and the dove becomes a Christian symbol for the Holy Spirit, but because a knowledge of Christian iconography is required to interpret the symbol, there is a much greater probability that people will either not understand or perhaps misunderstand the meaning of the symbol.

The degree of knowledge required to interpret the meaning of a symbol varies from rather basic and general knowledge to sophisticated and at times obscure knowledge. While there may be some "universal" symbols that require no previous knowledge or limited previous knowledge to understand, they are the exception.

Symbols as Expression

When we move to the level of symbols as expression, we move our focus from that of the viewer of the symbol to that of the creator of the symbol. Symbols as expression are not simply to provide basic information, but to present an idea or concept in such a manner that its message will be understood by the *intended* audience.

Symbols provide a variety of means for expressing an idea. A flag, for example, represents a nation. In the flag of the United States, the stars represent the states and the stripes represent the original colonies. There is no innate reason why the elements of the flag are what they are, arranged as they are, or are colored as they are. There were several flags in use throughout the American colonies before an official flag was adopted. In 1777, the first national flag adopted by Congress was a blue background with a ring of thirteen white stars and thirteen stripes alternating between red and white with a red stripe at both the top and bottom. The flag was changed in 1795, however, to reflect the addition of states to the Union. Since there were fifteen states, there were fifteen stars on the blue field arranged in rows of three with the second and fourth rows offset so that the stars were not directly over those in the preceding row. There were also fifteen stripes, still alternating between red and white with a red stripe at the top and bottom.

If we assume that the visual design of the flag had continued to follow the pattern of the first official flags, today we would have the blue field with fifty stars on it and fifty stripes alternating between red and white. We know that we have the fifty stars on the blue field, but we do not have fifty stripes. The third official flag that was adopted by Congress created a synthesis of the first two in that the stars continued to increase in number representing the number of states in the Union, but the stripes were limited to thirteen, as in the first official flag, representing the original thirteen colonies.

A flag is a symbol for a nation, and by association the people of that nation. It also takes on qualities that go far beyond a simple visual symbol. When soldiers go to war, they carry the flag with them as a symbol of their allegiance, and soldiers fallen in battle are buried in a flag-draped coffin. This is not "mere" symbolism; it carries a deep emotional meaning as anyone who has seen a husband or father buried with military honors can attest.

On the other hand, those who want to vicariously attack a nation often do so by burning the symbol of the nation, its flag. Nothing seems to rouse more anger than seeing the flag being burned in some foreign city by a foreign mob, and nothing can be more disturbing than to see those of ones own nation burning the flag in protest. Interestingly enough, the proper way to dispose of an old flag is to burn it. What begins as a simple symbol can rapidly become all pervasive in a society, even to the point of blind devotion.

The flag of any nation is not that nation any more than a portrait is the person being represented. Whatever emotional appeal a symbol carries is provided by the viewer, not the symbol. In order for the symbol to be a successful means of communication, it must have some association based on a knowledge consensus shared between the individuals involved in the communicative interaction.

Symbols as Control

Part of the emotional power of the symbol is its ability to serve as a control or power tool. Symbols are the basis for hegemonic action. We have already referred to the flag as an emotional symbol, but the flag can also serve a control function. If you will not pledge allegiance to a flag, many will question your patriotism and loyalty even though the Supreme Court has interpreted the Constitution as giving you the right to not pledge allegiance. Legal decisions aside, think about the relationship between symbol, word, and action when we say the pledge. It is in group situations where everyone can see whether you pledge or do not pledge allegiance. We hold our right hand over our heart as a nonverbal sign of our allegiance to the flag and the "nation for which it stands." There is a strong emotional control factor involved in the simple act of pledging allegiance.

Symbols that may have had little hegemonic force may take on strong emotional and control factors. The swastika is an ancient symbol, a form of mandala, that was part of the ancient cultures of China, India, and the Americas. During the 1930's and 1940's, however, it took on a role and significance that forever changed its meaning and power. Even when drawn incorrectly, most people associate it with Nazism and racism, with death and genocide. We treat control symbols differently depending on our depth of association with the symbol. While we can see and use the swastika in the United States, repugnant as it may be to most of us, it is illegal in Germany to use the swastika in any form for any purpose. This should not be so difficult to understand when we consider the historical significance and the hegemonic force it recalls.

Symbols in Political Cartoons

The political cartoon provides an interesting focus for understanding symbols. Studies have focused on symbols that frequently appear in political cartoons including Uncle Sam (Blevins, 1987; Ketchum, 1990), the Statue of Liberty (Fischer, 1986), John Bull (Mellini & Matthews, 1987; Taylor, 1992), Jimmy Carter and Ronald Reagan (Blackwood, 1989), James Watt (Bostdorff, 1987), and the Strategic Defense Initiative (Lilenthal, 1989).

Let's apply some of the concepts from the previous sections as they might be used in creating political cartoons.

Take a simple geometric shape like a triangle. In isolation it has no obvious social meaning. Place it on the head of a child and it becomes symbolic of the "dunce" or class clown. Place it on the head of George Bush and it can become a symbol of the failure of Bush to live up to his pledge to be the "Education President." It seems so simple an act, but the cognitive functions associated with it are quite complex. We must have some understanding of the significance of the pointed hat, recognize the caricature of George Bush, and make the association between the hat, the president, and his education promises and policies.

Now, take a common object, animal, or any other visual image. Cartoonists use common objects and images and visually transform them into symbols. Take a snail. What characteristics do we associate with the snail? How might we transform a simple snail into a political symbol? It could be done in an almost infinite number of ways, but two common solutions would be to transform the snail's shell into an image such as the dome of the capitol building to represent how slowly Congress moves on important legislation or some cutting issue such as Congressional ethics. If we give the snail the face of President Bush, we suggest that he has been slow to act on some issue.

Here are several examples of how political cartoonists have used symbols in their cartoons. First, you need to create a visual image in your mind about the setting of the cartoon. Second, you need to think about the symbols used in the cartoon and how they relate to basic communication, knowledge, expression, and control. Finally, if you feel the need to do so, go look up the reference for the cartoon and see if your image matches the image created by the cartoonist.

Cartoonist Steve McBride of the Independence (Kansas) *Daily Reporter* drew a cartoon about German unification (Brooks, 1991, p. 49). See Figure 1. Some of the symbols are seemingly insignificant at face value. One such symbol is a street sign, but even a simple iconic image of a post with the name of a street takes on symbolic value when the street is named "SUPER POWERS AVE." There on the

Figure 1. New Kid on the Block.
(Used by permission. Steve McBride, editorial cartoonist,
Independence, KS *Daily Reporter.*)

corner are two kids and a thug, but not just any two kids or any thug. Via the
symbol of the hammer and sickle, we recognize that one of the kids, a super
power, is the Soviet Union. The other, of course, is the United States represented
by Uncle Sam. The thug is appropriately labeled United Germany. Had McBride
chosen to use them, there are symbols available that could have been used, like
the hammer and sickle or Uncle Sam, to stand for Germany. What symbols
represent a United Germany? The German flag might have worked, but perhaps
most readers would not immediately recognize the flag and it would have
needed colors to be clearly identifiable as the German flag since there are several
European nations with similar flags. Certainly the swastika could have identified
the thug as German, but the meaning would have been significantly different.
The thug is a skinhead, often seen on the evening news as a potentially volatile
factor in German political life. The use of written language symbols adds to the
clarity of the cartoon since the United German thug says, "Move over boys! …
There's a NEW KID on the BLOCK!" Other symbolic references in the cartoon
that might be picked up by various readers would be the contrast between the
teen singing group New Kids on the Block, a clean-cut and good role-model
contrasted to the "typical" rock group like the United German thug.

How else might the potential threat of a United Germany be expressed in a political cartoon? Scott Stantis, formerly of the *Arizona Republic*, used the symbolic event of a marriage to express fears about the new nation (Brooks, 1991, p. 48). Stantis shows a dapper pair at the wedding altar, clearly German in the images of Hilda (East Germany) and the robust crew-cut groom (West Germany). The wedding takes place in a large church, symbolized by the arched windows and ceiling. The minister or priest (remember that Germany is part Catholic and part Protestant) says, "Anyone knowing of a reason why these two should not be united speak now or forever hold your peace." If that were all Stantis had put into his cartoon, the symbolism would have been evident, but when we see that the congregation at this marriage is a host of ghostly figures in prison uniforms wearing the Star of David, the character and tone of the cartoon changes radically. The sunken faces recall scenes of concentration camps, and the Star of David stands clearly as a religious symbol of past genocide and the potential of a future that repeats the sordid past.

Finally, consider a cartoon by Bob Dornfried of the Fairfield (Connecticut) *Citizen* (Brooks, 1992, p. 41). This is a simple cartoon of President George Bush. We know it is Bush because of the caricature and there are no ancillary cues such as labels or symbols. In reality, George Bush is known because of the way his chin and his glasses and his high forehead are drawn by most cartoonists. Going from one ear to the other is a clothes hanger. We know the clothes hanger is moving because of small "movement lines" symbolizing movement. What does the cartoon mean? The most potent symbol in the cartoon is, of course, the clothes hanger which represents a point of view about abortion. How should we interpret the cartoon? Is George Bush in favor of abortion or is he opposed to abortion? The clothes hanger usually represents pro-Choice groups, since they say that if abortion is made illegal, women will resort to less safe forms of abortion, including the use of tools like clothes hangers. George Bush has a dialogue balloon, signifying that he is speaking these words: "My views on abortion? ... Let me think about it!!!" The cartoonist might be saying that pro-Choice groups are playing with George Bush's thinking, or that George Bush has his ears closed to any pro-Choice arguments. We know where George Bush says he stands on the abortion issue, and we know the meaning of the clothes hanger as an abortion-symbol, but the meaning remains ambiguous and open to a wide range of interpretations. Symbols do not always clarify meaning, but sometimes ambiguity is an intentional strategy used by the cartoonist. On volatile issues, such as abortion, symbolic ambiguity is a device employed by the cartoonist to delay reader evaluation in order to get the reader to think about the issues.

Conclusions

The role of symbols in visual communication is certainly more expansive than can be covered in this one short chapter. The basic tools for understanding and creating visual symbols, however, have been presented. It is now up to the individual reader to further develop their ability to comprehend symbolic elements or create messages based on the use of symbolic visual communication.

References

Blackwood, R. E. (1989). Ronbo and the peanut farmer in Canadian editorial cartoons. *Journalism Quarterly, 66,* 453–457.

Blevins, T. H. (1987). The body politic: The changing face of Uncle Sam. *Journalism Quarterly, 64,* 13–21.

Bostdorff, D. M. (1987). Making light of James Watt: A Burkean approach to the form and attitude of political cartoons. *Quarterly Journal of Speech, 73,* 43–59.

Brooks, C. (1991). *Best editorial cartoons of the year.* Gretna, LA: Pelican Publishing Co.

Brooks, C. (1992). *Best editorial cartoons of the year.* Gretna, LA: Pelican Publishing Co.

Cassirer, E. (1944). *An essay on man.* New York: Doubleday & Co.

Cassirer, E. (1953). *Philosophy of symbolic forms.* New Haven, CT: Yale University Press.

Douglas, M. (1970). *Natural symbols.* London: Cassell Education Limited.

Firth, R. (1973). *Symbols: Public and private.* Ithaca, NY: Cornell University Press.

Fischer, R. A. (1986, Winter). Oddity, icon, challenge: The Statute of Liberty in American cartoon art, 1879–1986. *Journal of American Culture, 9* (4), 63–81.

Jung, C. G. (1964). *Man and his symbols.* Garden City, NY: Doubleday & Co.

Ketchum, A. (1990, April). The search for Uncle Sam. *History Today, 40,* 20–27.

Lilenthal, E. T. (1989). *Symbolic defense: The cultural significance of the strategic defense initiative.* Urbana, IL: University of Illinois Press.

Mellini, P., & Matthews, R. T. (1987, May). John Bull's family arises. *History Today, 37,* 17–23.

Morris, C.D. (1945). *Signs, language, and behavior.* Chicago: University of Chicago Press.

Peirce, C. S. (1958). *Values in a universe of change: Selected writings,* P. P. Wiener (Ed.). New York: Doubleday & Co.

Taylor, M. (1992, February). John Bull and the iconography of public opinion in England. *Past and Present, 134,* 93–128.

Ricoeur, P. (1976). *Interpretation theory: Discourse and the surplus of meaning.* Fort Worth, TX: Texas Christian University Press.

White, R. (1989, July). Visual thinking in the Ice Age. *Scientific American, 261,* 92–99.

Wileman, R. E. (1980). *Exercises in visual thinking.* New York: Hastings House.

Chapter Nine

Action and Object Language

David M. (Mike) Moore

Objectives

After reading this chapter, you should be able to:

1. *Define action (body) language.*

2. *Discuss action language by the following cues provided: reflexive actions, conventional signals, appearance, gestures, and role.*

3. *Identify Perception cues that are used to "group" people.*

4. *Discuss the impact of "personal space" in the role of communication.*

5. *Define object language.*

6. *Identify the utility, command, and symbolic functions of objects.*

Introduction

The leader of the 1992 Olympic Marathon was two to three hundred yards in the lead, seemingly running well and relaxed. Then, he began to look over his shoulder several times. The television announcer, himself a former runner, commented that the leader was tiring and probably would not finish the race. Sure enough, a short time later he was back in the pack and later dropped out of the race.

Two college students walked into the first class of the Fall semester, one looked at the room and the way the tables were placed and commented to his colleague, "I think I will like this class; the instructor obviously is laid back." As predicted, this turned out to be the case. Because of the nonverbal cues present in these two situations, the viewers were able to make a correct observation without any words being spoken.

The two instances above are examples of people able to "read" (understand) two forms of nonverbal communication, that of action and object language (Fransecky & Debes, 1972). These two forms of "language" are some of the most important types of nonverbal communication. People within a culture are generally alike both physically and emotionally. Because they have been exposed to similar experiences, situations, customs, religions, law, language, etc., they are able to sense and thus infer feelings and motives to others. Obviously, the most common of these experiences are the easiest to interpret (Hall, 1959).

Action or body language represents what some call the most universally understood language across all cultures and across time. However, all body or action language is not always understood and some actions, like words, have multiple meanings or no meaning at all. Are nonverbal language and verbal behavior related? Nonverbal language can be used in combination with verbal language or it can be independent of any verbal activity. It can replace verbal language, or it can clarify statements and conform thoughts and emotions. Many communication experts believe that action language is more accurate in the expression of emotion and attitude. However, nonverbal language is less able to express logical thoughts and sophisticated or creative ideas than verbal language (Wolfgang, 1979). Nonverbal language can be more ambiguous than verbal language and is more controlled by the setting and the culture of the participants. Ruesch and Kees (1970) state that body or action language has "a dual function: on one hand they serve personal needs, and on the other, they constitute statements to those who may perceive them" (p. 189). Action language involves all physical signals, both intentional and unintentional, to which an observer can make inferences (generally accurate) about the observed person's behavior.

On the other hand, the second type, Object Language, comprises all conscious and non-intentional display of "material things," which by their location or arrangement can convey information, commands, and a state of being (Ruesch & Kees, 1970). Both body and object language play powerful roles in human communication. While much time and effort are spent in schools in developing and refining verbal communication, little effort is expended to recognize and teach the wide range of messages coming from these nonverbal areas. However, the importance of nonverbal communication appears to be taking on additional importance, for one only has to look at textbooks on communication and speech to see increasing amount of pages devoted to these subjects.

Action (body) Language

It has been estimated that as much as 65 percent of the meaning gained from social interchange comes from nonverbal action language (Burgoon, 1978). The words "nonverbal language" have been used above to describe how people and even objects communicate without using words. Exactly what is language? Language is composed of many signs or symbols, of which their significance must be known to their interpreter. They must have patterns of use that have been agreed upon in advance (i.e., they must be a recognizable code) (Morris, 1946). "Any action or thing may have symbolic properties and represent some other event. Knowledge and information enable the human being to reconstruct past events, understand present events, and to predict and anticipate those of the future" (Ruesch & Kees, 1970, p. 7). Using these definitions, we see that nonverbal codes can be classified as a language. These nonverbal codes have much in common with their verbal cousins. They can be used with the verbal medium or by themselves. Verbal codes are very explicit and have many conventions, i.e., rules of grammar, syntax, etc. Nonverbal codes until recently did not have formal guidelines for their use and understanding, although they have been used effectively for thousands of years. Ruben (1984) indicates there is a perception that verbal language is a public or social activity and as thus is worthy of instruction. On the other hand, action language consisting of individual's appearance, movement and position, is considered to be a private experience, and thus, not a suitable candidate to be considered as a formal subject.

What does action language consist of? What is its purpose? Patterson (1983) classified the functions of nonverbal communication as follows:

1. Providing information
2. Regulating interaction
3. Expressing intimacy
4. Exercising social control
5. Facilitating service or task-goals. (p. 7)

Nonverbal language can be used for purposeful communication as is spoken communication, but generally has a more unconscious aspect than verbal language. Patterson (1983) identified 16 nonverbal actions used in communication. These actions include interpersonal distance, body orientation, hand movement, grooming behavior, object and self manipulation (e.g., fiddling with rings, self-touching), and gaze direction. These actions to be understood require both "sender and receiver to know the codes" of nonverbal communication. Communications experts feel that when body language is used in combination with words, the reading of the nonverbal codes is more powerful and more accurate than words in expressing emotion. Someone may say one thing, however, their actions, expression or gestures may unintentionally indicate something entirely different and chances are more truthful (Leathers, 1986). All human communication starts from some physical action. As well as body movement, both our voluntary and involuntary speech sounds convey meaning. Since emotional expression is difficult to hide or conceal, it can say much more than words. It "colors and influences the nature and tone of any message, and often contains explanatory clues about how such a message is meant or is to be taken" (Ruesch & Kees, 1970, p. 45). As indicated earlier, just as verbal communication has been codified using structure and syntax, nonverbal (body) language also can be categorized by type of cues presented. These cues include reflective actions, conventional signs, appearances, gestures, and the use of space.

Reflexive Actions

Probably the most basic and easily understood nonverbal cues are reactions beyond voluntary control. Morris (1977) suggests that we can only be certain of these involuntary actions in cases where movements are performed without any prior experiences such as with newborn or blind children. He speculates that our present nonverbal social interactions are not much different from those of our early ancestors. "We may have advanced with abstraction and artifaction but our urges and actions are probably the same" (p. 17). For example, the grimace of a person in pain, or the gritting of teeth of an angry person are cues to the person's real emotional state, no matter how much he/she verbally disavows the condition. Morris (1977) used the term "nonverbal leakage" to classify these nonverbal cues that give away our true feelings and attitudes without our knowing. The major culprit in giving our true emotions to others appears to be the general body position. "Whole-body lying is difficult for most of us because we lack practice" (p. 106-107). We learn nonverbal cues from personal experience and life-long observation. We apparently *understand* what others are truly feeling.

Conventional Signals

Another category of cues is signs or signals we have learned by convention, i.e., by social and cultural agreements or understandings. The signs used in the American deaf language are one example. Hand positions and facial expression are a vocabulary which to be understood must be taught, observed, and learned. The old hand signs used as traffic signals are another example. These signals have been codified, even though they may or may not have any visual connection with their function. These signals have been agreed upon and are expected to be used (by agreement or by law). Different professions have created their own signals because of necessity or convenience. These signals may not be known or understood by those not belonging to these groups. Many of these types of conventional signals were developed where speaking was impossible or impractical. There was a need for effective and efficient communication of which these signs provided a useful substitute for words.

Appearance

In all societies, personal appearance is a major aspect of social interaction. Personal appearance can convey both accurate or inaccurate information to and from the bearer and the observer. Clothes can radically change the self-perception of an individual or how he/she is looked upon. Clothes may establish a person's identity (e.g., police uniform), taste, status, well-being, values, personality, and his/her attitude towards others. We interpret much from another person's attire, from finding that person socially or sexually attractive to whether he/she will be employed in a particular job. Studies have shown that in situations in the workplace where people are available with similar qualifications, but with different wardrobes, the people most appropriately dressed will generally be hired. The concept of "power" dressing has long been known in business and politics. The neatness and stylishness of one's wardrobe can determine if he/she is accepted or rejected by others. The old saying "Clothes make the man" is generally a very accurate statement concerning these visual cues. Accessories, cosmetics, hair styles, and glasses are closely associated with clothing in providing cues. The presence of jewelry or a particular hair cut may indicate age, wealth, and status (Burgoon, 1978). Glasses and make-up can convey attitudes as well as serving practical needs. Appearance can affect that all important "first impression." However, as it commonly known, we must be very careful in "reading" the nonverbal codes of appearance. Appearances can, and are quite often purposefully changed, and the true meaning may be hidden or masked.

Physical Attributes

Closely connected to personal appearance are the physical attributes of an individual. Age, body build, sex, muscle tone, and posture all provide useful cues to a person's temperament and personality. "Thus everyone has a certain **identity**, known to himself and to others, that for all practical purposes remains stable regardless of the social situation in which he participates" (Ruesch & Kees, 1970, p. 57).

The human face probably has more communicative value than all the other physical attributes combined. Ruben (1984) indicates that the face is a system of interrelated components (eyes, nose, mouth, etc.), which collectively serve communicative functions that no one part could alone. The expressions of the face provide the best source of information as to a person's emotional state (e.g., happiness, sadness, anger, disgust, etc.) (Ekman & Friesen, 1969). The eyes in particular have a powerful impact on others in terms of communication. We even have "rules" of eye contact or avoidance. Whether or not a person is a friend or stranger determines how we conduct ourselves and the appropriate eye behavior, e.g., staring or not at another person (Ruben, 1984).

A person's posture can give many clues as to his/her age, health, mood, and attitude. One can tell if a person is tired or weary, or if he/she is expectant, if he/she has a positive or negative self-image, if he/she is bored or happy. The way people sit, stand or lean can tell us much about their feeling, disposition, age, and physical health. Physical aspects such as physique, muscle tone, and development give us clues as to a person's profession or vocation. Acquired (or lack of) features such as sun tans, wind burns, calluses, and bent backs can tell us much about what an individual has done and where. For example, Doyle's Sherlock Holmes often used clues such as these to solve his mysteries, which illustrated his power of observation.

Gestures

While much of the previously discussed nonverbal (body) language can either be intentional or unintentional, gestures are generally considered to be purposeful and are used primarily for intentional communication. (Please note that for this review unintentional gestures are placed in the category of reflexive actions. There is a fine line between voluntary and involuntary body language and the situation determines its role.) A gesture may be defined as intentional body or facial movement with the purpose of emphasizing a verbal point or to expressing an emotion or attitude. Figure 1 illustrates common facial gestures. It should be understood that these illustrations could also be examples of unintentional body language.

Gestures are used to emphasize, to explain verbal communication and generally cannot be separated from it. Verbal communication in most cultures needs to be supplemented by nonverbal actions. Thus, in many cases it is very

Figure 1. Facial Gestures.

difficult to isolate either action (Ruesch & Kees, 1970). Gestures, however, can be used without words to express ideas and emotions. They are usually performed by the face, hand, arm, and shoulder. Facial gestures are powerful cues accenting other body movements.

There has been much written on how gestures have been acquired. Morris (1977) for instance, suggests that gestures come from several sources, such as heredity, discovery, imitation (absorbency), and training. Gestures are determined by natural body movement and many are purposeful exaggerations of reflexive movements. Many gestures may come from activities developed during childhood. Because of this, many gestures that express anger, pride, anxiety, and pleasure are similar across cultures. Other gestures have been taught and imitated. Thus, their understanding and purpose may be culturally specific. Brannigan and Humphries (1969) noted there are many human gestures and have identified over 80 arising from the head and face alone. An additional 55 gestures are produced by the body and arms. Gestures are used in a variety of communication situations, but are primarily found in verbal conversations. However, these gestures can be somewhat limited in use because of the need to be in proximity to the other individual(s) involved in the conversation. Gestures are used to describe looks, feeling, or taste, or to emphasize some situation or event. The most common use is to express emotion or feeling. Gestures are also used to send and receive messages of liking, trust, approval, and dominance (Burgoon, 1978).

Some have argued that gestures could form a universal language because they have cross-cultural appeal. Gestures can be easily taught and can be refined or adapted. They have a potentially large vocabulary and they allow for special expressions. However, one must be careful not to judge other people from a single gesture because it takes practice to "read" gestures. Since people are complex, the gesture may not be telling the entire story (Ruesch & Kees, 1970). The "reading" of gestures and other nonverbal clues must be set in the *context* of the situation. What is the location? Is it formal or private? Who is involved? The nonverbal statement can be interpreted (or guessed at) by fitting together the situation, the individual (sender), and the particular gesture.

Roles

A necessary prerequisite to understand context and the general nature of the body language is to determine or understand the position (or role) of the sender as well as the observer. It is

> well to keep in mind that any kind of observation of behavior—occurs in two —person or group situations. The very fact of being observed changes through feedback, the actions and emotions of the observed individual; actions formally intended for self-consumption then become a statement to others. (Ruesch & Kees, 1970, p. 46)

Obviously, the location, situation, time of day, dress, implements of work or play, and background experience of the individual help determine the nature of a person's role or position. People play different roles, many at the same time. Because of experience, we expect a person in a hospital with a white robe to denote a particular position, such as doctor, nurse, or aide. The most common way to make judgments on other people's work or profession is to study the "tools of the trade" and the activities in which they are involved. However, all individuals assume different roles at home, work, on a vacation, etc. Props (both intentional and unintentional), like an armload of books, may signify a student or avid reader. The use of a shopping cart at a grocery store might indicate a person in the role of shopper. A woman with a small baby in a stroller might indicate a person in the role of a mother or a baby sitter. It is possible for person to be at the same time a father, a professor, or a scoutmaster. Many roles are permanent and long term in nature, such as an occupation, a citizen, or a church member. Other roles are temporary and easily changed, such as spectator at a sports event or a chef in a backyard cook-out. Many times roles, while concurrent with others, do *not* transfer their activities to the second or third role. A doctor as a little league coach may not be professionally recognized in the second role. However, the background or situation (e.g., baseball field), the dress (e.g., uniforms), and group (e.g., team) will help identify the individual's current role, however temporary. People move from everyday roles to other roles without difficulty or thought. Likewise, the background and the activity involved *do* change. As in roles, of which people have many, individuals are also members of many groups.

Groups

While people are members of many groups or organizations, they may not be identified as a member unless the group is present (e.g., a member of a fraternity). This, of course, is not always true. A person may be identified as a group member because of wearing a uniform, even if other uniformed members are not present. Another individual may be identified as a member of a political party by the campaign button he/she happens to be wearing at the time. See Figure 2.

Figure 2. Group Identification.

Activity and task are other perception cues that we use to group people into perceived units (Taylor, 1960). People can also be observed in loose groups, where as a member, they do not necessarily lose their own identity (e.g., a town council or a committee). See Figure 3.

Figure 3. Loose Group.

In other types of groups, individuals do lose their own identity at least while the group is present (e.g., baseball fans at a ball game). One of the easiest methods to determine the existence of a group is by the *proximity* of the individuals. Seeing the individuals in Figure 4, one might assume they are members of the same family because they are together (Taylor, 1960).

Figure 4. Group—Proximity.

Another way in which we identify groups, as noted earlier, is by *similarity* of the members (e.g., the same uniform of a baseball team). The group is identified by common features (uniform), location, and purpose of the various individuals. The members do not necessarily need to be physically close to make a determination that they are a group (team, unit, committee, etc.) only that they are similar. See Figure 5.

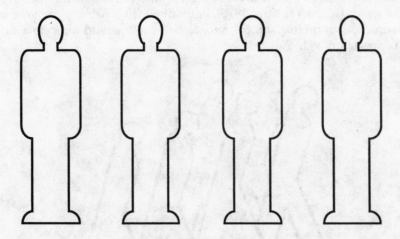

Figure 5. Group—Similarity.

Other examples of people identified by individual similarity include religious or ethnic groups. Individuals using common symbols and icons, dress, language, ritual, etc., thus, appear to be members of a particular group or religion. (Taylor, 1960).

Figure 6 illustrates an another way of grouping individuals, that of combining both the *proximity* and the *similarity* of individuals. Having both elements in combination is a powerful perceptual grouping cue (e.g., band members in a parade).

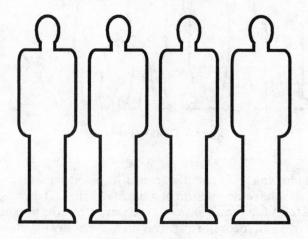

Figure 6. Group—Proximity and Similarity.

Common *movement* of individuals also is a technique for identifying a potential group (Ruesch & Kees, 1970). Individuals (in proximity) moving toward a common destination (e.g., an entrance to ball park) would indicate a common group of spectators as in Figure 7.

Figure 7. Group—Common Movement.

Other individuals moving at approximately the same *speed* and *direction* would indicate the formation of a group, however temporary (e.g., people hurrying to catch a subway car become a group of commuters).

Obviously, group body position gives cues as to the urgency of the situation or attitude of an individual or group. People "lounging" with hands in their pockets would imply a relaxed attitude, while others walking rapidly or running with arms pumping would denote some urgency. People moving on the same path would also indicate the formation of a loose, temporary group (e.g., students going to and from class). Therefore, movement, speed, direction, and path can provide cues that individually or in combination indicate people belong to a particular group (Ruesch & Kees, 1970).

Space

A key dimension in action language is the way people use and occupy space. The distance we maintain between ourselves and our reactions to appropriate spacing between strangers, friends, groups, and individuals convey much information about each other's attitudes and emotions (Burgoon, 1978). Hall (1959) in his important work *The Silent Language* stressed the importance of *culture* in the requirements for the amount of space an individual needs. A lack of understanding of an individual's need for personal space can cause considerable consternation among parties involved. In a broader sense, Hall felt that much of human history revolves around efforts to take space (territory) from others or to defend one's own area (i.e., a geographical area—land) from outsiders. This concept has been defined as territoriality. People appear to need two types of space; territory and personal space. Personal space is not territory or land but an "invisible bubble of space that an individual carries with him" (Burgoon, 1978, p. 130). When this bubble of personal space is violated, we tend to react with discomfort. If this violation of our space continues over time we may react with frustration or even aggression (McCardle, 1974). The concept of personal space and the act of distancing ourselves from others has often become a major factor in our ability or difficulty to relate to others. Hall (1966) noted that this need for space is culturally derived and he termed the concept as *proxemics*. Some of these space (proxemitic) variables include how well people involved know each other or not. Other variables include the allowable distance between the individuals, the speaker's orientation (e.g., the degree to which his/her body is turned toward, versus away from the listener), touching and eye contact between the speaker and the listener (Mehrabian, 1972). The concept of personal space takes into account variations of the posture, the distance between the speaker and listener, the degree of acquaintance, the topic of conversation, and the degree of personal liking or disliking. It appears that the more individuals like each other, the closer the personal space and the more open the communication. Hall (1966) notes that every culture (and even subcultures) has *implicit* norms regarding the proximity of individuals (speakers). For example, Hall has determined that there are four distinct communication distancing zones for Americans. These distancing zones can vary from one situation to another depending upon participant familiarity (McCardle, 1974).

1. Zero to one and one half feet for intimate relationships.
2. One and one half feet to four feet for personal relationships.
3. Four feet to ten feet for social consultative relationships.
4. Ten feet and over for public interaction (Hall, 1966, p. 126).

Observation can generally validate the accuracy of these 'zones.' Consider the distance between young lovers, a mother and daughter, an employee and his/her supervisor, or people waiting for a bus.

Fast (1970) indicates that the personal space of an individual in a crowd is destroyed due to the very nature of crowding. The amount of space invasion and circumstance determine the reactions to this intrusion. Reactions can range from avoiding eye contact to shifting the body away from the offenders, to creating "barriers" with objects (e.g., coats, books, packages), to glaring, to verbal or physical abuse, to leaving the scene (Patterson, Mullens, & Romano, 1971). However, in public places such as a crowded elevator or a subway station, people tend to react differently. They know the invasion of their personal space is unavoidable in these locations. People cope by treating the other individuals as non-persons or objects. This behavior appears to reduce their tension of others being in their personal bubble of space (Ruben, 1984).

> A non person cannot invade someone's personal space any more than a tree or chair can. It is common under certain conditions for one person to react to another as an object or fact of the background. (Sommer, 1969, p. 24)

People have strong space and territorial needs. The way people create, defend, or accommodate others within this space send powerful nonverbal messages to others, as do the distances which people adopt between themselves and others.

Object Language

In *Nonverbal Communication*, Ruesch and Kees (1970) identify object language as another major category of nonverbal communication. "Object language comprises all intentional and non intentional display of material things such as implements, machines, art objects, architectural structures ..." (p. 189). The way objects are displayed can, by their arrangement, their texture, their age, etc., convey information, instructions, usage or a state of being. Burgoon (1978) uses the term *artifacts* to define essentially the same concept of objects communicating (providing) information. Objects can and do provide information and insights to the user or observer of the objects. Objects can also provide the same type of information from years or even centuries past. Archaeologists primarily use objects in their study of past cultures. "Primitive and single objects give us information about the manual activities of the men who used them. ... Objects— some of them at least—are enduring, and the information coded in material items has survived for centuries" (Ruesch & Kees, 1970, p. 27). Object language obviously exists in nature because people learn to "read natural signs," such as storm clouds and changes in temperature, and then use that information to make judgments and plans based upon weather and seasons.

Although man does not control nature, much of what goes on in the environment is a result of human action. There are traces of man's past and present activity found at all levels. Some of these traces are permanent and others are temporary, but all can communicate a message about current or past events. Footprints and tire tracks in the sand on the beach can denote activity or presence. Trash strewn around a public area can denote not only activity but the character of the participants. Worn places on floors or door handles show evidence of heavy traffic. Mud and dust on cars may indicate where the occupants have been. Our buildings, offices, factories, and parks give cues of our society's purpose, thoughts, and activity. Much like body language, the decor of the home and workplace can tell us much about the occupant's personality, neatness, work and play habits, and his/her likes and dislikes.

Utility

Our surroundings can be designed for comfort, for ease of movement, for study, and for relaxation. For example, the type of chair found in a public area can determine it's use. Easy (soft) chairs are designed for comfort and invite people to spend time. Straight chairs convey a message of "sit here for only a short time." Architects and designers have long used the concept of utility in the design of buildings and their interiors. The reason we spend a short time in a fast food restaurant is by design. We have learned from various environmental cues to behave a certain way without being told. Placement and arrangement of objects can convey information beyond the objects themselves. Businesses can announce and comment on the value of their products by the way they use and place price tags. For example, large tags suggest inexpensive or cheap products while small tags with small print suggest expensive items, e.g., rings or jewelry. A display of a single item with a minute price tag may indicate an extremely expensive item (Ruesch & Kees, 1970).

We can tell from observation if an object is functional, decorative or both. We can tell if it is used or not by its arrangement, location, and content. We can tell much about a person's work habits by observing his/her tools and their condition. We can tell if a person is busy, neat, careful, or conscientious by looking at the way they have arranged their environment. The same is true of a carpenter, a lawyer, a doctor, a homemaker, or even a student.

Command

By the placement of a single object or combination of objects, we are directed (or influenced) to do or not do certain things. Figure 8 is an example of a non-verbal statement not to enter even though there is not a No Trespassing sign present.

Fences, doors, curbs, streets, and sidewalks are all examples of objects exerting control and indicating direction. Locks, stairs, and hallways within a building control our movement or indicate directions without anything being said. The way classrooms are furnished and the way the desks or chairs are placed, as noted in an earlier example in this paper, can influence the atmosphere of the class, its activity, and its decorum. Many manmade environments set the tone for the activity to take place. Business environments, for example, may regulate movement and interaction by the placement of furniture or counters. The type and placement of furniture are sometimes designed for the convenience of the

Figure 8. Object—Command.

custodians, not for the public, such as in the public waiting rooms of train
stations and hospitals. The placement of objects, thus, indirectly affects patron
interaction and mobility. Other examples of objects designed to give commands
are rural mailbox flags which give instructions "mail inside, please take." Filled
garbage cans on the curb request that the contents be carried away (Ruesch &
Kees, 1970).

Objects as Symbols

Ruben (1984) states that "structures and their contents, by virtue of their size,
shape, use of space, and decor may also have symbolic significance for us"
(p. 151). Some buildings and rooms are designed to inspire awe and reverence
(e.g., large cathedrals or a rotunda in a building of state). Monuments such as the
arch in St. Louis or the Washington Monument in the nation's capital have
become symbols for these cities. The Statue of Liberty is more symbolic than
functional. Figure 9 illustrates a well-known object used as a symbol.

Objects and furnishings can be symbols of status (or lack of), power, and
authority. In the business world, big desks versus small desks have significance.
The decor and structure of a courtroom (e.g., a judge seated higher and facing all
others) serve as symbols of authority and power. Rundown tenements in large
cities become a symbol of a society's problems or ills. Small objects also can take
on powerful symbolic meanings. Consider the flag of the United States, which is
the symbol of the entire country and its purpose and character. In many cases,

Figure 9. Object as Symbol.

objects like medals, trophies, and works of art have taken on a symbolic rather than practical, value.

Objects can acquire other symbolic attributes. For example, objects can become signs and symbols of professions or trademarks of businesses such as the barber pole for the barber and the mortar and pestle for the pharmacist. In abbreviated form the objects signify the concept of the profession or the nature of work and include all information needed for others to recognize this purpose.

Summary

Nonverbal communication plays a major role in the communications process. Some researchers estimate that more than 90 percent of an interactive communication situation results from nonverbal factors (Leathers, 1986). Nonverbal communication helps determine our interpersonal relationships and provides information that is not available from verbal communication alone. Some action (body) language appears to be universally understood, while at the same time, other action language is culturally specific. The context of events and knowledge of the culture must be known to accurately understand the communication process in a nonverbal setting. Action language can be better understood by studying its several categories including reflexive actions, conventional signals, personal appearance, physical attributes, gestures, interpersonal roles, groups, and personal space. Each of these categories illustrates ranges of the functions and impact of body language on the communication process.

The second type of nonverbal communication discussed in this paper is object language. The ability of people to "read" object codes is extremely important, for many times they set the stage for communication in a broader sense. Object language must be learned and understood for in some situations, verbal and even body languages may not be present or available. It might be necessary to rely on objects' codes in such cases. A person's well being might be in jeopardy if objects are "read" incorrectly. Object language can be studied and understood by looking at the utility, command, and the symbolic functions of objects.

Notes

Figures 2, 3, 9 are reprinted (adapted) by permission of the publisher.
    Modley, R. (1976). *Handbook of pictorial symbols*. New York: Doves Publications.

Figures 4–7 are adapted by permission of the publisher.
    Taylor, I. A. (1960). Perception and visual communication. In J. Balla & F. C. Byrnes (Eds.), *Research, principles, and practice in visual communication*. Washington, DC: Department of Audiovisual Instruction.

Illustrations by Don Inman.

References

Brannigan, C., & Humphries, D. (1969). I see what you mean. *New Scientist. 22*, 406–408.

Burgoon, J. K. (1978). Nonverbal communication. In M. Burgoon & M. Ruffner (Eds.), *Human communication* (pp. 129–161). New York: Holt, Rinehart, and Winston.

Ekman, P., & Friesen, W. V. (1969). The repertoire of nonverbal behavior: Categories, origins, usage, and coding. *Semiotica, 1*, 49–98.

Fast, J. (1970). *Body language*. New York: M. Evans and Co.

Fransecky, R. B., & Debes, J. L. (1972). *Visual literacy: A way to learn—A way to teach*. Washington, DC: Association for Educational Communications and Technology.

Hall, E. T. (1959). *The silent language*. New York: Doubleday & Co. (Fawcett Premier Book).

Hall, E. T. (1966). *The hidden dimension*. New York: Doubleday & Co.

Leathers, D. G. (1986). *Successful nonverbal communication*. New York: Macmillan Publishing Co.

McCardle, E. S. (Ed.). (1974). *Nonverbal communication for media, library, and information specialists*. New York: Marcel Dekker.

Mehrabian, A. (1972). *Nonverbal communication*. Chicago: Aldine-Alherton.

Morris, D. (1977). *Manwatching*. New York: Harry N. Abrams.

Morris, E. W. (1946). *Signs, language, and behavior*. Englewood Cliffs, NJ: Prentice-Hall.

Patterson, M. L. (1983). *Nonverbal behavior: A functional perspective*. New York: Springer-Verlag.

Patterson, M. L., Mullens, S., & Romano, J. (1971). Compensatory reactions to spatial intrusion. *Sociometry, 34*, 114–121.

Ruben, B. D. (1984). *Communication and human behavior*. New York: Macmillan Publishing Co.

Ruesch, J., & Kees, W. (1970). *Nonverbal communication*. Berkeley, CA: University of California Press.

Sommer, R. (1969). *Personal space*. Englewood Cliffs, NJ: Prentice-Hall.

Taylor, I. A. (1960). Perception and visual communication. In J. Ball & F. C. Byrnes (Eds.), *Research, principles, and practices in visual communication* (pp. 51–70). Washington, DC: Department of Audiovisual Instruction.

Wolfgang, A. (1979). *Nonverbal behavior*. New York: Academic Press.

SECTION IV

Visual Design

New technologies are making it easier for people to create visual images. However, ease does not imply effectiveness. Merton Thompson contends that if visuals are to convey the intended message, the designer must be familiar with the language of visuals and what he refers to as design considerations. These considerations are divided into two areas: design elements and design principles. Each is described and graphic examples are provided. The elements and principles, in and of themselves, do not represent strict rules but individually and collectively achieve appropriateness depending on the different characteristics of the learners and the type of educational objectives to be achieved.

Ann Saunders discusses graphic forms of visual communication in an attempt to advance the reader's understanding of how graphics are planned, developed, and implemented to communicate a specific message or general impression. She reminds us of the pervasive presence of the graphic form and that it is a mode of communication that relies on our most powerful sense, sight, for its visible composition and perception. Saunders concludes her chapter with a review of the processes, knowledge, and skills necessary for the development and implementation of a graphic.

Roberts Braden, in describing the relationship that exists between visual and verbal communication elements, uses many examples to point out that each has distinct features. The relative amount of visual and verbal elements in a specific message is dependent on the idea to be conveyed. Knowing how visual and verbal elements appear and relate to each other can provide the reader with a starting point to discover more about how positioning affects learning. He presents ideas on how to categorize, classify, or group different visual and verbal elements. Figures are included throughout the chapter to illustrate the verbal elements.

Using the assumption that electronically produced visuals require different design considerations than those in the print format, Nancy Knupfer discusses the role of images in this unique format. This format of computer graphics is viewed from several perspectives: the structure of the image, the meaning of the image, and the power of the image. Using examples, she explains that many factors influence learning. These factors include: good screen design, learner's perception and interpretation, and the emotional impact of the message. Knupfer also traces the concept of data visualization and how electronically produced visualization can add meaning for the potential user.

Chapter Ten

Design Considerations of Visuals

Merton E. Thompson

Objectives

After reading this chapter, you should be able to:

1. *List essential principles of visual design.*

2. *Discuss the differences between elements and principles of visual design.*

3. *Identify and provide an example of each element of visual design.*

4. *Explain how visuals are designed.*

5. *Explain how principles can be combined to develop effective visuals.*

6. *Explain how visual design is evaluated.*

Introduction

The advent of new technologies, including computer drawing programs, scanners, printers, plotters, and electronic photography has made it easier for people to create visual images. With these tools, it is now a simple process to create, enlarge, reduce, combine, and otherwise manipulate artwork and other visual materials. What has not changed with the widespread availability of these tools is the need to apply basic design considerations when creating visuals. If a visual is effectively going to communicate a message, the designer must still pay attention to the language of visuals or the design considerations. Ease of creation does not guarantee that a visual will be easily or appropriately interpreted by the intended audience.

Not only have new technologies made visual creation easier, they have also made possible a wide variety of special effects, such as color combinations and changes, movement, and changes of perspective. Designers must keep in mind that simply because something is possible does not mean it is either useful or effective. It is necessary to take to consider who the visual is designed for and what the visual is trying to accomplish. Creation of effective visuals depends upon the designer's understanding and applying the basic design considerations for visual materials.

For purpose of clarification, these considerations for visuals are divided into two areas: design elements and design principles. **Design elements** may be thought of as the building blocks or basic units of construction of the visual. All visuals are composed of one or more of these elements. **Design principles** are guidelines for using the elements and the resulting components of a visual to communicate the intended message. The principles are not inalterable rules, but are guidelines of effective ways visual materials may be put together. Creative and successful designers select appropriate design principles to apply to their designs. The items contained in these two categories have been an integral part of the language of visual design for many years. The attempt here is to provide a comprehensive list and description of these tools.

Design Elements

Point

The first element of visual design is the point. A point is actually a location and therefore has no length or width of its own. A point is often represented by a small dot or circle.

●

Point.

A single dot may serve as a focal point of a visual. This is often the portion of the visual that is most important. Several points in combination may be used to represent more complicated objects or ideas. An example of this is constellations of stars that have been given meanings by humans for centuries.

The Big Dipper.

Line

The second element of design is the line. A line may be thought of as a series of dots so close to each other that they lose their individual identity and form a new entity.

Line created from points.

This new entity has one dimension, length and, as a result, it has distinct beginning and ending points and a specific distance between those two points. A line may be straight, curved, or irregular.

Lines.

Humans tend to follow a line along its length and as a result lines are used to direct attention to a specific location in a visual. This application is most effective if another component of the design is located near the end point of the line, in other words, if there is something to gain the viewer's attention at the end of the line. With the left to right, top to bottom orientation taught to readers in western cultures, unless other factors interfere, most people will see the upper or left end of a line as the beginning and the lower or right end as the ending point. Lines can also be used to separate components of a visual from one another.

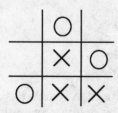 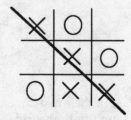

Lines can separate components of a visual...   or group components of a visual.

Lines and their placement can also take on other characteristics. Vertical lines, such as in towers and columns, are symbols of power and strength. Horizontal lines symbolize a restful or relaxing nature. A diagonal line, because it is perceived as being in an unstable position, symbolizes a dynamic, action-oriented visual.

Although lines technically have only one dimension, the mark that represents them in visuals does have a width or thickness. A thick, heavy line is seen as stronger or more powerful than a thin line

Shape

A line that continues until it reaches its starting point forming a closed figure or is perceived as a closed figure is called a shape. Shapes are composed of two or more lines or one line that changes direction at least twice.

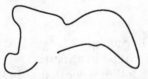

Shape created from a line.

Shapes have two dimensions, length and width. They may be regular or irregular in appearance.

Because of their two dimensions, shapes are often used in visuals to symbolize objects found in the world. They represent objects by defining or outlining the outer edge of the object. As with lines, the heavier the line used to create the outline, the stronger or more powerful the object is perceived to be.

Form

A shape that has additional lines or shapes to represent the third dimension, depth, is called a form.

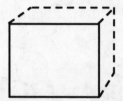

Form created from a shape.

Currently, most methods for viewing visuals are two dimensional and, therefore the visuals are two dimensional. The third dimension that distinguishes form from shape must be simulated. Forms, because they represent all three dimensions of nature, are seen as more concrete visuals than points, lines, or shapes. They are also the element most likely to be perceived as having mass.

Space

Space is the portion of a visual that is not filled by one of the other elements. Space in a visual is the one element that is defined by the other components of the visual. Viewed by itself, space has no meaning. Space is further defined as positive or negative. Positive space is the area inside a shape or form as defined by border lines. It is the interior of an object. Negative space is the area outside the lines making up objects. The most common application of negative space is the background of a visual.

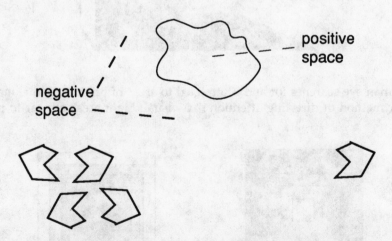

Space can be used to group or separate other components of a visual.

Texture

Texture is the visual equivalent of the sense of touch. It is how the object would feel if the viewer could touch or handle it. Texture is the element that makes an object appear to be smooth or rough, hard or soft, heavy or light, sharp or flat.

 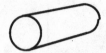

Texture adds realism to objects in a visual. With the element of texture added to objects, the viewer has a better sense of the objects and their characteristics. Texture also adds a psychological effect to the visual. Smooth objects have a positive reaction from most people while rough or sharp objects often attract attention but are repulsive. People are sometimes drawn to rough or sharp objects but are less likely to want to be personally involved with them.

Light

Light as a visual design element may be defined as the areas of greater brightness or whiteness. It is a representation of the level of illumination by the sun or an artificial source of light on the components of a visual. The right face or side of this cube is perceived as having more light falling on it that the other two visible sides. The area opposite the lit face is seen as a shadow of the cube.

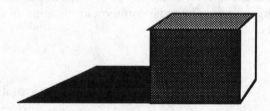

The human eye searches for and is attracted to areas of brightness, making light another method of directing attention in a visual. Light areas appear to project

 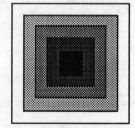

forward from a visual while dark areas tend to recede. The left drawing is likely to be viewed as a top view of a tower and the right drawing is viewed as a hole or well.

Light can be soft and even, uniformly illuminating a visual, or it can be harsh and create areas that are powerfully lit and other areas of deep shadows. This latter type of lighting is often used in film, television, and photography to add a dramatic touch to visuals.

Color

Color, as viewed by the human eye, is the characteristic of a visual that distinguishes it from black or white. Color is composed of three parts: hue, value, and saturation. Hue is the specific wavelength that human eyes perceive as color, i.e., red, blue, green, yellow. Value is overall lightness or darkness (brightness) of the color. A high value means the color is close to white, such as yellow. A low value means the color is close to black, such as navy blue. Saturation is the purity of the color. The more a color is mixed with other colors the less is its saturation. Highly saturated colors are brilliant in their effect while low in saturation color are more subtle.

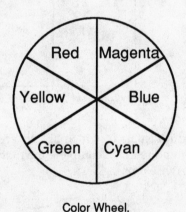

Color Wheel.

Color adds realism, making the visual a more concrete representation of the object. Color is also used to differentiate between portions of a visual: i.e., red lines representing arteries and blue lines representing veins in a diagram of an arm. Just as bright light attracts the eye and shadows do not, colors high in value and saturation attract the eye more than their counterparts. The flame orange of hunting vests and the yellow stripe marking the lanes on a highway were carefully chosen for maximum visibility. In addition, the hue of red attracts the eye, a fact that can be observed when looking at the colors of clothing of people in a stadium or by looking at the covers of magazines on display in a newsstand.

Colors also have psychological effects on people. Bright colors are seen as high energy or exciting. Pastels are more soothing and relaxing. Reds and yellows are energizing and uplifting, while greens and blues tend to be more peaceful (Fleming & Levie, 1978, 1993).

Motion

The final element of visual design, motion, is similar to form in that it is usually simulated in most media in use today. Motion is defined as the observed, implied or perceived change of position or location of an object in a visual.

Motion is useful for guiding the eye through a visual. The human eye tends to follow a moving object or the perceived path of an object in a still medium. For this reason, objects portraying motion should be positioned so they can move into the visual rather than out of the visual.

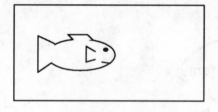
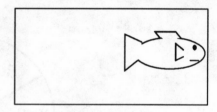

Good example.   Poor example.

Motion is also evident in visuals in which objects are portrayed in frozen or unnatural positions. The mind tends to complete the motion and see the object as jumping or falling or otherwise moving.

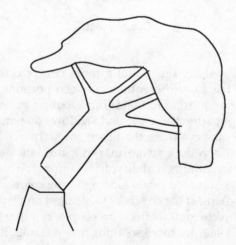

Design Principles

Simplicity

One principle to consider is simplicity. This guideline states that each visual should deal with only a single concept and only provide the essential information needed for the audience to understand that concept. Visuals are more likely to communicate the intended message efficiently if they contain only the essential details. A simple line drawing is often more effective than a photograph because the details included in a photograph may be distracting or misleading.

The medium chosen for the visual will influence the level of simplicity that should be maintained. Televised or projected visuals should contain less information than one distributed on a printed page because of the limited access the audience has to the projected image. The audience does not ordinarily control the conditions and time under which a projected visual is viewed as they do with printed materials. As a result, projected visuals should be quicker and easier to interpret than those in which the viewer controls the viewing.

An application of this principle is to provide one illustration per step in the instructions to assemble a bicycle or toy. Attempting to show several steps in one diagram usually leads to confusion and frustration on the part of the assembler.

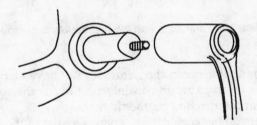

Step 5. Insert the crank on the axle.

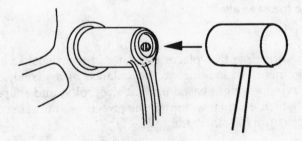

Step 6. Tap the crank lightly with a mallet to seat it.

Clarity

A second principle of design is clarity, which is the characteristic of a visual that ensures that the components have meaning to the intended audience. The information contained in the visual must be within the viewer's previous experience and be capable of being recalled by the viewer.

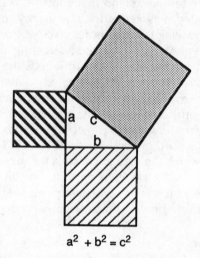

$$a^2 + b^2 = c^2$$

This visual is clear to an audience with the appropriate background knowledge.

This diagram of the Pythagorean theorem does not have clarity to an audience that does not have the background in interpreting mathematical symbols for squaring numbers or interpreting geometric shapes.

If visual designers do not consider key characteristics of the intended audience for a visual, the likelihood of successfully communicating the intended message is greatly reduced. A visual without clarity may lead the audience to interpret the message very differently than intended or to be so frustrated with the visual as to not interpret the message at all.

Balance

Balance is the principle that places the parts of the visual in an esthetically pleasing arrangement. In looking at the balance of a visual, each object is thought of as having a weight based upon it size, color, and shape. A balanced visual is one in which the total weight of the objects on one side equals the total weight of the objects on the other side.

There are two types of balance: formal and informal. Formal balance is an arrangement in which the two halves of the visual are mirror images. The human body can be viewed as an example of formal balance. This is the easier method of achieving balance, but it is often viewed as less interesting because of its overuse and predictability. As a result, the audience may not pay attention to the visual for a sufficiently long time for it to have the intended impact.

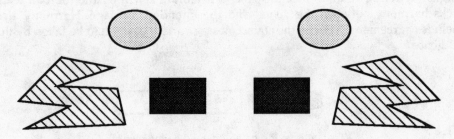

Formal balance.

Informal balance is an asymmetrical arrangement of the parts of the visual but one that still achieves balance. In this type of arrangement, the objects perceived as lighter are placed in the upper portion or away from the center of the visual. Heavier objects are placed near the bottom or center of the visual. Heavy objects are placed low because it is psychologically uncomfortable to have heavy objects placed in high positions. The farther objects are from the center of the visual, the more weight they appear to have. This is similar to two children of unequal weights at different distances from the fulcrum of a seesaw. Informal balance does a better job of holding an audience's attention because of the increased creativity needed to create the visual.

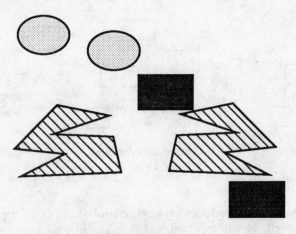

Informal balance.

Harmony

Harmony is the design principle that states that all the parts of the visual should relate and complement each other. This includes such considerations as the drawing styles, colors, textures, size, and lettering style of the visual. For example, a staff photo collage that is composed of a professionally done portrait of the president and snapshots of the clerical staff lacks harmony and may be sending a very different message than intended. Similarly, a poster that uses Old English lettering to announce a picnic to celebrate a win by the football team lacks harmony between the visual and the intended message. Harmony also includes agreement between the stated message and the action to be taken by the audience.

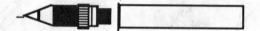

When refilling the cartridge, hold pen vertically.

This illustration does not show harmony between the layout of the visual and the text. The results are likely to be messy if the person filling the pen pays more attention to the illustrated orientation of the pen than to the written instructions.

Organization

Organization of a visual refers to the arrangement or layout of the components. This principle states that there should be a clear path for the eye to follow. This can be accomplished by capitalizing on the left to right, top to bottom orientation of readers in a western culture, by numbering the components or by using other visual cues such as lines or arrows to connect components in the desired order.

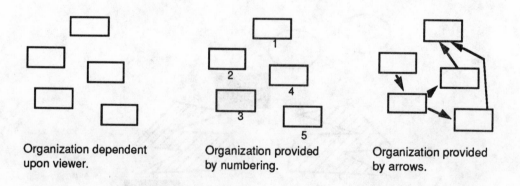

Organization dependent upon viewer.

Organization provided by numbering.

Organization provided by arrows.

An obvious organization reduces confusion and frustration for the intended audience and speeds the interpretation of the visual. It is important to note that the organization must be apparent to the audience, not just to the creator of the visual.

Emphasis

Emphasis as a design principle may be seen as an exception to the principle of harmony. The goal with emphasis is to make one component of the visual stand out from the rest. This should be the portion of the visual that is the most important, the focal point for the visual. The remaining components are included in the visual to support and help define the emphasized component. This is similar to the photographic concept of a center of interest. One portion of the visual dominates the rest. This guides the viewer through the visual and tells them which portion to pay the most attention to. Emphasis may be accomplished in a variety of ways, including the use of size, color, contrast, texture, pattern, space, or through visual cues such as arrows or circles.

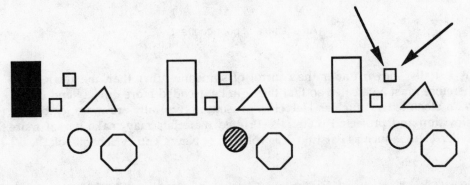

Color used to emphasize.   Texture used to emphasize.   Arrows used to emphasize.

Legibility

Legibility is the principle that states the visual materials are designed and delivered in such a manner that the audience can see sufficient detail to "read" the design. This relates to both the visual and words included in the design. The key considerations for legibility are size, contrast, letter style, and letter capitalization.

Size as a legibility consideration is largely dependent upon the medium used to display the design. For example, a 12 point letter that is approximately 3/32 inches high is legible on a printed page at a distance of approximately 12 inches. This size is much too small on a television screen that is normally viewed from a distance of 12 feet or more.

Contrast refers to the fact that the color and patterns chosen for the words and visuals stand out from those of the background. Colors of foreground and background need to differ significantly in hue, brightness, and value.

Letter style must be one easily decoded by the intended audience, one in which they have had sufficient experience differentiating among the letters. With television and projected media, there is less latitude in letter style than with printed materials because of the way television and projected materials are made available to the audience. Print materials are typically read and studied under the time and condition determined by the reader. Projected and television materials

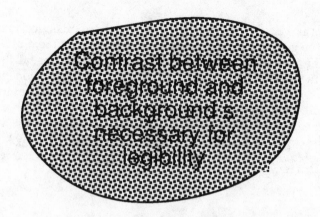

An example of poor contrast.

are usually shown under the control of someone other than the reader and therefore must be created so that they can be decoded more quickly and easily. Plain block letters, such as Helvetica or Geneva, typically are more legible for television and projected materials. Printed materials may make use of more stylized letters such as Palatino (this volume) or New Century Schoolbook.

Helvetica	Bookman	London
Geneva	New Century Schoolbook	Heidelberg
Avant Garde	Palatino	
Styles useful for projection and television	Additional styles useful in print media	Less useful or special purpose styles

A fourth consideration of legibility is the use of **capital letters**. The American educational system and the basic rules of English grammar teach that only the first letter of a sentence and the first letter of important words such as proper nouns are capitalized. Students learn to read words, sentences, and paragraphs written in this manner. As a result, it is more difficult to decode strings of letters when written in all capitals. The use of words written in all capitals should be reserved for short phrases such as a two or three word title or avoided altogether.

A SENTENCE WRITTEN IN ALL CAPITAL LETTERS IS DIFFICULT TO READ.

A sentence written using capitals and lower case letters is much easier and more pleasant to read.

An additional consideration for projected or televised visuals is to **limit the number of words** to 25 or less per visual. Because these types of visuals are not under the control of the reader, as indicated earlier, it is difficult for the audience to read and interpret long passages. These visuals are more effective when key words are used rather than phrases or sentences.

Unity

Unity is the design principle that relates to the placement of the components of a visual in such a way that they are viewed as a whole or a unit. This may be accomplished by the use of any of the design elements. For example, placing the components so that they touch or overlap each other makes use of the element of space. Placing the components on a common background makes use of shape and texture or color.

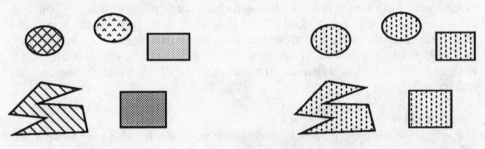

A visual lacking unity.   Unity achieved through use of a common pattern.

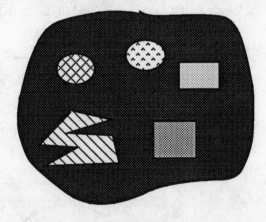

Unity achieved through the   Unity achieved through the use of a common
the use of space.   background.

Perspective

Perspective is the representation of the spatial relationship of objects in a way that is like they appear as actual objects to the human eye. The concept that converging lines are interpreted as objects receding into the distance, is key to the use of perspective. This is the principle that allows us to use form in a two-dimensional visual.

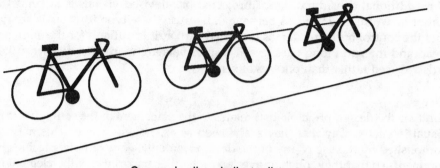

Converging lines indicate distance.

Perspective allows the designer to use the third dimension to place objects and draw the audience into the visual. It adds realism to the visual and makes the objects less abstract to the audience. This is an important factor when introducing new objects or concepts to an audience. The more concrete and less abstract a new concept is to an audience the easier it typically is to relate and to understand.

Point of view

Point of view is the apparent location of the viewer in relation to the visual. An objective point of view has the audience watching the visual as an outsider or uninvolved viewer. A subjective point of view places the viewer in the position of taking part, of being involved in the visual.

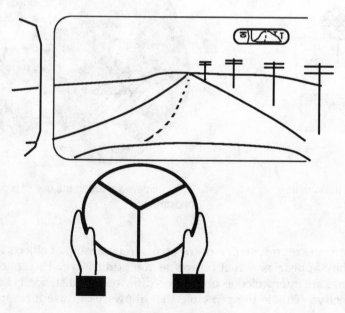

Subjective point of view.

In addition, the angle of view influences what a viewer perceives in a visual. A high angle of view, one that places the viewer higher than the subject of the visual, tends to make an object seem smaller, less significant, less in control of its world. Conversely, a low angle of view, where the viewer is below the object, looking up at it, makes an object seem larger, more powerful and in control.

Framing
Framing of a visual refers to the boundaries imposed by the creator of the visual. A visual includes a limited number of components and excludes the rest of the world. A frame may be an outer border such as the frame of a picture on a wall. This helps separate the visual from its surroundings, focusing the attention of the viewer on the visual.

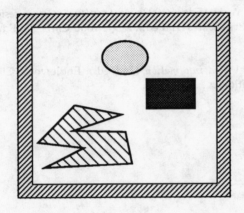

A frame may be included as a part of the visual itself. An example of this type of inner frame is a tree branch along the top of a visual. Inner frames are used to guide and focus attention upon specific components of the visual.

Conclusion
When creating a visual it is important to begin with a careful understanding of the audience and their characteristics as related to the topic. Materials used to introduce a new topic will need different characteristics and therefore be created differently than materials used to review a topic with which the audience is already familiar. A second consideration is what exactly the creator of a visual would like the audience to do as a result of being exposed to the visual. If the objective is for the audience to be able to apply a concept to a wide range of situations, the materials used again differ from a situation in which the objective is for the audience to be able to list the main parts of a concept. Once the audience is identified and the objectives established, it is then appropriate to proceed to select the most suitable media to deliver the information. If the creation of visuals is a part of this strategy, then the selection of design elements and principles to make the visuals as effective as possible is the next step.

Once the visuals have been created and used, it is important to evaluate their effectiveness. This should be done in relation to the original objectives with the specific audience identified. This is the time to determine if the audience was able to fulfill the objectives.

(Editors' note: Additional information on this topic can be found in Fleming & Levie (1993) and Pettersson (1993).)

References

Fleming, M., & Levie, W. H. (1978). *Instructional message design: Principles from the behavioral sciences.* Englewood Cliffs, NJ: Educational Technology Publications.

Fleming, M., & Levie, W. H. (Eds.). (1993). *Instructional message design: Principles from the behavioral and cognitive sciences* (2nd ed.). Englewood Cliffs, NJ: Educational Technology Publications.

Pettersson, R. (1993). *Visual information* (2nd ed.). Englewood Cliffs, NJ: Educational Technology Publications.

Chapter Eleven

Graphics and How They Communicate

Ann C. Saunders

Objectives

After reading this chapter, you should be able to:

1. *Define graphics as constituting a form of visual communication.*

2. *Distinguish and identify various graphic forms by name.*

3. *Distinguish and identify the various communicative functions of graphics.*

4. *Explain why we need to know about graphics.*

5. *Explain how the client communicates a message which has been translated into a graphic form and disseminates the message through the media to an audience.*

Introduction

Right from the beginning we need to clarify an issue that can easily be misinterpreted. The title of this chapter is "Graphics and How They Communicate." In fact graphics do not communicate! Graphics are merely a means through which human beings communicate! Human beings are responsible for graphics and what graphics say. The goal of this chapter will be to share an understanding of how human beings communicate through graphics.

To accomplish this goal, over the next several pages, graphics and graphic forms will be defined. The pervasiveness of graphics will be considered as well as how we manage to communicate through graphics. To understand how we communicate through graphics we must understand something about how graphics are specifically developed, how graphics are configured and used, and we must learn why graphics work so effectively.

It is important to note here that graphics, unlike other forms of communication, are generally a "one way" form of communication. Through graphics we send or deliver messages, but graphics generally do not allow for feedback from their audience in a similar form. As a result, they have limitations as a form of communication and are subject to misuse. This chapter, therefore, will discuss not only the role of graphics as a valuable tool in enhancing communication, but also the dangers inherent in their potential misuse, as well as their limitations.

Graphics (Graphic Designs) as Represented Through Print and Electronic Media

Definitions

Graphics may be simply defined as a *prepared form of a visual message* or a *visual form of communication*. Examples of other forms of visual communication that have been prepared or devised by humans include the signing language for the hearing impaired and architectural elements in the built environment. On the other hand, existing visual forms of communication to which human beings have given meaning include the signs we witness outdoors that signal a change of seasons, or how the changing light in the sky communicates to us the passing of day to night.

The common denominator for all forms of visual communication are: (1) they are seen and; (2) meaning can be extracted from them.

Historically, "graphics" was the term used for images prepared for use in printed materials, but today graphics are disseminated through printed material and other additional media such as:

—film,
—television,
—video,
—computer, and
—three-dimensional signage.

Transmitted through these forms of media, graphics are an important component in the mass-communication process.

In looking at the graphics communicated to an audience through television news, they include "all two dimensional visuals especially *prepared* for the television camera, such as studio title cards, illustrations, maps or charts, and electronically generated titles; charts or animation, even if appearing three dimensional, are also part of television graphics" (Zettl, 1984, p. 402).

Just as graphics may be categorized as a form of visual communication, the following may be categorized as forms of graphics:

—symbols (pictographic or abstract),
—maps,
—graphs,
—diagrams,
—illustrations or rendered pictures (realistic to abstract),
—photos (still or moving),
—three dimensional models (3-D),
—graphic devices and elements (may also be considered as symbols), and
—composite graphics.

Each of the graphic forms above was originally designed by a human being to function as a communication tool.

A **symbol** is a visual presentation that *signifies* something. As a communication tool it *identifies* an action, individual, organization, direction, concept, philosophy, or a thing. It may also serve as a form of notation.

Examples of symbols include our written or typographic alphabet. The alphabet is an abstract-symbol system that stands for, or represents, the sounds humans make and structure into words and sentences, etc. Another symbol is the pictographic logo that represents the Girl Scouts. This symbol identifies this organization through a recognizable physical representation of faces. Another abstract symbol is our nation's flag. Each visual element—color, lines, stripes, and stars—*represents* a different message and usually one which is more complex. For instance, the color red in the flag represents blood spilled in the quest for independence from England, while the 50 white stars on a blue background, or plane represent the union of our 50 states.

A **map** is a drawing or other representation of an area or surface. Maps were designed to *show relative position and size* of features or places. Examples of maps include the globe found in a 5th grade classroom or the city street map found in the local telephone directory.

A **graph** is a drawing that *presents the changes* of and the relationship between two or more things through the use of visual elements and various forms of visual notation. Examples of graphs can typically be found on the front page of the national daily newspaper *USA Today* or on one of the evening television news broadcasts. A graph on the evening television news often appears along with information on stock-market trading.

Diagrams include those visuals drawn to *represent and identify parts of a whole, a process, a general scheme*, and/or the flow or results of an action or process. An example is the printed visual set of instructions that accompany any product that requires assembly.

An **illustration** is a non-photographic picture that *represents* something in an accurate drawing or likeness. Most illustrations present one point of view, but illustrations can represent multiple points of view simultaneously, which is not possible in real life. This is, however, possible because the illustrator can manipulate the image in such a way as to create the illusion of simultaneous points of view.

Examples of illustrations are the rendered pictures that accompany stories printed in magazines or books. Illustrations are designed to provide a visual *explanation. They elaborate* on the written text. Illustrations may also serve as background to other information.

A **photo**—still or moving—*locates time and captures image*, thus representing both. Examples of photographs can be seen on various media, ranging from T-shirts, to billboards; from your drivers license to the backs of playing cards. Photos can be captured through the photographic process, a digitizing process or an analog process. They may be altered by hand or through computerized manipulation.

A **3-D model** is a *representation* that can be constructed and held or constructed through computer graphics and animation. A model can be seen from all sides or from all angles. An example of a real 3-D model is a mannequin. An example of a computer graphic animated 3-D model is a wire-frame structure, configured by using computer-graphics software to create an illustrated form that can be moved and rotated and is viewable from all sides.

A **graphic device** is a *visual indicator* that is used as a visual tool to grab or *direct one's attention*. It is best represented by asterisks, dots or arrows.

A **composite graphic** is a visual image made up of two or more graphics from the above list. An example of a composite graphic is a photo of a person with the symbol for Apple Computers rendered on his forehead, and a caption below that reads "apple head."

How Graphics Function as Communication Tools

Graphic functions, as suggested in the examples above, include: identifying, representing, locating time and capturing image, explaining, elaborating, creating an impression and serving as background.

The American Institute of Graphic Arts, in a brochure titled, "What is Graphic Design?," also included the following among the positive functions of graphics: informing, directing, exciting, inviting, explaining, entertaining, simplifying, identifying, educating, demonstrating, motivating, organizing, inspiring, selling, promoting, and warning. Functions of graphics that can be considered negative include persuading, distracting, propagandizing, manipulating, stereotyping, deceiving, trapping, and tricking.

Even with a sense now of what graphics are and a sense of how they function, one might still wonder why we need to know about graphics as a form of visual communication and why we need to know how communication is realized through graphic forms.

Graphics as a Form of Visual Communication:
Why We Need to Know
How Communication Is Realized Through These Forms

There are six reasons one needs to know more about graphics as a form of visual communication. Each one suggests why we need to know how communication is realized through graphics.

1. *Graphics* as visual units of communication *are pervasive and relatively easy to deliver to large audiences.* Graphics reflect our cultural symbols and social habits. They embody forms of sign, ritual, and token. Graphics are in some ways universal forms of communications because they are based upon those things that are seen. The technology to transfer and transmit graphic and other forms of visual communication instantaneously around the globe has made a large audience, which is often visually illiterate, available for communication.

Caroline Hightower current director of the American Institute of Graphic Arts reminds us graphics have a:

> ubiquitous presence in our daily lives that can engage and inform us or simply add to the visual morass of contemporary culture. Important and unimportant messages are graphically communicated throughout the day. From the face of the clock that wakes us, the morning newspaper and the subway or expressway signs on our way to work, to the weather map on the evening news and the preparation of dinner, graphics are a constant in the

lives of a captive audience unaware that the profession of graphic design exists and that quality can be of consequence. (Hightower, 1989, p. 7)

2. *Graphics* as visual forms of communication *can appeal to our emotions as well as to our intellect.* In addition to being everywhere, graphics can be designed to appeal directly to our emotions and/or our intellect. In some instances graphics are configured to appeal to our emotions first and then our intellect. This approach embodies a political philosophy advanced by Adolf Hitler with regards to the effective use of propaganda. In fact, Hitler believed propaganda should be designed and developed for that segment of the audience with the lowest intellect.

Graphics designed for political campaigns frequently appeal directly to our emotions as do graphics used to sell a product or service. To do this the graphic designer, on in behalf of the client, may design an image to convey a single overwhelming meaning or message, such as: "if you don't vote for candidate X you put the country at risk." An example of how a graphic was designed to generate an emotional response (fear) to trigger a vote in a specific direction is the now notorious use of Willie Horton and the revolving prison door advertisement used against Michael Dukakis in the 1988 presidential campaign.

3. *Graphics communicate.* Whether or not we correctly interpret a graphic, whether or not we pay a great deal of attention to it, if we see it we receive a message. Sighted people are constantly taking visual messages into their brains. Even if the messages don't consciously register, the information has been received and registered in the subconscious. This is how graphics or an individual graphic message communicate even if we don't.

4. *Graphics comprise a language and grammar of which most of us are ignorant and for which we are only just beginning to receive formal education.* In a study conducted by Foote and Saunders (1990) which was to document graphics used and seen daily in network television news, it became apparent that the coders for the study had no frame of reference for distinguishing and identifying graphic forms of visual communication. Though the coders were used to seeing these images on a daily basis, they found it difficult, until they were educated, to: (1) distinguish and identify graphic forms, (2) distinguish and identify graphic functions, and (3) accurately discern if the visual message re-presented the audio message.

Howard Levie points out how:

> research on the interpretation of graphic forms of information, such as pictorial clues and features, demonstrates that, without ample picture viewing experience, adults, as well as children, have difficulty decoding pictorial information which is abstract, complex, or represented in culture bound conventions. (Levie, 1987, p. 7)

While the world has seen an increase in the use of "pictures" to communicate (pictures that require that we study "seeing" to understand and use them), our educational systems have reduced the number of courses in art education, for instance, that can shed light on picture understanding. Further, the availability of courses in visual literacy that would advance seeing and interpreting what is seen are only recently finding support in the educational system. Our educational systems have been slow to recognize the increased complexity of the designed visual message, the ease of delivery of that message and the general lack of vision competencies in human beings.

When we are conscious of the message, its intent and its meaning we are said to be visually literate. Richard Sinatra (1986) explains visual literacy as: "the active reconstruction of past visual experiences with incoming visual messages to obtain meaning" (p. 5). He also states that because visual literacy emanates from a non-verbal core, it becomes the basic literacy in the thought process of comprehending and composing that underlie reading and writing. Fransecky and Debes (1972) further define visual literacy as:

> a group of vision competencies a human being can develop by seeing and at the same time having and integrating other sensory experiences. The development of these competencies is fundamental to normal human learning. When developed they enable a visually literate person to discriminate and interpret the visible actions, objects, and symbols natural or man-made, that he encounters in his environment. Through the creative use of these competencies, he is able to communicate with others. Through the appreciative use of these competencies, he is able to comprehend and enjoy the masterworks of visual communications. (pp. 1, 7)

5. For the most part, *graphics as presented through the mass media* (TV, books, magazines, advertising etc.) *are intentional one way communications.* They are *designed to be immediately perceived, comprehensible and emotionally moving in order to achieve the response the client desires,* like the purchasing of a product. Most graphic forms are *not designed to encourage feedback* from the audience, of any nature, *beyond that sought by the client.*

6. *Without a knowledge of how graphics function* (visual literacy) in the visual communication process or indeed an ability to communicate through graphic means ourselves, *we are left out of an important, powerful level of discourse.* We become subject to a one-way communication process in which we receive messages but have no parity in response. As a result we are visually illiterate and subject to manipulation, exploitation, and mental domination, as can be found in any dictatorship.

How We Communicate Through Graphics

As stated previously, graphic forms of visual communication are usually directed towards an audience of individuals through one of the many forms of mass media which can transmit, transfer, reflect or present imagery. As such the communication of a graphic can be represented through a diagram which suggests a hypodermic approach to communications. See Figure 1.

A diagram that reflects in more detail how human beings communicate and receive communications through graphics follows in Figure 2.

When attempting to understand how we communicate through graphics we must look more closely at what graphic designers know and do once they have been approached by a client with a message.

First the graphic designer considers several things that may help in rendering an appropriate graphic solution. Such information includes:

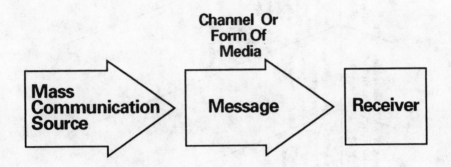

Figure 1. A Hypodermic Approach to Communication.

1. the message itself. Is it appropriate? Does it really meet the clients' needs? Should it be redefined?
2. existing knowledge of the message-factual, allegoric, mythical, metaphoric.
3. research of the message and related topics (historic and contemporary).
4. knowledge of materials and process that can contribute to the rendering of the message.
5. research of materials, processes, vehicles of dissemination (communication media), and solutions to similar problems.
6. current understanding and research of audience (psychological and sociological information, such as a knowledge of how colors or specific imagery will likely trigger a certain emotion in a targeted consumer group and/or consumer buying and spending patterns), including information on perception, and interpretation.
7. knowledge of visual language history—based on social and cultural subject and object recognition. Such subject-object recognition is established through the repetitive acceptance of visual messages.
8. knowledge and use of the design process and visualization skills which allows one to move an idea from the brain out to where it can be shaped and molded into reality as a final outcome like a poster or a brochure.
9. knowledge and use of graphic elements, forms, attributes principles, and techniques.

The preceding items (1–9) reflect the knowledge and components that a designer uses to configure a graphic. The visual **elements**, **forms**, and their **attributes** are specifically rendered or placed onto an apparent two-dimensional surface to create a graphic. In this one manner, one may consider the visual elements, forms, and attributes analogous to our alphabet.

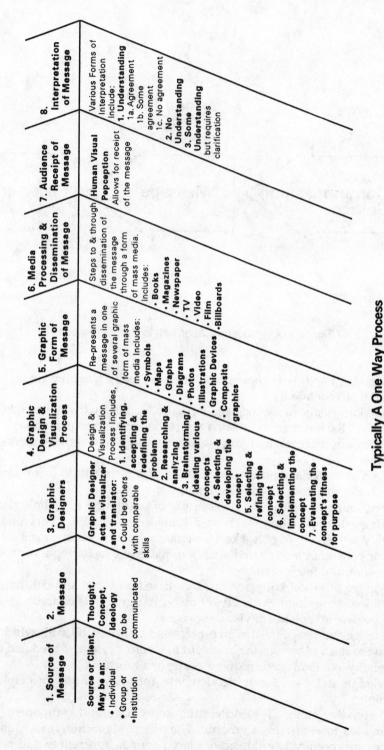

Figure 2. Graphics and How They Communicate.

The **elements** include the dot, line, and plane. **Form** is the primary identifying characteristic of volume. The elements and form can be manipulated and given **attributes,** including color, shape, proportions, texture, dimension, and direction.

Through our ability to perceive and our ability to render, copy, and create illusions, the attributes can appear to be affected by space, light, and dimension. Beyond this there are **perceptual** and **organizational principles** and **techniques** that can further affect the graphic which in turn alters the communication (Busic-Snyder & Wallschlaeger, 1992).

Such principles and techniques include:
—gestalt theory,
—figure-ground relationship,
—compositional relationship,
—spatial organization,
—acquired associations,
—closure and grouping,
—and symmetry.

Each element, form, attribute, principle, and technique can be further affected by things like **cultural bias** and **semiotics** or theories of sign. Additionally, the communication process, plus configuring and structuring, plus the medium on which the graphics is rendered or presented, plus the medium through which the graphic is disseminated, are all potential variables in the visual communication process.

As an example, take a simple straight line and draw it out in a number of positions. Make the line longer, shorter, thicker, thinner, then think of how you might vary the thickness and thinness you could have drawn. Give the line depth, illustrate how light from sources in various directions change the message. Now, separate the line into blocks. Where does shading occur? Where do the shadows fall? Now put texture on it and repeat this motif to fill a page, or construct the motif in such a manner that the textured blocks take on the shape of a bell or a boat. Now, color the boat with the colors used in the Italian flag.

All these changes and more could be made to the line; each change alters the message. Think now of the dots, lines, planes, forms, variables, and attributes which go into rendering an architectural blueprint or a self-portrait and think of the infinite number of ways this type of map could be altered. Each change representing a change in the graphic and a change in the message.

With a knowledge of the message, audience, graphic forms, design, and visualization skills, the graphic designer is able to produce a graphic form, which in many instances can convey a message better than words, and may often work where words cannot because of regional, national, and international language barriers. What was initially a problem of how to communicate a message becomes a graphic solution, which is then transmitted to an audience through various media.

Conclusion

This chapter's goal has been to define the true nature of the graphic as a prepared form of visual communication through which messages, which originate with an individual, group, or institution, have been translated and transmitted to an audience to address the issues, needs, wants or concerns of the individual originating the message. In addition to defining graphics, we explored their functions, pervasiveness, appeal, and power as a communication tool. Finally, we articulated the process by which graphics are developed, configured and disseminated, and the elements, forms, and attributes of which they are constructed. This was done to help develop an understanding of what we need to know about how human beings communicate through graphics and why it is so important that we know these things.

References

Busic-Snyder, C., & Wallschlaeger, C. (1992). *Basic visual concepts and principles for artist, architects, and designers.* Dubuque, IA: Wm. C. Brown.

Foote, J., & Saunders, A. (1990 Autumn). Graphic forms in network television news. *Journalism Quarterly, 67,* (3). 501–507.

Fransecky, R. B., & Debes, J. L. (1972). *Visual literacy: A way to learn—A way to teach.* Washington, DC: Association for Educational Communications and Technology.

Hightower, C. (1989). Foreword. In M. Friedman (Ed.), *Graphic design in America: A visual language history* (p. 7). Minneapolis, MN: Walker Art Center.

Levie, W. H. (1987). Research on pictures: A guide to the literature. In D. M. Willows & H. A. Houghton (Eds.), *The psychology of illustration: Basic research* (Vol. 1). New York: Springer-Verlag.

Sinatra, R. (1986). *Visual literacy connection to thinking, reading, and writing.* Springfield, IL: Charles C. Thomas.

Zettl, H. (1984). *Television production handbook.* Belmont, CA: Wadsworth.

Chapter Twelve

Visual Verbal Relationships

Roberts A. Braden

Objectives

After reading this chapter, you should be able to:

1. *Define in your own words the terms used to discuss visual-verbal relationships.*

2. *Identify and discuss the primary relationships between visual and verbal elements.*

3. *Discuss Wileman's typology as an organizing scheme for explaining the relationships of visual elements to verbal ones.*

4. *Discuss other organizing schemes for explaining visual-verbal relationships.*

5. *Identify and discuss examples of verbally dominated graphics.*

6. *Define and discuss the concept of visible language.*

7. *Decide when to illustrate text.*

Introduction

Definitions of the terms visual and verbal are subject to dispute. Operational definitions are offered because our purpose here is not to quibble about shades of meaning, but rather to be clear about the meaning denoted when we examine the relationships between the visual and the verbal. Sometimes those relationships are strong. Sometimes weak. In general, though, we can summarize all of the relationships between visual images and verbal elements with the conclusion that images complement words and vice versa. The natural tendency for visual and verbal components to be mutually supportive was labeled by this author a decade ago as visual-verbal symbiosis (Braden, 1983). When an image is mislabeled, words are not correctly illustrated, or when there is any other instance of showing one thing while saying another, the natural relationship is destroyed and the result is visual-verbal discontinuity. This chapter will concentrate more on the symbiotic relationships than the discontinuous ones.

Terms

The word "visualize" is a verb. Its noun form is "visualization." But what of the root word? "Visual" is listed in the dictionary as an adjective, but not as a noun. Thus adjectively we speak of the visual properties of objects, visual metaphors, visual skills, visual flight rules, and, yes, of visual language and visual literacy. While visual is not listed as a noun, common usage will soon change that. In education and the visual arts we now speak of visuals when we mean visual aids, or when referring to images of many kinds that are used to communicate. As a pseudo-noun visual is somewhat synonymous with image, picture, and illustration. In fact, the word visual has been used as a noun substitute for chart, graph, diagram, painting, and sketch. For the purpose of this discussion, let us consider visuals to be things that can be seen, things viewable, or visible things other than printed words that are used in a communication process. Clearly, the sense of sight is central to the concept of a visual.

Like visualize, "verbalize" is a verb. The adjectival form is "verbal," and "verbalization" is the comparable noun with regard to the preceding discussion. No pseudo-noun usage of the term verbal is common, however, so a complete analogy between the terms cannot be constructed. Thus, to facilitate discussion, the term verbal will be used hereafter not only as an adjective, but also as a noun, meaning verbal elements of any kind. Unlike "visualize," the term "verbalize" is most often associated with the acts of speaking and listening, and therefore is most closely related to the sense of hearing. But it is language, not the sense of hearing, that is central to verbal things. The operational definition must be extended so that verbal applies to written or spoken words, linked to either or both the sense of hearing and sight.

Jack Debes, the father of the visual literacy movement, and others (e.g., Pettersson, 1989, 1993) have referred to *visual language*. At the extreme, a visual language would imply a stand-alone grammar and a vocabulary of images, symbols and icons that are independent of the spoken and written language in general use.

After a luncheon speech given by Debes in which he extolled the notion of visual language, he was asked to give an example of a truly visual language. He responded that American sign language was a highly developed visual language, but conceded that it really was only a different way to "write" (with gestures) the English language. Pressed further he identified the captionless cartoon (he named the now extinct comic strip *Henry*) as an example of the use of visual language.

Pettersson (1989) says, "Symbols and pictures could be referred to as 'visual languages'" and he notes that "Paintings, drawings and other objects of art often stand alone" (pp. 202–3). Mostly, however, Pettersson deals with visual language only as a theoretical concept. He plugs visual language into a theoretical model in which three kinds of language—verbal, audial, and visual—are found in combinations.

Consequently, Pettersson's model results in the coining of new terms: **audio-verbal** refers to combinations of verbal language and audial language; **verbo-visual, oral-visual, and lexi-visual** all refer to combinations of verbal language and visual language; **audio-visual** represents the combination of audial language and visual language; and the combination of all three kinds of language is designated as **verbo-audio-visual.** For practical everyday use, Pettersson simplifies his theory thus, "Based on how the *verbal information* is presented to the receivers we can distinguish between two forms of verbo-visual information. We *read* text in **lexi-visual** representations and we *listen* to speech in **audio-visual** representations ..." (Pettersson, 1989, p. 204).

Types of Visuals

Visuals are categorized in several ways. They can be categorized by size: small, medium, and large. Or, they can be classified according to the end purpose: educational, promotional, entertainment, art. Or, visuals can be grouped according to the roles that they play relevant to text. Or, visuals can be sorted according to content. Visual literacy enthusiasts have found these and other classification systems useful.

Still another useful categorization scheme is one that groups visuals by outstanding characteristics of the visuals themselves. For instance, the terms static, dynamic, and personal may be assigned as categorizing rubrics.

- **Static visuals** include pictures and other printed or projected images
- **Dynamic visuals** include animation, video, and film
- **Personal visuals**, a subset of dynamic visuals, include pantomime, sign language, body language, and gestures

Following the same line of reasoning verbal elements can be categorized into one of two major classes, static or dynamic.

- **Written (Static) verbal elements** include words (text) in all of their forms, printed or projected. When numerals and other mathematical symbols are used as language they are included in this category.
- **Spoken (Dynamic) verbal elements** include the spoken language in audible form and visible forms of text that are metamorphosed or animated.

To create a useful matrix which displays the interactions of germane variables we need to ask which factors are known to support which others and to record how that support might be provided. In that context, Figure 1 is offered, which is more a description of the possible interactions than a set of ultimate examples.

The simplicity of Figure 1 is its greatest weakness. Obviously the cells are filled with only a few of the many examples that might have been chosen. More critically, the categories are so broad that only the broadest generalizations could be made. What about the degree of realism in visuals (see Knowlton, 1966; Levie, 1978; Levie & Lentz, 1982; Dwyer, 1968, 1978, 1987), the degree of visualization versus the degree of verbalization (Wileman, 1980, 1993; Braden & Beauchamp, 1987), and the characteristics of the particular visual genre, e.g., outline graphics? See Braden (1982).

Static Visuals	n/a	Rare. Use of video as a guide to an art museum.	Yes. Slide + Tape. Mediated lecture. Show and tell.	Yes. Story boards. Figures and pictures in newspapers. Magazine ads.
Dynamic Visuals	Yes. As objects shown in the dynamic medium, e.g., a chart in use in a filmed lecture.	n/a	Yes. The commentary which accompanies the pictures on the evening news.	Yes. Superimposed explanations on TV, e.g., the names of speakers on interview shows. "Crawl" messages at the bottom of the screen.
Spoken Verbals	Yes. Diagrams used in a chalk talk. Slides shown during a lecture. Charts used during a briefing.	Yes. The pictures which accompany the commentary on the evening news.	n/a	Yes. Handouts at a speech, lecture, or meeting.
Written Verbals	Yes. All kinds of images in books and journals which illustrate the subject of the text.	Unusual. A video or film of a story being taught as a book in a literature course.	Yes. A lecture which explicates a printed handout. Any speech which explains printed information.	n/a
Supported by →	Static Visuals	Dynamic Visuals	Spoken Verbals	Written Verbals

Figure 1. Matrix of Support Relationships with Selected Examples.

Degree of Realism

The most extensive research that has been done in the field of visual literacy has been the twenty-odd year series of experiments conducted by Francis Dwyer and his associates known as the Program of Systematic Evaluation (PSE). In one way or another most of the PSE experiments have been related to a set of visuals that depict the human heart. The illustrations range from realistic color photographs of a real heart to sketchy black and white line drawings. They span the spectrum of reality which can be displayed in printed images. Many of the experiments sought data on the effects of these images as they interact with verbal components such as labeling, parallel printed text, and oral commentary.

Degree of Visualization vs. Degree of Verbalization

Comic books are mostly picture stories with the dialogue of the principals lettered into speech balloons. Text books are mostly written sources of information with appropriate pictorial and graphic materials scattered around. The possibilities are endless as far as the ratio goes of visual to verbal material present in a book or magazine. For the most part, the role or purpose of the publication determines the ratio. The final ratio is determined as an editorial decision. You are looking at an example of how the purpose drives that editorial decision. Rational thought would lead us to expect that the editorial decision regarding *this text-book* would be to have a relatively high ratio of visual material to the verbal content. (**Editors' note:** This book contains approximately 150 illustrations.) Would the same decision be made if this were not a book about *visual* things? Probably not.

Visuals and verbals can be combined in any ratio—lots of one, lots of the other, or lots of both. An interesting (and challenging) set of possibilities occurs when the ratio involves visual and verbal elements displayed together in one medium. Posters, printed ads, billboards, computer graphics, and TV commercials are but a few of the examples we encounter daily wherein visual and verbal elements are displayed concurrently.

Wileman's Typology

Ralph Wileman has created a typology of verbal and visual image relationships. In his earlier work (Wileman, 1980) he called his seven image types "slides." Thus at one end of his spectrum were what he called reader slides, which were basically images of words—purely verbal. At the other extreme were pictorial or graphic symbol slides which were devoid of any typographical enhancement—purely visual. In his most recent version of the typology (Wileman, 1993), he uses the term "frame," reflecting the fact that slide-lectures and slide plus tape presentations are giving way in popularity to lectures illustrated with computer graphics and other forms of computer driven presentations (see Figure 2).

What Wileman has done is to identify the extremes, the middle (visual/verbal balanced frame) and then created arbitrary categories representing other degrees of dominance of either the visual or verbal component. His examples are appropriate, and the result is an extremely useful theoretical model.

Braden and Beauchamp (1987) approached the categorization task from an audio-visual perspective. The particular medium they chose to exemplify their theory was the slide plus tape. Consequently, they established two continua: one for what is seen, the other for what is heard. In contrast, Wileman's typology considers only what is seen. The four extremes of the two variables in Beauchamp and Braden's model are displayed as a 2 X 2 matrix in Figure 3. The matrix could, of course, have been expanded to show all seven of Wileman's types of slides (frames) and a comparable number of types of sound ranging from completely non-verbal to completely verbal. However, the resulting chart would have contained 49 cells and would have been much more difficult to comprehend.

The typical slide plus tape program contains a mixture of slide types and a mixture of sound variations. As a result, it is clear that an infinite number of possible combinations exist, and the relationship of visual to verbal elements in any given program is determined in large part by the purpose of the program and the preferences of the designer.

The Roles of the Visual in Text

Duchastel (1978) pointed out three roles of illustrations in text: the *attention role*, the *explicative role*, and the *retention role*. The first role or purpose is to attract or motivate, the second to explain (show) that which is difficult or impossible to describe, and the last is meant simply to be memorable.

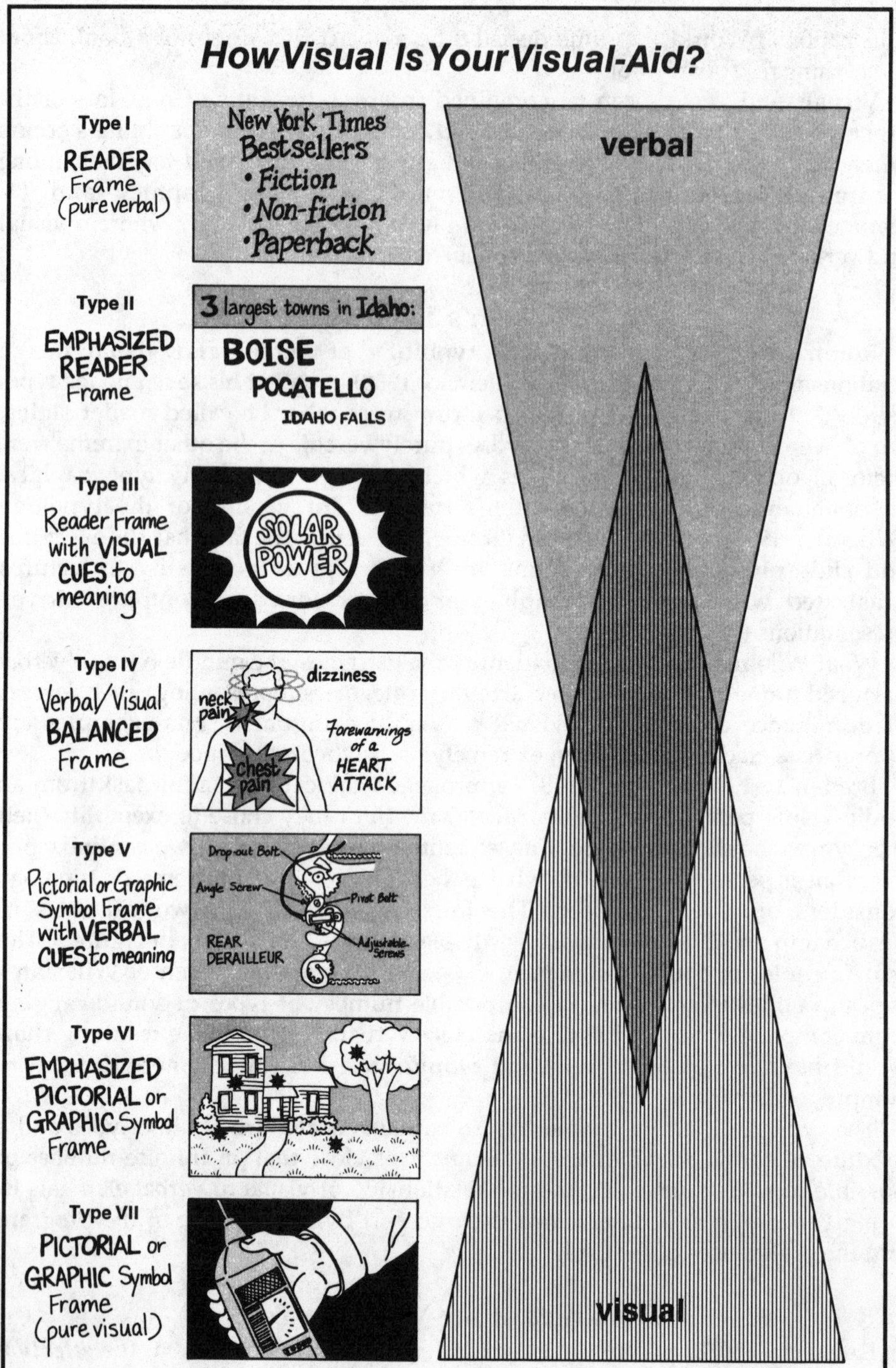

Figure 2. Wileman's Typology.
(Wileman, 1993, p.19.)

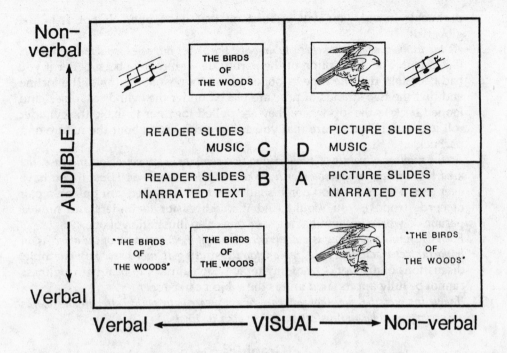

Figure 3. Beauchamp and Braden's 2 X 2 Visual Verbal Matrix.

All of Duchastel's three roles can be applied to the uses of text in learning, but they are equally appropriate to the field of advertising, business communications, and other textual applications. In essence the role of the visual is a projection of the intent or purpose of its creator. That being the case, let us simplify to a single role, i.e., that *illustrations in text are usually there to support the text* (and the text carries the author's message and agenda—whatever it may be). The rare exceptions are art books and specialized pictorial books where the role of the visuals is to *be* the message and to carry the author's agenda.

Duchastel and Waller (1979) indicated that we need "... a set of principles which relates illustrations to the potential **effects** they may have on the reader or learner." Wiley's Hierarchy of Visual Learning contends that the **effect** of visuals upon verbal information is a function of the visual maturity of the viewer (Bertoline, Burton, & Wiley, 1992).

However, the lack of proven principles regarding the use of illustrations and the confounding effects of obvious personal variables should not deter us from illustrating things in text. For lack of research data, this author will rely upon intuition to offer five flexible guidelines which seem to make sense regarding illustrating text:

1. *The more unusual the object, the greater the need for illustrating it.* For example, a verbal description of a **parbuckle** might be "a rope sling used for rolling cylindrical objects up and down an inclined plane." If you have ever seen a

parbuckle in use, you will understand that description. If not, it is just gibberish.

2. *As the number of words needed to describe the object increases, so does the need to illustrate it.* The description of the parbuckle would have been better if you had been told that the rope is looped around a post at the top of the incline and that the two strands of rope are placed under the cylindrical object and looped back to the top where they are pulled together to make the cylinder roll upward. [Chances are that you still are confused about the nature of a parbuckle.]

3. *As the number of points of similarity with a commonly known object increase, the need to illustrate an unknown or little known object decreases.* Thus, if you have ever seen a set of bamboo porch shades that roll up when you pull on a pair of cords (ropes), you would find it much easier to understand how a parbuckle works without having seen one or an illustration of one.

4. *Even when understanding is not a critical issue, if the appearance of the object is an important characteristic, the reason for illustrating it increases.* For example, discussions of art works or of any topic which alludes to beauty or ugliness cannot be fully appreciated unless the subject can be seen.

5. *If your instincts tell you that you can communicate your point better if your words are accompanied by an illustration, follow your instincts.*

Graphics

In both the Wileman typology and the Beauchamp-Braden matrix, the continuum of visual reality is anchored at one end by the pictorial and at the other by the imaged word. All of the points in between represent "graphics" in one form or another. Hartley categorized graphics as either iconic or digital. The more iconic, the more that the graphic resembles the subject; the more digital, the more the graphic is symbolically abstract. Of the several ways that have been suggested to label points along the icon-digital continuum, Wileman's is as self explanatory as any. Instead of iconic and digital, Wileman (1993) chose the terms pictorial symbols and verbal symbols. His scale of ways to represent an object is depicted in Figure 4.

Visually Dominated Graphics

The visual half of the graphic continuum is composed of the visual-verbal combinations in which the image predominates but is clarified by the verbal component. In spite of the old Chinese proverb that a picture is worth a thousand words, often it takes at least one word to complete the visual message. Frequently, the purpose of the verbal symbols is merely to point out one of many features in the illustration or to provide some clue for interpreting an otherwise complete visual message. In general the relationship of the verbal to the visual in this half of the continuum is one of providing whatever it is that is weak or lacking in the visual. That is, the *verbal symbols are provided to compensate for the languaging deficiencies of images.*

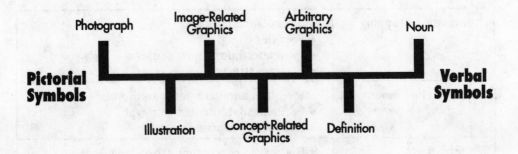

Figure 4. The Icon-Digital Continuum.
(Adapted from Wileman, 1993.)

Verbally Dominated Graphics

On the other half of the continuum the relationship is quite different. The verbal component usually contains all of the message and the function of the visual element is to facilitate the **display** of that message. An interesting aspect of the more verbal graphics is to be found in the specialized ways that they are employed. Many instructional and presentation strategies have been tied to formatting and display techniques, so that diagrammatic or other graphic conventions take on special meanings beyond the words that are displayed.

Pettersson (1989) coined the term **infography** to describe structured combinations of text, pictures, and graphic design. He described seven types of information graphics which are categorized according to end use. They are: Instruction[al] graphics, presentation graphics, explanatory graphics, news graphics, locating graphics, and expo [exhibition] graphics. Braden (1983) concentrated upon verbally dominated graphics which embody primarily only the elements of text and graphic design. Table 1 is both a display of information about verbally dominated graphics and an example of the genre. The matrix identifies nine types of verbally dominated graphics and lists some of the reasons why each format might be used. Because the terms and concepts are well within the knowledge level of the expected readers, the table is a parsimonious way of providing the information and of organizing it for the readers.

Information Mapping	• Unitizes information • Provides cuing • Facilitates information retrieval • Portrays structure
Multi-level Writing	• Identifies alternate paths and levels • Facilitates information retrieval • Enhances text visually
Pattern Notes	• Encourage conceptual networking • Display relationships • Provide holistic view
Outline Graphics	• Show organization • Display relationships • Reduce content to skeletal concepts • Provide holistic view
Matrix Display	• Provides a decision guide • Displays interactions • Segments, categorizes, and blocks information • Organizes data

Flowcharts
  Time lines
    GANTT charts
    PERT charts
    Algorithms
    Systems models
	• Highlight sequence
	• Show process steps
	• Record milestone events and elapsed time
	• Display routines (computer programs)
	• Display choices and decision points
	• Display relationships of activities

Schematic diagrams	• Symbolize functions • Show relationships of functional components
Logic diagrams	• Provide a decision guide • Identify interconnections • Identify logic functions

Hierarchical Displays
  Models
    Organization charts
	• Visualize hierarchy
	• Show levels of importance or degree
	• Infer conceptual networks
	• Display organizational structure

Table 1. Verbally Dominated Graphics.

The Printed Word

Of the many media combinations which bring visual material together with verbal elements, by far the two most influential and widely utilized are the printed page and the video screen. Of the two, the printed page remains the clear leader in terms of the amount of visual-verbal information disseminated. Print remains, therefore, of central concern to students of visual-verbal relationships.

Several major books have been written recently on the topic of text, and each devotes extensive coverage to the visual aspect of displaying text (Jonassen, 1982, 1985; Gropper, 1991; Misanchuk, 1992). "Text," of course, refers to **words** displayed in any of several printed forms, including books, magazines, newspapers, letters, pamphlets, and so forth.

A few books have also been published recently that deal specifically with displaying **visuals** in print. Commendable among the latter group are the books of Pettersson (1989, 1993), Tufte (1990), Wileman (1993), and Willows & Houghton / Houghton & Willows (both 1987). These books deal directly with the visual-verbal relationship. The books in the "text" category are all concerned with **visible language** itself, i.e., all of the visual aspects of written language.

Visible Language as defined here is any written or printed example of a verbal language—in any visible form. Today we have viewable electronic and projected displays of verbal language in addition to books, newspapers, and the like. As we think about the relationships of the visual to the verbal, there are four aspects of visible language that immediately come to mind. They are: typography, typographical cuing, printing conventions, and format & layout (page design).

Typography is concerned with the design, appearance, and use of type-faces— that is, the size, shape, and placement of letters on the printed page. It is concerned with line and word spacing, fonts, and how letters fit side-by-side (kerning). In short, there is an entire profession out there which is devoted to the visual aspects of letters and printed words. Typography is part of *visible language.*

Typographical cuing consists of a variety of visual techniques which are used in printing to direct the attention of the reader. Visual impact is gained through the use of capitalization, font size, underlining, italics, boldness of letters, lines, rules, arrows, bullets, and even of the use of white space on the page or screen.

Printing conventions are the "rules" which govern letter placement and other visual considerations during printing. When cuing is artfully combined with printing conventions, the visual aspect of typography may take on near-equal status with the verbal component. We take these conventions for granted until we see them violated. Consider the following block of text:

SeLeCtEdPrInTiNgCoNvEnTiOnSHeAdInGsSkIpTwOlInEsPrIoRsKiPoNeLi
NeAfTeRsEtOfFwItHcUInGwOrDsPaCeBeFoReAnDaFtErInItIaLcApItAlIzA
tIoNfOrPrOpErNoUnSpHrAsEbIuNdArYpUnCtUaTiOnExTrAsPaCe*SeNtEn
CeBoUnDaRyInItIaLcApItAlIzAtIoNfInAlPuNcTuAtIoNmArKsExTrAsPaC
e*PaRaGrApHiNdEnTaTiOnSkIpAlInE*bOlDfAcEiNiTiAlChArAcTeReNlArG
eDeTceNdOfLiNeRiGhTaNdLeFtJuStIfIeDhYpHeNInDiCaTeSwOrDdIvIsIoN
*iNbOoKsUsUaLlYnObEcOnSiStEnT

The information in that string of letters can be made much more readable if we observe only three printing conventions—those of capitalization, punctuation, and word spacing. (See the next example.) While we may still experience difficulty deriving clear meaning from this block of text as a whole, at least we can easily read the words and phrases.

> SELECTED PRINTING CONVENTIONS Headings Skip two lines prior Skip One line after Set off with cuing Word Space before and after Initial capitalization for proper nouns Phrase boundary Punctuation Extra space* Sentence boundary Initial capitalization Final punctuation marks Extra space* Paragraph Indentation Skip a line* Bold face, initial character enlarged, etc. End of line Right and left justified Hyphen indicates word division *In books, usually no. Be consistent.

The string of letters makes more sense as a string of words, but even more meaning is possible when the words are powerfully displayed. For example, you can add visual cuing and arrange the words into a display format to create an all-verbal figure that draws much of its strength and meaning from the layout, the fonts, the bullets, or other sight cues. Figure 5 illustrates how one might display the information in our example at hand (see Braden, 1982; Haber & Haber, 1981). Any number of equally effective or more effective layouts are possible.

SELECTED PRINTING CONVENTIONS

HEADINGS
- Skip two lines prior
- Skip one line after
- Set off with cueing

WORD
- Space before and after
- Initial capitalization for proper nouns

PHRASE BOUNDARY
- Punctuation
- Extra space *

SENTENCE BOUNDARY
- Initial capitalization
- Final punctuation marks
- Extra space *

PARAGRAPH
- Indentation
- Skip a line *
- Two or more sentences

END OF LINE
- Right and left justified
- Hyphen indicates word division

* In books, usually no. Be consistent.

Figure 5. Formatting Example. Compare with Previous Text Blocks.

An obvious attribute of Figure 5 is the hierarchical structure of the content. Because the information is outlined, it can be abbreviated and displayed as shown. The outline graphic is a particularly powerful form of visible language.

Outline Graphics

An outline graphic (OG) is any outline done in any graphic form (Braden, 1982). Outline graphics are worthy of special consideration in the discussion of the relationships of visuals to verbals. To begin with, the outline in any of its forms is essentially verbal. A graphic is essentially visual. The OG retains all of the content features of the simple textual outline and enhances them by embellishing the way in which they are displayed. The essential characteristics of OGs are that they are **skeletal, orderly, holistic,** and have a **visual** component (see Figures 6 and 7).

These two examples of outline graphics are designed to illustrate how the same content may be graphically presented in various ways. Figure 6 is dominantly verbal. The only distinguishing visual enhancements are the box in which the words appear, the use of more than one type size, typographic bullets, and indenting. The same words appear in Figure 7, but the visible hierarchical arrangement of Figure 6 has given way to a networked display with a focus upon one central concept.

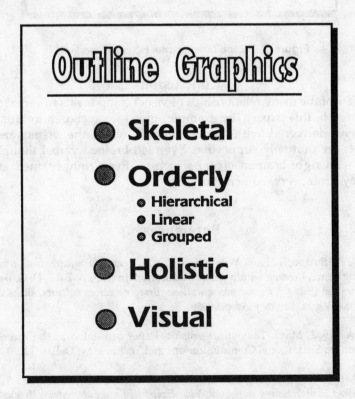

Figure 6. Minimal Outline Graphic.

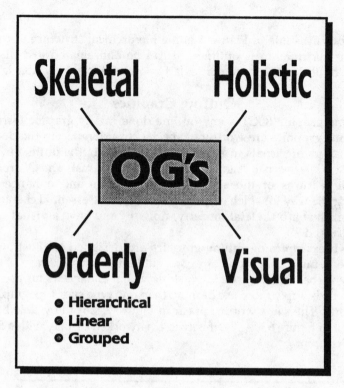

Figure 7. Outline Graphic with Holistic Emphasis.

Conclusion

Only a few of the many relationships of visual components to verbal ones have been explored in this paper. The examples given were chosen to illustrate that ideas can be delivered with greater impact when the visual and verbal components are mutually supportive. Even left-brained verbal thought can be enhanced with right-brained visual structure. Even right-brained art can be enhanced by strong verbal description.

References

Bertoline, G. R., Burton, T. L., & Wiley, S. E. (1992). Technical graphics as a catalyst for developing visual literacy within general education. In J. Clark-Baca, D. G. Beauchamp, & R. A. Braden (Eds.), *Visual communications: Bridging across cultures*. Blacksburg, VA: International Visual Literacy Association.

Braden, R. A. (1982, May). *The outline graphic*. Paper presented at the meeting of the Association for Educational Communications and Technology, Dallas, TX.

Braden, R. A. (1983). Visualizing the verbal and verbalizing the visual. In R. A. Braden & A. D. Walker (Eds.), *Seeing ourselves: Visualization in a social context*. Blacksburg, VA: International Visual Literacy Association.

Braden, R. A., & Beauchamp, D. (1987). Catering to the visual audience: A reverse design process. In R. A. Braden, D. G. Beauchamp, & L. W. Miller (Eds.), *Visible and viable: The role of images in instruction and communication*. Wolfe City, TX: International Visual Literacy Association.

Duchastel, P. (1978). Illustrating instructional texts. *Educational Technology, 18*(11), 3–6.

Duchastel, P., & Waller, R. (1979). Pictorial illustration in instructional texts. *Educational Technology, 19*(11), 20–25.

Dwyer, F. M. (1968). Effect of cognitive style and learning passage organization on study technique effectiveness. *Journal of Educational Psychology, 71*, 620–626.

Dwyer, F. M. (1978). *Strategies for improving visual learning*. State College, PA: Learning Services.

Dwyer, F. M. (1987). *Enhancing visual instruction*. State College, PA: Learning Services.

Gropper, G. L. (1991). *Text displays: Analysis and systematic design*. Englewood Cliffs, NJ: Educational Technology Publications.

Haber, R. N., & Haber, L. R. (1981). Visual components of the reading process. *Visual Language, 15*(2), 149.

Houghton, H. A., & Willows, D. M. (Eds.). (1987). *The psychology of illustration: Instructional issues* (Vol. 2). New York: Springer-Verlag.

Jonassen, D. H. (Ed.). (1982). *The technology of text: Principles for structuring, designing, and displaying text*. Englewood Cliffs, NJ: Educational Technology Publications.

Jonassen, D. H. (Ed.). (1985). *The technology of text: Principles for structuring, designing, and displaying text* (Vol. 2). Englewood Cliffs, NJ: Educational Technology Publications.

Knowlton, J. Q. (1966). On the definition of "picture." *Audio Visual Communication Review, 14*, 157–183.

Levie, W. H. (1978). A prospectus for instructional research on visual literacy. *Educational Communications and Technology Journal, 26*(1), 25–26.

Levie, W. H., & Lentz, R. (1982). Effects of text illustrations: A review of research. *Educational Communications and Technology Journal, 30*, 195–232.

Misanchuk, E. R. (1992). *Preparing instructional text: Document design using desktop publishing*. Englewood Cliffs, NJ: Educational Technology Publications.

Pettersson, R. (1989). *Visuals for information: Research and practice*. Englewood Cliffs, NJ: Educational Technology Publications.

Pettersson, R. (1993). *Visual information* (2nd ed.). Englewood Cliffs, NJ: Educational Technology Publications.

Tufte, E. R. (1990). *Envisioning Information*. Cheshire, CT: Graphics Press.

Wileman, R. E. (1980). *Exercises in visual thinking.* New York: Hastings House.

Wileman, R. E. (1993). *Visual communicating.* Englewood Cliffs, NJ: Educational Technology Publications.

Willows, D. M., & Houghton, H. A. (Eds.). (1987). *The psychology of illustration: Basic research* (Vol. 1). New York: Springer-Verlag.

Chapter Thirteen

Computers and Visual Learning

Nancy Nelson Knupfer

Objectives

After reading this chapter, you should be able to:

1. *Name and describe components of computerized images.*

2. *Discuss essential elements of good computer screen design.*

3. *Discuss the most important factors in creating realistic data displays. Why are they important?*

4. *Describe data visualization.*

5. *Explain why electronically-produced visual images can be considered powerful.*

6. *Discuss the power and potential of artificial reality as it relates to computer screens and visuals.*

Introduction

This chapter addresses visual displays produced with computers. It assumes that electronically-produced media require different design considerations than print-based media. Further, it approaches information display from three perspectives: the structure of the image, the meaning of the image, and the power of the image. It is the structure of the image that contains the essential elements of good screen design. These elements can enhance the learner's ability to interpret the intended message, thus perceiving the images and creating meaning for the given context. Finally, images add power to text-based messages. Not only do the images visualize the message, but they come loaded with the potential to add emotional impact. The combination of structure, meaning, and power of computerized images draws upon creativity and strives to design

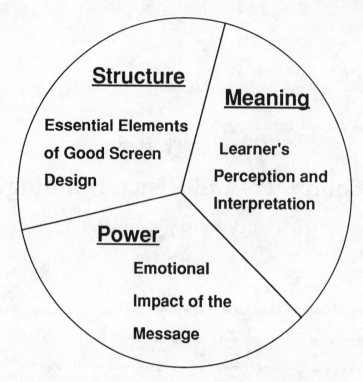

Figure 1. Effective Instructional Images.

coursework which is visually stimulating while it enhances the instructional objectives (see Figure 1).

As computers become more popular and available, larger numbers of people are spending more time reading and learning from computer screens or projected computerized images. Because computers provide a form of visual communication, the increased use of computers in various settings magnifies the importance of well-designed screen images. These images can help to guide the user through a mix of text and graphics to gain insight and realize meaning. However, if poorly designed, the images can interfere with the processing of information, thus providing an obstacle to understanding the message.

Computer-displayed images are no longer limited to monochromatic text nor to static graphics nor even to completely digitized signals. Instead, computer monitors have the power to incorporate colorful graphics in both static and dynamic modes. Computer-controlled multimedia presentations can display images that are either digitized, such as those on CD-ROM, or analog format, such as those played from a videodisc. Some equipment even allows a mix of both analog and digital displays on the same screen by placing computer-generated graphics over a videodisc image.

Computer screens are similar to television screens. The monitor is limited by the same aspect ratio and requires consideration of common design techniques for successful information display. Oftentimes a presentation mixes images from a computer with images from a videodisc, television camera, or other projected image. This technique is becoming quite popular and generally follows the rules of video screen design.

Structure of the Image

The structure of the image first considers the visual as a whole, then its components, and finally the elements of good screen design. In order for the various image components to work together as a whole, elements of well-planned screen design must weave the components together. Thus, one must consider both the image and the screen design.

The Image

The image contains a mix of components such as text, graphics, color, animation, and multimedia influences. These components can work alone or together to modify the intended message. Try to visualize the possible image variations as you read this section about the various components, beginning with text.

Text. Recently Soulier (1988) observed that text makes up the main body of most computer-based instruction, averaging 80–90 percent of the display. This emphasizes the importance of designing text displays that communicate clearly to the reader. Computer screens work very well for presenting limited amounts of text that incorporate appropriate fonts and spacing. But large amounts of text are likely to cause eye fatigue (Hathaway, 1984; Mourant, Lakshmanan, & Chantadisai, 1981) and are more likely to be forgotten (Wager & Gagné, 1988). When large amounts of text are necessary, it would be better to supply that information in printed form (Soulier, 1988).

Several researchers have investigated the effects of upper-case and lower-case, text density, and typographic cuing within computer screens (Hartley, 1987; Hathaway, 1984; Morrison, Ross, & O'Dell, 1988; Ross, Morrison, & O'Dell, 1988). Generally, the text should contain a mix of upper and lower case letters; the exception to this could be titles, headings, or special effects. Text can be mixed on the screen in a variety of font sizes and densities to create a light airy feeling or a bold, forceful message. Text can be plain and thus depend upon the reader's attention to each word, or text can be suggestive in its very structure, using font shape and size, degree of boldness, or even word direction to add meaning to the text image (see Figures 2 and 3).

No matter what the screen design, legible text requires an appropriate font that is properly spaced. The appropriateness of particular fonts has caused some debate and there remains disagreement about whether to use serif or sans serif type faces. Some authors claim that fonts with serifs, as opposed to block-style lettering, are a better choice for computer screens (Soulier, 1988). Yet others believe that sans serif fonts with proportional spacing provide a cleaner effect that is easier to read than their seriffed counterparts (Gibson & Mayta, 1992; Kemp & Dayton, 1985). Fonts with small serifs can add interest to the display, while elaborately-seriffed fonts are difficult to read.

Text legibility also depends upon the point size of the font. The point size of text on a computer screen can range from 12 to over 100 points per inch and remain legible. However, one should consider the intended usage when selecting

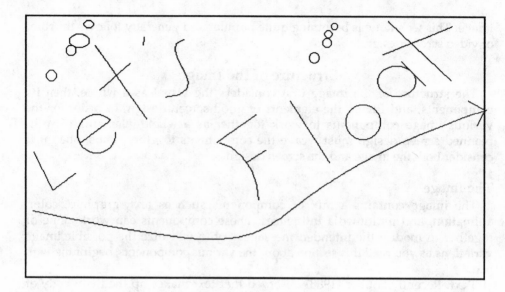

Figure 2. Light, Airy Text.

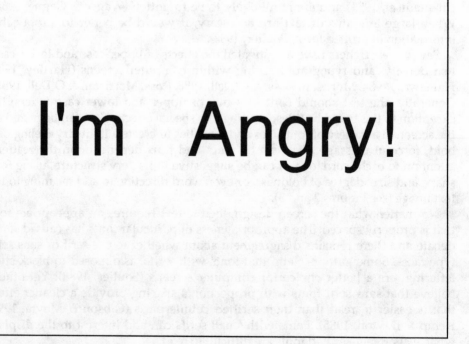

Figure 3. Bold, Forceful Text.

point size. Images that are likely to be projected for large audience reading should not use a point size smaller than 26 (Gibson & Mayta, 1992) and images that are not likely to be projected will seldom require an extremely large font. Also consider the age of the user; when designing screens for young children, use a larger font.

In addition to style and size of the font, the weight of the typeface, line length, phrasing, and spacing between lines of text affect the legibility of computer screens. The weight of a font can vary from light, narrow, fine lines to heavy, broad, bold lines. A medium to bold weight is very good, depending upon the mix of elements on the screen. Gibson and Mayta (1992) recommend that bold typeface be used throughout all computerized screen images so that the text shows up against the graphics. At the least bold fonts should be used for all titles and headings as well as for particular words that need emphasis.

Because computers, monitors, software, and projection systems are becoming more capable, perhaps it is not as critical to adhere precisely to recommendations about font style and weight as it was in the past. An important contributing factor is the availability of good resolution provided by a VGA monitor and a quality projection device. But even the best resolution will not suffice if the print is too small or if the text layout seems awkward for the reader. Layout that works well depends upon an aesthetic mix of text and graphics.

Graphics. Graphics combine with text to enhance the image and add another opportunity to suggest meaning to the reader. With graphics the screen image can be more interesting because of increased visual variety (Kemp & Dayton, 1985). Possible graphic treatments range from simple to complex, from small monochromatic embellishments to dramatic, richly-colored, full-motion video images complete with sound effects. As personal computers become more powerful and easier to use, designers can incorporate graphics more easily than in previous years.

Soulier (1988) comments that some graphics can be described as visual metaphors. Like verbal metaphors, visual metaphors can help us to understand an unfamiliar concept. Metaphoric graphics may be used to clarify a meaning within the computerized message, or they can steer the user through the mechanics or functionality of using the software. For example, an international symbol such as a steep hill might represent content that refers to the terrain while icons from a computer desktop, such as a wastebasket or stop sign, symbolize the functionality of the software. Figure 4 shows a metaphor of a library which could actually serve as a menu for a database.

Computers vary in their graphic ability. Some are limited by text-only capability or by lack of image clarity or color. Some systems which have considerable graphics capability, might be limited by extremely difficult program operation. Yet other computer systems have the capability of easily producing images for use on the computer screen as well as producing images for transfer to other media such as transparencies, camera-ready art, computer-designed slides, animation, video segments, and so on.

One type of graphic application that is commonly produced beyond the original computer screen is the common tabulated data graph. Graphs that

Figure 4. Visual Metaphor of a Database.

represent data need to be clearly designed so the reader can interpret the meaning based upon the legend, scales, symbols, and other provided cues.

Graphs that display data depend upon the reader's thought processing, interpretation, and comprehension; to be effective they must consider the intended visual message carefully. All graphics do not require such clarity. For example, some graphics might not influence comprehension one way or the other. Simple graphics at the pictorial level might not make a difference in the user's comprehension of surrounding information, but graphics that are designed to suggest inferences, generalizations, and evaluative interpretation can help a student grasp the meaning of the overall and detailed messages with the support of the higher-level graphic display (Reinking, 1986; Singer & Donlan, 1980).

Further, research on learning suggests that designers should address cognitive processes by developing materials for graphic thinkers, not just graphic readers (Boyle, 1986). More sophisticated instructional graphics, such as symbolic, schematic, or figurative displays can be effective in teaching, and the visualization of abstract ideas through figurative displays may very well enhance learning (Nygard & Ranganathan, 1983). The computer screen is an excellent tool for creating and manipulating such visual aids.

Obviously, this tool can be put to better use with a few guidelines. Soulier (1988) suggests several tips for using computerized graphic images as follows:

1. Keep illustrations appropriate for the audience. Adults will react differently to humor or cartoons than will children.

2. Use simple, line drawings instead of complex pictorial illustrations. If more complex images are needed, then build them incrementally and highlight important areas of complex graphics.

3. Design graphics to appear quickly unless there is a specific reason for slowly revealing parts of the graphic. By preloading graphics into the computer's memory and using a "quick draw" programming technique, the user will have less waiting time for the graphic to appear.

4. Use standard symbols and symbolic representations whenever possible. Visual literacy is a learned skill and it is important to make sure that the audience will recognize the symbolism.

5. Place graphics close to their corresponding text, but never on the screen before the text appears. If the graphic must be split from the text, then place it on the following screen.

These few tips can greatly improve the look of a finished graphic and promote clarity of the message. Additional cueing can be added by using color.

Color. Although color has the potential to greatly enhance the text or the graphic, a little color goes a long way. Dwyer (1978) found that specific educational objectives can be enhanced by using color in visual illustrations. But it is important to use color cautiously and to pay attention to its effect. Color should assist the user in focusing on the material; it should never be a distraction (Gibson & Mayta, 1992).

Choose a few colors that have good, but not extreme contrast values. Good contrast values will permit the colors to show up as distinctly different when using a monochrome monitor, but an extreme contrast like stark white on a black background will cause bleeding and illegibility. It is better to use a light gray instead of the white. Also avoid high values of red and orange because they can bleed into the surrounding colors.

In addition, certain colors that look ideal on an individual computer screen tend to flare or wash out when they are projected to a large screen or transmitted over a distance. To avoid disappointment it is best to experiment with a few color combinations using the equipment that will support the image when it is actually used. Complementary colors with low saturation should have a good chance of working.

On computer screens, always use color with care. Too many colors can be confusing while a few colors can cue the learner about the intended message. For example, Hannafin and Peck (1988) suggest using a bright color like red to cue the learner for new information, while presenting the remainder of the information in standard colors consistent with the rest of the screen. When color is used for coding, always check the program on a monochromatic monitor and also use a pattern as a backup technique (Soulier, 1988). Even though the color scheme may appear to be good for both monochromatic and colored monitors, some people are color blind and will see it differently. A pattern will help those individuals to distinguish between objects on the screen.

Animation. Most computer software allows the use of simple animation to illustrate a motion, provide interest, or draw attention to particular areas of the screen (Kemp & Dayton, 1985). Those who have access to digital video effects (DVEs) might find it tempting to create and overuse computerized graphic animation, using it for "fluff" instead of substance. Use animations only when appropriate and keep them short (Soulier, 1988).

Choice of graphic animation can be touchy. Only animate graphics that will aid the user's comprehension of the situation at hand, for example by gaining attention or illustrating a concept. Although animations can be highly effective for attracting attention to a specific portion of the screen, they can become irritating if left on too long and they can be distracting or disruptive to the thought process. Whenever possible, allow the user to interrupt the animation.

Multimedia. As the name implies multimedia presentations can be a mix of various types of media. This discussion assumes the use of computer-supported visuals, such as digital computer images and analog images. It is possible to obtain these images from a computer, a compact disc, a video disc, or even from a computer-controlled multi-projector slide and video show. The possible styles range from single computer screen, to projected computer screen, to 360 degree "theater in the round" displays.

A very popular instructional practice is to support lectures with images from a videodisc or compact disc driven by a computer program. Using this technique, a hypertext program controls the display with various mixes of video images and text. Despite its great potential of rich imagery, this delivery method often falls short of expectations because of cluttered screens or inappropriate lesson delivery. One of the greatest problems in actual usage is the size of the text. Instructors frequently depend upon the high-tech imagery to relay the message, but forget that a student audience cannot read text from a distance unless it is enlarged. A second common problem is washed out colors in the computer graphics; color selection that does not hold up during projection.

When designing multimedia presentations do remember to follow some of the strategies for making text and colors work over a projection system. Also remember that even though this type of presentation might work well for group instruction, one of the advantages of computers is the ability to provide interactive, individualized instruction. The general tips for computer screen design found below may be applied to various forms of multimedia displays as well as straight computerized images.

Screen Design

Screen designs that work well combine the individual features of text, graphics, animation, and multimedia components into a whole, cohesive screen. To visually aid the learner, it is necessary to consider both the general layout of well-designed screens and the various elements of good screen design.

Good Design of Screen Layout. Good screen design uses the visual to portray the message to the reader. It aids the learner by clarifying information through a visual interpretation. Research on layout and graphic design emphasizes the importance of balancing text with white space, improving the aesthetics of the page, and positioning graphics as the dominant visual element (Parker, 1987). The computer screen design should never be visualized as a printed page filled with text. Instead it requires variation within a consistent protocol and layout based upon legibility, spacing, aesthetics, and the purpose of the particular frame. Avoid cluttering the screen with too many images. Provide hard copies of complicated images that are important to remember.

One of the most powerful elements of face-to-face communication is silence and, like silence, empty spaces can be used to advantage on the computer screen. For example, the screen can be used to organize or highlight information, to draw attention to particular parts of the frame. For example, the mix of graphics and text can provide a visual cue; so can boxing and grouping of information. Partitions, borders, standard icons, and consistent placement of common elements will visually aid the reader.

While partitions and borders can draw attention to an area, artistic sense can still flourish. Figures 5 and 6 show a screen layout that protects a bordered area for graphics. In Figure 5 the designer has incorporated two borders, one within the other. The image is allowed to overflow the internal border while being contained by the external border. Figure 6 uses the same general format, but incorporates a different shaped border to accommodate the graphic.

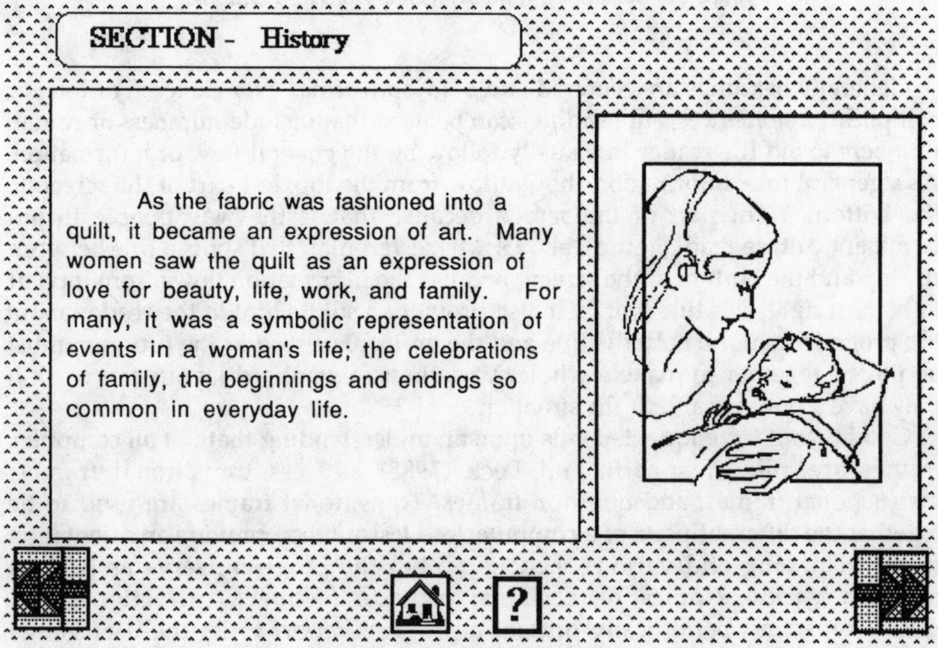

> **SECTION - History**
>
> As the fabric was fashioned into a quilt, it became an expression of art. Many women saw the quilt as an expression of love for beauty, life, work, and family. For many, it was a symbolic representation of events in a woman's life; the celebrations of family, the beginnings and endings so common in everyday life.

Figure 5. Positioned Frame with Double Bordered Graphic.

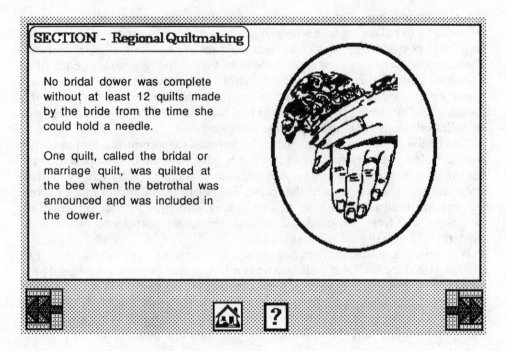

Figure 6. Positioned Frame with Oval Bordered Graphic.

Generally headings are centered and bold, sometimes even boxed. For long or complicated sequences, subheadings can be used that include numbers or roman numbers to aid the reader in visually following the general flow of information. As a general rule, information should flow from the top, left part of the screen to the bottom, right part of the screen because that is the way people in our dominant culture read. Figure 7 shows artistic variation that splits a title between the top and the bottom of the screen. Because the information flows from top left to bottom right, this title works. It also provides a subtle hint to the reader about the program content; both the title and the quilts discussed in the program must be pieced together to make a whole. Variations in standard layout can work if they have a purpose and fit the situation.

Good layout technique depends upon an understanding that not all computer frames are alike. Hannafin and Peck (1988) address transitional frames, instructional frames, and question frames. Transitional frames are used to tie together the different parts of a computerized lesson: they provide an orientation to the beginning and various sections within the program; serve as bridges between various topics or sections; provide feedback, directions, and instructions; and periodically present a progress report to let the user gauge success.

Instructional frames present basic information to the learner: these frames can alert the student to a need for prerequisite information; provide links between

A History of

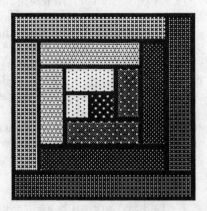

Quiltmaking

Figure 7. Left to Right Title Split.

relationships from past and current learning; and provide definitions, examples, and rules.

Question frames or criterion frames solicit input from the student to help individualize the instruction; these frames are usually based upon a true or false, yes or no, multiple choice, completion or short answer, or a constructed response which is considered to be a more open-ended answer.

There are also variations to the general type of frames. For example, some screens provide both instruction and a question on the same frame. Copy frames, prompt frames, hint frames, and interlaced frames are some types of variations (Hannafin & Peck, 1988). Copy frames provide information and a question about that information in the same screen. This type of format can be helpful in directing student attention, emphasizing important points, and for assuring a high degree of success for particular students. But because they are so obvious, copy frames are considered very elementary and need to be used sparely.

Prompt frames direct the learner to supply input; these can be used effectively for question or instructional screens. Hint frames are usually provided after a student has failed to enter an expected response; they offer guidance but do not supply the correct response. Interlaced frames are hybrids which combine various components from the standard frame types; they might include instruction, question, and feedback all on the same screen. This design can appear cluttered if not presented carefully but it has the advantage of allowing the student to visually examine and compare the question and feedback.

Each type of frame depends upon grouping of information in a way that visually aids the reader. To make optimal use of visual cues, it is helpful to design standard protocol for each type of frame and use it consistently throughout the program. Whatever protocol is chosen will need to comply with the overall program design. Programs that vary the screen location of pertinent information or procedures used to advance throughout the program can be confusing and frustrating (Mackey & Slesnick, 1982). Although standard protocol is necessary (Heines, 1984; Lentz, 1985; Simpson, 1984) designers can provide artistic variation to other parts of the screen. A comfortable mix of standard protocol and aesthetic variation will consider particular elements of good screen design.

Elements of Good Screen Design. Although variety is essential to stimulate the learner and obtain clear message delivery, there are several characteristics of good screen design that one needs to consider. This section presents several of the elements of optimal screen design. Many are equally important so these elements are not necessarily in any particular order. As the information is pieced together, remember that the desirable end result is a simple, consistent design that provides enough information while not being cluttered.

Unlike printed material which can be skimmed backward and forward for hints, the computer screen limits the reader's view of the overall content. This makes it particularly important to maintain clear, consistent frame protocol. Screen designs that make learners search for functions are frustrating while those that are simple, straight forward, and consistent can more easily lead to a successful experience. This does not mean that individual frames need to be boring; any graphics can certainly range from simple to complex without affecting the basic simplicity of the frame layout and user options.

Always available user options such as status lines, inform the reader of progress but perhaps even more important, they allow the reader a certain amount of control over the program direction. Status lines at the top or bottom of the screen should remain constant so that users always can know how to move about in the program and be able to determine their status in relation to the whole.

Menus should be clear, concise, uncluttered, and consistent. Icons within menus can be very helpful if the meaning of the icon is readily apparent; international symbols can work well. Menu screens can become cluttered and menuing systems can become excessively layered when providing for all of the possible choices. One partial solution to keeping menuing systems easy to use and looking clean is to design menus that pull down, temporarily revealing a selection of appropriate choices within any particular function. Shading of menu choices will quickly give a visual cue about which choices are currently available within any pull-down menu.

Text display can be difficult to read or easy to read, depending upon the font, the screen layout, and the contrast provided. To improve readability, text should be left justified, and limited to about 65 characters per line. Centering will work for lists, diagrams, or graphic mixes.

Ross and Morrison (1988) suggest using low-density text display, reducing sentences to one main idea, stripping off all extra wording, and using a hierarchical text display which is vertical and uses indentations similar to an outline. Soulier (1988) reminds us to use care when splitting lines so that phrases remain complete. Personal preference varies concerning single or double spacing of text; a good rule of thumb is to provide text breaks where the content allows.

Crowded, small text, or text that has either too sharp or too little contrast to the background can be difficult to read. Eyestrain cannot be blamed entirely on the text since the graphics and screen background can also influence legibility. Like video images, computer screens that use cool, neutral background colors like gray or blue are easier to read that those that use bright, very light, or very dark backgrounds.

Some tips from video production should be taken seriously and applied to computer screens as well. For example, text enhancements like drop shadows can make the text more legible; this is particularly true when using outline-style lettering (see Figure 7). Inverse lettering which switches the background and foreground colors can work well to briefly draw attention to a particular area of the screen. The same is true of flashing text but it can be irritating if it is overused, so proceed with caution and use this technique rarely.

Special techniques like zooming, panning, and tilting can vary the viewer's perspective of the image. These techniques originated with motion picture camera angles but can also be applied to computer screen design. For example, a particular section of the screen can be enlarged to give the user a close-up view of particular details while maintaining perspective on the whole image. Panning and tilting call for animating the image so that the viewer has a sense of following the image to the left, right, up, or down.

When computer graphics are broadcast for distance education, overscan and underscan considerations become important. These features are among those inherited from the world of broadcasting. Overscan and underscan are ways of adjusting the screen image so that edges of the frame look good no matter what small adjustments happen as the image is displayed on various equipment.

Overscan fills the screen beyond the edges so that no blank space will show around the edge later when the program is being used. Computer graphics need to be produced in overscan mode so that no blank edges or distracting video signals will show around the edges during transmission (Gibson & Mayta, 1992). Underscan protects a blank area around the screen edge so that images don't get cut off the transmission process; important information should be placed within a safe area, usually the middle two-thirds of the screen (Kemp, 1980). It is important to pay attention to both overscan and underscan because the desired result is neither an empty pocket around the around the screen nor loss of important information around the edges. One way to handle overscan and underscan variations is to use a border around screen; this fills the screen edge completely while marking the safe area.

Rate of display and pauses can influence the effectiveness of the program. The reader should control the rate when possible so that there is adequate time to read the text, interpret the graphics, and consider the meaning of the message.

Meaning of the Image

Information becomes valuable as it takes on meaning for an individual. Since visuals are meant to aid in the discovery of meaning, it follows that well-designed visuals will help students interpret the meaning.

Learning from the Image

Computer images have a wide variety of possible designs and implications for usage. Images can be portrayed as static or dynamic, concrete or abstract. An image can change as a result of user interaction with the program. To make effective use of images, designers need to consider the intended message, the type of graphic, and the influence of layout on the impact or interpretation of the image.

Layout must consider the principles of perceptual organization, which include similarity, proximity, continuity, and closure (Bloomer, 1976). These four processes, by which the mind organizes meaning, depend on how physically close the objects are, how similar they are, whether there is a continuous line to guide the eye, and whether the minimal amount of information is present that is necessary to obtain meaning or closure. Comprehension is directly affected by the way the mind organizes meaning from the placement of graphics and text.

Computer Creation of Data Displays

Powerful computer software allows for the creation of visual data displays that were difficult or impossible to produce in the past. Computer-generated graphs are being presented on screens within computer-based instruction and they are being produced on other media by using the computer as a production device. Since the graphic software is publicly available, anyone can produce data graphs; the practice is no longer limited to use by trained professionals. Special applications are the exception. For example some scientists, medical personnel and other select specialists now can visualize data that was previously limited to numerical reporting. It follows that some design guidelines are needed.

Computer Graphs. There is a wide selection of software that produces graphs to tabulate or represent data. These data displays can take the form of circle or pie graphs, bar or chart graphs, line graphs, histograms, and scatterplots, among others. The ease of creation does not always result in good, meaningful graphics. It is important to follow some common-sense approaches to graphical data display, whether the information is to be used on or off the screen.

Edward Tufte is an expert on the visual display of quantitative data. Tufte (1983) states that simple is better when displaying data; use only those dimensions and colors that are necessary to convey the message. Three–dimensional graphs should not be used unless the third dimension represents a third aspect of the data interpretation. Likewise, color should not be used for prettiness, but because of a need for contrast or to aid the reader to obtain meaning. To help illustrate the point, some poor graphs and some better graphs are provided, each presenting the same information in a different way.

The various graphic examples all illustrate the rate of ticket sales at Kansas State University (KSU) over the last twenty years. The horizontal scale reflects two-year intervals and the vertical scale shows increments of 5,000 tickets sold.

Figure 8 displays the original graph printed in a local newspaper (Seaton, 1992). It is cluttered, numerals are redundant, the horizontal scale is inconsistent, the title is within the graph, the legend is scattered throughout the data, and the accompanying article disagrees with the displayed information (the full text of the article is not contained here, only the title). The caption below the graph appears to be not centered but that is not a flaw; it is the title of the accompanying article in its original placement on the newspaper column. The reason that it appears here is because it does not match the information provided in the graph. The article title and the text of the article claim that football ticket sales have increased for the 1992 season over the 1991 season. However, there is no data provided for the rate of 1992 ticket sales within the graph nor within the article.

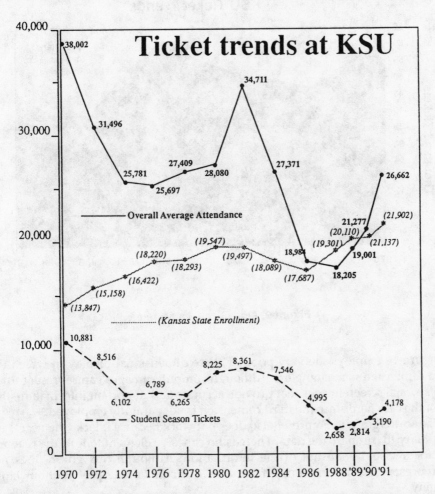

Ticket sales show increase over 1991

Figure 8. Cluttered Graph.

It is confusing that the graph goes out of its way to vary to horizontal scale, yet omits 1992 information. What has happened here is that an article has been written and uses a graph for supportive visual information, but that visual information is unusable due to lack of complete data. The reader must sift through unnecessary visual clutter and hope to properly interpret the graph, only to find that the comparative information is missing in the end.

Figures 9, 10, and 11 provide alternate displays to the same information. All three are poor representations. Figure 9 uses an area map that confuses the data points needed for proper interpretation. Area maps are often substituted for line graphs, probably because people like the way they look but they fail to interpret the information.

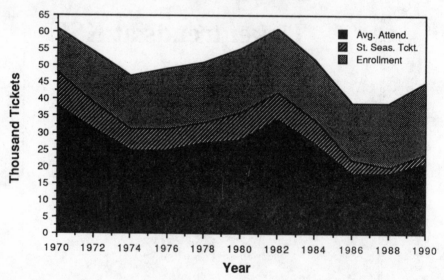

Figure 9. Area Graph, Inaccurate.

Figure 10 employs the very popular three dimensional display in which the third dimension is meaningless. Although computer images can represent three dimensional screen images that provide accurate and important information, that is not the case here since the third dimension is not gainfully employed.

The scattergram in Figure 11 also does not work because it lacks the necessary continuity to compare the data. There is no cohesive element to lead the reader's eye for a visual snapshot of the information. Although this graph does not misrepresent the information, it remains difficult to interpret without close scrutiny.

As a contrast to those graphs that do not work well, the graphs in Figures 12 and 13 work better. Although they are not perfect, each of them presents the three pieces of information in a way that can be interpreted from the visual pattern. Both are a visual improvement over the original graph presented in the

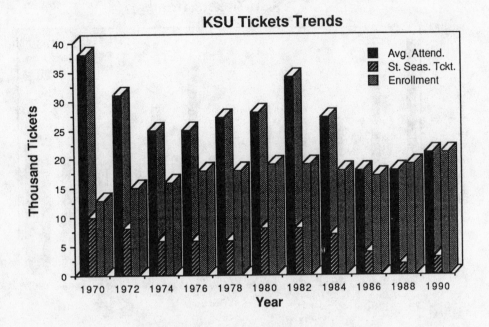

Figure 10. Graph with Excessive Dimensions.

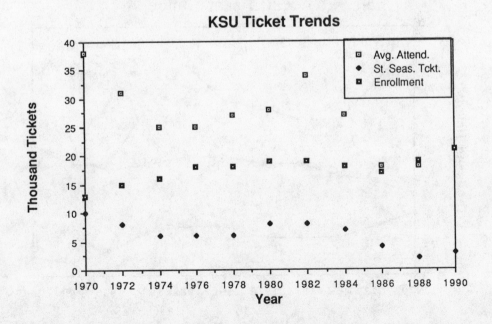

Figure 11. Scattergram, Lacks Continuity.

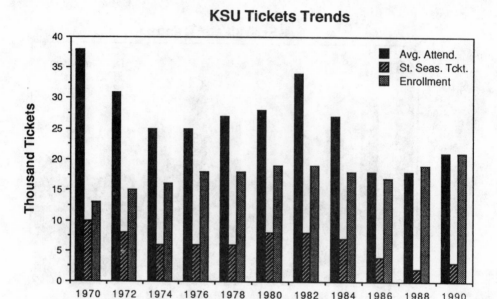

Figure 12. Chart Graph.

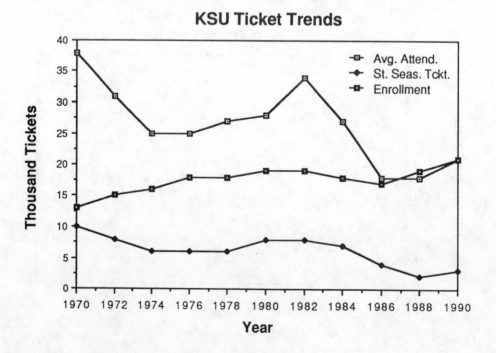

Figure 13. Line Graph.

newspaper, but neither presents the necessary 1992 data which remains a mystery.

The critical point here is that visual information is frequently misrepresented by lay people who produce data graphs without the benefit of being visually literate. This practice can be dangerous since it can confuse and mislead consumers. Computers are not responsible for poor visual design, but they make it possible for uninformed users to produce inadequate products. Let's look now at another type of computer graphic display called data visualization.

Data Visualization. Data visualization is a way of capturing data as it is produced and recording it in a digitized format that can be displayed as an image instead of a series of numbers. With this type of procedure, data from scientific events can be visualized in a symbolic, digitized way that can seem more understandable to the lay audience and to professionals who prefer to interpret data visually as opposed to numerically. For example, data visualization can show a tornado in action. Instead of seeing only the result of a tornado, the visual display of the tornado's dynamics allow scientists to study the patterns of wind, motion, and behavior of tornadoes in a way that could only be interpreted before from numerical recordings. The visualization shows the tornado in action, by using digitized computer imagery.

There are several applications of data visualization, with more being developed every day. Some examples of data visualization are: recording and visually displaying symbolic imagery about specific atmospheric information which is collected from another planet via satellite measurements; visualizing the result of a simple physics experiment by collecting the data points and visually displaying of the upward and downward trajectory of a ball as it is tossed into the air from a moving object, such as a train traveling at a certain speed; visual display of possible outcomes of automobile accidents occurring between a certain number of automobiles with specific characteristics, traveling at a particular speed under given road conditions, etc. This last sort of visual information could be used to solve mysteries about how accidents happened for law enforcement or insurance purposes, or it could be used by automobile manufacturers who seek to design safer vehicles.

The difference between data visualization and display of graphic data in the standard types of graphs is that data visualization displays images of an event in action, while a data graph displays patterns of numerical information resulting from the event. Data visualization is creating somewhat of a controversy because some scientists do not want to accept it as a valid method of displaying scientific data. Even though the general public can better understand a data visualization than a set of numbers, certain scientific purists claim that visualization is inferior to the numerical measurement displays. These objections are not necessarily well grounded, but they most likely reflect a set of values that fear removal of the traditional professional skill required to interpret the standard numerical data.

People need to know that there is something between the two extremes of data visualization and lists of numbers; in the middle lie the various common graphs that so many people have come to rely upon. However, those graphs cannot display the type of information discussed here.

Power of the Image

Computer graphics and appropriate screen display lend power to communications by adding an image to the text. Images can represent realistic data or they can conjure up imaginary situations through artificial imagery called virtual reality.

Realistic Data Display

Visual images can aid message interpretation and enhance learning. They can also add power to the message by providing an emotional element that is beyond that of other communication strategies. Realism can be enhanced by providing a graphic component.

Because computers support visual images from other sources, it is possible to display still or dynamic photos of real events. These events and their results can combine with text and audio segments to provide a sense of realism to the user that otherwise would not be possible. For example, the *ABC News* videodisc provides real news footage, not just of newsroom reporting but of visual field events. Visual display of these events add realism and understanding, but beyond that they can stir emotions for various reasons.

Tapping the Imagination with Artificial Reality

Virtual reality offers the opportunity to remove a person from the real environment and create a feeling of living within an artificial mode. Some examples of this sort of application include specific video arcade games, airplane simulators, and architectural design software. All of these examples have one thing in common, that which makes them virtual reality environments.

Within virtual environments created by the computer, participants become part of the software environment and feel as though they are within the computerized image that is displayed. Rather than viewing the image from without, the participants change perspective and view the image from within the software.

For example, arcade games in which the player becomes part of the game, as opposed to manipulating the game as a viewer, employ virtual reality. Instead of manipulating a lever and observing the result of its movement on a screen-displayed baseball game, the player might wear a viewing device over the eyes and a manipulative device such as a data glove to control a particular action within the game. The viewing device limits the player's view to the three-dimensional image of the game and the data glove produces simulated movements within the game based upon a realistic motion of the player's hand or arm, such as throwing a ball. This produces the feeling of actually playing the game.

Virtual reality is used within high-class pilot training in which the trainee obtains the feeling of actually flying the aircraft. Placed within a simulated cockpit the realistic knobs, switches and levers (pilot control devices) become the input devices, while the flight control panel and the windshield become the viewing devices where the pilot observes the effect of control movements. Not only does the control panel light up appropriately, but its gauges reflect the trainee's actions at the flight controls, while the control panel displays various maps of the flight path and even simulates a radar screen. All the while, the pilot views the surroundings through the simulated windshield and can observe other airborne craft in the immediate area as well as the appropriate ground activity based upon the altitude, speed, weather conditions, and general visibility being simulated. This type of pilot training usually progresses in stages from standard classroom training, to traditional computer-based training, and then on to the flight simulator for the artificial practice flight, prior to engaging in a training sortie in a real aircraft.

The third virtual reality example, architectural software, produces the ability for the common consumer to obtain the feeling of entering and moving around within an environment prior to its actual construction. A good example of this type of application is a department store which creates custom-designed kitchens. A customer can don a viewing helmet and a body movement probe in order to try out a new kitchen prior to its actual construction. Sophisticated software allows the customer to try different room arrangements while doing such things as stretching to reach the highest shelf or testing the comfort of the counter height and drawer positions.

These virtual environments are digitized images that not only display information to the visual senses, but allow the user to participate in the resulting display by contributing other communication strategies such as movement or speech. These images can get very complicated and can stray from the standard rules of computer screen design. Certainly artificial reality opens new doors for visual communications with computer input and display devices.

Summary

This chapter has addressed instructional design of effective computerized images from the standpoint of structure, meaning, and power. The structure of the image considers both the components of computer images and the elements of good screen design. It is the interplay of both that produce effective computer displays.

Sophisticated software, a wide variety of media options, and knowledge learned about computer communications offer the ability to improve screen design as well as products produced with the aid of computers. Today, more graphics are mixed with text than in the past but text display remains a very important part of computer communications.

Meaningful communication occurs when the message impacts the reader from a cognitive or visual perspective. In order to embrace some degree of meaning for the user, computer graphic displays need to follow some rules of good design.

Finally, computer imagery lends power to the message through the visual element of understanding and emotion. The imagery can represent real situations or it can create an artificial situation that appears to be real. Still in its infancy, artificial reality is limited in applications and accessibility, yet its future potential is tremendous in terms of visual communications.

Figures 5, 6, 7 with permission of Barbara E. Menzel.

References

Bloomer, C. M. (1976). *Principles of visual perception.* New York: Reinhold.

Boyle, M. W. (1986). Hemispheric laterality as a basis of learning: What we know and don't know. In G. D. Phye & T. Andre (Eds.), *Cognitive classroom learning: Understanding, thinking, and problem solving.* San Diego, CA: Academic Press.

Dwyer, F. M. (1978). *Strategies for improving visual learning.* State College, PA: Learning Services.

Gibson, R., & Mayta, M. (1992, August). *Designing computer-based instructional graphics for distance education.* Paper presented at the Eighth Annual Conference on Distance Teaching and Learning, Madison, WI.

Hannafin, M., & Peck, K. (1988). *The design, development, and evaluation of instructional software.* New York: Macmillan Publishing Co.

Hartley, J. (1987). Designing electronic text: The role of print-based research. *Educational Communications and Technology Journal, 35*(1), 3–17.

Hathaway, M. D. (1984, January). Variables of computer screen display and how they affect learning. *Educational Technology, 7–11.*

Heines, J. (1984). *Screen design strategies for computer-assisted instruction.* Bedford, MA: Digital Press.

Kemp, J. (1980). *Planning and producing audiovisual materials* (4th ed.). New York: Harper & Row.

Kemp, J., & Dayton, D. (1985). *Planning and producing instructional media* (5th ed.). New York: Harper & Row.

Lentz, R. (1985). Designing computer screen displays. *Performance and Instruction, 24* (1), 16–17.

Mackey, K., & Slesnick, T. (1982). A style manual for authors of software. *Creative Computing, 8,* 110–111.

Morrison, G. R., Ross, S. M., & O'Dell, J. K. (1988). Text density level as a design variable in instructional displays. *Educational Communications and Technology Journal, 36*(1), 103–115.

Mourant, S. J., Lakshmanan, R., & Chantadisai, R. (1981). Visual fatigue and cathode ray tube display terminals. *Human Factors, 23,* 529–540.

Nygard, K. E., & Ranganathan, B. (1983, Spring). A system for generating instructional computer graphics. *AEDS Journal, 16*(3), 177–187.

Parker, R. C. (1987). *The Aldus guide to basic design.* Seattle, WA: Aldus Corporation.

Reinking, D. (1986). Integrating graphic aids into content area instruction: The graphic information lesson. *Journal of Reading, 30*(2), 146–151.

Ross, S., & Morrison, G. (1988). Adapting instruction to learner performance and background variables. In D. H. Jonassen (Ed.), *Instructional designs for microcomputer courseware* (pp. 227–245). Hillsdale, NJ: Lawrence Erlbaum Associates.

Ross, S. M., Morrison, G. R., & O'Dell, J. K. (1988). Obtaining more out of less text in CBI: Effects of varied text density levels as a function of learner characteristics and control strategy. *Educational Communications and Technology Journal, 36*(3), 131–142.

Seaton, J. (1992, September 4). Ticket sales show increase over 1991. *The Manhattan Mercury*, p. 7.

Simpson, H. (1984). A human-factors style guide for program display. In D. F. Walker & R. D. Hess (Eds.), *Instructional software: Principles and perspectives for design and use.* Belmont, CA: Wadsworth.

Singer, H., & Donlan, D. (1980). *Reading and learning from text.* Boston, MA: Little, Brown.

Soulier, J. S. (1988). *The design and development of computer based instruction.* Newton, MA: Allyn & Bacon.

Tufte, E. (1983). *The visual display of quantitative information.* Cheshire, CT: Graphics Press.

Wager, W., & Gagné, R. (1988). Designing computer-aided instruction. In D. H. Jonassen (Ed.), *Instructional designs for microcomputer courseware* (pp. 35–60). Hillsdale, NJ: Lawrence Erlbaum Associates.

SECTION V

Use of Visuals

Barbara Fredette states "The use of visuals in schools is most frequently related to their significance as exemplars of knowledge. ..." The use of visuals in schools as a basis for problem solving for thinking at higher levels is evident less frequently. TO SEE IS TO THINK should be encouraged as a complement of equal status to TO SEE IS TO KNOW. Her chapter has three major sections. The first section introduces the reader to the visual environment of schools and of classrooms. Section two presents six aspects of using visuals in schools. Fredette refers to this as the "6w" approach.

The third section introduces the notion that although visuals in schools are thought of as tools for teaching and learning, images can and should be considered as objects in and of themselves. A systematic approach to 'reading pictures' that has been developed and used by the author is described in detail.

Robert Griffin contends that there is widespread use of visualization in the business and industrial community to communicate information. Because of this, emphasis should be placed on understanding how to use visuals effectively. Several media formats are discussed and it is noted that although the overhead slide (transparency) is currently the most used business visual, the electronic visual is becoming increasingly popular.

Since many people are not familiar with business presentations as a form of communication, Griffin addresses five of the most commonly asked questions:

- How important are visuals to the business presentation?
- What are the most common types of business visuals?
- What purpose do visuals serve in the business presentation?
- What are computer generated business graphics?
- How do business people learn to visualize?

Richard Couch, Edward Caropreso, and Helen B. Miller in their chapter emphasize the need for better prepared visual consumers. They begin their discussion of creativity and visuals by pointing out the degree to which the visual media permeate our lives and explain that our interpretation of these visual messages influences our daily behavior. As media become more sophisticated, technically and visually, it is imperative that we learn how to interpret these messages in meaningful ways. By its very nature, making meaning is a creative process.

Creativity is defined in terms of two models of creative thinking and is operationalized in relation to visual learning. The discussion defines visual literacy and proceeds to focus on specific ways in which people can enhance their ability to become effective visual consumers. The authors outline four steps related to becoming more creative "consumers" of visual messages.

Chapter Fourteen

Use of Visuals in Schools (Curriculum and Instruction)

Barbara W. Fredette

Objectives

After reading this chapter, you should be able to:

1. *Name the different types of visual images accessible to classrooms.*

2. *List several uses of visuals for instructional purposes.*

3. *Analyze the content of a visual (be able to identify meaning dimensions that are available in it).*

4. *Describe as well as use a systematic approach to interpreting visuals.*

5. *Consider developmental differences in selecting visuals.*

6. *Discuss the selection of visuals for specific learning purposes.*

Introduction

TO SEE IS TO KNOW. Walk into any school. What you see tells you immediately what is valued in that setting. Enter a classroom in that school. There you will see the extent to which the selection and use of visual materials is based on conscious deliberate decisions or, instead, on the accidental or incidental opportunity to display visuals. When you see what visuals are given prominence and when you see how teachers use visuals in their classroom you know something about the importance of visuals in that setting.

TO SEE IS TO THINK. Visuals should be selected to encourage students to think about what they are seeing in relation to the content they are learning. The selection process is guided by teachers' understanding of the types and functions of visuals as well by their knowledge of contents and the developmental levels of their students.

The ability to learn from visuals is determined by two important factors; what the learner knows and what skills the learner has acquired for 'reading' the meanings encoded in visuals. Another important factor is the strategy the teacher uses to guide or direct the learner's perceptual attention to the critical attributes of the visual material.

> the better an object or event is perceived, according to the ... principles of perception, the more feasible and reliable will be further cognitive processes....
> (Fleming & Levie, 1978, p. 88)

This chapter is arranged around three major components which include; the effects of the visual environments of schools, the uses of visuals in schools which is organized around six questions about selecting visuals, and a consideration of visuals as objects which includes a description of a systematic approach to reading pictures. For the purposes of this discussion the term 'Visuals' refers to pictorial and graphic representations of information as well as three-dimensional objects/ displays but not to alpha-numeric materials.

The Visual Environment of Schools

A school's values are made explicit in the visual 'face' that is put forward for public view. When you enter a school the first sensory impact you may receive is the smell of the disinfectant used to cleanse the halls, but the one that remains longer in memory is the visual information you receive. In high schools you will probably find trophies representing the athletic prowess of past students. Portraits of administrators or others who have had a major impact on the school may also be present. If you want to see the work of students you will probably have to find the art room or 'suite' where current work may be displayed in the hall outside of it. I recently found an exception to this usual scene. The art room was located across from the office and the entry hall was lined with cases displaying students' art work. This school is an exception, it is not the rule.

Art rooms, where most of the explicit instruction in visual literacy takes place, are seldom close to the school's entrance because as we all know art is noisy and messy. In some schools you may find the work of contemporary artists or reproductions of well-known artists' work. If these are located in the halls for all students to see, it tells us one thing; if they are found only in the administrative offices, it tells us another. The excuse for visually sterile halls as a way of circumventing vandalism is an empty one. Everyone can identify at least one example where the most recalcitrant students learned to value and respect their own and others' visual products.

Elementary schools usually provide a different 'face' to visitors. While the visual sterility of some schools can be blamed on the janitor or the fire marshal, in many more you will be likely to find children's work displayed. The type of work that is displayed will give you an important value message. Does the work displayed show individually different ideas or does it represent repetitions of a single idea? I recall a late September visit to an elementary school. The vision of

26 versions of three sprigs of goldenrod assails my visual memory. Another example that comes to mind involved one of my young students who described to me his summer camp experience where he was instructed to use a pattern to make a Scotty dog tie holder. With eyes wide he told me; "You wouldn't like it at all, the only way you could be creative was if you made a mistake!" Visual materials which encourage stereotypes must be discouraged. See Figure 1.

Figure 1. Visual Materials Which Stereotype Must Be Discouraged.

In contrast to these examples in many elementary schools you can find delightful displays of individually different expressions. Through the products they display in the schools' halls teachers demonstrate to their students as well as to the public which they value more: individually different visual ideation or the importance of following directions.

The same criteria holds true when you visit an elementary classroom; do the childrens' products reflect individual visual problem solving or are they versions of the teachers directed or dictated ideas? Another aspect to consider about the visuals in an elementary classroom is quantity. How many does it take to make the room visually alive? When it comes to visuals in the classroom some may be good, but more may not be better. I have visited some visually impacted early childhood and elementary classrooms where I have been tempted to shut my eyes just so that I could concentrate on what was being said. As a result of these experiences, I have wondered whether the cumulative impact on students of excessive visual noise in their learning environment should be studied. It is common knowledge that students can concentrate on content in aurally noisy environments (doing homework with music blaring) but is the same true of visual noise? It is possible that the developing selectivity of the perceptual process may counter the effects of what this viewer sees as excessive visual stimulation for young learners. However, a caution is in order. The influence of the quantitative visual effects of the learning environment on their students' perceptual development should be considered by teachers as a factor in the 'deciding what to show' process. An informal assessment of what children can recall seeing may help in these decisions.

The Visual Environment of Students

Our students' environment is multidimensional. One of the most important dimensions is that of the information which they must access for a variety of living and learning purposes. The world of information for today's students is very different from what it was twenty or even ten years ago. At that time most of the significant information was in verbal form. That is not true today. White (1987) spoke of the "need to redefine and to rethink the nature of information itself" (p. 41). She went on to say that "the change in information is a shift from print to imagery as the medium for information delivery, transformation, and exchange" (p. 41). This relocation of emphasis onto imagery, she says, "is affecting deeply how we see our world, how we think about it, and therefore how we behave toward it" (p. 41).

White (1987) suggests that public education does not seem to be aware of the significance of these changes. As she puts it: "if these changes were taken as seriously as they should be, they would require us to rethink the heart of education itself. Instead education is treating the technologies as just another adjunct to the traditional triad of textbook, teacher, and test" (p. 57). She proposes that a specific curriculum should be "designed to educate for these changes" (p. 41).

Learning from images is different from learning from print. In print we learn from static lines which are dictated by the technology of the printing press. We learn to sequence information and as a consequence to think in linear, sequential ways. On the other hand, electronic imagery is transient. In order to comprehend imagery we must be able to process images simultaneously or to use a computer metaphor, we must process them in a parallel fashion (White, 1987).

These are two different ways of learning and, as a result, two different ways of thinking. The traditional way of thinking in a linear fashion, represented by an hierarchical outline may be replaced, or at least complemented, by a relational, interdependent mode of thinking with interactive images. Salomon (1979) acknowledged this effect when he determined that different media lead to different ways of knowing as well as to different knowledge. Another way of putting it is to suggest that a technology is not only a window through which we may learn but that the learning itself is a mirror image of the technology. In conclusion, White (1987) suggests an important position for teachers to take in acknowledging the visual imagery world of their students.

> Whether imagery proves to be the fruitful tool we wish, or not, it is certain to become the major information carrier—in fact, it already is. We need to recognize that fact, educate our society to understand imagery as we once taught the reading of print, and begin serious analysis of what it means for a world to learn about itself from images. (White, 1987, p. 60)

Use of Visuals in Schools

In an attempt to help the reader to acquire a clear picture of a complex subject, I have devised the "6W Approach to Using Visuals." The six areas or topics that comprise this system are listed below with brief descriptions of the related content that will be selectively covered in each of them.

1. WHAT TO USE—characteristics of visuals, types of visual media
2. WHEN TO USE—selection based on teaching/learning objectives
3. WHY TO USE—purposes for selecting visuals
4. WAYS TO USE—teaching strategies, tasks
5. WHO WILL USE—developmental and individual differences in students
6. WHERE TO USE—environmental considerations in selection

It is expected that elaborating on each of these areas or topics will result in a comprehensive view of the subject. Although the six are given in a linear list there is little basis for assuming a hierarchical relationship among them. This is a morphological rather than an operational construct. There is obvious overlap between and interaction among these topics. It is also acknowledged that a comprehensive coverage of each would result in a complete text rather than a chapter. What follows is a selected sample of significant information for each topic.

WHAT Types of Visual Media to Use

Many different types of visuals are accessible to most classroom situations. They may be categorized by their major presentation characteristics. For example, Seels and Glasgow (1991) identify traditional visual media options as: Projected Visuals: Static which includes opaque or overhead projection as well as slides and filmstrips. They identify film and television as Projected Visuals: Dynamic. Non-projected Visuals are identified as pictures, photographs, charts-graphs-diagrams, and displays (which includes feltboards and bulletin boards). Locatis and Atkinson (1984) have two categories for essentially visual media, they are: Graphic and Object Media and Photographic Media. For their purposes Graphic Media are identified as two dimensional (pictorial) illustrations and (three dimensional) Objects are the real thing or representations of it. (Note: Many references refer to objects as "realia.")

In the Locatis and Atkinson text photographic media are categorized into still (print and projected) and motion. The characteristics and forms or formats of all of these visual media are described with many exemplars in this text. Anderson (1983), in *Selecting and Developing Media for Instruction*, classifies visuals as Projected Still Visuals and Motion Visuals. He includes drawings and photographs in Printed Material.

Categorizing visual as well as all other media in terms of their physical attributes is a common practice for those who wish to guide the media selecting process. See Seels and Glasgow (1991) or Gagné, Briggs, and Wager (1979) for more systematic approaches to the Instructional Design process. In some ways these lists are similar to the printed pads which list all the categories of items you might wish to buy in a supermarket. They help to nudge your memory of the scope that is accessible but they don't do much in the way of helping you to choose, to make a specific selection. Other facets of the instructional uses of visuals must enter into the decision-making process, for example, the goals or objectives of the instruction.

WHEN to Use Visual Concept Acquisition

Visual instructional materials are called for in many different learning situations. Traditionally visual media have been suggested when students need to learn concrete concepts (such as identification or classification) or when they must identify spatial relationships. Motor or process skills are also best learned as demonstration shown through visual media. Whenever visual distinction must be made visual media are appropriate memory.

Visuals are very useful in learning tasks which involve memory. The information received from visuals appears to remain longer in memory. Baggett (1989) tells us that information obtained visually is more memorable, or in her word, "bushier." "Visual material creates in memory far broader nets of associations for already learned concepts. There are more connections in the memory representation when the input is visual" (Baggett, 1989, p. 119). Kozma (1991) contends that the "bushier nature of representations derived from the visual symbol systems are better for building mental models of the situation than are representations based on audio-linguistic information" (p. 192). Visuals are shown to assist the recall of verbal material by helping the learner establish associated mental images. Levie (1987) cites Levin and Pressley's studies which show that mnemonic pictures are useful in tasks which require rote or list learning such as capitals of states or U.S. presidents.

Much research supports the contention that our recognition memory for pictures is far superior to our memory for words. While this factor may support and encourage the instructional use of pictorial materials, it should be noted that though recognition is an act of remembering, we should not confuse it with our power of recall. Many variables may influence the outcomes of visualized instruction, especially when it is recall and not recognition that is desired. The amount of detail to include is one of these variables. This variable comes into play when the teacher must decide whether the learning objectives call for a richly detailed photograph or, instead, a simple graphic representation such as a line drawing.

Dwyer's extensive research in visualized instruction is reviewed by Levie (1987) who cites the general finding (from over 200 different experiments) that "pictures are most helpful in achieving objectives that entail visual discriminations (such as studying the parts of the heart). Line drawings are more effective when study time is limited but more realistic versions can be effective when the student has more time to spend with them" (p. 16).

Many of the visual materials used in schools will be found in conjunction with words and, especially in the upper grades, most of these will be found in textbooks. Showing the relationship between words and things through pictures is a practice which has an historic precedent originating with Comenius who created *Orbis Pictus* to help his students learn Latin vocabulary. The contemporary use of illustrations in texts serves several purposes although Peeck (1987) writes that two characteristics of text pictures comprise all of the roles and effects of illustrations. The first characteristic is that they illustrate some aspects of the text. The second is that they add something to what is found in the text alone.

This added something has been investigated by Levin, Anglin, and Carney (1987), who in the analysis of text illustrations found that they served five functions. These are: decoration, representation, organization, interpretation, and transformation. Except for the first, decoration, these functions serve to assist the student in constructing knowledge from the text materials. Illustrations that 'tell' essentially the same story of the text are representational. This category could coincide with Knowlton's Realistic Pictures, but illustrations may be representations of imaginative constructs, in which case they would not be iconic or realistic. The organization function is served by illustrations which show the relationship between several parts or steps in a process described in the text. Step by step diagrams or consecutive pictures of procedures or illustrations of complex objects which have been described in detail are referred to as organizational because they assist the reader in acquiring an internalized image. Knowlton exemplified his 'logical pictures' with abstract graphs or diagrams which were abstract representations of organization. However, illustrations which serve an organizational function may be realistic representations as when a sequence of photographs shows how to bake a cake or a set of drawings illustrates the steps in the etching (drypoint) process (see Figure 2).

Interpretational pictures help to clarify conceptually dense prose. Visual analogies are often used as interpretational pictures because they are a way of giving concrete form to abstract concepts or ideas. For example, in order to help students to consider long term versus short term basis for decisions they may be asked if they would go with the ants working toward a goal in the future or seize the day and play with the grasshopper (see Figure 3).

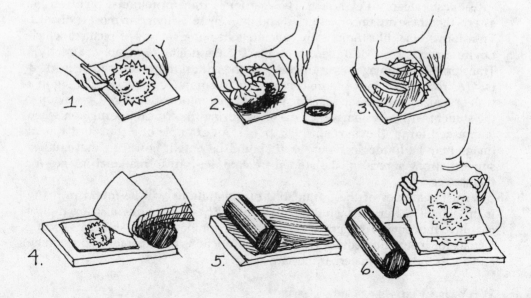

Figure 2. Illustrations Serving an Organizational Structure.

Figure 3. Example of an Interpretational Illustration.

Knowlton's category of Analogic pictures is interpretational. "A visual analogy is a picture of one thing used to explain something else ... the thing that the visual analogy describes may be a concrete object, a process, a concept or an idea" (Visual Education Curriculum Project, 1981, p. 14).

The last category Levin *et al.* (1987) offer is transformational pictures. He asserts that these are unconventional and unlikely to be found in most textbooks. Transformational illustrations are concrete mnemonic images or pictures which Levin asserts are "designed to impact on student's memory directly." Transformational images assist memory of the critical information to be learned by "(A) recoding it into a more concrete and memorable form, (B) relating in a well-organized context the separate pieces of that information and (C) providing the student with a systematic means of retrieving the critical information when later asked for it" (Levin *et al.*, 1987, p. 61). An example of a transformational image may be found in Figure 4. It should be noted, however, that studies suggest stronger recall if the students create the transformational images for themselves.

Visual examples of these functions of illustrations will be found in many instructional materials including textbooks. These functions also exemplify cognitive functions. Teachers who are interested in developing skills in selecting visuals for instruction could use these five functions of illustration to examine and assess the visual materials they are using.

WHY Use Visuals

To a large extent this topic overlaps with that of the former one—when to use visuals. However, in this section, I intend to be more specific in terms of

Figure 4. Example of a Transformational Illustration.

instructional purposes which may be served with visuals. Another way of differentiating between the two topics is to recognize that in WHEN TO USE VISUALS, I addressed the learners' mental functioning in relation to visuals, while in this section, I will pay more attention to the teaching purposes. I will address the utilization of visuals as teaching tools.

In 1978, a survey of 72 sixth through ninth grade teachers in Adelaide, Australia revealed the purposes for which pictures (in this case, photographs) were used in their classrooms. An informal replication of this survey has been conducted by students in my classes in Visual Thinking with surprisingly similar results.

- For display only, to add decoration   40%
- For motivation, stimulate incidental learning   22%
- To illustrate selected main points   30%
- To supplement verbal through elaboration   6%
- As a main information source   2%
  (Visual Education Curriculum Project, 1980, p. 20)

It is obvious that there is a potential for the extended use of pictures in classrooms which has yet to be realized. A heightened awareness of the possibilities or potential uses of visual material is needed. Toward this end I have developed the following checklist which I use with teachers to encourage them to examine their own practices with regard to visual images—pictures and photographs—in the classrooms. See Figure 5.

USES OF IMAGES FOR LEARNING

I use images:	frequently	often	sometimes	seldom	never	Briefly identify a specific instance- content or concept
• as illustration						
• as a source of stimulation						
• to solve problems						
• to build new experiences						
• to provide background information						
• for verification and additional research						
• to encourage the expression and clarification of opionions						
• to assist in concept development						
• as a source for comparison and contrast						
• to prevent and correct misconceptions						
• to summarize a topic						
• for evaluation of learning						

Figure 5. Checklist of Visual Images in the Classroom.

The list is a synthesis of lists found in Dwyer (1978, p. 12) and in the Visual Education Curriculum Project (1981, p. 20) with my experience observing the visual environment of classrooms. The checklist serves the purpose of awakening teachers to the potential uses of visuals. Specific examples of the ways teachers have put these uses into practice are also productive.

WAYS to Use Visuals

Levie (1987) reviews theoretical positions on what it means to 'perceive a picture.' Winner (1982) reviews these theories with more examples, in a chapter entitled "What's in a Picture." Because of the seeming simplicity of the perceptual process of seeing a picture, it is important for teachers to have some notion of the actual complexity of the process to 'ground' their picture-using practices with students.

Visual materials such as photographs or pictures may be used at each level of a plan for instruction. They may be used for motivation or to stimulate student interest in a topic. A history lesson is introduced several days in advance by a portrait posted on the bulletin board with the caption: "Do you know this person, and what she did?" Student curiosity may be aroused by pictures showing unusual views or extreme close ups of common objects. Closeups encourage close observation, an important visual skill (see Figure 6).

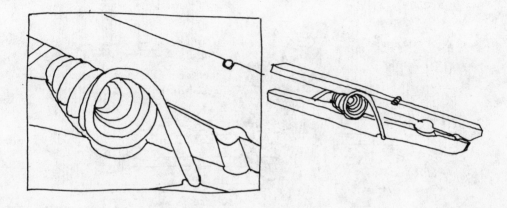

Figure 6. Closeups Encourage Observation.

Visual materials are often used for induction activities in a lesson but teachers with awareness of the potential for visualized instruction also use them for transitions as well as for the major focus of the learning activity itself. Visualized closure (feedback) for a lesson has been found to be satisfactory to a greater number of students than an oral closing statement. Visualized evaluation (testing) is being used more often, perhaps as a result of easier reproduction technologies for visuals. It is appropriate and essential to test visual learning by visual means.

New patterns of classroom interaction, such as cooperative learning, are suitable for practice in visual problem solving. An inquiry process centered on a picture or photograph can require close observation of detail and interpretation of findings. Cooperative learning is a good strategy to use for this purpose. Pairs of students in a class studying local architecture were given enlarged photos of local structure and a set of questions posed as though they were interviewing the building itself, e.g., "How old are you?" See Figure 7 for an example used with students studying Grecian History.

Imagery related thinking is apparent in new strategies for teaching higher level thinking. The inquiring school approach engages the students in creating webs of meaning for target concepts. From the web, related ideas are woven together in a process called weave. The teachers who use this approach identify these forms as "images used for learning" (personal report). An extensive

Figure 7. Example of Visual Used in a Cooperative Learning Setting.

examination of graphic forms which represent many types of thinking processes may be found in Clarke (1990).

Visual aids which are designed for specific instructional purposes are usually limited to those uses. In contrast, complex visual images such as works of art, or non didactic films or videos, can be used for different purposes by different teachers. For example, a film of France can be shown by a social studies teacher without the sound track so that the teacher and the students can add explanation to the imagery. The art teacher can focus on segments of the same film which show the great cathedrals of France.

In discussing ways to use visual images as teaching tools it may be useful to consider those particular types of (static not dynamic) images which are most accessible to classroom teacher. I am referring to 'found images,' that is, the images that are found in periodicals, newspapers, magazines, junk mail, and any other source of pictorial material. It is quickly apparent to any school visitor that, except for the student work, 'found images' are the largest source of static, or still, pictorial material in the classroom. Among the 'found' images that may be considered useful in the classroom are advertisements. These can actually be one of the most useful image sources for instruction. Language teachers find them particularly useful and not just for vocabulary. Advertisements are also cultural messages—a comparison of advertisements from two different countries will quickly reveal that aspect of them. Advertisements are also effectively used by teachers to teach about values and stereotypes. Found images tend to be fragile, so if they are going to be handled, they need to be mounted and laminated before being used for instructional purposes.

WHO Will Use the Visuals

When a group of 35 elementary teaching interns were asked what they would expect to find in an article written to help them select visual materials for the classroom, over a third of them expected to find information about developmental differences in the use of visuals (from a survey by author during 1992). Young children, even those not exposed to pictures, can recognize the objects that are shown in pictures; they do not have to be taught to do so. Winner (1982) cites evidence of studies with infants which suggest that this capability may even be present at birth. However, it must be kept in mind that the pictures used in these studies are simple realistic representations. Pictures which are limited, that is "impoverished" depictions or pictures that are ambiguous, are difficult for young children to interpret without guidance. Cultural conventions, such as the depiction of motion, are also difficult and must be learned. Winner (1982) suggests that the problem of 'reading' these aspects may be the result of young children's lack of "systematic scanning strategies" (p. 117).

Children are also less able to judge distances, or depth, depicted in pictures. Winner (1982) cites evidence that young children are able to "perceive relative depth" in pictures but that they "have a much greater difficulty determining precisely how far away a pictured object is meant to be relative to other objects in the picture" (p. 121).

Reading the expressive qualities of pictures is another area in which children seem to require time and tuition to develop skill. Studies of the ability of children to perceive expressive qualities of pictures show that children cannot respond to the mood expressed in pictures until elementary school. However, preschoolers can perceive the expressive properties of such things as single lines or color samples. The aesthetic aspects of pictures, that is—expression, composition, and style—are not noticed by preschoolers or early elementary level children. Children of six or seven can begin to notice these aspects, especially through the sensitive guidance of teachers, but it is not until adolescence that they will spontaneously respond to these aspects (Winner, 1982).

All of these findings suggest that vision, especially the perception of complex picture meaning, is essentially a cognitive ability. Seeing pictures appears to be a simple matter, but it is not. The very act of seeing itself is cognitively driven. When people view pictures they are not looking for specified targets. They make spontaneous eye movements in order to determine the content of the picture. In many studies these movements have been recorded so that we have a record of the visual attention given to various perceptible qualities of the picture.

Eye movements are necessary when looking at a picture, and these movements are different from the movements used in reading words. Picture viewing is more exploratory than reading (Matlin, 1983). Information in a picture is more directly visual. Fixation durations are generally longer in picture viewing. Studies reveal that in viewing pictures, viewers of all ages do not divide their attention equally among the different areas to be seen. Winner (1982) found that the scanning patterns of young children are controlled by what catches their eye, followed by a downward movement from that. Things above are not seen by the child.

While adults look first at the area of greatest contrast they also focus on what catches their attention but then scan all around the picture to establish what the picture is about. But not all regions are scanned even by adults. Some are returned to frequently in the scanning process but others are ignored. One of the most important aspects to remember about this process is that instructions influence the pattern of picture viewing (Matlin, 1983). Teachers can and should guide attention to what it is important for students to see in the picture, if, through inquiry, it is revealed that students have not noticed these aspects.

Preference for Visuals

In their selection of visuals, teachers may also acknowledge their students' preferences. Hurt (1987) analyzed the results of 12 picture preference studies that were available. He assessed the results in relation to conditions and variables in the studies to attempt to find consistencies across the data. He found that four pictorial variables had the most impact on student's picture preferences. Fidelity and chromatic color appeared to be significant determinants of preference common to all students studied. High fidelity or "a great amount of resemblance" (Hurt, 1987, p. 89) shown in a picture is preferred. The students' perception of fidelity is related to their familiarity with what is portrayed.

> It is also important to consider that children's perception of fidelity in a picture depends in part upon recognition of the objects or information represented in the picture ... The greater the amount of identification a child has with a picture, the more the child will prefer that picture." (Hurt, 1987, p. 91)

Some interaction between fidelity and age is that the older the student it appears the more they will prefer greater fidelity. Chromatic color (realistic color) is also a basis for positive preference. Chromatic color adds to fidelity and also to complexity through the addition of more information, however this is not a problem for students when the color is naturalistic or what is expected, 'the way things really look.' Unusual or unnatural colors are generally not preferred. Familiarity seems to be the key in these cases. Some interaction appears between age and color preference (Hurt, 1987).

> Within the bounds of colors that are accepted as natural, primary-aged children appear to prefer bright, saturated colors, while intermediate-aged children prefer light tints, earthtones, and pastel colors. (Hurt, 1987, p. 92)

Many media guides suggest that 'less is more' when the teacher is deciding how much detail to include in a visual illustration he or she will use for instruction. Anderson (1983) tells us that "Graphics should be as simple and bold as possible," and further that, "visuals should not be busy or cluttered, to insure that the intended communication is clear to the viewers" (p. 39).

Locatis and Atkinson (1984) suggest that the amount of detail should be determined by the instructional objectives but "unless detail is crucial, make every effort to simplify. Simple line drawings should be used when they can suffice, and the illustration should be uncluttered" (p. 142). Fleming and Levie (1978) state it in another way: "Learning is facilitated where criterial cues are salient (dominant, apparent, conspicuous). Add non-criterial cues only if and as necessary" (p. 115). In contrast to these suggestions, Dwyer (1978) tells us that "recent research investigating learner preferences have found that students across a wide age range express a consistent preference for complexity and variability in visualization" (p. 150). He qualifies this, however, by citing research showing that student preferences for visual materials may not relate positively to their learning achievements through the use of those preferred types of visualization materials. On the other hand, the cited research is over 20 years old and the visual environments of our students, especially in relation to the information they receive through imagery, has changed considerably in those years. From a motivational point of view it may be that the learners' personal preference for specific characteristics of pictures may contribute to the effectiveness of those types of pictures for instruction.

WHERE to Use Visuals

The following table (Visual Education Curriculum Project, 1981, p. 44) is an adaptation of one which was found in a teacher's guidebook for the use of photographs in the classroom (see Figure 8).

PICTURE RESOURCES / CLASSROOM ORGANIZATION	Resource Booklet	Poster Size Image	Image Shown by Opaque Projector	Single Copy Resource (Books, Etc.)	Whole Class Projected Slide of Image	
Whole class, same image	A	B	A	C	A	A = Appropriate
Whole class, different image	C	C	C	A	C	B = Limited to very few uses
Small group, same image	A	D	A	C	A	C = Not appropriate
Small group, different image	C	A	C	A	C	D = Dependent on multiple copies being available

Figure 8. Guide for the Use of Photographs in the Classroom.

Anderson (1983) provides guidelines for legibility in the use of projected images (except video) by offering another use of 6W. In this case it refers to a formula for determining the requisite size of the projected image for specific viewing distances. He asserts that "All projected visuals—excluding video—are based on the premise that one foot of screen width is required for each six feet of viewing distance from the screen" (hence the 6W) (p. 40–41). Anderson provides other guides and formulas for the use of visuals that could be useful to people who are interested in the optimal conditions for visualized instruction.

These two examples provide some awareness of the contextual or environmental decisions that contribute to the effectiveness of the use of visuals. It is important to remember that in order for students to learn through or about visuals it is necessary that they see them, and see them well.

Museums are rich sources of visual experience for students. The artifacts and art work provide an authentic window on diverse contents that are more often talked about than seen in schools. The value of museum objects to visual education and to the development of visual skills is evident. What can also be observed is the practice of higher level thinking skills when students are engaged productively in making visual discoveries in museum galleries. Many museums have educational departments or curators who are very interested in helping teachers and their students have access to the rich visual material in the museum. Many school subjects can be made more 'alive,' and consequently more memorable, with these visual resources.

A Systematic Approach to Reading Pictures

Visuals as Objects vs. Visuals as Tools

To a large extent, the discussion thus far has focused on the use of visuals as tools. We have looked at visuals as a medium or vehicle for learning, that is, we have concentrated on learning through visuals rather than about visuals. This section will focus on a visual media, specifically pictures, as subject. This will be done by describing a systematic approach to 'reading' pictures which addresses the visual symbol system they exemplify. This symbol system is encountered through the description of the visual elements and their syntactical organization which may be seen as composition in the pictures that are 'read.'

In the selection of pictures for classroom use, teachers, like the general public, look at and select pictures for what they explicitly represent. This 'factual' aspect determines the use of the picture which, as we saw earlier, is most often for decoration or because it directly illustrates content. Other possibilities of use may be overlooked. Pictures can provide a major source of information for study if teachers learn to recognize and select pictures on a basis other than that they illustrate simple, recognizable fact. Except for content controlled visual aids, pictures have multiple meanings which may be utilized in the instructional process.

A systematic approach to reading pictures was developed to provide teachers with a heuristic approach to unpacking the meaning dimensions of pictures. As a consequence it encourages more extensive use of visualized information, especially that which may be found in paintings or photographs.

Background

This systematic approach to reading pictures gradually evolved as the result of a desire to find an effective way to assist teachers in making intellectual contact with the multiple meanings of pictures. The pictures used as a focus for the development of the systematic approach were works of art. This selection was made for two reasons: first, to make art more accessible through familiarity and second, because works of art have dense meaning structures including the aesthetic. The Krietlers (1972) refer to the multiple meanings of a work as *multileveledness*, while Goodman (1968) uses the term *density*. A visual analogy of this density may be found in Figure 9, which illustrates the several layers that make up the complete mandala.

Figure 9. A Visual Analogy of "Density."

Initially I studied the way novice aesthetic perceivers confront a work of art, how they extract information from it, and what types of information they tend to focus upon. Their common response strategies were identified inductively. These strategies helped to determine which ones to select and focus upon educationally so that the novice perceivers could be more effectively use of pictures as tools for learning. These selected strategies became the basis for the stages in the systematic approach.

The conceptual foundation for this systematic approach was based, in part, on Feldman's 'Critical Performance Method' (1973) and was enriched by several studies including those by Woods (1978) and Koroscik (1982). Its roots may also be found in Broudy's 'aesthetic scanning' (1988). Many variations of systematic attention to the properties or qualities of pictures, including works of art, may be found in the literature.

The graphic form shown in Figure 10 represents the approach to "reading" pictures that identifies the levels of information which are to be sequentially addressed. Although each of the levels of this system could represent a separate and distinct approach to works of art, the levels are combined to form a single, sequential approach. As they are sequentially addressed, the levels represent an increasing depth in the mental processing of the visual information. (The spatial metaphor for thinking abounds; thinking 'in depth' is also considered 'higher level thinking.') The solid line dividing the system into two sections visually represents the differentiation between response tasks. Some tasks refer to visual attributes 'possessed' by the art object—what it is, while others require a mental stretch into the symbolic (expressive) nature of the visual qualities of the work— what it means.

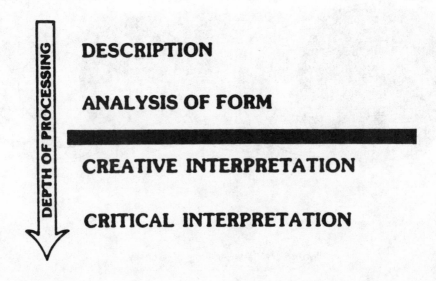

Figure 10. Levels of Information to Be Sequentially Addressed.

Description of the Levels of the Systematic Approach to 'Reading Pictures'

First Two Levels: Description and Analysis of Form

The response tasks identified in the top section of Figure 10 deals with information that is directly accessible through the senses. The visual skills of observation, of seeing details, and of analytic perception of the overall pattern, are practiced through the Description and Analysis of Form levels of the system.

This attention to sensory and formal properties is especially important for novice viewers. Perkins' (1983) analysis of the problem these viewers have with art concludes that they don't really see it. They don't see the art that is embedded in the perceptual form. "They recognize the cows, the trees, but not the form or the style" (p. 39). Perkins (1983) suggests that the first goal in reading works of art becomes simply making the art in art visible. In the perception of objects, many novice viewers treat the surface properties as though they were transparent. It appears that these viewers process such information automatically in their effort to find meaning to recognize and label. They continue to do this unless they are taught to pay conscious attention to the sensory and formal properties of the art object. It's not that they have to learn something new. In a sense they already know what they are to be taught. However, this implicit knowledge has to become explicit to become an object of attention in its own right (Olson, 1983). As novice viewers learn to attend to these various properties, they may also begin to develop the skill of analytic seeing. Arnheim (1979) defines the skill of analytic seeing as the ability to perceive essential structure. He describes it as the understanding of visual relations of what things—or parts—do to one another. McKim (1980) describes analytic seeing as seeing the interrelatedness of parts and wholes. This is the skill of perceiving pattern, of perceptually organizing and reorganizing the given information to find the key to its coherence—what makes it hold together. This skill is identified by Gardner (1982) as the capacity to look beyond the dominant figure or gestalt, to pay attention, instead, to the fine details or microstructure which cut across figure and ground. The development of this skill builds upon the natural tendency to organize what we look at into coherent patterns by perceptually grouping or combining parts to "make sense" of what we see. This pattern-seeking effort is a perceptual tension which craves resolution. Resolution comes when meaning can be assigned to what is seen. By attaching meaning we assure its place in our memory. To view aesthetically is to see the form and how it contributes to the meaning rather than to simply see through the form to the meaning (Olson, 1983). It is this holistic perception of form and content which is encouraged and developed in novice viewers through this approach to 'reading pictures.' Through deliberate attention to the visual form, managed by the tasks of the first two levels, the novice viewer is encouraged to develop more complex anticipatory schema as preparation for the subsequent tasks.

Bottom Levels: Creative and Critical Interpretation

The response tasks of the next two levels of the system involve extracting symbolic (expressive) connotations from visual art objects, which requires the mental stretch called interpretation. Using a spatial metaphor for activity of the mind, interpretation is referred to as deeper processing. Sequential attention to the system's levels requires processing efforts that involve further or deeper exploration of the mental schemata which are called to mind by the visual material in the art. Prior knowledge, time involved in looking, and the task or activity demands are critical aspects of the process. The bottom portion of the diagram (Figure 10) involves two types of interpretation of the art object. The first is Creative Interpretation, which consists of generating personal expressive associated meanings for the visual content—a sort of mental elaboration through personal association—resulting in an initial hypothesis of meaning. This effort is followed by Critical Interpretation, which entails an assessment of the hypothesized meanings through criteria derived from outside knowledge sources.

My study of the responses of novice viewers led me to divide interpretation into two types. The two different response types are labeled Creative Interpretation and Critical Interpretation. Creative Interpretation permits a response option in which the work of art may serve as a limited projective device—an opportunity to draw upon the rich differences of experiential background to derive personalized meanings. This response level serves a useful purpose in making visual content personally accessible and not gated by authority. It is 'gated,' however, by a sensitive and sensible 'reading' of the form from which an hypothesis of the expressive meaning is derived as a creative interpretation. Olson (1983) presents evidence which suggests that the expressive function of symbols in thought precedes the knowledge function, and it is for this reason that creative interpretation is addressed before critical interpretation in the design of this system.

The second type of interpretation, Critical Interpretation, involves response to certain types of visual content which directly illustrates or metaphorically symbolizes aspects and ideas of the cultural, socio-political context of the work. The windows and mirrors of the visual arts provide access to a wide range of abstract human ideas in concrete visual form. Ideas in visual form are the knowledge cues which are used for Critical Interpretation. Students using this approach are encouraged at this step to search for information that is available from experts. Application of the knowledge results in the corroboration or revision of the hypothesis of meaning developed in Creative Interpretation. Critical Interpretation brings to closure the process of 'reading,' or unpacking the multiple meanings of the systematically accessed content of the work of art.

All visual materials can be viewed as examples of visual elements organized in a particular way for a purpose. The systematic approach described above has recently been used with visual materials, including photographs, and advertisements, which are not ordinarily considered to be works of art. It appears to work in a similar manner when contextual information about the creation of the selected image is introduced, or made accessible through references, at the critical interpretation level. It has been shown to be particularly useful when introducing unfamiliar multicultural images to students. They are encouraged to use their own eyes, and minds to make 'sense' of the work, to hypothesize what it means, and then to engage in research which reveals the cultural intent and meaning. This problem-solving process centered on visuals has more educational value than a teacher 'show and tell' event.

The use of visuals in schools is most frequently related to their significance as exemplars of knowledge, of what facts are to be learned and associated with them. The use of visuals as a basis for problem solving, for thinking at higher levels, is evident less frequently. TO SEE IS TO THINK should be encouraged as a complement of equal status to TO SEE IS TO KNOW.

Illustrations by Karen Lawson

References

Anderson, R. H. (1983). *Selecting and developing media for instruction*. New York: Van Nostrand Reinhold.

Arnheim, R. (1979). *Art and visual perception*. Los Angeles, CA: University of California Press.

Baggett, P. (1989). Understanding visual and verbal messages. In H. Mandl & J. Levin (Eds.), *Knowledge acquisition from text and pictures*. Amsterdam, The Netherlands: Elsevier.

Broudy, H. (1988). *The role of imagery in learning*. Occasional Paper I, Getty Center for Education in the Arts. Los Angeles, CA.

Clarke, J. H. (1990). *Patterns of thinking*. Boston, MA: Allyn & Bacon.

Dwyer, F. M. (1978). *Strategies for improving visual learning*. State College, PA: Learning Services.

Feldman, E. B. (1973). *Varieties of visual experience*. New York: Harry N. Abrams.

Fleming, M., & Levie, W. H. (1978). *Instructional message design: Principles from the behavioral sciences*. Englewood Cliffs, NJ: Educational Technology Publications.

Gagné, R., Briggs, L., & Wager, W. W. (1979). *Principles of instructional design*. New York: Holt, Rinehart, and Winston.

Gardner, H. (1982). *Art, mind, and brain*. New York: Basic Books.

Goodman, N. (1968). *Languages of art*. Indianapolis, IN: Bobbs-Merrill.

Hurt, J. A. (1987). Assessing functional effectiveness of pictorial representations used in text. *Educational Communications and Technology Journal, 35* (2), 85–94.

Koroscik, J. S. (1982). *Verbalization in visual art information processing*. Paper presented the meeting of National Art Education Conference, New York, NY.

Kozma, R. (1991). Learning with media. *Review of Educational Research, 61*, 179–211.

Krietler, H., & Krietler, S. (1972). *Psychology of the arts*. Durham, NC: Duke University Press.

Levie, W. H. (1987). Research on pictures: A guide to the literature. In D. M. Willows & H. A. Houghton (Eds.), *The psychology of illustration: Basic research* (Vol. 1). New York: Springer-Verlag.

Levin, J. R., Anglin, G. J., & Carney, R. N. (1987). On empirically validating functions of pictures in prose. In D. M. Willows & H. A. Houghton (Eds.), *The psychology of illustration: Basic research* (Vol. 1). New York: Springer-Verlag.

Locatis, C. N., & Atkinson, F. D. (1984). *Media and technology for education and training.* Columbus, OH: Charles E. Merrill .

Matlin, M. W. (1983). *Perception.* Boston, MA: Allyn & Bacon.

McKim, R. H. (1980). *Experiences in visual thinking.* Monterey, CA: Brooks/Cole Publishing Co.

Olson, D. (1983). The role of the arts in cognition. *Art Education,* March, 36–38.

Peeck, J. (1987). The role of illustrations in processing and remembering illustrated text. In D. M. Willows & H. A. Houghton (Eds.), *The psychology of illustration: Basic research* (Vol. 1). New York: Springer-Verlag.

Perkins, D. (1983). Invisible art. *Art Education,* March, 39–41.

Salomon, G. (1979). *Interaction of media, cognition, and learning.* San Francisco, CA: Jossey-Bass.

Seels, B., & Glasgow, Z. (1991). *Exercises in instructional design.* Columbus, OH: Merrill Publishing Co.

Visual Education Curriculum Project. (1980). *What a picture! Learning from photographs* Canberra, Australia: Curriculum Development Centre.

Visual Education Curriculum Project. (1981). *Pictures of ideas: Learning through visual comparison and analogy.* Canberra, Australia: Curriculum Development Centre.

White, M. A. (Ed.). (1987). *What curriculum for the information age?* New York: Columbia University Press.

Winner, E. (1982). *Invented worlds: The psychology of the arts.* Cambridge, MA: Harvard University Press.

Woods, D. (1978). Reading pictures and words: A critical review. *Review of Research in Visual Arts Education, 9,* 11–38.

Chapter Fifteen

Use of Visuals: Business and Industry

Robert E. Griffin

Objectives

After reading this chapter, you should be able to:

1. *Describe why visuals are important to the business presentation.*

2. *Name and describe the common types of business media.*

3. *Name, order, and describe the classifications of business visuals and name the classification most often used.*

4. *Name the type of visuals used to show the outline of the presentation.*

5. *Name the type of visuals used to sustain the statements of the presentation.*

6. *Describe how business people currently learn about the concepts of visual literacy.*

Introduction

Most business presentations today use some form of visualization in order to communicate their message. Unfortunately, most people who are not regularly employed by a business don't get a chance to see business presentations. This is due in part to the confidential nature of most business presentations. Most people only get to see the outward trappings of business communication, that of advertising. Advertising and business presentations are entirely different forms of communication. Because people don't understand business presentations, they often have many questions about this form of communication. Five of the most commonly asked questions are:

- How important are visuals to business presentations?
- What are the most common types of business visuals?
- What purpose do visuals serve in the business presentation?

257

- What are computer generated business graphics?
- How do business people learn to use visuals?

Understanding the answers to these questions will help us understand the complexity of the business visual. Let's explore each in detail.

How Important Are Visuals to Business Presentations?

Visuals are used in every part of society but they seem to have found a special home in business. Visuals have become a necessity in business communication today. For example, board rooms in modern corporations are equipped with the latest in projection equipment, as are conference rooms and other corporate meeting rooms. Business graphics software is a major product line of computer software. Additionally, although it has yet to reach major proportions, business students are being trained in the use of visuals in their written and oral communication. Business has recognized the value of complete communication skills because they have found that good communication is profitable.

The use of visualization in business presentations is not a modern innovation. Using visuals has been commonplace for many years. Consider these examples. In the 1960's and 1970's, companies like *IBM* and *DuPont* were known for their use of flip charts in business presentations. Stories are told at *DuPont* of how critical it was to always have an artist available in case you were called on to make a presentation to management. Later, photographic companies, notably *Eastman Kodak*, gained communication prominence for promoting the use of 2 x 2 slides for business presentations. Likewise, for many years, *3M* has had a reputation for research and study about the overhead projection medium. Clearly business and industry are major contributors to the visual communication revolution that we witness today.

Using visuals in business presentations is popular. From Griffin (1989), we know that more business people use visuals than do not. This survey was conducted with 272 managers who were enrolled in Penn State's Executive Management Programs. When asked, "Do you use visuals in your business presentations?" 92 percent of the manager's responded that they use visuals always or sometimes. This data is shown in Figure 1.

Indications are that the percentage of people using visuals will continue to increase. Also from Griffin (1989), we know that the average business person gives 12 presentations per year. Each of these presentations reportedly lasts about 20 to 25 minutes. It is obvious that the business presentation is an important tool.

From Griffin (1991a) we have also learned that the overhead projector seems to be today's choice of presentation medium. This study surveyed 141 managers. The results from this research are shown in Figure 2.

The overhead projector is the dominant presentation medium for business. The reason for this premier position most likely stems from the ability of most major computer graphic programs to produce high-quality overhead transparencies very rapidly. Adding to this popularity is the fact that most transparencies can be produced at a manager's desk rather than in a more sophisticated art or visual production area using the fine overhead transparency production equipment which is available today. However, the overhead projector has not always been the medium of choice in business. During the 1970's, 2 x 2 slides were the

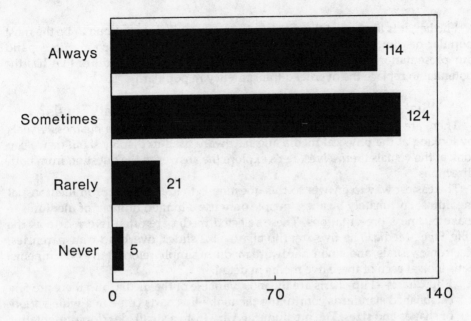

Figure 1. Do You Use Visuals in Business Presentations?

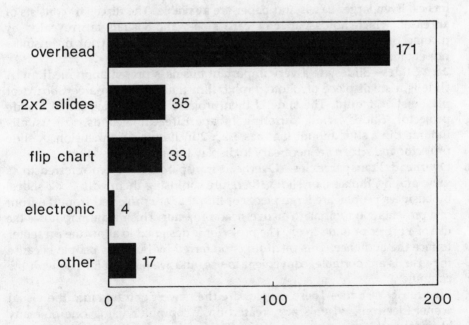

Figure 2. What Medium Is Most Often Used in Business Presentations?

dominant medium. It should be pointed out that the popularity of slides has not diminished from that time. They have simply been surpassed by overhead transparencies.

Further, it is likely that the overhead projector will not continue to be the most popular medium. New technologies are emerging that offer promise to expand our presentation ability. The electronic visual is one such medium that has the potential to replace the overhead transparency in popularity.

What Are the Most Common Types of Business Visuals?

There are two ways to answer this question. We can discuss business visuals by looking at the physical media and hardware used to display them or we can look at the visuals themselves. Let's explore the answer to the question from both directions.

The easiest way to answer to this question is to identify the prominent visual mediums. Fortunately business people only use a limited number of mediums to make business presentations. These selected media are often referred to as the "Big Five" Media. The five are: flip charts, 2x2 slides, overhead transparencies, electronic visuals, and a non-hardware medium simply referred to as documents. Let's look at each of these five media in detail.

1. **Flip Charts**—Flip charts are the most variable of the media, and there are few established standards controlling the tool. Flip charts come in a wide variety of shapes and sizes. The medium can vary from a small, desktop presentation easel to a more typical floor stand easel holding paper that is 22 inches x 28 inches. Even larger easels and paper are available. The flip chart consists of an easel, which holds paper or card stock, and visuals are revealed by turning or flipping pages. The flip chart is a proven warrior of business presentations.

2. **2 x 2 Slides**—Slides are a very important business presentation medium. A slide is a small piece of photographic film that is held in a cardboard or plastic slide mount. The slide is then projected in a device called a slide projector. Slides, while differing in aperture dimensions, are usually mounted in a slide mount that has a 2 x 2 inch outside dimension. A slide projector and screen are necessary to display this medium.

3. **Overhead Transparencies**—Overhead transparencies, often referred to as view graphs, flimsies, or slides (therefore confusing them with 2 x 2 slides) by business people, are large pieces of film that are projected from the front of a presentation room with an overhead projector. This medium requires the use of a projector and screen. The projector is designed to allow the presenter to face the audience. This medium is preferred by business people because the visuals are portable, convenient to use, and well-suited for use with the computer.

4. **Electronic Visuals**—These devices are the newest entrants into the visual scene. Electronic visuals are created on a computer using one of many business graphics software packages. These visuals are then displayed using a computer, projection panel, and an overhead projector. An alternative to using this equipment is to connect the computer to a video projector and project an image on a conventional screen. This medium does not require a tangible visual but rather relies on visuals stored on a computer disk. Although the cost of using this medium is still high, the technology is rapidly becoming more affordable.

5. **Document Visuals**—Documents are different from the previous four mediums. Until the advent of desktop publishing and word processing software, it was difficult to include visuals in documents. Usually they had to be inserted by an old-fashioned cut and paste method, where the visual was glued into a spot which had been left in the text or placed in an appendix at the end of the document. Desktop publishing now allows us to create visuals using business graphics software and then insert the visual in a typed document electronically.

These five mediums, the "Big Five," carry most of the burden in business presentations. These media must be mastered by today's business people. But looking at the physical media and hardware that is available to present visuals is not the only way to determine the common types of business visuals. We must also look at the forms the physical media take. What does the overhead transparency display? Is the transparency a word visual, graph, or some other visual form? To see the visual make-up of a business presentation, we need to turn to one of the few studies done on the topic. Due to the confidential nature of business, researchers are not normally invited into business presentations. For this reason it has been difficult to get an inside perspective on the business presentation. In considering this problem, one researcher (Griffin, 1988) turned to a professional meeting attended by engineers and scientists in order to gather data. At this meeting the technical presenters made highly sophisticated presentations to their peers regarding updates of products which their companies had developed. This study surveyed 31 presentations and categorized the visuals used during these presentations into five classifications; word visuals, graphs, diagrams, maps, and other. The average distribution of these five categories of visuals at these presentations is shown in Figure 3.

All the presentations included in Griffin's study were analyzed for the types of visuals used. As can be seen in Figure 3, word visuals were the dominate type. Within the category of word visuals the most frequently used type was the word list with bullets. An example of a typical bullet visual is shown in Figure 4.

Presenters seemed to use this type of visual as a substitute for speakers' notes or when they were not sure what other type of visual to use. The study suggested that word visuals were over used in business presentations.

Diagrams accounted for the second largest category of business visualization noted in the study. Diagrams viewed during the study usually consisted of block diagrams and other creative attempts at modeling ideas. These diagrams were intended to help an audience understand the steps in the thought process that were used to reach a conclusion. An example of a diagram is shown in Figure 5. In this diagram the author of the visual is showing the five companies that compete with *Centre Manufacturing* and the degree of competition each company provides. While the discussion that accompanies the visual is very complex, the purpose of the visual is to cut through that complexity so that the words can be better understood.

Graphs were the third most common form of visualization in the study. It should be pointed out that graphs may be more common in business presentations than this study shows. Because of the nature of this particular study, most of the presentations were not financial in nature. However, many presentations

word
54.3%
diagrams
15.1%
graphs
10.8%
maps
0.8%
other
19%

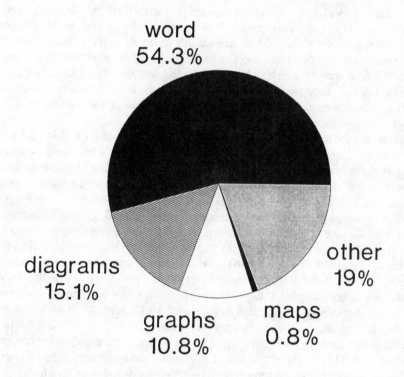

Figure 3. Types of Visuals Used in Business Presentations.

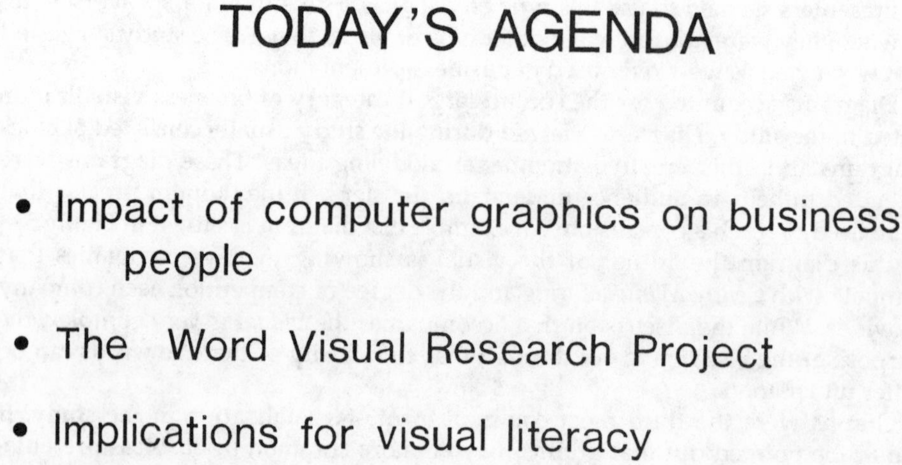

TODAY'S AGENDA
• Impact of computer graphics on business people
• The Word Visual Research Project
• Implications for visual literacy

Figure 4. A Word Visual.

CENTRE MANUFACTURING
Our Competition

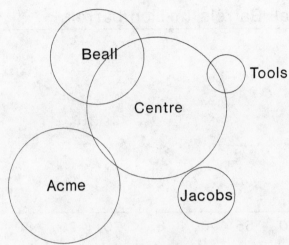

Figure 5. A Diagram.

done within companies focus on financial aspects and these financial presentations usually rely heavily on graphs. For these reasons, graphs may be more common in business presentations than this study indicates.

The most common types of graphs used in presentations are line and column graphs. These two types of graphs are shown in Figure 6a and Figure 6b.

The line and column graphs share a common axis structure. Line and column graphs are created so that the X axis displays time while the Y axis displays amount. While this rule is sometimes broken, it is this constant that separates these two graph forms from the others.

Both line and column graphs are used to show function over time. Line graphs are used to:

• emphasize a trend;
• give a cumulative picture of all components;
• compare several time series;
• to make projections.

Column graphs are often confused with their cousins, the bar graphs. Column graphs are vertical while bar graphs run horizontal. Column graphs are used for a distinctively different purpose than bar graphs. Column graphs are used to:

• emphasize numeric data;
• make data appear less statistical.

The second most common group of graphs used in business presentations are bar and pie graphs. These two graphs are shown in Figure 7a and Figure 7b.

Bar graphs are not column graphs set on their side. Bar graphs are used when:

• data does not fit the time and amount axis which is common in line and column graphs.

TOTAL U.S. PRODUCTION OF MALTED BEVERAGES

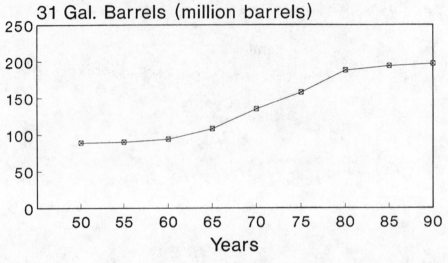

Figure 6a. A Line Graph.

GALLUP CORPORATION
First Quarter Sales

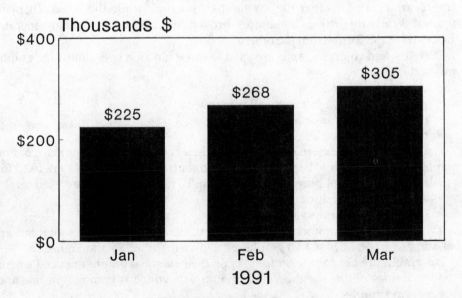

Figure 6b. A Column Graph.

TOP 3 BREWERS - 1990

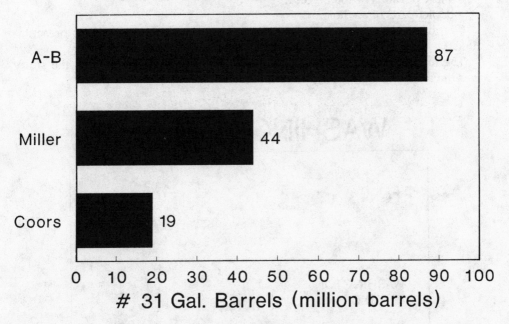

Figure 7a. A Bar Graph.

BURGER-STEAMWAY CORP.
Market Share

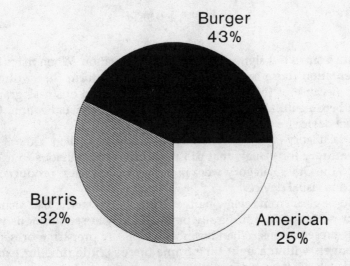

Figure 7b. A Pie Graph.

Pie graphs are a uniquely distinctive form of graphs. Pie graphs are used to:
- show portions of 100 percent;
- depict parts of a whole.

Graphs are important and necessary and appear in most business presentations.

The fourth most common category of visualization discovered in the study was the map. An example of a map is shown in Figure 8.

WASHINGTON D.C.

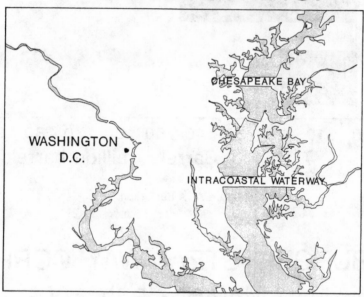

Figure 8. A Map.

Maps are a small but significant type of visualization. When maps are needed in a presentation there is no other type of visual form that will adequately substitute. Because of the availability of computerized business graphic maps, they have become an increasingly important form of visualization. Computers are a perfect device for generating precise map visuals.

The final category of visualization in this study was called 'Other.' This was a catch-all category for visuals that did not fit into the previous four categories. Included in the Other category were pictures of plant sites, products, and other miscellaneous visual devices.

It should be clear from reviewing the Griffin (1988) study, that visuals used in business presentations are surgically precise. Rarely are superfluous visuals part of business presentations. When business people are preparing presentations on limited budgets within a tight time frame there is little time for extra visuals. Business visuals get the job done.

What Purpose Do Visuals Serve in the Presentation?

Now to the question of what purpose do visuals serve in a presentation? All the visuals used in a presentation can be divided into one of two forms, linking visuals and supporting visuals. Linking visuals are a form of visual designed to show the audience the outline or organization of a presentation. An example of a linking visual is shown in Figure 9.

MODES OF TRANSPORTATION

- Air

- Water

- Rail

- Truck

- Pipeline

Figure 9. A Linking Visual.

Linking visuals are used to maintain the continuity of a presentation for the audience. These visuals often are done as word visuals or diagrams. When consecutive versions of this visual form are interspersed through a presentation at planned intervals, they provide continuity to the presentation and keep the audience on track. A linking visual sequence is shown in Figures 10a, 10b, 10c, 10d, and 10e.

Each of the visuals in this sequence serves a purpose. The initial linking visual serves to introduce the agenda to the audience. The linking visuals (three in this case) are used to introduce each of the major points of the message. Finally the concluding linking visual is used to wrap up the presentation. Each visual carries part of the organization load of the presentation.

The second type of visual is the supporting visual. Supporting visuals are the visuals used to sustain the statements made by the linking visuals. The visuals shown in Figures 5 through 8 are all examples of supporting visuals. Supporting visuals include all types of graphs, diagrams, or other visuals which support the statements made by the linking visuals. Supporting visuals are the visuals that carry the proof of the presentation.

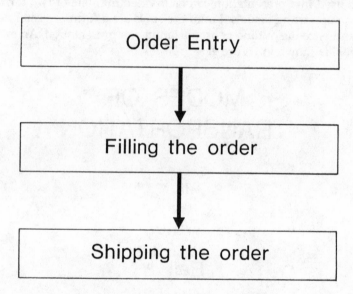

Figure 10a. A Linking Visual Sequence.

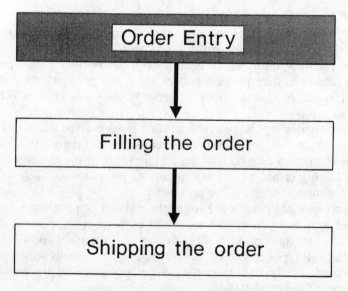

Figure 10b. A Linking Visual Sequence.

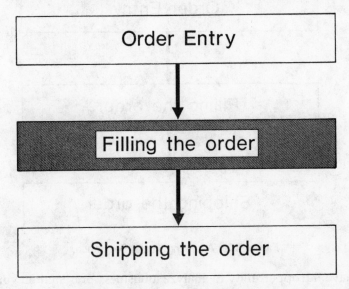

Figure 10c. A Linking Visual Sequence.

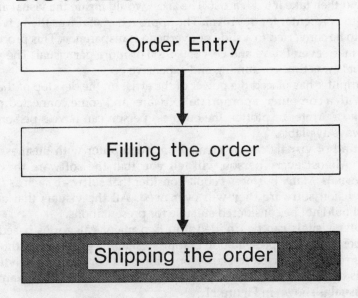

Figure 10d. A Linking Visual Sequence.

DISTRIBUTION PROCESS

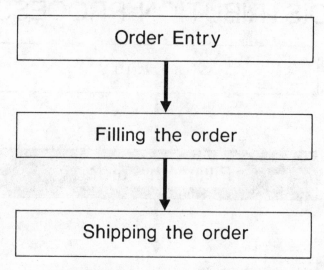

Figure 10e. A Linking Visual Sequence.

If you have the opportunity to analyze a business presentation you will find that all business visuals can be categorized into one of these two visual forms, linking or supporting visuals.

What Are Computer Generated Business Graphics?

The computer has changed the way business people create and produce visuals. Before business people had business graphics software and personal computers, business people would develop an idea that they wanted to turn into a visual and then take it to an artist. The artist would create the visual and deliver a copy to the presenter for approval. The approved visual was then given back to the artist to be converted to a slide or overhead transparency. This process would normally take several days and cost $50–$100 or more per visual. The process of using visuals was time consuming and expensive.

The computer has placed the power of the artist on the desktop of the business person. With a computer, appropriate software, and some connected peripheral devices like a printer or plotter, the business person can have a personal artist's studio always available.

What kind of visuals can be created on a computer with business graphics software? Almost every person will tell you that the software they use will produce visuals. Many business people consider that software such as *Lotus 1-2-3* is all the visual software they will ever need. All the visuals that computers produce should not be considered suitable for presentations.

Computer visuals can be divided into two major categories based on their appearance; analytic or presentation graphics. Analytic graphics are those visuals which are principally used to clarify or evaluate a condition. Analytic graphic software is often found accompanying spreadsheet software. An example of an analytic visual is shown in Figure 11.

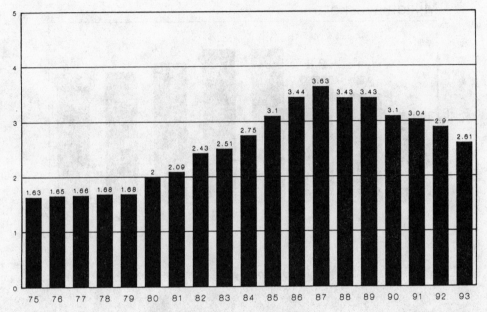

Employment In The Defense Industry
From 1980-1993
Millions of Workers

Figure 11. An Analytic Visual.

Figure 11 is an analytic visual used to determine the trend of the data, calculate future directions, or make predictions. Good visual design is not essential for analytic visuals. A person viewing an analytic visual does not require that the visual be highly legible. If you can read an analytic visual—that's good enough. Factors such as color, font style, and simplicity are not important to this form of visual. Visuals such as the one shown in Figure 11 are normally studied on a computer screen or looked at in a study document. They are rarely used in a presentation to others.

The second category of computer graphic is the presentation visuals. Griffin (1991b) stated that presentation visuals must embody the qualities of a good visual such as; legibility, simplicity, and clarity. These qualities are important because presentation visuals must be viewed and understood by an audience. An example presentation visual is shown in Figure 12.

If you compare Figure 11, an analytic visual, and Figure 12, a presentation visual, you can see the purposes of the two visuals. Figure 11 is used to present a comprehensive look at all the data. Precise, non-rounded data is presented to the viewer. In Figure 11 any element that might help the viewer interpret and analyze the data is allowed to remain. An assumption is made in an analytic visual that the viewer will take all the time needed to view the visual. Figure 12 is designed for a different purpose. The presentation visual is designed for a specific communicative purpose. Presentation visuals are meant to be looked at

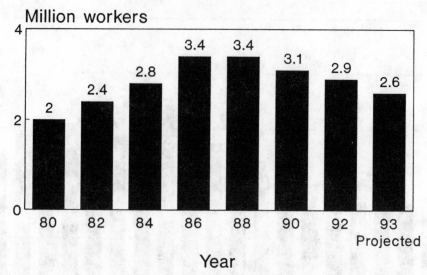

Figure 12. A Presentation Visual.

quickly, usually in sequence with other visuals. Presentation visuals are usually easy to read and instantly recognized by the audience.

It is important to understand that neither visual is better than the other. Analytic visuals are perfect for what they do—analyze. Presentation visuals are properly suited for use in presentations, but are usually too simple for complete analysis. Each visual form does its own job well.

A question that is usually raised about computer generated business graphics concerns output. What is the most common form of computer graphics output? This answer, which comes from an unpublished survey by Griffin of 67 managers, is shown in Figure 13.

It is easy to see from this data that overhead transparencies are the most common output from business graphics software. It is also interesting to note the black and white laser printer is the most popular output device. The laser printer is a popular device for producing black and white overhead transparencies. It should also be noted from this data that color devices are gaining in popularity but continue to lag behind monocolor devices.

Business graphics software packages have allowed business visuals to become powerful tools for business people. Anyone who is interested in studying the use of visuals in business needs closely to examine the impact that business graphics software has had on business communication. Through the 1960's visualization in business was an artist-based business. Business people developed visual ideas, but these ideas were turned over to an artist to interpret and develop. The 1970's saw the development of computer graphics software, but this software ran

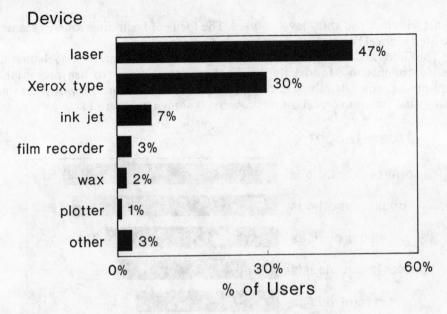

Figure 13. Common Forms of Computer Output.

largely on bulky mainframe computers. Output had to be sent to remote printing locations and was often not good enough to be of use in a presentation. The 1980's brought the personal computer and bestowed its power on the individual. Individual presenters were now able to develop visuals that could compliment either a written or oral presentation. Visual power was given to the user.

The 1990's will surely see an expansion of the advances made in the 1980's. Software programs will be made easier to use and more powerful. Presenters will find that visual horizons are limitless.

How Do Business People Learn to Use Visuals?

An important question that should concern all people interested in visualization is how business people are learning to use visuals. If visuals are important to business people and presentations, business people must be learning to master the methods of visual design and use. Unfortunately this is not correct. Gibbs and McKendrick (1991) investigated how business communication is taught in colleges and universities. Their findings indicate that not much is being done in training business people to use visual communication properly.

The Gibbs and McKendrick (1991) study surveyed major business programs throughout the United States. These researchers found that only two percent of the surveyed schools taught anything about visualization in communication courses. Most of the respondents who did not teach visualization said they assumed that students learned visual communication skills in other public speaking or technical writing courses. This also proved to be a false assumption. The Gibbs and McKendrick study found that visual material was not normally dealt with in those entry level courses. The focus of beginning courses seems to be on rhetorical basics; speech making and basic writing.

The Gibbs and McKendrick (1991) study found that business schools that did teach students to use visuals taught them mainly how to use presentation equipment rather than how to design proper visuals. A summary of what these few visual communication courses covered is shown in Figure 14.

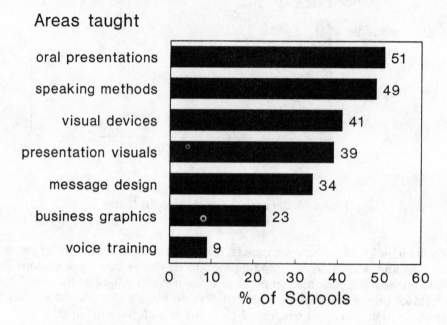

Figure 14. Topics Taught in Business Communication Courses.

To give an example of the sparse attempts at giving visualization skills to business people, in one program surveyed, MBA students were taught to use the overhead projector. However, they were only given a few rules about how to design visuals for the machine. These students became hardware users, but not visual communicators. Clearly, the Gibbs and McKendrick (1991) study points out the need for improving the visual literacy of business people.

What Does the Future Hold?

It should be evident from the facts and stories presented here that visuals are an important aspect of business presentations. Visuals are used every day in business in a variety of forms. Today's business leaders are eagerly attempting to learn the intricacies of the visual use. Advocates of visual literacy must share their skills with those communicators who use visuals every day.

References

Gibbs, W. J., & McKendrick, J. E. (1991). A study of communications in business colleges. In D. Beauchamp, J. Clark-Baca, & R. Braden (Eds.), *Investigating visual literacy* (pp. 51–60). Blacksburg, VA: International Visual Literacy Association.

Griffin, R. E. (1988). A comprehensive study of the types of visuals used in business and engineering presentations. In R. Braden, D. Beauchamp, L. Miller, & D. M. Moore (Eds.), *About visuals* (p. 172). Blacksburg, VA: International Visual Literacy Association .

Griffin, R. E. (1989). Important facts about business presentations. *Advanced printing of paper summaries* (Vol. 2), (p.108). Boston, MA: BISCAP International.

Griffin, R. E. (1991a). The visual business presentation: An international comparison. In D. Beauchamp, J. Clark-Baca, & R. Braden (Eds.), *Investigating visual literacy* (p. 107). Blacksburg, VA: International Visual Literacy Association.

Griffin, R. E. (1991b). *Harvard Graphics 2.3: Creating effective visual presentations.* Boston: Course Technology.

Chapter Sixteen

Making Meaning from Visuals: Creative Thinking and Interpretation of Visual Information

Richard A. Couch

Edward J. Caropreso

with

Helen B. Miller

Objectives

After reading this chapter, you should be able to:

1. *Explain why visual literacy is important in today's society.*

2. *Compare and contrast differentiation and interpretation of visuals.*

3. *Define creativity as it relates to interpretation of visuals.*

4. *Describe the social psychology model of creativity (Amabile).*

5. *List ways that an individual can be a more creative visual consumer.*

6. *Define differentiation in terms of visual literacy.*

Visual Media: The Common Denominator

Over the years all media have become more sophisticated, technologically and visually. No longer is our information exclusively transmitted visually via text or verbally via radio. Those media have become entertainment media. Who has time to read in-depth newspaper articles? Instead we "look at" *USA Today*, whose policy is that they will not continue an article on the "next page." Most radio programming is designed for musical entertainment. Our magazine choices have changed as well. Most of our magazines are like *People*, pictures connected with a small amount of text. Our news comes to us via television in graphic visual detail. The two-dimensional video images tell the real story; the person reading the TelePrompTer merely enhances the picture. Even our political process has in some cases become a choice between two people who spend much time on their visual image and prepare very carefully for each two minute "visual-image bite" on television. See Figure 1.

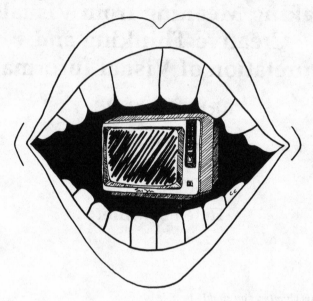

Figure 1. Visual-image Bite.

As members of a society which increasingly relies on visual messages, we must learn how to interpret these messages in a meaningful way. When we allow ourselves to become passive participants in visual media we lose control over information which impacts our lives. Through time we become less and less able to filter truth from fiction. We eventually lose both the opportunity and capacity to interpret visual information meaningfully. 'Making meaning' out of visual images can often determine how our lives are conducted, even how fulfilling our experiences will be. By its very nature, making meaning is a creative, constructive process.

The authors will therefore define creativity in terms of two models of creative thinking and operationalize that definition in relation to visual learning. Creativity can be applied to visual learning in many ways, the creating of visual messages, the interpretation of visual messages, and the criticism of visual messages. However, we have chosen to explore creativity in terms of how we learn from interpreting visual messages. The discussion will then focus on specific ways in which people can enhance their ability to become an effective visual consumer. The first step in understanding the connection between creative thinking and visual literacy is to understand the two stages of visual learning. Understanding these two stages will prepare readers to incorporate creative thinking into their own interpretation of visuals.

Decoding Visuals: Differentiation and Interpretation

Visual literacy involves the ability to learn from visual messages. The ability to learn from visual representations involves two components. The first involves the process of gaining or enhancing a person's awareness of the meaning of visuals. The second involves the process a person uses to interpret the meaning associated with a given visual message (Heinich, Molenda, & Russell, 1985).

When a person decodes a visual message for the purpose of learning or for the purpose of gaining information, a complex relationship involving two interdependent steps is established between the viewer and the visual message. The first stage of visual learning is differentiation. Differentiation is the critical or analytical component of decoding during which relevant information is identified or recognized and classified into categories. This decoded information becomes the basis for the "intended message" or the literal message. This information stimulates in the viewer's consciousness important or relevant meanings or networks of meaning (schemata). This is often the case with the viewing of abstract art. Unless one is trained to view the artwork, there is little meaning in the literal viewing of the painting, except perhaps for the vitality or colorfulness. The extent to which information can be appropriately categorized determines how effectively the viewer of visual information will be able to integrate the intended messages with meaningful interpretations. If the reality or the facts in the visual are discordant, unfamiliar, or cannot be categorized, the viewer will tend to ignore or misinterpret the message and little learning will take place. In essence, differentiation, the analytical component of decoding, extracts relevant information from visual messages. This information can be described as the factual, realistic, or literal elements of the visual. It represents the important information upon which the viewer will establish or build a sense of comprehension and meaning.

The second stage of visual learning is interpretation of the visual message. Viewers cannot interpret a visual message unless they can extract the factual or realistic information, that is, the literal meaning of the visual. Interpretation involves synthesizing the analyzed factual or realistic information, connecting the new or unfamiliar information with existing knowledge, and then making inferences and judgments about the new and newly integrated information. A person may see a picture of a lighthouse on a sandy peninsula of land. In the differentiation stage the viewer grapples with the elements of the painting, for example, sea grass, barber-pole stripe on the lighthouse, sea gulls, and so forth. The interpretation stage involves synthesizing the data from the painting and making meaning by extending it with existing networks or adding new information to the "lighthouse schema." After synthesizing the new information, the viewer can elaborate or enhance the new information and make further cognitive connections to give it personal meaning. Such elaboration and interconnection make this information more deeply integrated with prior knowledge. It also helps in making the information more accessible for use in decoding future visual experiences. See Figure 2

Figure 2. Lighthouse Schema.

This second stage in the visual learning process, interpretation, involves some of the essential skills typically associated with creative thinking skills such as synthesis, originality, and elaboration. Based on individual conceptions of the literal meaning of the visual, that is, what we extract during the differentiation stage, creative thinking skills can be applied during the interpretation/ integration stage of visual decoding. The creative use of the visual information identified through differentiation will be limited only by the extent of the viewer's ability to think creatively.

The connection between creative thinking and visual literacy often occurs during the interpretation stage of the decoding process. When we look at visual information, whether video, computer graphic, painting or print, we first decode it literally. We may even list all the components. In fact, parents and teachers often train children to differentiate when we ask them to tell us what they see in a picture. We make sure the child points out every detail. This literal decoding may require persistence on the viewer's part. It can be a very sophisticated cognitive skill, but not necessarily a creative experience. A creative viewer can apply creative thinking skills to the interpretation of the visual, which, in turn, enhances his/her understanding of the meaning of the visual. Creative thinking skills are intrapersonal skills which we can apply to develop various interpretations of visual information. Creative thinking is a powerful tool for making meaning. But what is creativity and how can it be developed? These two questions will be addressed in the following sections.

What Is Creativity?

Creativity has been studied formally for over thirty years. One of the ways creativity has been studied has been to investigate those people who have demonstrated a capacity for creativity in many different fields, including scientists, artists, and architects. What personality characteristics make these individuals creative? Amabile (1983) asked these individuals to describe the processes which they used to develop innovative products. Data from these interviews was used to develop a creative process profile. This research has resulted in a series of observations on the nature of creativity. The first observation is that talent, education, and cognitive skills do not by themselves appear to be sufficient for high levels of creativity. Creative ability is found on a continuum within a population and it appears to be a normally distributed trait among the population. Everyone has some degree of creative potential that can be identified and enhanced. Second, creative individuals demonstrate a high degree of self-discipline, the ability to delay gratification, perseverance when frustrated, independence of judgment, a high degree of autonomy, absence of sex-role stereotyping, an internal locus of control, a willingness to take risks, and intrinsic motivation. Third, high levels of creativity seem to occur when a match between individuals and domains exists. Individuals often have a special talent in a certain domain such as music or chess. High levels of creativity often appear to be manifested within specific contexts. They are domain-specific rather than general dispositions applied to many different contexts. Torrance (1983, 1987) refers to this as passionate involvement or love of a particular interest that results in long-term commitment and high levels of creative performance. Finally, creativity is ultimately judged by output, the product. In order to produce a creative product, the process by which the product is developed needs to be explored. Novelty or uniqueness separates creative products from ordinary ones. Value or usefulness also helps to describe a creative product.

An awareness of how we as individuals can realize these creative personality characteristics can help in developing our own ability to apply creative thinking to visual learning. Several simple recommendations follow: Be persistent when viewing visual information. Don't be satisfied with the first view. Delay gratification and continue to experience the visual as often as possible before making a final judgment or interpretation. As an additional framework for considering creative thinking and visuals two other models of creative thinking will be explored in the following section.

Two Models of Creative Thinking

There are two traditional models of creative thinking. Guilford, whose work is cited in publications of the Open University (1972), and Torrance (1962, 1979) define creativity as proficiency in four distinct categories: fluency, flexibility, originality, and elaboration. Fluency refers to the ease with which we use stored information when we need it. The following exercise is an example of fluency of thinking:

Write as many synonyms for "light" as you can think of in 30 seconds. (Some examples appear at the end of the chapter.) See Figures 3 and 4 for additional exercises.

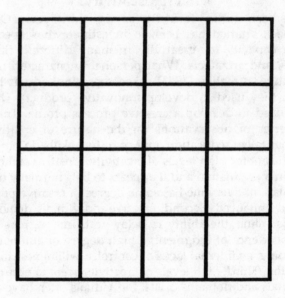

Figure 3. How Many Squares Are in This Picture?

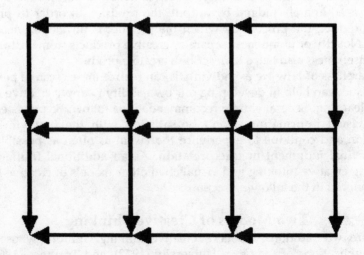

Figure 4. Remove Four Arrows and Leave Three Squares.

The second proficiency is flexibility. This is described by Guilford (1968) as "freedom from rigidity." This involves the restructuring of the material in ways which require freedom from convention. One way of assessing flexibility is to ask individuals to do the following two exercises. (Possible answers appear at the end of the chapter.)

Guilford used the following task to measure originality: *What would happen if the volume of water in the sea decreased by 10 percent?*

Guilford determined a recognized level for these two categories, originality and elaboration, by comparing an individual response to a set of norms thus determining the degree of creativity expressed. Norms were established by giving the same problem to a large number of participants to determine the type and range of responses to the same stimulus. By comparing the new responses to the norms he could determine the relative level of creativity demonstrated by the new individual. For example, on the elaboration exercise below, the "normal" response may be a simple drawing of a face. Highly creative individuals will produce unusual and/or detailed drawings incorporating the simple shape.

Elaboration is also measured by comparing individual responses to norms. Elaboration is the creative individual's ability to produce large numbers of additions to "basic" material. The following is an example: Elaborate on the drawing in Figure 5.

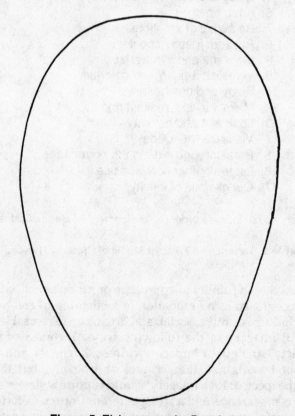

Figure 5. Elaborate on the Drawing.

None of these four skills lend themselves directly to visual literacy in terms of visual applications or interpretations, however, using any of the four skills can enhance our visual learning. Fluency can be used in generating multiple interpretations of visual information, flexibility in avoiding a conforming mind set, originality in the way we look at a conventional visual message, and the ability to elaborate can effect "potential meanings" of visual information. Several researchers have attempted to operationalize these four skills as measures of creative thinking (Torrance, 1966; Welsh, 1975).

Torrance (1979, 1992) has continued to develop and elaborate upon his model of creativity to include 17 creative thinking skills (see Table 1), but he has emphasized the tremendous potential which the stimulation of creative thinking has derived from visual experience. Within his theoretical model, three specific skills reflect creative visualization: visualize it richly and colorfully; look at it another way; and visualize the inside.

1. Problem awareness and definitions
2. Consider and produce many alternatives
3. Be original
4. Highlight the essence
5. Elaborate-but not excessively
6. Keep open
7. Be aware of emotions
8. Put your ideas in context
9. Combine and synthesize
10. Visualize it-richly and colorfully
11. Enjoy and use fantasy
12. Make it swing; make it ring
13. Look at it another way
14. Visualize the inside
15. Breakthrough-extend the boundaries
16. Let the humor flow-and use it
17. Get glimpse of infinity

Note. Numbers do not indicate order of development or hierarchical relationship.

Table 1. Torrance's 17-Factor Model of Creative Thinking.

Torrance noted that the ability to appreciate or produce rich, colorful imagery has long been recognized as a foundation or wellspring of creative behavior in many fields, including scientific, social, and artistic endeavors. He has described rich and colorful imagery in the following ways. Richness of visual images involves its variety, strength or impact, vividness, liveliness, and intensity. Rich images need not be original, that is, rare or unlikely, but they should be uncommon or unexpected. Rich imagery should capture a viewer's interest, have a clear distinctive appearance, and a strong effect or impact. Colorful imagery has sense-appeal. Colorfulness involves exciting, unusual or unexpected images that stimulate one or more sense modalities. Colorful images appeal to viewers' emotions primarily through the sensory stimulation or excitation. Rich and colorful images break away from the typical or expected, grab a viewer's attention through their distinctive appearance, and stimulate interest and curiosity through their sensory and affective appeal. By knowing this information about richness and colorfulness, we can be more effective consumers of visual information. We can interpret visuals based on our understanding of the use of color and vividness. See Figure 6.

Figure 6. Rich, Colorful Imagery.

As part of the normal processes of development, people learn to look for and expect patterns in virtually all sensory experiences. Development involves a continual limiting of perceptual experience to bring order and coherence to our experiences. However, the extent to which people perceive their world in terms of routine or in terms of expected patterns may inhibit their ability to view their experiences from new and unusual perspectives. Torrance has suggested that the ability to develop unusual visual perspectives may be one of the strongest indicators of creative behavior. Creative people appear to be able continually to return to common objects or experiences and develop new, different, and exciting perspectives. Therefore, Torrance (1979, 1992) has highlighted the need to encourage people to develop the capacity to reexamine both the objects and experiences that fill their world. He has focused on the need to break away from initial perspectives and develop alternative images and points of view. A wealth of new and unexpected information about both the image or experience and the perceiver may be gained through the ability to try alternative perspectives. See Figure 7.

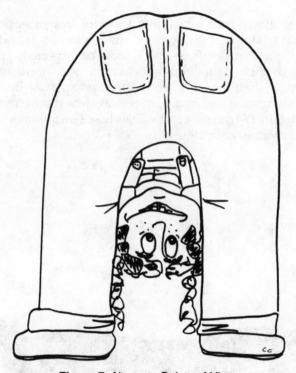

Figure 7. Alternate Points of View.

The third visualization skill discussed by Torrance involves the ability to visualize the inside: of objects, of experiences, of the world around us. Torrance indicated that highly creative and productive people seem to be able to visualize the internal appearances or dynamic processes of objects or experiences. This skill reflects the need to look beyond surface appearances for hidden information, to make explicit any implicit but important, information not immediately apparent. By looking to the inner core of objects or experiences, we deepen our perceptual engagement and interaction with the objects or experiences. This in turn increases our opportunity to identify relevant and important information that may influence our understanding and interpretations of our perceptual experiences. These three skills considered together reflect Torrance's belief that, of the sensory modalities, visual perception strongly influences our experiences and, therefore, our ability to make meaning out of our world. Intentionally cultivating and manipulating these skills will enhance our opportunities to maximize the amount and type of information derived from visuals, the richness of meaning of visual experiences and, therefore, the richness of the interpretation of the visual world in which we live. Ultimately, the use of these creative thinking skills will help us interpret information in an informed and productive manner. See Figure 8.

Simply knowing more about creative thinking processes does not insure that we will be more creative visual consumers. The viewer can take certain steps which can ensure that they can start to become a more creative thinker and in

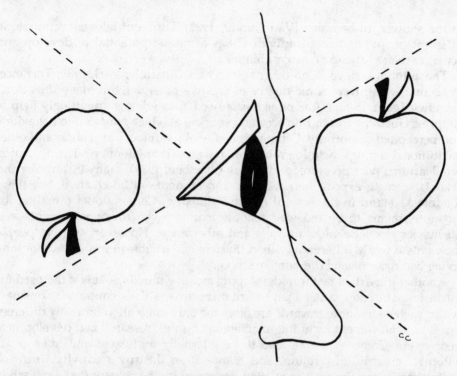

Figure 8. Creative Thinking Skills and Interpreting Information in a Productive Manner.

turn become more able to interpret visual information in a more successful manner. Before describing these steps, we would like to give an operational definition of creative thinking as it applies to visual learning in the context of this chapter. **Creative thinking is an individual's ability to interpret a visual product in a novel, unique, and useful way which allows that individual to avoid conventional interpretation of visual information.** Conventional thinking may lead to conformity of behavior and, therefore, conventionality of expectations. Are all paintings of lighthouses the same? Do they all have the same meaning or the same interpretation? This cycle of conventional thinking must be interrupted to develop and apply creative thinking skills to visual information and indeed to all aspects of our experience. Can you apply creative thinking skills to the interpretation of visual information? If not, can creative thinking be taught? That difficult question will be addressed in the following section.

Can Creative Thinking Be Taught?

The argument has been addressed by scholars for years—perhaps since or even before the beginning of formal studies in creativity—as to whether creativity can be taught. The argument against teaching creativity goes something like this. Creativity is spontaneous and unpredictable; it can't be forced to happen in a given place at a given time, and stressful situations are anathema. Truly creative people get their best ideas at the most peculiar times—

in the shower, in bed, etc. (Van Gundy, 1992). Different talents are innate in different people and each individual has a unique potential to develop and actualize their particular creative abilities.

The authors believe as do other researchers (Amabile, 1983, 1989; Torrance, 1992) that we all have some degree of creative potential, but most of us don't acknowledge it. In fact, it is often suppressed. Our schools unwittingly help to suppress creativity through structured experiences which may lead to behavioral and perceptual conformity. Other unintentional roadblocks in schools and other institutional settings include evaluation, reward, competition, restricting choice, rote learning, peer pressure, and failure (Amabile, 1989). Many businesses and schools seem to expect their workers and students to be creative, but these roadblocks stand in the way of creative thinking. Conventional thinking, for example, seems to be the way schools maintain control over students and businesses restrict choices in dress and other areas. However, creative people look at their world differently. Albert Einstein had trouble in school. Author John Irving had dyslexia and did not like school.

Another important factor in developing creative thinking skills is the need for intrinsic motivation rather than external rewards. This is contrary to business settings where financial rewards are often the only motivation for many different levels of achievement including management, sales, research and development people, etc. Creative people tend to be internally motivated and often times external rewards, evaluation, and competition destroy creativity. Intrinsic motivation in creative people is often destroyed by the content that we teach in school and the way we ask children to learn. Rote learning and memorization create a sense of learning useless facts. There is no connection between the content and the children's lives. Students should be encouraged to ask, "Why are we learning this?" Finally, we restrict choices in both schools and in the work place in the name of control or in the name of making the teacher's job easier. A good analogy here is the military; the military doesn't want creative soldiers— many schools and businesses don't want creative students or creative employees. Creative individuals are hard to control. Two of the first steps in learning to use creative thinking in the interpretation of visual information are to recognize these roadblocks and to avoid them at school and in the workplace.

The answer to the question, "Can we teach creative thinking?" may be another question. "Are we willing to do what it takes to become creative thinkers?" It is difficult because we must first recognize the need for creative thinking, and then learn as much as we can about creative thinking. In addition we have to practice overcoming the roadblocks to creative thinking. What can we do to enhance creative thinking and to consume visual information in a more creative manner?

What Can We Do to Enhance Creative Thinking?

To improve our ability to think creatively, we must examine or at least consider our daily routines. The first step in being creative is to be willing to recognize the need to think creatively. It sounds very simple, but how many of us try to interpret a visual message with the kind of openness that allows us first to develop the relevant knowledge base needed to make meaningful interpretations? How often do we question the visual information being presented to us? The second step is to find the essence of the visual information. This means to seek and define a core problem; then seek alternative solutions always remaining open to possibilities, not jumping to the solution of a problem which may be superficial or may not even exist. Be aware of your own emotional responses to visual information. We all have emotional triggers; many of those triggers can be set off by certain images, colors, or other sensory experiences. To think creatively about visual messages, one must produce as many alternative interpretations of the visual information as possible. Do not be judgmental about them; withhold judgment for as long as possible. Another step in learning to think creatively is to imagine looking at the visual information from a different point of view, as if you were another person. For example, ask yourself, "How would Aunt Martha view this information?" Similarly, use fantasy; ask yourself, "What would happen if ... ?" Place yourself in the visual image. Use alternative thinking modes; for example, act out the visual or use abstract music to help stimulate your thinking about the interpretation. And, finally, use humor. Humor contains many of the elements of creative thinking: surprise, unusual combinations, insight, playfulness. Do not expect humor to conform; the essence of humor is its spontaneity. Once we start using these creative strategies in our normal, daily experiences, how do we apply these skills to interpretation of visual information?

Creative Visual Consumers

Creative thinking used to interpret visual information is a skill needed in today's information culture. At some point in everyone's life interpretation of visual information will become important, whether deciding to vote for a political candidate, buying a product, or reading the newspaper. Creative thinkers analyze what they see in the various media, distinguish between fact and fiction, make informed judgments, and express thoughtful evaluations of their perceptions. They will be better prepared to make intelligent use of their leisure time which may include visual media. However, to accomplish each of the above goals the creative viewer must understand the role of visual media in society, must understand the techniques used by visual media, and must understand how visual media continues to evolve (Hefzallah, 1986).

In order to interpret visual information in a creative manner, we must first learn how each of the media work. For example, read about how billboards and magazines sell their advertising. Why does the facing page of a magazine cost more? Learn the vocabulary of the visual media—a pan, a tilt, a fade, etc.—and how each affects the differentiated meaning and how each affects the interpretation of the visual information. Learn to distinguish between reality and fantasy in advertising. Learn about journalism and the "news." What is editorializing and what is straight news? Is there such a thing as straight news? Learn how stories are written and chosen for the magazine, newspapers, and for the evening news. Realize that the stories chosen often express the producer's values. Realize that human beings create these programs and advertisements. Understand that visual images are chosen to arouse interest and keep the viewer's attention. Learn how commercials are made and learn about the different types of commercials. Analyze the types of characters seen in ads and on television. How do certain characters become role models that we may sometimes imitate? Watch for stereotyping that may lead to simple solutions to complex problems solved in visual media. Even a billboard can tell a story—why is a certain malt liquor advertised on billboards in African–American neighborhoods? Why is it that children can identify "Joe Camel" more often than they can identify some politicians? By learning more about the various visual media, people can use their creative skills to interpret the information.

The total integration of creative thinking skills into people's lives should be a long-term goal. Creative thinking skills can enhance every aspect of a person's life. Differentiation and interpretation of visual information are only a small part of the world in which we live. But because our world is becoming increasingly more controlled by visual information and those who manipulate it, we need a population of creative thinkers and creative visual consumers.

Visual consumers, in order to maximize their interpretations of visual messages, must follow four steps. First, they must recognize the need to apply creative thinking in the differentiation and interpretation of visual information in their lives. Second, they must learn as much as they can about creative thinking and how they can apply it to visual learning. Third, they must develop those thinking skills necessary to be able to interpret visual information more effectively and extend those skills to other areas of their lives. Finally, visual learners must apply the creative thinking skills which they learn to the realm of visual learning and, coincidentally, apply them to the rest of their lives as well. The authors believe that if we all follow these four steps, our visual learning and our lives will be enriched.

Some possible answers to the FLUENCY TEST:
bright (as in color)
easy (as in light task)
illumination (as in a bright light)
insight (as in seeing the light)
slender (as in light build)
example (as in a shining light)

Answer to NUMBER OF SQUARES:
At least 30 squares, 16 small squares, one large square, the upper left four squares combined are one square, all combinations of four, and combinations of nine squares, etc.

Answer to ARROW PROBLEM (see Figure 9):

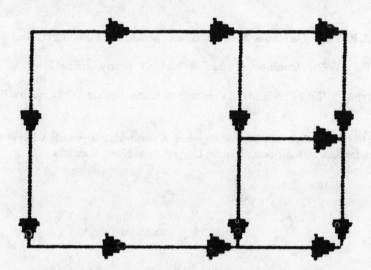

Figure 9. Answer to Arrow Problem.

Illustrations by Carter Caropreso.

References

Amabile, T. (1983). *The social psychology of creativity*. New York: Springer-Verlag.

Amabile, T. (1989). *Growing up creative: Nurturing a lifetime of creativity*. New York: Crown.

Guilford, J. P. (1968). *Intelligence, creativity, and their educational implications*. San Diego, CA: Knapp.

Hefzallah, I. M. (1986). The why of studying critical viewing. *International Journal of Instructional Media, 13*, 93–103.

Heinich, R., Molenda, M., & Russell, J. D. (1985). *Instructional media and the new technologies of instruction* (2nd ed.). New York: John Wiley & Sons.

The Open University. (1972). *Creativity*. Walton Hall, Bletchley Bucks, Great Britain: The Open University.

Torrance, E. P. (1962). *Guiding creative talent*. Englewood Cliffs, NJ: Prentice-Hall.

Torrance, E. P. (1966). *The Torrance tests of creative thinking: Technical-norms manual* (research ed.). Princeton, NJ: Personnel Press.

Torrance, E. P. (1979). *The search for satori and creativity*. Buffalo, NY: Bearly Limited.

Torrance, E. P. (1983). The importance of falling in love with "something." *Creative Child and Adult Quarterly, 25*, 55–62.

Torrance, E. P. (1987). *The blazing drive: The creative personality*. Buffalo, NY: Bearly Limited.

Torrance, E. P. (1992). *The incubation model*. Buffalo, NY: Bearly Limited.

Van Gundy, A. B. (Ed.). (1992, May). *Creativity in action*. Buffalo, NY: Creative Education Foundation.

Welsh, G. S. (1975). *Creativity and intelligence: A personality approach*. Chapel Hill, NC: Institute for Research in Social Science, University of North Carolina.

SECTION VI

Cultural, Social, Political, and Technological Aspects of Visuals

How we come to think about ourselves and others is the product of cultural and historical factors. Ideology and discourse provide the horizons and means for the transmission and reproduction of world views and senses of reality. Semiotics and postsemiotics offer models for the analysis of visual representations. Realistic representations are pictures that stand in place of what is assumed to be. Robert Muffoletto, through an analysis of representation and meaning, explores the historical, ideological, and social implications of representations. Models for the unpacking of representations and meanings from a postsemiotic perspective are also presented.

Andrew Yeaman has designed his chapter to stimulate thinking about deconstruction and visuals. Deconstruction, initially a particular way of thinking about the world developed for examining text, has subsequently been applied to the visual media. Yeaman introduces deconstruction as an intellectual alternative to the commonsense, "telephone" model of communication. He raises important questions: Are visual media limited to reinforcing the current sociocultural agenda? Since visuals deconstruct like language, can viewers go beyond receiving the *correct* message? Many citations are provided to exemplify the issues. Visuals are deconstructed and the creation of the deconstructive visual message is demonstrated. Practice exercises and suggestions are provided for further experience with concepts introduced in this chapter.

Mass media exerts an increasingly powerful influence. Gretchen Bisplinghoff contends that images surround us and are mediating our view of the world. Currently the most popular forms of mass media are film and television. The images of film and television represent a version of reality that has been selected and interpreted for our consumption. The total communication process of creating, sending, and receiving mass media images involves the process of encoding and decoding. However, the elements of this coding process often remain unrecognized, first because the images look "real" and second because of cultural conditioning.

The physical perception of the image, the material in the image, and the way that we read the image all involve coding. The brain and the eye create motion and meaning from symbolic codes of dots, lines, and still photographs. We learn how to read these images through Western conditioning and media selectivity that trains us to look for and expect certain elements, such as a three-dimensional perspective. Artistic codes of structure, such as invisibility and continuity, *determine* what we see. Cultural codes of action and narrative, historical reference, and symbolism determine how we *interpret* what we see.

Chapter Seventeen

Representations: You, Me, and Them

Robert Muffoletto

Objectives

After reading this chapter, you should be able to:

1. *Define semiotics.*

2. *Identify and describe ways of thinking about representations.*

3. *Explain what is meant by social and political implications of representations.*

4. *Discuss the basic "issue" that exists between representations and reality.*

5. *Explain what is meant by poststructural thought.*

Introduction

This chapter is as much about representations as it is about ourselves.[1] It is my position that "who" we are, "what" we are, and who "they" are, are the results of discourse. A discourse is situated in historical, social, political, and institutional relationships. The meanings and interpretations about the world and our role in it that emerge from those relationships construct a sense of "self" and other(s). Representations, taking the form of photographs, paintings, drawings, videos, films, and holograms, to name a few, are social and historical objects that have been assigned meanings, values, and functions through already established and maintained codes of discourse and meaning. The purpose here is to situate realistic representations, as pictures that stand for what "is," within a social, political, and historical landscape. The implications for positioning representations within a social landscape and not a neutral naturalistic one, places pictures, as well as other forms of representations, within a political and epistemological landscape. Once arriving at that position, the realistic image may be deconstructed and then reconstructed presenting a different world view and a different voice.

Our experience with representations is dependent on their constructed nature and use within social arenas. Once we arrive at an understanding that representations are socially constructed objects full of intentions and purposes, the asking of questions that focus on the control over the production of meaning by both producers and readers becomes critical to our inquiry into how we come to know and express ourselves to the world around us, and how it is expressed to us. In attempting to understand the nature of representations as social artifacts, we move our inquiry from a position of common sense that infers that representations mirror reality and truth, to a social critique of representations and the production of meaning.

Representations and images function not only to provide forms of expression for the dissemination of information, but they also construct, with other social experiences, individuals as subjects. "Subject" refers to how individuals think about whom they are and how they should act in relationships to others. Social institutions, like families, religions, and education, work to inform the individual when they are in relation to the other. Mass media, as well as educational media, deliver messages to individuals from various sponsors who all want to inform and influence their audiences as they would like them to be. Considering the nature of communication, before a message is created, the perceived receiver is constructed. How we think of ourselves as individuals is the result of a historical discourse controlled by others through language and discourse. In that sense, the "self" is a social construction (Atkinson, 1985; Belsey, 1980; Berger, Berger, & Kellner, 1973; Ellsworth & Whatley, 1990; Popkewitz, 1991).

This construction of a "self" is accomplished through the formation of psychological relationships between others and self through the recognition of what we are not (Belsey, 1980). Words and pictures mean something only because "we" are placed in a historical, social, and epistemological relationship to them. Pictures form us as subjects, who we think we are, as much as we form them as pictures. Pictures look the way they do because, first, we have learned how to make and look at them (Berger, Blomberg, Fox, Dibb, & Hollis, 1972; Postman, 1992); and second, pictures within the realist tradition, hold some resemblance to perceptual experience.

Again, I am not suggesting that realist pictures, or our relationships to them are natural. I am suggesting just the opposite, that representations and our relations with them are social constructions. This chapter will argue that pictures are constructed "texts" which are meant to be experienced or read by some reader. A text is anything produced to be experienced by others, it is similar to a "text" that has a writer/producer and a reader/interpreter. A text is what is experienced. These constructs, experienced as intended texts or messages, have emerged out of social and political worlds and discourses that over time has worked, as part of a larger social experience to form our understanding of self and other. It is in this analysis of self as a representation, that we can begin to find the effects of ideology. It is through the non-acceptance of self as seen, but as constructed, that the meanings and forces of an ideology will begin to appear (Nichols, 1981; Weedon, 1987).

Ideology and Discourse

The relationship between ideology and discourse is an important one to understand. For "Ideology is inscribed in discourse in the sense that it is literally written or spoken in it; it is not a separate element that exists independently in some free-floating realm of 'ideas' and is subsequently embodied in words, but a way of thinking, speaking, experiencing" (Belsey, 1980, p. 5). We cannot escape ideology(ies); every culture to function must have them, some of which are competing. One is usually dominant, marginalizing others. How we think and act, how we make meaning, is the result of an ideology that is embedded within the language/discourse in use. "The operation of ideology in human life basically involves the constitution and patterning of how human beings live their lives as conscious, reflecting initiators of acts in a structured, meaningful world. Ideology operates as discourse, addressing or ...interpolating human beings as subjects" (Therborn, 1980, p. 15). Discourse refers to systems and rules over what is said (Cherryholmes, 1988). Discourse practices, language in use from a realist perspective, attempt to define an ideology of reality. Discourse is a "domain of language-use, a particular way of talking (writing and thinking). A discourse involves certain shared assumptions ..." (Belsey, 1980, p. 5).

Discourses exist because of ideology.[2] It is only through the study of discourse, visual, verbal, or spoken, that the common-sense view of language as neutral, truthful, and transparent, becomes a mirage existing in the imagination. The point here is that language itself is ideologically based. Language itself is a closed system with ways of thinking, acting, and experiencing the world embedded in it. Every sentence that is spoken, every photograph or video that is made is a form of expression that reflects a way of thinking and understanding. Realistic representations attempt to make the image and the story transparent and absent of human intervention or authorship. The realistic image, the narrative provided by an author understood to be a distant neutral reporter, is seen only as a window to the world and not as a window with a view (Muffoletto, 1991).

Photographs as Ideological Representations

The following discussion and the examples in this chapter refer to photographs that present a realist or iconic representation of a constructed reality.[3] The assumption here is that our notion of reality is itself constructed. Reality exists only as we think of it. It is how we come to think about reality that is of interest here.

There are two generalized ways of thinking about photographic images (again, the discussion is limited to the classic iconic realist image). First, photographs work on a technical-pictorial level, merging knowledge about science and a technology of production with an interest in showing things the way they are or the way we want others to see them. This form of representation is usually referred to as realism or functionalism. Documentary, journalistic, and commercial images use realistic representations to represent the world. From a realist perspective, the world is as given, removing the form of presentation (discourse) and the language used from any ideological referents. The visual language is understood to be transparent. Realist images appear as news photographs, family snapshots, and as advertisements. This method of re-presenting is grounded in a positivist science where reality is assumed to be set and knowable (Berger *et al.*, 1972; Newhall, 1964; Popkewitz, 1991; Therborn, 1980). The emphasis here is on the "assumption" and "taken for granted likeness" of the photograph's ability to mirror reality. It, the photograph, looks like what I have experienced before.

Secondly, photographs have provided to those of us living in developed countries a format or vehicle to record moments and passages of our personal lives. (We cannot forget that there are people where the economic ability to produce and own photographs is still limited.) Photographs, film, television, and holograms, as examples, are very effective communication media based in realism for the dissemination of ideas, information, and stories about the world. The emphasis here is on the social message of the realist or mirror image rather than the technical aspect. It is through the realism of the mirror and its constructed message that we come to understand one perspective or story about the world (Muffoletto, 1991). As we are told various stories about the world, the narration becomes authorless. The subjectivity of the author is missing from the realist image; we are shown reality, not told about it (Belsey, 1980). Except in cases of aesthetic or historical considerations, the photographer is unimportant; it is the image that we are concerned about, not who made it.

Realist images consume us because they speak to us from a position of authority. They speak to us in a way that is familiar; we know the world that is being recreated for us because we live in it. The power of the realist image, photograph or otherwise, is its ability to re-create the world as we know it and have experienced it before. The frame of the lens becomes our eye and we believe what we see, and we see what we believe. The individual participates as a willing partner in the discourses presented through the constructed image. By identifying and participating with the realistic image we place ourselves in a subjective relationship to the world being presented. The mirror quality of the photograph not only shows us a constructed world, but a constructed "self" as well. This construction of "self" is accomplished because we are spoken "to" as autonomous individuals and our eye is the lens. The image as part of a discourse has defined us as a subject. The image does not speak to us as individuals, but as a mass.

The problem in thinking about photographs in this manner is that it is too simple. Thinking about, making, and looking at photographs is a complex and dynamic activity. The process of image production and reading/interpreting (creating meaning) cannot be taken as common-place or innocent. Pictures mean something because we believe they do and were made to look that way based upon that belief (Nichols, 1981). How we come to believe that pictures, as well as anything else, are meaningful, is a result of our relationship to the image. A socially constructed object came into existence because it had a social purpose. It remains part of our social landscape because it still serves that purpose. Who or what controls that production and dissemination process in a very real way controls how we think, act, and relate to the world. The "who" then refers to whom controls the discourse. Controlling discourse includes framing what can and cannot be said, who can and cannot speak. In considering pictorial, verbal, or written discourse, it is important to be aware of what is being said, what is not being said, who is and is not saying it, who is listening, and who benefits from what is being said (Cherryholmes, 1988; Goffman, 1974).

Before the development of the automated photographic process (cameras, films, and processing), the ability to make representations of oneself and others was in the hands of the artist/craftsperson/technicians. Emerging out of an interest in realism caused by oil painting and positivist science, photographs, like paintings, reflected frameworks for looking at the world (Berger *et al.*, 1972). As we experience images it is important to note that the way we currently understand and look at photographs is the result of historically looking at other forms of representations. The codes for realism were set before the shutter clicked (Goffman, 1974).

Our way of looking emerged out of one-point perspective. One-point perspective placed the viewer, the reader of the text, within the eye of the painter. The world we see is not of our own choosing, it was constructed for us as a technology of vision, and as a way for seeing what we see.

It was only after the invention of still photography that it became possible for a society to record, and in a real way construct, itself.[4] That has interesting implications, for it is in notions about the constructed "self" as a subject that we find the effects of ideology (Berger & Luckmann, 1966; Goffman, 1974; Nichols, 1981; Popkewitz, 1991; Weedon, 1987). It is in "ideology" that we find notions about the self as a constructed subject (Coward & Ellis, 1977; Feenberg, 1991; Therborn, 1980).

As discussed earlier, ideology forms our relationship to representations. As a set of beliefs, a way of knowing, our common sense and ideology form the landscapes and the horizon line by which we come to understand and make sense of the phenomena that comprise our daily experiences. In doing so, it also creates us as a subject in relationship to the dominant way of thinking and acting.

There are dominant and struggling ideologies. There are conflicts between ideological frameworks for the minds and souls of the people they touch. Images and representations (private or mass mediated) reproduce, maintain, and struggle against dominant ideologies. Hegemony, the consumption of others into domination, uses forms of mass representation to reproduce and maintain the dominant ideological framework. As Feenberg (1991) suggests, "An effective hegemony is one that need not be imposed in a continuing struggle between self-conscious agents but is reproduced unreflectively by the standard beliefs and practices of the society it dominates" (p. 78). The role of mass mediated images has been to reproduce the dominant ideology and knowledge so that it is natural and correct. Personal representations (photographs, videotapes, films) also reproduce the dominant ideological perspectives on family, gender, work, consumption, and ownership of material, images of self and others as reflections of the self, knowledge, and power. It is important to realize that "knowledge is socially constructed and the methods and forms of conveying knowledge shape knowledge itself" (Berger & Luckmann, 1966; Ellsworth & Whatley, 1990, p. 3).

At times, alternative perspectives appear which resist the dominant ways of thinking. It is at this point that the ideological framework becomes apparent to those who are able to ask critical questions about the status quo. To ask those questions, the individual as a subject must realize that there are other ways of being and that common sense, reality as we know it, is a social construction (Berger, 1963). It is a construction that is controlled through social institutions and representations. Those who control the ways of knowing and the forms of discourse, in effect, consume us as subjects, transforming us into objects.[5]

Producer, Text, and Reader

Representations, especially realistic images, not only present likenesses that point to a time and place, but also refer to various relationships between the photographer/producer and the "object" pictured. Images also refer to the perceived viewer as a reader of the image (Berger *et al.*, 1972; Fish, 1980; Monaco, 1977; Muffoletto, 1984). It cannot be overlooked that representations, as a product of some intention, are made for someone to experience including the producer and the reader of the image.

The producer of any representation is its first reader. The first consideration by any producer is to think about the question, "Does the representation communicate what I intended?" The reader, on the other hand, experiences the representation as something to be read, and asks, "What does this mean?" The way a representation comes to be meaningful to both producer and reader is a result of historical social, political, and economic relationships between the producer and the reader of the representation (Freund, 1987; Holub, 1984). To understand this connection between producer and reader, the connection must be positioned within existing institutional and knowledge relationships. Meanings are produced and reproduced because of those social and power relationships. The individual and our notions about what it means to be an individual, are the results of those institutional affiliations (Berger & Luckmann, 1966; Bronowski, 1965; Eagleton, 1984; Popkewitz, 1991).

Codes and Meanings

Photographs, as well as other forms of representation, are about the existing codes of meaning, the producer (background, intent), the technology used to produce the image (camera, lens, film, paper, chemistry, etc.), the reader/viewer of the image, and the historical and geographical moment.[6] It is through ideology, the relationship to the "way" things are perceived to be, that the individual comes to know her/himself.

Those forms of perceptions are, in a sense, given to the individual at birth (socialization) through both a verbal and visual language and a discourse in practice. It is because of the ideological basis of knowing that we must address representations not as neutral objects produced by a technology, but as subjective historical processes based in political, institutional, and social relationships (Berger, Berger, & Kellner, 1973; Berger & Luckmann, 1966; Bernstein, 1975; Popkewitz, 1984, 1991).

Representations

Representations, as institutional manifestations, are both material and non-material. They stand in place of "real" objects and ideas. Representations refer to something other than themselves. For example, a photograph of Uncle Joe refers to a real person; a road sign refers to a rest area along the highway; and a national flag refers to a concept of government.[7] Each of these representational forms is a real object that refers to something else. Depending on the context they may refer to many different things and meanings. Representations or signs are constructed and used with the intention of communicating meaning between a producer and a reader (Monaco, 1977; Nichols, 1981; Wollen, 1969). In order for communication to occur, representations or signs must be meaningful. The problem arises when, as we will see later, the meaning of the sign is understood to be real, fixed, and not socially produced. The sign is understood to be the object or concept itself and not what it is, a social construction that exists within a historical social world full of conflicts and struggles over the meanings of representations. It is in the notion of common sense and truth that ideology may be unmasked.

Semiotics as a Model for Understanding Communication

Semiotics as a model for understanding the communication process may shed some light on this constructive process (Muffoletto, 1984, 1991; Nichols, 1981; Wollen, 1969). Semiotics, as a model for understanding the communication process, holds a structuralist view of the world. It assumes a correspondence between meanings and materials that exist because of their structural relationship. This structural relationship is based upon difference—this is not that.

Semiotics is based on the notion of the sign (a representation) which is the result of the combined actions of the signified (the concept, the referent) and the signifier (material, sound, gesture) on each other that form their marriage, the sign. See Figure 1. The sign, which stands for the "thing" it represents, is the result of that relationship formed between the signifier and the signified. It is the joining of concept and material through a historical, social, and cultural process that create meaning. Language in use, both visual and non-visual, in this semiotic model, sets the meaning of the sign. From this historical perspective the meaning of the sign appears to be natural. We do not normally think about the constructed nature of words and the meanings assigned to them as we read any text. The reader of the text, as well as its producers, from a semiotic model of communication, reproduce the already fixed and existing meaning of the sign (Hawkes, 1977; Muffoletto, 1990; Weedon, 1987).

The sign has meaning because of its historical uses in practice resulting in a seemingly fixed meaning, which has become part of a system of signs or codes. Signs have been organized around three basic categories: iconic, indexual, and symbolic. Iconic signs, like photographs, hold a perceptual and technical relationship to experienced reality. Signs become meaningful because they "look like" what they depict. There depiction has become meaningful to the reader of the text through experience with other social texts.

Index or indexual signs point to or refer to something else in an abstracted or conventional manner. Thus a road sign may not look like a railroad crossing but "we" must all agree that it refers to one. The symbol, as Langer (1942) suggests, is an "instrument of thought." Symbols in this manner refer to broader more

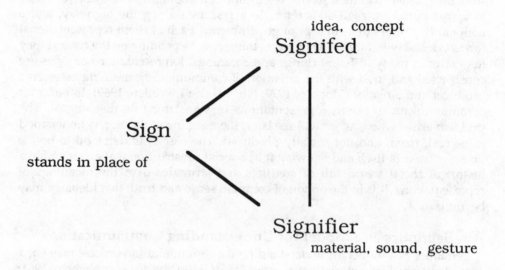

Figure 1. The Sign Is the Result of Combined Actions of the Signified and the Signifier.

universal concepts. A picture of a flag may denote a flag but it also refers to the symbolic nature of the flag to represent nationalism as well as liberating or repressive government powers.

Signs are further organized into systems of meanings or codes. Codes create the context and set the limits for the production and reception of the text. It is the produced text, the production of intentions, that is experienced by the reader of the text.[8] In this way signs appear to mean what they do because of their context—their relationship to other signs within a coding system. A dash (–) or a dot (.) have different meanings in different contexts. Morse Code uses dots and dash's to represent letters and numbers. In the writing of this text dots and dashes are used for different reasons. It is the context, the code, which sets and limits the meaning.

Having assigned a set of meanings to colors, objects, relationships between objects, as well as, genders, races, and ages, the picture (now a collection of signs placed in relationship to each other) takes on meaning(s). It works because it looks so natural (Goffman, 1974). The picture, now an organization of signs within a codified system of meanings, may denote relationships to a place, a person, or an object, but it also connotes much more. It refers to social uses, implications and multiple interpretations. A text is also produced to speak to a reader. Not only does the text position you outside, looking in, it also constructs you as a reader. Advertisements on television construct their viewer in terms of gender, economic class, race, age, and need. The commercial speaks to you because it has defined you.

As mentioned above, signs are placed in relationship to each other within the text, combining their meaning(s) and result in the formation of a text or message intended to be experienced by others. This message gains its significance because it was constructed within the parameters of a code. Codes, like signs, are socially produced. They define their meanings over time. They exist and have significance only within that context. Thus, an object in one context may refer to garbage, but in another context refer to artistic expression. Bodily movement in one context is an erotic dance, in another it is labeled as a sign of insanity. It is when codes bump into one another that conflict appears. Is it pornography or is it Art? Is it dance or is it delirium? For our purposes here, codes are best understood as part of a system of connotations drawing their strength and meaning from their relationship from within the text and from other texts.

Intertextuality

Intertextuality refers to the relationship, the historical ideological play between different texts.[9] The relationships between various texts and ideology is important to consider. For as Ellsworth and Whatley (1990) suggest, ideologies are "constructed from within particular perspectives, historical contexts, and economic, political, and social interest. They "work" to serve the interest for and from which they have been constructed by offering individuals a perspective on the world, a position from which to make sense of the world and act in it in ways that serve the interest of a particular social position. The perspectives and interest embedded within a particular ideology are presented in texts as if they were natural, given, and those of the individuals being addressed" (p. 4). If texts are ideologically based, that is, their meanings present certain perspectives of the world and not others, then the relationships between texts may work to reproduce, reinforce, and maintain certain ideological perspectives. If this is the case, then those who control the production of the various forms of representation control the way individuals construct themselves and their world as they make meanings out of it. It is in this manner that photographs and other forms of representation are grounded in social, political, and epistemological struggles. It is a question of control (power) over the control of the generation and dissemination of texts. Who is allowed to speak, and who is allowed to hear?

This is not to say that there is no resistance to the ideological messages embedded in the text. Various ideological communities resist the dominant or common sense meanings by offering other interpretations of the text. Television programs are deemed sexist or racist, photographs are dismissed as being fabricated (as if they were real to begin with) to serve the interest of one group or another, or films are seen as politically based providing one a world perspective in an attempt to legitimize the actions of a government or a political movement.

Postsemiotics

We come to know everything through a language form, its representation, and discourse. The correspondence between the inferred object, its representation, and its meaning, is part of a community "belief system, its cosmology" (Goffman, 1974, p. 27). A photograph of a shoe is more than just the shoe it denotes. Shoes have a history and a social function. Shoes have various referents. They may refer to certain type of work or life style. For example, dress shoes refer to social situations, play shoes refer to notions of leisure and competition, and every shoe refers to its means of production and to those who produced it. What may appear to be a simple and fixed meaning (after all, it is a picture of a shoe) becomes a web of intrigue in a postsemiotic, postmodern form of analysis. See Figure 2.

Photo by Robert Muffoletto

Figure 2. A Shoe?

Poststructuralism (departing from the structuralist notion of semiotics) proclaims not one truth or one meaning, but multiple meanings and interpretations providing more than one text to be experienced (Fish, 1980; Freund, 1987; Hall, Hobson, Lowe, & Willis 1980; Holub, 1984; Macintyre, 1984; Muffoletto, 1990; Weedon, 1987). Poststructuralism does not except the non-neutrality of language, visual or verbal. It situates the text as experience between the intent of producers and the receptiveness of readers. Poststructuralism does not position the reader of the text as one who is searching for the absolute truth of the text, but one who is an active partner in the creation of meaning. From a poststructuralist model the reader is understood (as well as constructed) to be a social agent who does not just receive messages as experiences but interprets them from their historical social position.

This model differs from the structuralist or semiotic perspective in that meaning is not fixed. The meaning of a gesture, a color, a word, will not only vary within time and space but also within economic, gender, and racial settings. Meaning from this perspective is not found within the relationships constructed within the text. Meaning is created, from a poststructuralist position, somewhere between the text as an intended social construction and the reader of the text who is also socially constructed. See Figure 3.

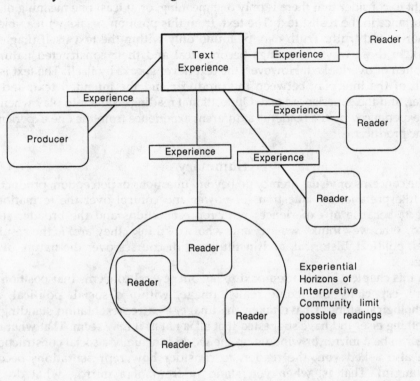

Figure 3. Meaning for the Producer and Reader Is the Experience of the Intended Text or Representations.

Poststructuralism offers another way of understanding the meaning of the image. It is a way that situates the image in a changing and conflicting world. It questions the common sense interpretations and meanings held to be truthful. It considers who benefits from the relationships depicted through representations and who does not. In short, poststructuralism does not take anything for granted, it rejects the meanings put forth by the dominant ideology as being only one interpretation that benefits some and consumes others. By rejecting the dominant ideology, the reader is providing an oppositional reading or ideology. In this light, the reader providing an oppositional interpretation of the text, deconstructs the naturalism of representation and the common sense truth of the image.

In Figure 2 we did not have a shoe but an image or picture of a shoe. It was an image made with certain intents and attitudes, with a knowledge about what pictures look like and how technically to make them.[10] In short, the image was constructed within a certain framework or paradigm. That paradigm itself defines the possibilities of interpretations and uses (Berger & Luckmann, 1966; Goffman, 1974). A poststructuralist model for understanding the meanings of images requires of the reader of any text an understanding of the construction of meaning as being not set or natural (Atkinson, 1985; Berger & Luckmann, 1966).

Intended meaning from a realist position is very well controlled. Readers are taught to consider that there is only one meaning, or at least one meaning of any importance in the realist text. The text from this position speaks with a voice of authority and truth. Truth may be found only within the text itself (Eagleton, 1984). In these ways, meanings become real and their constructed nature is forgotten or overlooked. However, the text never speaks by itself. The text is the result of the interplay between the producer and the intended text, and the reader, and the experienced text. Oppositional readings come into play when the text experienced by the reader is a different experience from the one experienced by the producer.

Summary

The concerns of visual literacy go beyond questions of perception, production, and interpretation, to questions of power and control over the formation of subjects because of experiences with representations and the broader social world. Who we "think" we are, and who we "think" they are, is the result of social, political, historical, and institutional discourses over the nature of our being.

In this chapter, I have attempted to lay out several concerns that position the image, especially the iconic realist image, within a social, political, and psychological arena. I have taken the image, as a representation standing for something else, and have suggested that all is not as it may seem. That what may appear to be a mirror or window on the world is actually a social construction. I have also asked you, the reader, to consider how representations become meaningful. That is, when you stand in front of a mirror, what do you understand, and why do you understand it in that particular way? When you view (read) texts, how do those texts become messages that mean something to you. For example, the photograph, as document, is seen from a modernist perspective as truthful, representing "the" reality that existed at some time and geography. Rarely do we as consumers of images delivered over television, in films, or found in newspapers or magazines, raise the question concerning why the image makes sense to us; or why it is meaningful at all. Do we ever ask the question: Is it truthful? Seldom do we as consumers of images ever consider the influences working on the photographer when he or she decided to "click" the camera, or where one decided to stand to make the picture. Where one decides to stand, both physically and politically, is a factor in what the photograph looks like as much as the technology of the camera and process of reproduction and dissemination (Szarkowski, 1973). What is viewed as a documentary image, as truth, as a window to the world, is in the end a result of economic, social, historical, political, and technological factors and interest. Therefore, the only "truth" we can confront with any representation is the "text" itself, not what it depicts or what it means.

As consumers we normally take the representation of things as fact. Consider the marks on this page, the sounds you are making in your mind as you "read" them, and the meanings (sense making) you are arriving at as the experience unfolds. It seems natural, unless your attention is directed to it; those marks become letters and then words. The words have sounds, and the sounds have meanings that emerge out of your experiences in the social world. In this chapter, I have asked the reader to consider them differently. I have asked you to consider them as representations that exist within a discourse full of intentions, assumptions, and other texts which inform you about "who you are" and "who they are."

Considering yourself as a subject formed by various discourses is the first step in the unpacking of the role of representations in our culture (as well as other cultures). Coming to an understanding that within any language is found ideology, moves you the reader into a reflective mode, asking critical questions not only about the various texts experienced, but how those texts function with other social texts to form how I act, speak, and think about myself and others.

Very importantly, we come to know the text through our experience with it, with the sense of knowing constructed somewhere between the intended text and its reader— experience. Those who control the meanings of representations, and this goes beyond notions of individuals and communities to include ideology and consciousness, control who you and I think "we" are. Underlying that position is the concern for whom benefits from those ways of thinking, knowing, and being.

End Notes

[1] I will be using the terms representation, image, and photograph interchangeably. The term representation refers to something that stands for something else. A photograph of a cloud is not the cloud but stands in place of it. Words are not the things they refers to, but in place of them. I understand the problems in using the above terms interchangeably, but for the purpose and scope of this chapter I have not found another way around it. No matter, pictures, photographs, and images are representations. Also, my use of representation draws from the interest in realism and positivist science.

[2] There may be multiple ideologies supporting various discourses. It is here where concerns over whom is being allowed to speak, what is being said, and who is allowed to listen, become critical.

[3] I use the word "constructed" to suggest that the reality we perceive and take for real is constructed out of our perceptual/cognitive system and how we have learned to understand or interpret what we believe we experience.

[4] It is later that we find the development of super-eight movie camera, the camcorder, and most recently the electronic-imaging camera as devices for recording events.

[5] I am using "who" here, not as a person or as a group but as a consciousness. Positivism has formed part of that who.

[6] The reader of the text is constructed as a subject who may hold membership in various interpretative communities. This membership provides the ideological framework for producing or constructing various meanings.

[7]Of course these examples may refer to other things as well. The photograph may refer to notions about uncleness, a historical period, or a person.

[8]I use the term reader here to imply an active participant. Many communication models refer to the reader as a receiver. In actuality the reader of texts creates the meaning of the text as experienced. I suggest referring to an excellent book by Stanley Fish (1980) that discusses the notion of interpretive communities.

[9]Instead of separate texts referring to each other, reproducing the viewer as a subject in relationship to all the texts, all the texts may be understood as "A" text. Thus all representations concerned with gender in some way may be considered as one.

[10]The image was made as part of larger art exhibition referring to the image as metaphor. The way the picture looks was determined by the function it would serve. It is Art.

References

Atkinson, P. (1985). *Language, structure, and reproduction: An introduction to the sociology of Basil Bernstein*. London: Methuen.

Belsey, C. (1980). *Critical practice*. London: Methuen.

Berger, J., Blomberg S., Fox C., Dibb M., & Hollis, R. (1972). *Ways of seeing: Based on the BBC television series with John Berger*. London: British Broadcasting Corporation and Penguin Books.

Berger, P. L., & Luckmann T. (1966). *The social construction of reality: A treatise in the sociology of knowledge*. Garden City, NY: Doubleday & Co.

Berger, P. L. (1963). *Invitation to sociology: A humanistic perspective*. Garden City, NY: Doubleday & Co.

Berger, P. L., Berger B., & Kellner H. (1973). *The homeless mind: Modernization and consciousness*. New York: Vintage Books.

Bernstein, B. (1975). *Class, codes, and control: Towards a theory of educational transmissions*. London: Routledge & Kegan Paul.

Bronowski, J. (1965). *The identity of man*. Garden City, NY: The Natural History Press.

Cherryholmes, C.H. (1988). *Power and criticism; Poststructural investigations in education*. New York: Teachers College Press.

Coward, R., & Ellis J. (1977). *Language and materialism: Developments in semiology and the theory of the subject*. London: Routledge & Kegan Paul.

Eagleton, T. (1984). *The function of criticism*. London: Verso.

Ellsworth, E., & Whatley, M. H. (1990). *The ideology of images in educational media: Hidden curriculums in the classroom.* New York: Teachers College Press.

Feenberg, A. (1991). *Critical theory of technology.* New York: Oxford University Press.

Fish, S. (1980). *Is there a text in this class? The authority of interpretive communities.* Cambridge, MA: Harvard University Press.

Freund, E. (1987). *The return of the reader: Reader-response criticism.* London: Methuen.

Goffman, E. (1974) *Frame analysis.* New York: Harper & Row.

Hall, S., Hobson D., Lowe A., & Willis P. (1980). *Culture, media, language: Working papers in cultural studies, 1972-79.* London: Hutchinson.

Hawkes, T. (1977). *Structuralism and semiotics.* Berkeley, CA: University of California Press.

Holub, R. C. (1984). *Reception theory: A critical introduction.* London: Methuen.

Langer, S. K. (1942). *Philosophy in a new key.* Cambridge, MA: Harvard University Press.

Macintyre, A. (1984). *After virture: A study in moral theory.* South Bend, IN: Notre Dame University Press.

Monaco, J. (1977). *How to read a film: The art, technology, language, history, and theory of film and media.* New York: Oxford University Press.

Muffoletto, R. (1984). *Towards a critical pedagogy of media education.* Unpublished doctoral dissertation, University of Wisconsin, Madison.

Muffoletto, R. (1990). Media education as critical pedagogy. *Journal of Thought, 25 (1&2),* 99–112.

Muffoletto, R. (1991). Technology and texts: Breaking the window. In D. Hlynka & J. C. Belland (Eds.), *Paradigms regained: The uses of illuminative, semiotic, and postmodern criticism as modes of inquiry in educational technology* (pp. 141-150). Englewood Cliffs, NJ: Educational Technology Publications.

Newhall, B. (1964). *The history of photography: From 1839 to the present day.* New York: The Museum of Modern Art.

Nichols, B. (1981). *Ideology and the image: Social representation in the cinema and other media.* Bloomington, IN: Indiana University Press.

Popkewitz, T. S. (1984). *Paradigm and ideology in educational research: The social functions of the intellectual.* London: The Falmer Press.

Popkewitz, T. S. (1991). *A political sociology of educational reform: Power/knowledge in teaching, teacher education, and research.* New York: Teachers College Press.

Postman, N. (1992). *Technopoly: The surrender of culture to technology.* New York: Alfred A. Knopf.

Szarkowski, J. (1973). *Looking at photographs: 100 pictures from the collection of the Museum of Modern Art.* New York: The Museum of Modern Art.

Therborn, G. (1980). *The ideology of power and the power if ideology.* London: Verso.

Weedon, C. (1987). *Feminist practice and poststructuralist theory.* New York: Basil Blackwell.

Wollen, P. (1969). *Signs and meaning in the cinema.* Bloomington, IN: Indiana University Press.

Chapter Eighteen

Deconstruction and Visuals: Is This a ~~Telephone~~?

Andrew R. J. Yeaman

Is it certain that to the word communication corresponds to a concept that is unique, univocal, rigorously controllable, and transmittable: in a word, communicable? (Derrida, 1972/1988b, p. 1)

As to the question "Who would be able to read it?," there is no pregiven response. By definition the reader does not exist. Not before the work and as its straightforward "receiver." (Derrida, 1992, p. 74)

Objectives

After reading this chapter, you should be able to:

1. *Describe what is meant by deconstruction.*

2. *Explain how deconstruction is applied to media.*

3. *Discuss the relationship that exists between deconstruction and communication.*

4. *Explain what is meant by critical theory.*

5. *Define postmodernism and poststructuralism.*

6. *Identify authors who are major contributors to the literature related to deconstruction and visuals.*

Introduction: Deconstruction in Perspective

–O, rocks! she said. Tell us in plain words. (Joyce, 1922/1986, p. 52)

Deconstruction is, I suggest, one of the most interesting and useful intellectual developments ever known. Drawn by Jacques Derrida in the 1960s out of the philosophical writing of Heidegger (Derrida, 1978), this way of knowing typifies French poststructural and postmodern thinking. Derrida's ideas rapidly spread via the Yale School so that by the 1980's English Departments in U.S. higher education included deconstruction as a major literary theory. Important understandings of literature grew from this infusion, and there is a comparable influence on the social sciences. Not only are documents being deconstructed but also social actions are read as texts and deconstructed. The metaphor of deconstruction has a particular appeal for architects and the critics of architecture. The refreshing efforts of postmodern design are the result. The appearance of deconstruction in visual and performance art has been rather different from the stereotypical new wave. Deconstructive meanings are not just conveyed by *avant garde* media. The ironies of deconstruction are depicted in mainstream techniques such as realistic painting and linear narrative. Through the current rethinking by the deconstructive movement, the humanities have regained their theoretical importance in human endeavors. Deconstruction is the core of the postmodern questioning and rejection of the engineering defects of modern science. However, these exciting recent events, with their sociopolitical overtones, tend to obscure that deconstruction has ancient and venerable roots in the tradition of critical theory.

Thinking Otherwise: Critical Theory and Deconstruction

The imperative for many cultural agents in the era of concentration camps and nuclear weapons has been to think "otherwise," to transgress the coherent unity of a metaphysics that has proven inadequate to the problems we face. (Ulmer, 1986, p. 27)

The critical theory approach is philosophical, literary, and sociopolitical in its epistemology. Critical theory dates back at least to Socrates privileging the reality of ideas or forms over the reality of appearances (Adams, 1971). Over the millennia this debate on interpretation, representation, and media became the intellectual foundation of philosophy, Christian theology, literary criticism, linguistics, psychology, communications, and education. In this century the literary focus of critical theory in North America was augmented through importing the European emphasis on sociological analysis and the critique of ideology (Adams & Searle, 1986).

There is no unified critical theory but critical thought is nevertheless influential. Despite their disagreements, critical theorists tend to concur that reality is socially constructed, that the positivistic labeling of people is not natural, and that scientific explanations of human behavior lack objectivity (Gibson, 1986). Contemporary texts produced by critical theorizing are viewed not as derivative, secondhand literature but as original, primary works actively confronting real problems (Eagleton, 1983; Hartman, 1981; Ulmer, 1986).

Current scholarship in education takes this point of view, especially *Critical Theory and Education* (Gibson, 1986), *Postmodern Education: Politics, Culture, and Social Criticism* (Aronowitz & Giroux, 1991), *Postmodernism, Feminism, and Cultural Politics* (Giroux, 1991), *Power and Criticism: Poststructural Investigations in Education* (Cherryholmes, 1988), and *Theory in the Classroom* (Nelson, 1986). Direct application to visuals in education is made by *The Ideology of Images in Educational Media* (Ellsworth & Whatley, 1991) and *Paradigms Regained: The Uses of Illuminative, Semiotic, and Postmodern Criticism as Modes of Inquiry in Educational Technology* (Hlynka & Belland, 1991).

Beyond this point some clarification of terminology is needed. Despite a heritage stretching back across millennia, critical theory is sometimes used in the context of neoMarxism to refer to the Frankfurt School alone and not to the wider perspective described in this chapter. Critical thinking, the recent pedagogical movement advocating teacher centered questioning for the development of student thinking skills, should not be conflated with critical theory. However, what was known in the last two decades as radical or liberatory pedagogy (Giroux, 1983) has been greatly influenced by present day philosophers, such as Baudrillard, Derrida, Foucault, Habermas, and Lyotard, and now refers to itself as critical pedagogy. Two more terms related to deconstruction and criticism need to be explained: postmodernism and poststructuralism.

The Department of Postmodern Languages

Postmodernism is critical theory that is "post" to the beliefs of the modern age of industrial, scientific, positivististic enlightenment. Jencks (1989) classifies societies by their major forms of production: premodern-agricultural (10,000 BC–1450), modern-industrial (1450–1960), and postmodern-information (1960 to the present) (p. 47). This runs parallel to the historical descriptions by Foucault (1977) of sovereignty giving way to disciplinary society, and to Deleuze and Guatarri's (1983, 1987) description of the current state of social control. Although "the notion of postmodernity becomes a parody of the notion of modernity" (de Man, 1986, p. 120), postmodernists question whether progress really exists. They observe changes in consciousness due to the automation of knowledge and the treatment of education and training as commodities (Lyotard, 1984).

Postmodern and poststructural are often used interchangeably as synonyms. The concepts overlap and both acknowledge the humanizing directions of modernism and structuralism. Their intentions are "post" in seeking to regain the initial courses of these endeavors. The original purposes had been lost in the institutionalization that caused the earlier efforts to stagnate.

Distinction is possible between the two but this demands much generalization. Postmodernists and poststructuralists converge in their questioning of the myth that science, technology, and knowledge are value free and neutral. Nevertheless, the postmodern focus is more social and political whereas poststructuralists are more concerned with understanding and the formation of meaning. In the late 1960's political neutrality became suspect and poststructural advocates gained credibility due to their sympathy with the postmodern.

Poststructuralism is "post" to structuralism. Building on the early 1900's lectures by Ferdinand de Saussure in linguistics, structuralist thought has influenced many fields: anthropology, the psychology of cognitive development, literary criticism, Marxist criticism, sociology, mathematics, and education (Cherryholmes, 1988, p. 16–30). The meaning of language at any one time is seen as both frozen and socially constructed. Structuralist themes were drawn together by Lévi-Strauss (1989) in language, kinship, social organization, magic, religion, and art. Beliefs collected by structuralist anthropologists were sorted into binary categories. This structure of oppositions makes all narratives appear grammatical in the way they generate meaning. As in decoding tribal myths, the unacknowledged assumption of any structuralist reading is that the task is a matter of mapping the signs and their relationship to each other.

Literary theorists of the 1960's questioned their formalist tradition and welcomed structuralism with a Johns Hopkins University conference on the importance of the structural enterprise. At this conference Derrida presented his paper on *Structure, Sign and Play in the Discourse of the Human Sciences* that identified paradoxes in structuralist reading. It is collected into *Writing and Difference*, published in translation in 1978. The provocative commentary revealed the pretense of contextual stability and introduced a new term: deconstruction. In *Speech and Phenomena*, originally published in 1967, Derrida addressed the reality of communication and thought modeled on the immediacy of speaking (1973). In *Of Grammatology*, also published in 1967, Derrida (1976) took this further by using Heidegger's X-ed out word as a visual sign that signs themselves are unstable and changed as soon as they are understood. While language itself may be endlessly self referential, it is still possible to continue thinking linguistically, grammatalogically but only with uncertainty. In this critique of Western metaphysics, Derrida was important in "leading" the French poststructuralists and postmodernists, but valuable, original contributions also came, at that time, from Roland Barthes, Jean Baudrillard, Hlne Cixous, Michel Foucault, Julia Kristeva, and Philipe Sollers among others (Adams & Searle, 1986).

Theory

Deconstruction subsequently affected literary interpretation and analytic philosophy. The result was a profound change in understanding; that what is signified by a Saussurian signifier is not always constant. Norris explains: "To 'deconstruct' a text is to draw out conflicting logics of sense and implication, with the object of showing that the text never exactly means what it says or says what it means " (Norris & Benjamin, 1988, p. 7). Thereby, all meanings are destabilized and better understandings are those which acknowledge this instability of meaning.

Derrida used deconstruction in 1966 to signal going beyond structuralism: "It is a question of explicitly and systematically posing the problem of the status of a discourse which borrows from a heritage the resources necessary for the deconstruction of that heritage itself" (Derrida, 1978, p. 282). These ideas were first presented in his introduction to Husserl's *Origin of Geometry* (1962/1989) where he addresses the phenomenological authority for obtaining meaning that rests with readers and, as a radical critique of Western metaphysics, suggests the impossibility of determining absolute, historical truth. Subsequent to this early excursion with text, language, and visualization, deconstruction has been translated to other areas such as painting (Derrida, 1987b), architecture (Norris & Benjamin, 1988), video (Ulmer, 1989), and cinema (Brunette & Wills, 1989).

In an extremely wide sense, deconstruction describes Derrida's lifelong intellectual adventures. It often implies what someone supposes Derrida would think, say and write as deconstruction. For example, the concept of polarities was taken by structuralists as central to how people think. The activity of poststructuralists in looking for exceptions to structural polarization, such as undecidable situations, and then emphasizing the gaps is taken as deconstruction.

Even this history deconstructs because poststructuralists can be thought of as continuing the structuralist tradition by refining it. Barthes (1968, 1973a, 1973b, 1984, 1987, 1988) performed definitive work in structuralism and used structural opposition to build his semiotics. Today, Barthes is remembered more as a poststructuralist for repeatedly observing discontinuities such as the labeling of cultural things as natural. This deconstructive breaking apart of mind and meaning is not mere technique.

When asked to help in translating deconstruction into Japanese, Derrida (1988a) wrote this:

> Deconstruction is not a method and cannot be transformed into one....The word "deconstruction," like all other words, acquires its value only from its inscription in a chain of possible substitutions, in what is blithely called a "context." For me, for what I have tried and still try to write, the word has interest only within a certain context, where it replaces and lets itself be determined by such other words as "écriture," "trace," "différance," "supplément," "hymen," "pharmakon," "marge," "entame," "parergon," etc. By definition, the list can never be closed.... (pp. 3–4)

Norris (1989) offered this summary as introduction to a video interview with Derrida. This was recorded for the March, 1988 Tate Gallery symposium on Deconstruction in Art and Architecture in London:

> Deconstruction locates certain oppositions or binary structures of meaning and value that constitute the discourse of 'Western metaphysics'. These include (among other) the distinctions between form and content, nature and culture, thought and perception, essence and accident, mind and body, theory and practice, male and female, concept and metaphor, speech and writing etc. A Deconstructive reading then goes on to show how these terms are inscribed within a systematic structure of hierarchical privilege, such that one of each pair will always appear to occupy the sovereign or governing position. The aim is then to demonstrate—by way of close reading—how this system is undone, so to speak, from within; how the second or subordinate claim in each pair has an equal (maybe a prior) claim to be treated as a *condition of possibility* for the entire system. Thus writing is regularly marginalised, denounced or put in its place—a strictly secondary, 'supplementary' place— by a long line of thinkers in the Western tradition, from Plato and Aristotle to

Rousseau, Husserl, Saussure, Lévi-Strauss, and the latter-day structuralist human sciences. But just as often—as Derrida shows in *Of Grammatology*—writing resurfaces to assert its claim as the repressed other of this whole logocentric tradition, the wandering 'outcast' scapegoat or exile whose off-stage role is a precondition of the system. And this curious 'logic of supplementarity' operates wherever thinking is motivated by a certain constitutive need to exclude or deny that which makes it possible from the outset. (p. 71)

More Theory

Deconstruction is a particular mode of mind for experiencing ideas. At first developed by Derrida (1989) for examining texts, it has since been applied to other media. Visuals, the concern of this chapter, deconstruct like language and also differently from language. Iconic and pictorial representations and texts are all visual. Regarding visuals as language means considering them in the context of the Western philosophical tradition, from Plato to Rousseau to Kant, whereby all communication media are representations of how people think. It is a logocentric tradition that valorizes speech over writing and painting. Derrida's program is to refute the assumption that spoken language, the most abstract of communication media, can be accepted as the closest representation of thought. For Derrida it is a non-neutral medium shaped by ideology and preconceived bias. No way of communicating, whether in speech or writing or painting, for example, is more or less direct. No way of communicating is unequivocally better for obtaining a convergence of minds than any other. It is a fallacy to think of thought as language because, in itself, language is undecidable. Ironically, this may only be made clear in the next few paragraphs if you resist the temptation to skip forward or to fall

          a
                  s
                        l
                                          e
                                                  e
                                                          p.

Derrida (1987a) repeatedly examines a picture from a medieval manuscript in *The Post Card from Socrates to Freud and Beyond* and deconstructs the postal metaphor of communication. The picture is sold as a post card and he buys "a whole supply of them" (p. 10). In the post card, the philosopher Plato appears to be dictating to a scribe. Surprisingly, the scribe is Socrates who is known for condemning written communication to Phaedrus in favor of speech. Derrida extemporizes and deconstructs the picture of Plato and Socrates, bringing metaphor up against fact: postcards are seen and not heard.

Deconstructing Communication as a Telephone Conversation

As we heard ourselves say, the telephone is a synecdoche for technology. (Ronell, 1989, p. 20)

The depth of deconstruction is greater than dialectic, than each position invoking a paired opposite. It is impossible to find a position totally outside of the text or the picture or any message. Many interpretations are possible. Some appear to different readers/viewers as more defensible than others. For example, Gardner, Howard, and Perkins (1974) compare symbol systems by their degree of notationality. They use this to distinguish pictures as visuals from texts as visuals: "It cannot be anything intrinsic to the symbols themselves if only because "oo" may function as letters in the alphabet in one system and as Little Orphan Annie's eyes in another" (p. 31). Deconstructors identify double codings in symbol systems, often working with dimensions of notationality and nonnotationality in visuals. These are most detectable when media are mixed. Pictures have inherent nonnational qualities and these interact with the literalness of notationality. When they are juxtaposed, speech and text will deconstruct each other, as will words and pictures.

The value in this active reading of visuals is in looking past the socially accepted *right answer.* The search for meaning may be the reward. This is illustrated here by deconstructing (after Derrida, 1976, p. 69) Shannon and Weaver's ubiquitous telephone metaphor from *The Mathematical Theory of Communication* (1949) and subsequently used in many educational media textbooks.

Consider deconstructing technology because telephones epitomize technological devices. According to Rogers (1983), "A *technology* is a design for instrumental action that reduces the uncertainty in the cause-effect relationships involved in achieving a desired outcome" (p. 12). This is a definition of technology that means more than hardware. It relates hardware and software directly to their affect on people. Therefore technology is always social technology.

Similarly, *The Post Card from Socrates to Freud and Beyond* examines who is doing what to whom. Derrida invokes the technology of visual representation as a social technology transmitting the authority of speech across generations. Due to its inherent quality of undecidability, the postal metaphor deconstructs in the context of social technology: "The entire history of postal *tekhnë* tends to rivet the destination to identity" (Derrida, 1987a, p. 192). This is also true of the seemingly innocuous issue of post office computerization and telecommunications. However, presenting communication as a telephone conversation is a modern myth that gives engineering decisions the status of being inarguably natural. Orality and aurality are favored as immediate representations of consciousness but speech cannot guarantee perfect understanding. The meaning of messages is shaped by emphasizing the authority of the speaker and the role of listeners as recipients is diminished. Technology, therefore reads as a social craft that allows the designers of machines and software to do things to other people.

A Deconstruction of Communication

One characteristic of those who live in a Technopoly is that they are largely
unaware of both the origins and the effects of their technologies. (Postman,
1992, p. 138)

"**Communication** is the process of sending and receiving a message," state
Fales, Kuetemeyer, and Brusic (1988) in their text on technology education for
teachers (p. 25). Their analogy is literally drawn from the Shannon and Weaver
model for transmission of data by telephone lines. The illustrative figure on the
same page shows two people in profile facing each other, eye to eye. By their
short hair and angular facial features they appear to be white males such as the
stereotype corporate soldier. The one on the left is open mouthed and speaking
into a microphone attached to a headset with a stick. A tube connects to the
headset of the one on the right. The tube has one loop in it and appears to be
plugging straight into the person's head at the left ear. The male on the right is
almost a mirror image of the one on the left except that his thin lips are together
to indicate listening activity.

The visual image suggests the hydraulic flow of words straight from one brain
to another. The artist has drawn not a telephone coil cord or a wire to connect the
two heads but a pipe like surgical tubing. The caption repeats the section
subheading that asks, "What is communication?" and the text definition hangs in
the air between the two figures at shoulder height. Unlike the text, the lettering is
sans serif and modulated in bold. The words are reversed as white on dark and
have added capitalization:

Communication
is the Process of
Sending and Receiving a Message

The pictures on the top half of the page have this caption, "In technology,
what can be imagined can very often be achieved." The archival cartoon on the
left shows a mustachioed gent walking and listening to an imaginary, futuristic
music box through the antennae sprouting from his stove pipe hat. The
contemporary photograph on the right shows a young woman listening with
headphones to a portable cassette player such as a *Sony* Walkman.

The deception here is not so much in obscuring the visions that never
materialized, such as helicars, but in blindly accepting that achieving
technological imaginings is always desirable. To describe communication as a
telephone call lacks caution. The analogy of human activities to machine
processes seduces intellect. According to the equipment-minded definition,
understanding is not necessary for communication, only the transmission and
reception of data. This suggests that meaning is unequivocable, plain, and
undeniable; that communication is principally one way; that it is something
people should do to other people because there are leaders who have voice and
followers who hear and obey; and that these cultural conventions are the natural
state.

An alternate interpretation of the profiled men hooked together by telephone is that they are not people at all. Instead they are styrofoam heads such as are found modeling hats or wigs in department stores. Perhaps they are on display in the window of an office equipment supplier to demonstrate telephone headsets. (It is paradoxical that computer operators use these to free their hands for keyboard input yet automobile drivers use hand held telephones while steering.) A further elaboration puts the dummies in a case at a museum to introduce a high tech exhibit. Like silhouettes frozen in time on the side of Grecian urns, there is a small loudspeaker in the mouth of one figure to "speak" prerecorded sounds into the telephone which conveys them to its fellow: "Watson, come here! I want you!" says Alexander Graham Bell in witless double entendre (Ronell, 1989, p. 228).

Communication is uniquely human and to give the power of communication to inanimate objects is to commit the anthropomorphic fallacy (Minsky, 1986, p. 318). There is self delusion in technological metaphors because technological imaginings are inherently cultural. Just as dance fads can be used to explain society, the myths can become real and, when technological dreams come true, technological nightmares roam the streets. Like the modern figure of Kilroy that came from the wartime schematic for a bandpass filter (Pynchon, 1964, pp. 435–436), the DOS computer face of the global search for all files represents the postmodern condition: *.* Unlike Kilroy, who complained, the DOS face only watches and listens and tinkers with the personal desiring machine: a television set (Deleuze & Guattari, 1983, p. 236). Placid, unquestioning, the DOS face viewers rotate through the programmed channels searching for the lost file, looking for meaning and escape while masturbating to reruns (Pynchon, 1990, p. 83).

It is not, as Fales, Kuetemeyer, and Brusic (1988) write, that cars send messages to people when their dashboard buzzer buzzes to remind them to fasten seat belts (p. 25). It is that automobile designers send messages to people by creating seat belt buzzers. Similarly, it is not even this printed page that communicates but the writer who speaks to your eyes. Readers may, of course, interact with things such as this page. If you ask this page, "Are you deconstructing yourself?" only you can answer the question by using your own intellect. That is interaction. If you write a letter and ask that question about what is meant or, more precisely, if what was meant at the time of writing is remembered, any reply you receive would be likely to confirm a suspicion that communication takes place only between people:

OPERATORS
ARE
STANDING
BY.
Let's put them to work.
Call now to subscribe
to The Wall Street Journal.

This crossed relationship between speech and print suggests that visual communication is also more a ~~telephone~~ than a telephone. Negroponte (1991) tells a naïve story that compares ideal visual communication to a wink (p. 106). However, the deeper meaning of winks is that they are undecidable. In addition, they may only be blinks. This is given in Ryle's parable of thick description and reported by Geertz (1973) in an ethnographic context (pp. 6–10). What Negroponte skips over are the difficulties with understanding any nonnotational medium. In contrast, it is important to acknowledge that communication can fail just as a telephone may become a ~~telephone~~. Anderson (1983) specializes in recording these events :

> I know this English guy who was driving around in the South. And he stopped for breakfast one morning somewhere in southeast Georgia. He saw "grits" on the menu. He'd never heard of grits so he asked the waitress,
> "What are grits, anyway?"
> She said, "Grits are fifty."
> He said, "Yes, but what are they?"
> She said, "They're extra."
> He said, "Yes, I'll have the grits, please" (no page number).

Postmodern Resistance *with* Media

> Rorty [1989] suggested that I can use a screwdriver for turning a screw, for opening a package and to scratch my ear inside. This is not proof that everything goes but rather that objects can be focused from the point of view of the relevant features—or pertinences—they display. But a screwdriver can also be black, this feature being irrelevant for any purpose (except perhaps if I have to use it to scratch my ear during a formal party in a dinner jacket). (Eco, 1992, p. 145)

What do you do with deconstruction? You resist. You might apply the deconstructionist concept of teletheory to question the current sociocultural agenda or even the possibility of receiving a *correct* message (Ulmer, 1989). In teletheory, people liberate themselves by accepting and making the most of undecidability in their visual communication. The self contradiction of questions such as, "What is deconstruction?" and "What is the formula for doing a deconstruction?" becomes clearer.

Memoirs of an *ERIC Digest*

The creation of a deconstructive visual document for ERIC (see Figure 1 and Figure 2) shows the context of postmodern resistance (Hlynka & Yeaman, 1992). On an intellectual level it continues the dialog on blank text which began in *ECTJ* (Hlynka, 1989; Moore & Garrison, 1988; Garrison & Moore, 1989) but it moves to a sociopolitical level. There is a longstanding tradition of this use of media; see Scott's (1990) *Domination and the Arts of Resistance: Hidden Transcripts*. Contemporary examples are described in *Technoculture* such as AIDS treatment activism (Treichler, 1991) and the appearance of slash media sexualizing *Star Trek*'s Kirk and Spock into lovers (Penley, 1991).

ERIC Clearinghouse on Information Resources

Syracuse University
School of Education • School of Information Studies
030 Huntington Hall
Syracuse, New York 13244-2340
(315) 443-3640

August 1992   EDO-IR-92-5

Postmodern Educational Technology
by Denis Hlynka and Andrew R. J. Yeaman[1,2]

Introduction

Postmodernism is a contemporary philosophic approach concerned with the multiple and contradictory ways of knowing in this historically postmodern time (Jencks, 1989). As such, the postmodern condition is becoming a significant force in educational technology, especially when instruction and training are treated as commodities (Fox, 1991).

Definitions

Postmodernism is "post" to the modernity of the industrial age. To Habermas, modernism is an incomplete project which relates a culture to its past through a transition from old to new (1983). Modernity to Lyotard means any scientific or technological activity legitimized by a grand myth or "metanarrative" (1989). The defining characteristics of modernity seem to be a faith in science, in the positive benefits of technology, and in the belief progress is inevitable and good.

Given the above definition of modernism, what is postmodernism? To Habermas, postmodernism is "antimodernism." To Lyotard, postmodernism is an "incredulity towards metanarratives" (mythlike social justifications). The defining characteristics of postmodernity are plurality, ironic double-coding, critique of metanarratives, and recognition that if there are multiple ways of knowing then there must be multiple truths.

There is much dissatisfaction with the modernist, positivist, scientific world. Science and technology had their chance but failed to deliver. They were accompanied by unexpected side effects. Nuclear energy was to provide cheap, clean power and not cause the Chornobyl disaster. Household cleaners and fuels were to make things better and not create a hole in the ozone layer. Similarly, ethnocultural groups which had once been defeated and conquered have re-emerged. As a consequence it is no longer a question of whether my view is more useful than yours. No longer does "might make right." At the very least, postmodernism confronts and exposes political overtones within information.

Postmodern Educational Technology

Producing information is a major economic force that ties postmodern theory to educational technology. The computerized society discussed in Lyotard's foundational report (1989) requires a postmodern educational technology. The field of educational technology was built on the positivist, modernist search for a best medium towards universal communication and the teaching of predetermined behavior and thinking patterns. Once it was thought to be motion pictures, then television, then programmed instruction and today it is hoped to be instructional systems development, intelligent tutoring systems and microcomputers. The past emphasis of educational technology on automated delivery systems favors the biases of the industrial, scientific, modern era. However, the postmodern is a philosophic approach that questions all dimensions, including the positivist, scientific paradigm of linear progress. In the postmodern context there is no one best way to communicate and to educate. To realize this is to begin to think as a postmodernist.

How to be a Postmodernist

1. Consider concepts, ideas and objects as texts. Textual meanings are open to interpretation.
2. Look for binary oppositions in those texts. Some usual oppositions are good/bad, progress/tradition, science/myth, love/hate, man/woman and truth/fiction.
3. "Deconstruct" the text by showing how the oppositions are not necessarily true.
4. Identify texts which are absent, groups who are not represented and omissions, which may or may not be deliberate, but are important.

[1] The order of names is alphabetical.

[2] This Digest's parallel structure is intended to be both explanatory and postmodern. Our ideal is for every reader to identify gaps and paradoxes.

First Subheading

How can a linear medium such as an ERIC Digest represent the postmodern? The Digest genre frames postmodern educational technology inside tradition. The unity of traditional text, one item followed by another, must be challenged here by textual interplay.

Our purpose is to give you a taste of the postmodern. Your reading should be an experience in going beyond control and prediction. On the page you see not one seamless piece of joint authored prose but two columns that convey difference. Does reading this affect your reading of that? The visibility of separate texts as graphic elements may bring you to participate in the message. How do the stories on this sheet of paper relate to each other? Do you seek another tale of limp french fries (Hlynka, 1991) or are your eyes drawn to computer screen experiments XXXX XX XXX XXXX XXXXXX XXXXX? Should   be left for your metaphysics? Should that be ▓▓▓▓▓▓▓▓▓▓▓▓▓? Can you feel the postmodern irreverence for modernistic oppositions?

Communication as a convergence of minds is an ideal seldom reached. What is remarkable is the agreement that it happens. Often the telephone metaphor of communication breaks apart and the unified text of authority is revealed as an illusion. Similarly, the commonsense of the systems approach to message design may be questioned. Although educational technology manipulates behavior into performance, it seeks to manipulate thinking, too. Why is there this belief that telling people something changes what they do, say and think? Postmodern dilemmas like

Figure 1. First Page of *ERIC Digest.*

Characteristics of Postmodern Educational Technology

1. A belief in pluralism. There is no one best technology of communication in education.
2. An emphasis on criticism rather than evaluation. Educational technology needs critics to turn its innovations upside down, backwards and forwards. We need to find dysfunctions as well as functions.
3. A focus on constantly rethinking and deconstructing our beliefs, tools and technology.

Conclusion

Postmodern thinking has entered the mainstream of educational technology theory and practice. Recently 26 major critical writings were assembled that address the postmodern interpretation of educational technology (Hlynka & Belland, 1991). Educational technology can no longer be perceived as neutral or as leading inevitably to progress.The hidden power within educational technology influences education, training, curriculum and people. Yet educational technology can make a difference through rigorous philosophic thinking, rethinking, deconstructing and criticizing. In short, educational technology is becoming postmodern.

References and Additional Reading

Bowers, C. A. (1988). *The cultural dimensions of educational computing: Understanding the non-neutrality of technology.* New York: Teachers College Press.
Damarin, S. K. (1991). Feminist unthinking and educational technology. *Educational and Training International, 28,* 111-119. [Also in ERIC No. ED 323 925]
Ellsworth, E. & Whatley, M. H. (Eds.) (1990). *The ideology of images in educational media: Hidden curriculums in the classroom.* New York: Teachers College Press.
Ethics scenarios: A critical theory symposium. (1992). *Proceedings of selected research presentations at the 1992 Annual Convention of the Association for Educational Communications and Technology.* (ERIC No. IR 015 709. ED number pending.)
Fox, S. (1991). The production and distribution of knowledge through open and distance learning. In D. Hlynka & J. C. Belland (Eds.), *Paradigms regained: The uses of illuminative, semiotic and post-modern criticism as modes of inquiry in educational technology: A book of readings.* (pp. 217-239). Englewood Cliffs, NJ: Educational Technology Publications.
Habermas, J. (1983). Modernity: An incomplete project. In H. Foster (Ed.), *The anti-aesthetic: Essays on postmodern culture.* (pp. 3-15). Seattle, WA: Bay Press.
Hay, K. E. (1991). *Postmodern theory, computer technology, and education: Looking forward to a postmodern education.* Unpublished doctoral dissertation. Ohio State University.
Hlynka, D. (1991). Applying semiotic theory to educational technology. In D. Hlynka & J. C. Belland (Eds.), *Paradigms regained: The uses of illuminative, semiotic and post-modern criticism as modes of inquiry in educational technology: A book of readings.* (pp. 37-50). Englewood Cliffs, NJ: Educational Technology Publications. [Also in ERIC No. ED 308 805]
Hlynka, D. & Belland, J. C. (1991). *Paradigms regained: The uses of illuminative, semiotic and post-modern criticism as modes of inquiry in educational technology: A book of readings.* Englewood Cliffs, NJ: Educational Technology Publications.
Jencks, C. (1989). *What is post-modernism?* New York: St. Martin's Press.
Koetting, J. R. & Januszewski, A. (1991). The notion of theory and educational technology: Foundations for understanding. *Educational and Training International, 28,* 96-101. [Also in ERIC No. ED 334 991]
Lather, P. (1991). *Getting smart: Feminist research and pedagogy with/in the postmodern.* New York: Routledge.
Lyotard, J. (1989). *The postmodern condition: A report on knowledge.* Minneapolis, MN: University of Minnesota Press.
Mlodzinski, L. (1991). *Teachers, technology, and patriarchy: Feminist discourse in educational technology.* Unpublished masters thesis. University of Manitoba.
Muffoletto, R. (1990). Media education as critical pedagogy. *Journal of Thought, 25* (1 & 2), 99-112. [Special issue on educational technology edited by R. S. Robinson.]
Nichols, R. G. (1990). Reconciling educational technology with the lifeworld: A study of Habermas' theory of communicative action. *Ohio Media Spectrum, 42* (3), 32-39. [Also in ERIC No. ED 308 805]
Ulmer, G. (1989). *Teletheory: Grammatology in the age of video.* New York: Routledge.
Yeaman, A. R. J. (1990). An anthropological view of educational communications and technology: Beliefs and behaviors in research and theory. *Canadian Journal of Educational Communication, 19,* 237-246. [Also in ERIC No. ED 335 025]
Yeaman, A. R. J. (1992). Seven myths of computerism. *Tech Trends, 27* (2), 22-26.

This digest was prepared for the ERIC Clearinghouse on Information Resources by Dr. Denis Hlynka, Professor, University of Manitoba, Winnipeg, Canada and Dr. Andrew R. J. Yeaman, Consultant, Yeaman & Associates, Denver, Colorado, USA. Authorship responsibility is equal.

For more information about ERIC or about obtaining ERIC articles and documents, call ACCESS ERIC, 1-800-LET-ERIC.

these cause educational technologists to read present day philosophers such as Jean Baudrillard, Jacques Derrida, Michel Foucault, Jürgen Habermas and Jean-François Lyotard.

Second Subheading

It is also appropriately postmodern to have and to establish biases: Who is doing what to you? While the advantages of systematic design are clear to its advocates, instruction is not a science but is creative and artistic (Yeaman, 1990). Talk of scientific paradigm shifts in educational technology sounds like a suspiciously modernist metanarrative. In contrast, the postmodern view supports a humanistic way of knowing with criticism as its mode of operation.

The humanities are the major source of postmodern thought. Consequently it is in teaching English, languages, literature, social studies and related subjects that the largest influence is felt. The postmodern in the classroom fits with liberatory, radical instruction as critical pedagogy. Postmodern perspectives on media and communication are thereby developing new sensibilities for educational technology to consider. Philosophy, once safely imprisoned in higher education, has escaped into our schools and training centers.

Third Subheading

This essay closes with the self consciousness of author-reader relations. Looking into the future, someone may greet us like this at a conference:

"Good to see both of you. I enjoyed your ERIC Digest on postmodern educational technology."

"Thank you."

"Tell me, is postmodernism the latest paradigm for the field or has something else come along?"

One of us makes an ironic joke about modernism:

"We are considering a new computer model for educational efficiency and productivity. It shows the square root of the instructional material covered is proportionate to the sum of the baseline interactivity and the cognitive architecture. It's based on the early research by Pythagoras with right-angled triangles."

Everyone laughs (but at different jokes) and the other of us concludes:

"However, linear, homogeneous, authoritarian versions of reality are drawing postmodern responses known by ambiguity, multiplicity and imagination."

This publication was prepared with funding from the Office of Educational Research and Improvement, U.S. Department of Education, under contract no. RI88062008. The opinions expressed in this report do not necessarily reflect the position or policies of OERI or ED.

Figure 2. Second Page of *ERIC Digest.*

Fortuitous events also contribute to the meaning of this *ERIC Digest* on *Postmodern Educational Technology*. Somehow in the ERIC Clearinghouse at Syracuse University the footnotes became entangled in the text, giving the dreamlike effect of a restaurant's order by number menu: 1, 2, 3, 1, 2, 4. The text had already split and the self-referential writing runs over the margins of marginalization (compare with the usual product) so what reason could there be for the ERIC Clearinghouse to adjust the interline spacing when readers will read in between the lines:

The end of linear writing is indeed the end of the book, even if, even today, it is within the form of a book that new writings—literary or theoretical—allow themselves to be, for better or worse, encased (Derrida, 1976, p. 86).

At What Temperature Do Computers Catch Fire?

—One must still know how to "let it blaze." One must be good at it. (Derrida, 1991, p. 67)

Memoirs of The *Post Post News*

There are nominal problems with announcing the message senders' own intentions after the fact, as discussed in Memoirs of an *ERIC Digest* (Hlynka & Yeaman, 1992, p. 43). The enhancement can actually cause distortion. This is like writing and talking about visuals being understood as a measure and visual literacy becoming consequentially transformed into the ability to write and talk about visuals. (For a thoughtful analysis of visual education see Cochran, 1991.) It is like running a digital image processing program again and again until something recognizable appears (Hoagland, 1987) and the tabloids report the face of Senator Kennedy is found on Mars ("Ted Kennedy's face," 1991).

The *Post Post News* (see Figure 3) is humorous but the deconstructive intent is to convey resistance *with* media. Different from the cliché resistance to media that supposedly should be overcome, postmodern resistance is redefined by Aronowitz and Giroux (1991) as positive:

By challenging the commonsense assumptions that are inscribed in the dominant ideology of discourse and power, it becomes possible for administrators and teachers to reconstruct their own theoretical frameworks by adding new categories of analysis and by rethinking what the actual purpose of their teaching might be. (p. 93)

The *Post Post News*

The text and its graphic form serve reading by deconstructing each other. The *Post Post News* is made from an *Aldus PageMaker* template for a newsletter. The dark square in the top left corner is a graphic place marker in the template. It is there only to be replaced by a logo but the layout indicator was not replaced. Instead, it remains to show the artificiality of PageMaker and of the newsletter as a product. A visual clue is thereby provided as a reminder that the text was simply poured into a preexisting page format. This electronic palimpsest was then edited to fit.

POST POST NEWS

OPINION OPINION
Subhead Heads Text

By Robert James

I am thinking of the essay on Tristan Tzara that makes up chapter two of Philip Beitchman's 1988 book *I Am a Process with No Subject.*

Chapter two begins with a quotation from Jürgen Habermas but more to my point it contains a translation of the speech Tzara was not allowed to give at the Eighth Dada Evening (April 9, 1919).

This appears in a footnote on pages 34-35:

   ...The talent THAT YOU CAN LEARN makes of the poet a shopkeeper
   ...SUPERMARKET OF GUARANTEED IMMORTALITY
   Nothing is important. Our art is neither transparent nor apparent.
   MUSICIANS BREAK YOUR BLIND INSTRUMENTS on stage
   ...I write naturally, like I take a piss
Art needs to be operated on
   Art is
PRETENSION...hysteria born in the atelier...
   we're looking for NOTHING
   we affirm the VITALITY of every moment

Profs Commit Microcomputer Massacre: Computers in Schools a Waste of Taxes

In medieval times books were burned but in Indiana an informal group of educational technology scholars set fire to a pile of microcomputers. Their justification? That the educational uses of computers are oppressive and a waste of public money.

When informed of the professors' actions a junior high math teacher burst into tears.

"Really, if only they could have been more thoughtful and asked Doctor Papert from MIT for his opinion. I'm really sure he would have advised them to do something really constructive and hand the computers over to a school like mine."

"I've been using Logo for seven years to teach geometry. And now I'm really teaching. No more pencils, rulers and protractors. They really keep getting lost. I've got Logo really well worked into the district curriculum but I could really use a few more computers. It's really hard to control a classroom when there aren't enough computers to go round because it means the students aren't really concentrating on doing their own work."

Commented Bloomington Fire Chief, Trebor Semaj, "They had a permit to burn and that's all that concerns me."

"It doesn't matter to me what they burned. What do you think this is? It's not like the book you read in high school, *Fahrenheit 451.*"

But some ecologically minded attendees at the professorial retreat objected to the contamination of the atmosphere with carcinogenic hydrocarbons released by combustion. However, the Program Committee came up with a compromise solution. They temporarily suspended the burning and hired a bus to take the objecting academics on a factfinding mission to Gary, Indiana. While they were away the computer burning took place as scheduled.

When asked for a comment, an IBM spokesperson declined to comment but a high ranking Apple employee who wished to remain anonymous said, "Bizarre, totally bizarre."

Figure 3. Sample Copy of *Post Post News.*

What does the black square indicate? That the black box metaphor in human information processing is not an explanation. A similar black square appears as an ultimate cybernetic machine in Barthelme's futuristic dialog *The Explanation* (Barthelme, 1970, pp. 69–80). Maybe it is a panel from a 70 year old constructivist painting by Rodchenko such as *Pure Red Color, Pure Yellow Color, Pure Blue Color*, see Strigalev (1990, pp. 33, 47). (Also see Papadakis, Cooke, and Benjamin (1990) for the constructivist origins of deconstruction.) It could be one of the seven sprocket holes, perhaps meant as nothing more than graphic punctuation, appearing between sections of *V* (Pynchon, 1964). More capricious meanings of the square graphic might be: a symbol of infinity, a piece of a chessboard or a checkerboard, a black hole as in science fiction, the black flag of anarchy, a postage stamp or the place to stick one. It may be the object of unbounded interpretation: a signifier with nothing signified. See Figure 4.

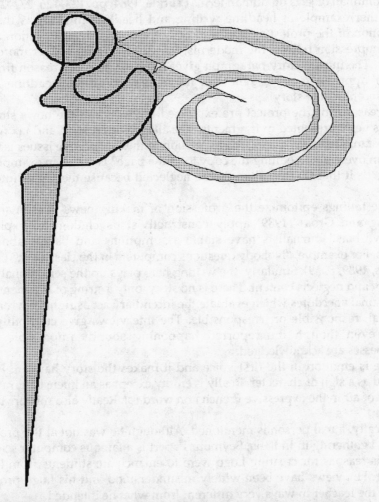

Figure 4. This is an example of a signifier with nothing signified (except to signify that there can be a signifier with nothing signified except to signify that there can be a signifier with nothing signified except to signify that there can be a signifier ...).

Dominating the page stands the feature news story which is ostensibly factual. It becomes obvious that the news story is a fiction because it is so extreme. The recounted event is reminiscent of the myths about English workers whose political acts included breaking weaving frames in the 1810's (Linton, 1985). In contrast, the story describes staid conservative figures as protesters. They will not be imprisoned then executed and scorned for generations. These professors have reached such a degree of understanding of technology that they are no longer zealous advocates but media ecologists and they seek to erase technology's emblem: computers.

The story presents bites of information like bursts of computer data. The compressed headline distorts values. The computers were not merely burned, they were given the status of people and massacred. This anthropomorphism with computers frequently happens just as it does when humans try to relate to any nonhuman objects on human terms (Turkle, 1984, pp. 123–126, 271–275).

Another example of headline writing and headline thinking is the partial description of the protest's causation. Only the economic justification appears. This compression reflects the modernist valuation of money over more human aspects. The introductory paragraph gives oppression as the reason first listed. Neither oppression nor a synonym for it appears in the headline, thereby misrepresenting the story.

No reasons for the protest are explained anywhere in the news story. This satirizes news presented in fragments. The alleged oppression and tax waste are not substantiated with detail. The expansion of these evocative issues is missing. Is this an oversight in editing the copy to fit the page? Is it just an example of bad writing? Is it that these challenges are neglected because they have intellectual depth?

These failings epitomize the profession of making news (Tuchman, 1978). Stocking and Gross (1989) apply constructivist psychology to explain this cognitive bias. Journalists have stable assumptions and beliefs about story subjects. For example, "Nobody questions computers in the classroom" (Stocking & Gross, 1989, p. 59). Similarly, the writing here plays up the sensational parts of the story and neglects content. There is no story, only a string of fragments. These are personal anecdotes which evaluate the incendiary act as right or wrong, legal or illegal, responsible or irresponsible. The interviews give credibility to the events even though the reported happening sounds impossible and no eyewitnesses are acknowledged.

There is emotion in the first voice and it makes the story happen. Really is repeated as a sign of character. Really is empty except as an intensifier, rather like the puff of air in the expressive French non word *bof*. Really also mirrors the story as fiction.

Ironically, a real person is mentioned. Although he was not at the professor's weekend gathering in Indiana, Seymour Papert is a famous computer scientist at MIT. His reasons for creating Logo were to emancipate students from lockstep learning. His views have been widely misunderstood and his Logo program is used by the teacher in ways very different from what he intended.

The Fire Chief legitimates the professors' act of burning: "They had a permit." This approval apparently does not satisfy the journalist. It is clear from the context of the second quotation that a question had been asked suggesting the response. The quotation is presented as a statement but it is a solicited response to one or two questions. It would not have been said without prompting. The Fire Chief rejects the unreported question but the invisible viewpoint is discernible as missing information. In this way the comparison with burning books, mentioned in the opening sentence, is reinforced by the Fire Chief's statement, even though it disagrees. The journalist's mind is already made up. With script in mind, the journalist knows what facts are needed for a good story and makes sure they are provided at the risk of coming close to invention. The Fire Chief, in consequence, is framed by a question.

There is more than irony in drawing on the legitimacy of fact. Consider this oblique reference to a genuine item: the classic science fiction novel *Fahrenheit 451* (Bradbury, 1953). The Fire Chief's speech, which actually is a fiction, is made more real by calling upon a work of imagination. To many this representation seems reasonable, just as educational technology is often accepted as its contemporary symbol: computer learning stations.

Deconstructing the Dominant Narrative

The *Post Post News* works as a demonstration of resistance by deconstructing the dominant narrative of computers in education.

> The challenge that a critical postmodernism has to face in education is represented in part by the power of dominant narratives to frame the questions, issues, and problems of the day in ways that exclude oppositional and radical discourses and movements. For example, the national media consistently portrays the current educational reform movement as if it were exclusively about the discourse of accountability, certification, and testing. (Aronowitz & Giroux, 1991, p. 189)

The ending of the article, cut due to circumstance by a production department editor needing to fit it to the space available, again satirizes the way that journalists think they know the truth and mean to proclaim it to readers. The writer or writers of the story sought authority by eliciting comments from computer manufacturers, possibly by telephone calls. The Rabelaisian tone of the fantastic is maintained and the stuffed shirt corporate public relations officers will not lend their names to this tale. Possibly it would be more than their jobs are worth. Here the text shows reversal of the name dropping technique used to generate an illusion of reality earlier. This switch actually increases the verisimilitude. The ordering of the fragments has become absolutely essential. The ending commentary by corporate authority would mean almost nothing if placed earlier.

As a tale this story is unsatisfactory. It lacks the concrete details of motivation. It lacks a photograph to make the event concrete. Neither of these deficiencies ever prevents news from being reported. Partial reports can be improved for the next edition or updated, on television and radio, for more news on the next hour.

The missing view of what must have been a visual event will be handled in the same way that newspaper and television news compensate for that deficiency. (Except when bigger news creates a squeeze on space and the less exciting stories simply drop out of sight.) If photographs are unavailable or the subject is too complex, computer graphics are used. Usually the illustrations are icons such as stylized flames and a clip art computer station. As there were no pictures taken of the professors either, their academic standing might have been conveyed by a stereotype head and shoulders portrait of a black gowned figure wearing a mortar board. A face might be unnecessary. Blips of visual information such as these could have *improved* the layout of the one page newsletter.

Postpedagogy

The Tristan Tzara column is headed OPINION OPINION. The redundancy indicates a mundane typing error, a double, twins, a two-sided something, a double opinion, an opinion of an opinion or the necessity to process carefully as when reading "Paris in the the Spring." In the style of Kafka, Borges, and Barth, the factual is mixed together with the fictitious. Similarly, Pynchon's (1990) postmodern novel *Vineland* which credits Deleuze and Guattari (1983) as the authors of *The Italian Wedding Fake Songbook* (1990, p. 97). Despite its suggestive title, *I Am a Process with No Subject,* is a published book that can be purchased in academic book stores and found in many libraries (Beitchman, 1988). The quoted footnote is genuine and Tzara was an actual living person. Like the Genet of *Glas* (Derrida, 1986), Tzara led a passionately unconventional life as an artist. Scholes, Comley and Ulmer (1988) refer to this tradition in French literature in their *TEXT BOOK* and identify the American peers of Tzara as Miller and Burroughs (p. 263).

In the left column a non-event is reported. Tzara published this speech, with the words given graphic emphasis in the lettering, but it was never delivered as a speech. Reputedly this emotional passage has inspired rock musicians for the last 25 years to smash electric guitars, attack musical equipment and televisions with chainsaws, and leap into the audience. This speech that was not a speech represents the poststructural deconstruction of the privileging of speaking over writing by Socrates and Rousseau. Derrida (1976) and de Man (1983) extensively analyze the tradition of making speech and text into opposites. They claim there is a self contradiction in writing about the supposed primacy of speaking and that this is a cover up for the non-neutrality of language as a medium.

The situation of Tzara's speech as an authentic non-event also applies to the newsletter itself. Because of communication difficulties stemming from unfamiliarity with poststructural literature and postmodern thinking, the newsletter may be unreadable to many without this descriptive essay. The usual emphasis in education on communication and clarity, as in technical writing, may preclude acceptance of communication as art. This was already considered in the act of composition. If the newsletter drew heavily on the early work of Derrida, then definitions of special words and phrases would be necessary to convey the concepts. That would still feed the technical mind set. Instead the style of Derrida's later writings, *Glas* (1986), *The Post Card From Socrates to Freud and Beyond,* (1987a), and *The Truth in Painting* (1987b), provides impetus for a more organic, quilted text in the newsletter, rather like the Dublin of *Ulysses* (Joyce, 1922/1986). On the back cover of *Truth in Painting* (Derrida, 1987b) a photograph of Derrida shows him in front of trees with wintry bare branches visible against the dark sky. Looking directly into the camera, his expression is quizzical as if to question the artificiality of the portrait. The setting is unusual but the moment is not unfamiliar. There seems to be humor for he is poised between two ornately carved wooden posts: the poststructural and the postmodern?

Between the Posts

> What is the purpose of placing these two texts there, and of placing them in that way, at the opening of a question about what goes (on) or doesn't go (on) between [entre] literature and truth? (Derrida, 1981, p. 183)

These are the two columns of text in *The Post Post News*. They can be read as interrelated and as interpretations of each other. This intertextual expression comes from Derrida's *Glas* (1986) where writings selected from Hegel and Genet are meaningfully juxtaposed with commentary. (Yes, the same saintly Hegel who was intellectual parent to the Dewey of Education and the same sinful Genet who continued the dark tradition of de Sade, Baudelaire, and Lautreaumont.)

In the left column page one begins:

> what, after all, of the remains(s), today, for us, here, now, of a Hegel?
> For us, here, now: from now on that is what one will not have been able to think without him.
> For us, here, now: these words are citations, already, always, we will have learned that from him.

In the right column page one begins:

> *"what remained of a Rembrandt torn into small, very regular squares and rammed down the shithole"* is divided in two.

The structure here is circular, like *Finnegan's Wake* (Joyce, 1939/1967), in that the text starts mid sentence and ends mid sentence so the beginning may be preceded by the end.

In the left column page 262 ends:

> A time to perfect the resemblance between Dionysus and Christ.
> Between the two (already) is elaborated in sum the origin of literature.
> But it runs to its ruin [perte], for it counted without [sans)

In the right column page 262 ends:

> What I had dreaded, naturally, already, republishes itself. Today, here, now, the debris of [débris de]

These last sentences finish on the first page, as does *Finnegan's Wake*.

Chance connections play a part in this sort of creation. The newsletter texts were originally written in a letter to Dr. Randy Nichols (see elsewhere in this volume). The letter was a follow up to a lunch dialogue in Bloomington, Illinois.

Half a year later in Bloomington, Indiana, where Dr. Nichols was again present, further discussions took place and the letter was reformatted as *The Post Post News*.

Resistance

A postmodernism of resistance argues that traditions should be valued for their attempts to name the partial, the particular, and the specific; in this view traditions demonstrate the importance of constituting history as a dialogue among a variety of voices as they struggle within the asymmetrical relations of power. (Aronowitz & Giroux, 1991, p. 116)

Radical things happen when resisting. To become authentic in oneself requires acknowledging the physical side of life such as the necessity of body and sexuality. The sobriety of the occasion in questioning basic assumptions is shown by breaking taboos as in ceremonies conducted by a shaman—see Ulmer (1985) on Beuys. Therefore, consider rereading the male priest's cassock as female attire. Like the accounts of desiring machines in Deleuze and Guattari's (1983) *Anti-Oedipus*, the text contains vulgarity describing basic body functions. This aspect of resistance ridicules authority. Similarly, at a conference session an Army representative unwittingly distributed a paper on Media Elimination. The ambiguity amused some anti-military participants in their scatological reading.

Postscript and Signature

"What is meant by exploiting one's own name?" ask Scholes, Comley, and Ulmer (1988) of undergraduate English students and suggest literary experiments with one's own signature (pp. 236–285). Who is Robert James? The flip side of Fire Chief Trebor Semaj is an extension of Ulmer's (1989) active version of teletheory as mystory. The telling of my story is changed by mystory as a portmanteau word. It is like the feminist replacement of history with herstory. In mystory, the personal, the subjective, the imaginative and the emotionally authentic is valued over the impersonal, the ostensibly objective, the commonsense and the superficial. This personal aspect, too, is political and postmodern. The dramatic convention of the pen name allows a wider voice through a multiple self. Hidden behind the mask of a pen name is an author who can put aside self censorship. The novelist Anthony Burgess is the person within John Wilson. His full name is John Anthony Burgess Wilson. Likewise, the author's full name also contains enough for an inner person: Andrew Robert James Yeaman.

Exercises

1. The fictional newsletter is meant as an example of what can be done in the name of resistance. Simply, people have some opportunity to take the power of communication back from centralized institutions such as newspapers and broadcast media. You do not have to be programmed with mass media programs and publications that tell you what to think about. Just as guerrilla media abandoned 16 mm Scoopics for *Sony* portable video cameras and 1/2 in video recorders in the early 1970s, word processors, page layout

programs, laser printers, and photocopiers allow more people (but not everyone) the authority of a page that looks good and reads well. The content can be nontraditional such as imaginative writing, perhaps short pieces, possibly fiction, possibly freewriting which is the descendant of surrealist automatic writing. Find your own use for a fictitious newsletter as a way of writing, printing, publishing, and resisting.

2.   Try an experiment to investigate how text and pictures deconstruct each other. Go to an art gallery and find out if you usually read the words in the title before you look at the visual work of art. If you discover that your understanding is driven by the labels then deliberately stop reading. Look first from a distance and then give your own names to the pictures. The last step, after going around a room of pictures, is to walk in close to the wall so you can read the officially assigned titles and make a comparison with what you thought. Alternately, if you find out that you are the type of person who looks at the image and then the title, observe your own cognitive processes to see if reading the title first changes what you understand from a picture.

3.   Try another experiment to investigate how text and pictures deconstruct each other. Quickly create some abstract art with a photocopier. (Why abstract?) First make a background by copying some bubble wrap or a towel or the texture of the bathroom mat. Set the copier on light if the background appears at all dark. Next, arrange some objects on the copier that will give form such as strands of yarn, crumpled colored paper, noodles, bread or almost anything that is photocopyable and not easily recognizable in itself. Copy these onto the sheet of background by putting your first copy through again and printing over it. Make at least three copies. Prop the copier lid up just a little to create some shadows for interest. Last, clip out two newspaper or magazine headlines and copy each onto a light area of your picture. Now you have three versions of the same abstract picture: one with some text, one with some other text and one without text. These three pictures are the stimulus materials which you will show to people.

Tell your subjects you want to learn how a visual affects them. Ask them to say anything that comes into their minds. When they agree to this, show them just one of the pictures. How you carry on from here is your business. You could be rigorous and record every word or you could make notes or you could just see what happens. Probably some sort of record keeping is best but it does make the data collection much more formal and you will worry about the theoretical aspects of verbalizing visuals.

There will be personal differences between people, but what you want is an overall impression of what is said in response to each of the three pictures. By reviewing what your respondents said, you can organize categories of responses and then generate hypotheses about their interactions with the visuals you have shown them. By making comparisons between the two conditions of picture with text and the picture with no text, you will be able to develop your own understanding how text and pictures deconstruct.

4.   Here is a normal instance of the subtle contribution of pictures to persuasive communication. The "America's Shame" *Macworld* came out in September, 1992. Its story is that a "technological underclass" is being created that "may never effectively compete in our technological world." This modernist message deconstructs around "competing"– because if there is competition then most people will not be allowed to win anyway, for one reason or another and whether they can do computer things or not. However, the text and the pictures deconstruct each other, too. The gray illustrations are unusual in that *Macworld* has full color pictures throughout the rest of the magazine. The text here has moody, Casablanca style photography to show that schools need to buy more computers. The pictures are printed as sepia tone black and white shots. There is only natural light which gives dark shadows and makes faces grotesque. It gives a Depression era feel to the

classrooms. In the text, *Macworld* tells readers what the solution is to these grim scenes, after all, *Macworld* exists for two reasons: To sell boxes of computer products and itself.

In advertising you can easily spot verbal messages, similar to *Macworld's*, that are supported by visuals but it is more challenging to look for contradictions in public policies. You can also act when there is an inequity, where the verbally declared intent and the visually declared intent do not correspond. You may uncover a sanctioning announcement that does not reflect actual policy in practice. Read institutional declarations of egalitarian intentions and analyze the pictures that go along with them. Obtain printed materials such as public relations brochures and then look for paragraphs like this: "... has a strong institutional commitment to the principle of diversity. In that spirit, we are particularly interested in receiving applications from a broad spectrum of people, including women, members of ethnic minorities, veterans, and disabled individuals." Then see what stereotypes the pictures show. You may locate a flyer for an instructional technology masters degree program in corporate training that only has depictions of men. The same department has a flyer for a masters degree program in school library-media that only has nineteenth century pictures of women with their hair tied back in buns.

Award yourself extra credit on this exercise if you not only find a visual disjunction but also do something about it.

References

Adams, H. (Ed.). (1971). *Critical theory since Plato*. San Diego, CA: Harcourt, Brace, Jovanovich.

Adams, H., & Searle, L. (Eds.). (1986). *Critical theory since 1965*. Tallahassee, FL: Florida State University Press.

America's Shame. (1992, September). [Special issue]. *Macworld*.

Anderson, L. (1983). *United States*. New York: Harper & Row.

Aronowitz, S., & Giroux, H. A. (Eds.). (1991). *Postmodern education: Politics, culture, and social criticism*. Minneapolis, MN: University of Minnesota Press.

Barthelme, D. (1970). *City life*. New York: Farrar, Strauss, & Giroux.

Barthes, R. (1968). *Writing degree zero*. New York: Noonday Press.

Barthes, R. (1973a). *Elements of semiology*. New York: Hill and Wang.

Barthes, R. (1973b). *Mythologies*. London: Paladin.

Barthes, R. (1984). *Camera lucida*. London: Fontana.

Barthes, R. (1987). *Criticism and truth*. Minneapolis, MN: University of Minnesota Press.

Barthes, R. (1988). *Image music text*. New York: Noonday Press.

Beitchman, P. (1988). *I am a process with no subject*. Gainesville, FL: University of Florida Press.

Bradbury, R. (1953). *Fahrenheit 451*. New York: Ballantine Books.

Brunette, P., & Wills, D. (1989). *Screen/play: Derrida and film theory*. Princeton, NJ: Princeton University Press.

Cherryholmes, C. H. (1988). *Power and criticism: Poststructural investigations in education*. New York: Teachers College Press.

Cochran, L. M. (1991). Visual education. In A. Lewy (Ed.), *The international encyclopedia of curriculum* (pp. 711–713). Oxford, UK: Pergamon.

de Man, P. (1983). *Blindness and insight: Essays in the rhetoric of contemporary criticism: Second edition, revised*. Minneapolis, MN: University of Minnesota Press.

de Man, P. (1986). *The resistance to theory*. Minneapolis, MN: University of Minnesota Press.

Deleuze, G., & Guattari, F. (1983). *Anti-Oedipus: Capitalism and schizophrenia*. Minneapolis, MN: University of Minnesota Press.

Deleuze, G., & Guattari, F. (1987). *A thousand plateaus: Capitalism and schizophrenia*. Minneapolis, MN: University of Minnesota Press.

Derrida, J. (1973). *Speech and phenomena and other essays on Husserl's theory of signs*. Evanston, IL: Northwestern University Press.

Derrida, J. (1976). *Of grammatology*. Baltimore, MD: Johns Hopkins University Press.

Derrida, J. (1978). *Writing and difference*. Chicago: University of Chicago Press.

Derrida, J. (1981). *Dissemination*. Chicago: University of Chicago Press.

Derrida, J. (1986). *Glas*. Lincoln, NE: University of Nebraska Press.

Derrida, J. (1987a). *The post card from Socrates to Freud and beyond*. Chicago: University of Chicago Press.

Derrida, J. (1987b). *The truth in painting*. Chicago: University of Chicago.

Derrida, J. (1988a). Letter to a Japanese friend. In D. Wood & R. Bernasconi (Eds.), *Derrida and différance* (pp. 1–5). Evanston, IL: Northwestern University Press.

Derrida, J. (1988b). *Limited Inc*. Evanston, IL: Northwestern University Press. (Original work published 1972.)

Derrida, J. (1989). *Edmund Husserl's origin of geometry: An introduction*. Lincoln, NE: University of Nebraska Press. (Original work published 1962.)

Derrida, J. (1991). *Cinders*. Lincoln, NE: University of Nebraska Press.

Derrida, J. (1992). *Acts of literature*. New York: Routledge.

Eagleton, T. (1983). *Literary theory: An introduction*. Minneapolis, MN: University of Minnesota Press.

Eco, U. (1992). *Interpretation and overinterpretation*. New York: Cambridge University Press.

Ellsworth, E., & Whatley, M. H. (Eds.). (1991). *The ideology of images in educational media: Hidden curriculums in the classroom*. New York: Teachers College Press.

Fales, J. F., Kuetemeyer, V. F., & Brusic, S. A. (1988). *Technology: Today and tomorrow*. New York: Glencoe/McGraw-Hill.

Foucault, M. (1977). *Discipline and punish: The birth of the prison*. New York: Pantheon.

Gardner, H., Howard, V., & Perkins, D. (1974). Symbol systems, a philosophical, psychological, and educational investigation. In D. R. Olson (Ed.), *Media and symbols: The forms of expression, communication, and education: The seventy-third yearbook of the National Society for the Study of Education: Part I* (pp. 27–55). Chicago: University of Chicago Press.

Garrison, J. W., & Moore, D. M. (1989). Comment on Hlynka's much ado about educational technology: A response to Moore and Garrison: An existential, postmodern, and postliterate visual parable. *Journal of Visual Literacy, 9* (2), 91–92.

Geertz, C. (1973). *The interpretation of cultures: Selected essays*. New York: Basic Books.

Gibson, R. (1986). *Critical theory and education*. London: Hodder & Stoughton.

Giroux, H. A. (1983). *Theory and resistance in education: A pedagogy for the opposition*. New York: Bergin & Garvey.

Giroux, H. A. (1991). *Postmodernism, feminism, and cultural politics: Redrawing educational boundaries*. New York: SUNY Press.

Hartman, G. H. (1981). *Saving the text: Literature/Derrida/philosophy*. Baltimore, MD: Johns Hopkins University Press.

Hlynka, D. (1989). Much ado about educational technology: A response to Moore and Garrison. *Journal of Visual Literacy, 9*(1), 47–57.

Hlynka, D., & Belland, J. C. (Eds.). (1991). *Paradigms regained: The uses of illuminative, semiotic, and postmodern criticism as modes of inquiry in educational technology: A book of readings*. Englewood Cliffs, NJ: Educational Technology Publications.

Hlynka, D., & Yeaman, A. R. J. (1992). Postmodern educational technology. *ERIC Digest* EDO-IR-92-5.

Hoagland, R. C. (1987). *The monuments of Mars: A city on the edge of forever*. Berkeley, CA: North Atlantic Books.

Jencks, C. (1989). *What is postmodernism?* New York: St. Martin's Press.

Johnson, B. (1982). Teaching as a literary genre. *Yale French Studies, 63*, iii–vii.

Joyce, J. (1967). *Finnegan's wake*. New York: Viking Press. (Original work published 1939.)

Joyce, J. (1986). *Ulysses*. New York: Vintage Books. (Original work published 1922.)

Lévi-Strauss, C. (1989). *Structural anthropology*. New York: Doubleday & Co.

Linton, D. (1985). Luddism reconsidered. *Et cetera, 42* (1), 32–36.

Lyotard, J. (1984). *The postmodern condition: A report on knowledge*. Minneapolis, MN: University of Minnesota Press.

Minsky, M. (1986). *The society of mind*. New York: Simon & Schuster.

Moore, D. M., & Garrison, J. W. (1988). The contribution of metaphysics to instructional technology: An existentialist perspective based on Sartre's being and nothingness. *Educational Communications and Technology Journal, 36*(1), 33–34.

Negroponte, N. P. (1991). Products and services for computer networks. *Scientific American, 265* (3), 106–113.

Nelson, C. (Ed.). (1986). *Theory in the classroom*. Urbana, IL: University of Illinois Press.

Norris, C. (1989). Jacques Derrida in discussion with Christopher Norris. In A. Papadakis, C. Cooke, & A. Benjamin (Eds.), *Deconstruction: Omnibus volume* (pp. 71–79). New York: Rizzoli.

Norris, C., & Benjamin, A. (1988). *What is deconstruction?* New York: St. Martin's Press.

Papadakis, A., Cooke, C., & Benjamin, A. (Eds.). (1990). *Deconstruction: Omnibus volume*. New York: Rizzoli.

Penley, C. (1991). Brownian motion: Women, tactics, and technology. In C. Penley & A. Ross (Eds.). *Technoculture* (pp. 135–161). Minneapolis, MN: University of Minnesota Press.

Postman, N. (1992). *Technopoly: The surrender of culture to technology*. New York: Alfred A. Knopf.

Pynchon, T. (1964). *V.* New York: Bantam Books.

Pynchon, T. (1990). *Vineland*. Boston, MA: Little, Brown.

Rogers, E. M. (1983). *Diffusion of innovations* (3rd ed.). New York: Free Press.

Ronell, A. (1989). *The telephone book: Technology, schizophrenia, electric speech*. Lincoln, NE: University of Nebraska Press.

Rorty, R. (1989). *Contingency, irony, and solidarity*. Cambridge, UK: Cambridge University Press.

Scholes, R., Comley, N. R., & Ulmer, G. L. (1988). *Text book: An introduction to literary language*. New York: St. Martin's Press.

Scott, J. C. (1990). *Domination and the arts of resistance: Hidden transcripts*. New Haven, CT: Yale University Press.

Shannon, C. E., & Weaver, W. (1949). *The mathematical theory of communication*. Urbana, IL: University of Illinois Press.

Stocking, S. H., & Gross, P. H. (1989). *How do journalists think? A proposal for the study of cognitive bias in newsmaking*. Bloomington, IN: ERIC Clearinghouse on Reading and Communication Skills.

Strigalev, A. (1990). The art of the constructivists: From exhibition to exhibition, 1914–1932. In R. Andrews & M. Kalinovska (Eds.), *Art into life: Russian constructivism 1914–1932* (pp. 15–48). New York: Rizzoli.

Ted Kennedy's face found on Mars. (1991, August 13). *Sun*, pp. 4–5.

Treichler, P. A. (1991). How to have theory in an epidemic: The evolution of AIDS treatment activism. In C. Penley & A. Ross (Eds.), *Technoculture* (pp. 57–106). Minneapolis, MN: University of Minnesota Press.

Tuchman, G. (1978). *Making news: A study in the construction of reality*. New York: Free Press.

Turkle, S. (1984). *The second self: Computers and the human spirit*. New York: Simon & Schuster.

Ulmer, G. (1985). *Applied grammatology: Post(e) pedagogy from Jacques Derrida to Joseph Beuys*. Baltimore, MD: Johns Hopkins University Press.

Ulmer, G. (1986). Sounding the unconscious. In J. P. Leavey, Jr. (Ed.), *GLASsary* (pp. 23–139). Lincoln, NE: University of Nebraska Press.

Ulmer, G. (1989). *Teletheory: Grammatology in the age of video*. New York: Routledge.

Chapter Nineteen

Cultural and Technological Coding of Mass Media Images

Gretchen Bisplinghoff

Objectives

After reading this chapter, you should be able to:

1. *Determine the pervasive influence of mass media.*

2. *Identify elements affecting mass media communication.*

3. *Identify the biological processes involved in reading images.*

4. *Explain the impact of Western cultural conditioning on perception.*

5. *Discuss the levels of cultural coding of mass media images.*

6. *Explain the structural and technical codes shaping perception.*

Introduction

We come home after work or school, open the door, go inside and turn on the TV. We catch up on the day's news in front of the television with a TV dinner. We plan our evenings around "what's on." Or we rent a tape. Or go out to catch the latest blockbuster on the big screen. The presence and influence of mass media is often so pervasive in our lives that it has become our lives; incorporated with an unexamined, uncritical acceptance of its role. We wear ad logos as fashion statements and carry our own personal mass media access systems of Walkman radios and Watchman televisions wherever we go. We watch instant replays and slow motion touchdowns as we sit on the fifty yard line. We rely on the mass media increasingly for information, recreation, and companionship. We rely on it for our perception and understanding of the world. Donald Bellisario, creator and executive producer of the television program "Quantum Leap," found this affecting him on a personal as well as a professional level. He created a program about Lee Harvey Oswald because his twelve-year-old son saw *JFK*: "And no matter how I tried to explain the facts, he said, 'No, Dad, I saw it in the movie.' I realized that years from now, *JFK* will become the definitive story on this" (Holbert, 1992, p. 37).

Mass media, by definition, affects large numbers of people and how they experience the world. It includes those types of communication which are disseminated through the use of technology to a mass audience. This definition may include newspapers, magazines, books, radio, films, and television. Currently the most popular forms of mass media images appear in film and television. These images act as mediator and interpreter of "reality" in our lives. Because of the inherent nature of their systems, they focus our attention on certain elements while filtering out others. They thus select from, interpret, and re-present the world. They present an illusion of "reality" on many levels. Understanding this transformation process in film and television images and how we learn to assimilate their messages is the focus of this chapter. The transformation process involves coding of mass media images. Though this coding may evolve over time and across cultures, it is crucial for us understand the defining elements of this cultural and technological coding.

Media Communication Model

The total process of producing and receiving film/television messages (and all the visual and aural elements which make up those messages) includes mechanisms working within film and television (form and content), as well as those that operate as a context (systems of distribution, audience expectation, etc.). Figure 1 illustrates the ongoing relationship between the parts of the total process of creating and receiving mass media messages (Lesage, 1974).

The parts of the system include the following elements: environment one (the context prior to and within which the messages are created), the creators who work within this cultural and economic framework, the product, the audience (both individual and collective), the audience's environment (its difference in space, time, and experience from the maker's), and the production/distribution system. This is an ongoing cultural/artistic process; its parts influence each other in terms of context and feedback. The model both isolates the elements and demonstrates the interactive nature of this communication process.

This framework also shows the ways in which cultural and technological structures affect our individual and collective perceptions of mass media. Specifically, these structures create ways of seeing. "Seeing" means both the perception and interpretation of mass media images. For example:

> In watching a film, the audience draws on its knowledge of the convention of the Glamorous Woman, a convention they know has a history. The way a Glamorous Woman is portrayed comes from structures or conventional attitudes in the director's mind, structures in the form/content of the film, conventional expectations (structures in the audience's mind), and structures and institutions in milieu. (Lesage, 1974, p. 14)

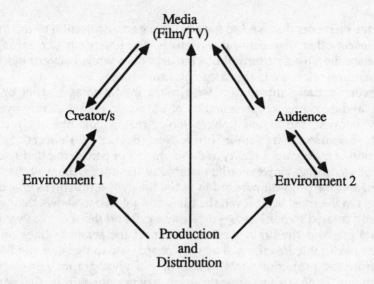

Figure 1. Media Communication Model.

Structures Exist in Each Part of the System

The production/distribution/consumption system affects all of the other elements. The system under which mass media images are produced, distributed, exhibited, and consumed works to institutionalize certain ways of creating mass media—they become standardized. Again, in film, for example: "In most countries, film production has been institutionalized so that feature films are made in remarkably similar ways" (Lesage, 1974, p. 15). These standards are different depending upon the basis of the system. The structures of mass media operate according to a Western perspective or basis in the U.S. This basis/bias becomes invisible because of our training. In the West, the intrinsic property of the camera's ability to reproduce a naturalistic image has been exploited and developed as the dominant mode of image production. Other modes, formalist or formativist, are possible, but are usually labeled avant-garde, experimental, out of the mainstream. Thus, Western structures of media images present illusions of reality which hide their construction.

Encoding and Decoding

As we grow up, we devote a large percentage of our time, formally and informally, to attaining literacy in the language of our culture. The educational system enforces the necessity, and recognizes the difficulty of this undertaking, with years of classes. In order to communicate, we need a command of this language. In studying its alphabet, vocabulary, syntax, grammar, and spelling, we soon grasp the nature of language as a coded system. WE see a structure of signs or symbols that the culture has created to use to refer to things, to represent something else. Our job is to learn how to encode and decode our thoughts, our expressions, and those of others, by using this culturally agreed upon system of referents. There is no difficulty in recognizing the symbolic basis of this system because the elements that we use have no apparent connection to the thing that they represent other than cultural consensus. The letters c,h,a,i,r, arranged in a sequence are literally a pattern of black marks on a white background until we learn its cultural reference in the category of furniture.

However, in daily interaction with mass media images, this process of encoding and decoding a representation of the world is consistently overlooked precisely because the visual images look "real"; look like their referents. Primarily because of its iconic properties (Becker & Roberts, 1992), the construction of mass media reality and the process of perceiving that reality isn't recognized as coding. However, the material of the image, the way that we read the image and the physical perception of the image itself involves encoding and decoding. On the most basic level, the films and television shows that we watch are literally created in our heads—they don't exist on the screen as we perceive them. The eye and the brain work to interpret the separate lines on the TV screens as intelligible images, just as they coordinate to perceive the illusion of motion from the projection of 24 frames of still photographs per second on a movie screen. Then, in fact, the program exists only within the perception processes and the mind of the person watching.

Physical Factors and Processes

Two perceptual processes work together to "see" motion in film and television: persistence of vision and the phi phenomenon. Of the elements that came together during the nineteenth century to begin motion picture history, the key factor was the investigation of the idea that the human eye could perceive motion from a quick succession of still images. This "trick" of the eye had been exploited in optical toys for centuries. However, Peter Roget's paper on "Persistence of Vision with Regard to Moving Objects" in 1824 began an intensive investigation into this process of perception. This theory proposed that an image was retained on the retina of the eye for a fraction of a second after its source was removed. If one image was replaced by another quickly enough, the images would seem to merge, as when a light source whirled around at the end of a string appears as a continuous circle of light. The eye "ignores" the blackness between the individual images. As a result of the article, there was an explosion in the number of optical devices invented to exploit this phenomenon, first using animation and then photographic stills of successive frames of movement (Wead, 1981). However, later investigation revealed that the eye still sees one frame after another in this process. It takes the brain making a cause-effect connection (I've seen a hand change positions like this before so that film character's hand must be waving) that the element in the frame must have moved (or the phi phenomenon) that allows us to see motion (Kawin, 1987).

This physical process of creating the moving image through the interaction of persistence of vision and the phi phenomenon also occurs at the basic levels of reading the television screen. The image on the screen consists of lines of black and white or color made up of linear sequences of scanned electrons. These fragments are organized and interpreted by the perception processes of the eye and brain; they create the message of that image at its most basic level. See Figure 2.

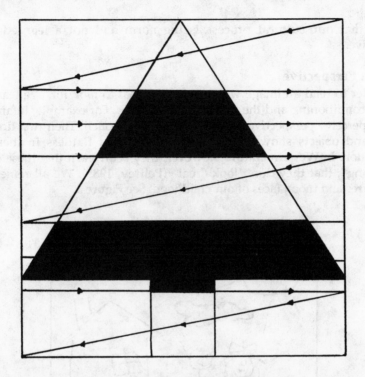

Figure 2. Phi-Phenomenon–Television.

Thus, we see the news anchors at their desks, not horizontal lines or dots of red, blue, and green. Also, because they smile, lean forward, and gesture, in their presentation of breaking stories, the principles of the persistence of vision and the phi phenomenon are also at work here in order for us to "see" their motion on the screen. The work of Lichtenstein and others who use dot matrix (also used in newspaper and magazine illustrations) to create "pop art" images acknowledges the central role that the physical perception of the consumer plays in the creation of mass media images.

Cultural Conditioning
The process of perception is basically a system of organization. The brain is confronted with the task of making sense out of the chaos of the world of everyday reality. Thus, the brain must constantly select out, focus on and organize the myriad of details that bombard us daily. The most basic of these organizational levels are the physiological ones just described through which we all receive the messages of the mass media as images. However, beyond the physiological organization, our reading of the images is also organized by cultural conditioning. What we see, how we see it, and what it means to us is focused, concentrated, and conditioned by our cultural connections. The "reality" of the mass media images is created out of a system of cultural conventions that we all learn by growing up in a particular culture and absorbing its rules, including those about how images should be made and read. As Americans, we

assume that our cultural process is the norm and not a learned Western perspective.

Western Perspective

In order to read an image we must know what to look for. We learn this by cultural conditioning and the pre-existence of cues. For example, infants do not initially perceive perspective; they learn it through touch. Their first drawings of people and objects show a different orientation, a flatness in their spatial presentation. In Western culture, however, they soon learn that these drawings are "wrong"; that they don't look "real" (Pelfrey, 1985). We all remember the stick figures and moon faces of our childhood. See Figure 3.

Figure 3. First Drawings.

And most of us remember when we concluded that we couldn't draw because we couldn't master the art of creating three dimensional perspective on a flat surface through shading and other techniques. An artist such as Grandma Moses is labeled "primitive" because of her deviation from three-dimensional perspective; however, many non-Western artistic depictions of the world do not incorporate this as a necessary element of a "realistic" portrayal. This is particularly important regarding perception of mass media images because it does involve creating for, and reading of, a flat two-dimensional surface. Western cues for creating and reading this image come from Renaissance painting techniques for creating three dimensional space using a horizon line and vanishing points, converging lines, etc. See Figure 4. This learned response imposes a Western "way of seeing" the world.

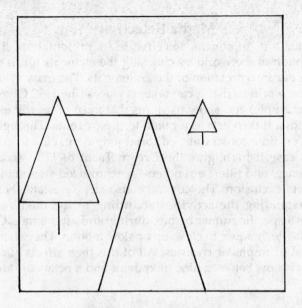

Figure 4. Western "Way of Seeing" the World.

Cultural Pre-existence

Filmic and televised reality, of course, is created out of the objects, gestures, dress, artifacts, and interactions of a culture, and have a pre-existence within that culture. And conventions, attitudes, and behaviors have been established regarding that existence. The elements of the scene seem part of the naturalistic detail, but we have a learned response both from growing up in a particular culture and from past experiences with the mass media's presentation of those elements. Even so basic and seemingly neutral a detail as soil is coded by human interaction:

> For example, soil existed before human practice, but soil as an object for human consideration (and how else can we know it?) cannot exist apart from the context of human practice. Within this context of human practice there are definite configurations of shared perceptions, ideas, and experiences which are expressed by systematic patterns of communication. This is what is known as coding. Soil is coded by all its cultural, agricultural, historical, political, economic, etc., characteristics: all the ways in which people have related to it. Therefore, reality itself is already coded. (McGarry, 1975, p. 50)

And the context of our experience with other films and TV programs guide our readings of the coding of soil; close-ups of the pioneer's plow breaking through virgin prairie sod to "tame" the West, U.S. soldiers "digging in" and dying on foreign soil, the centrality of land ownership in countless narratives from *Dallas* to *The Grapes of Wrath*. Thus, we know how to respond to these images because we are conditioned to read them as they are en-coded by our experience with their cultural pre-existence and through media selectivity.

Media Selectivity

The mass media is, of course, selective in its presentation. It mediates the viewer's perception of the world by choosing the elements for us to focus on, as well as guiding our interpretation of those elements. The mass media operates as a window on the world in that it can take us places (the 1992 Olympic Games in Barcelona, for example) and show us sights that most of us will experience only through the media. It then acts as a guide to these events. Through the selection process (based on time constraints, editorial judgment, etc.) it focuses on some events (in this case it highlights the Dream Team of U.S. basketball for the American audience) and filters out others (synchronized swimming), sometimes to their complete exclusion. The coverage also clearly establishes signposts or cues for understanding the activities according to the media interpretation. Cameras isolate a specific runner before, during, and after a race. Commentators point out running techniques in close-up or slow motion. They show background clips of personal triumphs or rivalries. All of this then affects our experience of that race, which is now between nine unknowns and a personal story.

Cultural Bias

In each country the filter tends to work along a cultural bias in the content that is emphasized versus that which is excluded. Thus, we may be experiencing more of the world via satellite and cable, but this material is still selected, organized, focused, and interpreted through a Western mass media perspective of what's "important" and what's not. We would, perhaps, expect this cultural bias in the nationalistic arena of the Olympic Games and "approve" the central focus on the role and activities of U.S. athletes to the exclusion of other countries (although we are a nation of immigrants from other countries) as "natural" under the circumstances. But this naturalness depends on cultural expectations which have been developed over the years concerning the interpretation of the role of the Games and national image, pride, and rivalries. The cultural focus also focuses on the visual story as the important story. The mass media of television and film are primarily visual media. They depend on, search for, and create visual images which will draw the viewer to the screen. The computer-generated pyrotechnics of *Terminator 2* and the opening and closing spectacles of the Olympics that become more lavish and elaborately staged each session are both examples.

Social Context

Although we apparently experience a different relationship to the media whether we choose to watch TV or decide to go out to a movie, there is overlap and consistency in this aspect also. When we go to a movie, we go out of the house to a darkened auditorium full of strangers to focus on and be immersed in a larger than life experience as part of a social event. We watch television, however, as part of the ongoing stream of our lives. Its small screen competes for our attention visually with the surrounding furniture, the movement of people across the room and ongoing conversation. These differences indicate that we respond to the movie with a more continuous look or gaze while the television has to compete for our glance (Edmonds, 1982). However, in the cross-integration of the two mass media, the large screens at the local cineplex have been getting smaller and the small screen in living rooms has been getting bigger. And the interaction with the screen and each other in the movie audience has been getting more vocal and more physically active. Overlapping and cross-referencing of experience also occurs whenever we watch a made for TV movie of the week or rent *Jaws* for home viewing.

In both cases, the coding of both film and television position us overall in relation to the text so that it is easy to read. In general, we are presented with a "world that is coherent, well-ordered, and already meaningful" (Mayne, 1976, p. 42). Even in seemingly unusual approaches (*MTV*), there is consistency in difference, i.e., a discontinuity of images, and borrowing from other familiar codes (Hollywood stereotypes and story):

> When music videos first began to appear in the early 80s, a ripple of excitement moved through the avant-garde film community. Here, at last, was a kind of commercially sanctioned American movie-making that broke with the tyranny of plot and characters, opening the way for a formally inventive, non-narrative cinema that could be seen and appreciated by a wide audience ... It didn't take long for the spirit of experimentation to wane, and for standard formulas and standard styles—every bit as codified as those that rule feature filmmaking—to settle in. (Heim, 1988, p. 14)

This consistency in the mass media is created out of a complex system of social and artistic codes. The interaction between these layers of codes creates the meanings we receive. Artistic codes of structure and technology determine what we see; social or cultural codes determine how we interpret what we see. Structural, technical, and cultural coding levels interweave and interact. The artistic codes are established and interpreted in relation to cultural coding and the cultural codes are supported and reinforced by the artistic codes.

Cultural Coding Levels

Cultural codes interact on five main levels. These coding levels include: Enigmatic and Action Codes of the narrative, Historical Reference Codes, Semic Codes, and Symbolic Codes (Lesage, 1976). The Enigmatic Codes are the unanswered questions which shape the narrative and our expectations throughout the story. The cause and effect relationship that the script sets up and manipulates for interest, suspense tension, etc., by withholding or retarding the revelation of the answers. And Action Codes prescribe what action is appropriate and expected during the working out of the narrative (kissing during a romantic scene) and how much of any particular action will be presented to establish the storyline. Our expectations for this action depend on our cultural knowledge of film/TV structure. This structure selects what's "necessary" to move things along; what's representative and what can be left out (most preparation of food, sleeping, etc.) as unnecessary to the story. In both of these codes, the basic underlying cultural assumption is that both film and television are based on codes of narrative realism—the fact that we automatically expect these forms to tell a believable story and to focus on that story while hiding the artistic process of the telling.

Historical Reference Codes

Historical Reference Codes are the text's explicit use of the established knowledge about the world of one's environment. They may make specific reference to areas such as science or history, as well as make assumptions about popular knowledge or common sense ("what people know"). Some of these codes the text explains, some it assumes that we know (definitions of masculinity/femininity, personality types of people of certain ages, ethnic backgrounds, etc.), and some it just mentions in passing (Lesage, 1976, p. 49). In a science fiction film, for example, great care is often taken to provide plausible details of scientific knowledge: equations, formulas, technical expertise—both to establish the verisimilitude of the world and to set up the action that will follow in this high tech environment. Use of this type of knowledge is then central to the development of the narrative.

Semic and Symbolic Codes

Semic Codes and Symbolic Codes work in an inverse relation to define structures. Semes work through an accumulation of specific detail, of labels (primarily about characters) to connote meanings. Symbolic codes work in a broader, less direct manner, often through continuing motifs or archetypes common to the whole culture. Semic codes define characters through conventions of dress, gesture, movement, etc.—the person presented is a "collection of semes, the sum of which identify character" (Lesage, 1976, p. 48). We read these codes based on the text and our cultural/media experience of the use of those elements—we label these characters (as "good," "evil," "sexy") and anticipate their behavior. All of these details of character and their setting accumulate to connote meaning in a specific scene. However, the Symbolic Codes establish meaning for the overall presentation on the broader level of working out basic cultural conflicts such as the values of civilization vs. wilderness or nature, male vs. female, etc.

Structural Coding

Structural codes are based on constructing a narrative and telling a story. The earliest film images were primarily very brief documentations of everyday life or filmed theatrical acts (a train pulling into a station or Chinese acrobats performing). When the initial novelty of witnessing motion began to wane, the incorporation of a story or narrative line brought audiences back into the theaters to see *The Great Train Robbery* or *Rescued by Rover*. The narrative form became the dominant form. The conventions which developed to focus on the storytelling ability of the media still persist as the dominant artistic mode which shapes our expectations. Television has also developed forms of performance in the "rhetorical mode" which directly address the audience (such as game shows, news programs, and talk shows) in addition to the "cinematic" mode or narrative mode used in soaps, dramas, TV movies, etc. However, most TV presentations are narratives and those that aren't often use narrative structures of presentation—the evening news is a series of news stories and music videos often recreate the story of the song's lyrics:

The only television formats that consistently eschew narratives are those that are highly structured according to their own alternate rules: game shows, exercise shows, sports contests, news conferences, talk shows, musical performances. Yet even in such forms one can often spot narrative infiltration: talk show guests frequently answer their host's questions with stories.... (Allen, 1992, p. 43)

Invisibility

Structural codes creating film/cinematic TV narratives include four basic conventions that guide our expectations and interpretation. These conventions include first the Invisibility of the process based on conventions of editing of space and time. The dominant structure which developed focused on developing the narrative and hiding the process. The techniques are not foregrounded, but rather are made as unobtrusive as possible (editing on action so that the action disguises the cut, for example). The audience's focus is on what happens to the characters in the unfolding action. The editing is seen, but not noticed. Thus, this also means that audience readings of film/TV shows occur in terms of the stories that they tell, even in case of recent films in which the visuals have become the experience of the film (the robotic transformations of the Terminator 1000 in *T2*). The established conventions contribute to the difficulty of going beyond the story to study techniques and even the resistance to analysis of this media. We are encouraged by our trained response to close-ups, subjective point of view shots, dark shadowy lighting, and a pounding score to identify with a character's peril, to immerse ourselves in their story. Their story becomes our reality. It requires an effort to go beyond this level of response.

Continuity of Space

The storylines are constructed out of manipulations of space and time which have been developed over time as the norm for establishing a narrative. We expect a continuity of space which we, again, often create in our minds based on conventionalized cues. In this continuity system, space is presented through patterns of consistency; consistency of background, and consistency of direction and action on screen. These patterns are literally based on "rules" of filmmaking (which are established for beginning artists in classes and texts). First, according to these rules, action should be staged and shot so that it doesn't violate the 180 degree line rule. This rule is the basis for consistency within the presentation of space. It is defined as "the imaginary line that passes from side to side through the main actors, defining the spatial relationships of all the elements of the scene as being to the right or left; the camera is not supposed to cross the axis at a cut and thus reverse those spatial relations" (Bordwell & Thompson, 1990, p. 408). We expect the consistency that this system provides of seeing the same background behind the actors (although from slightly different angles). And if they move, we expect the consistency that this positioning provides in screen movement, and we expect that we will have "matching" action on screen.

Visual Time Cues

Manipulation of time is also indicated through conventionalized Visual Time Cues. Usually the cues indicate time left out. The story is told primarily through time compression; representative events are chosen as the key elements to establish the storyline (leaving out all the boring stuff in between). Cues such as cuts, fades, or dissolves indicate to us whether time passes quickly or slowly. Often they also indicate how much time has passed. Time may pass instantaneously with a cut, or slowly with a fade out and fade in to the next scene. Time can stop in the freeze frame of two lovers' kiss, or expand in the slow motion death of a young cowboy. The depictions of time passing through editing or composition (actors aging, calendar pages turning) are conventions for structuring the narrative.

Verisimilitude

We also expect that rules of Verisimilitude will be operational in the created narrative world in terms of the selection of visual detail and the motivation of the characters and action. The created world will be believable. It will have verisimilitude within its own parameters, whether it's depicting downtown Burbank or an outer moon of the planet Tatooine. We expect consistency within the visual presentation of this world. Reviewers often measure the success of presentations by how completely and consistently the details of a fictional world have been fabricated. We also expect cause and effect rules to apply concerning characters' actions and relationships. And we expect the physical laws of the world they inhabit to apply. Thus, we look for the results of actions. We anticipate the reaction shot of a character's face when she learns of her lover's infidelity, or we wait for the fireball to fill the screen after the hero dives out of a crashing car. We are conditioned from other movies/TV to expect cars to automatically blow up—not a natural consequence in real life.

Technical Coding

The technical codes which build this structural system include framing (composition), photographic (angles), editing (length, placement, and connections of shots and sequences), and mise-en-scene (costume, decor, settings, gesture). These techniques are also conventionalized to the extent that textbooks can teach aspiring directors and camera people the correct techniques. Texts explain how to plan visual images. They give guidelines for the use of elements based on conventional usage in constructing a story. Rules for learning continuity editing to create a smooth flow of space and time to support the development of narrative constitute the basics for learning editing: "it is important to learn the basics of continuity editing before attempting to disrupt it. Beginning video and film directors need to first acquire some appreciation of the difficulty inherent in trying to maintain continuity and in meeting conventional viewer expectation" (Kindem, 1987, p. 118).

Composition

Elements of framing are based on composing an image within the space of a rectangle so that it creates a 3D perspective. Although the eye sees space in a somewhat diffuse oval shape, the camera frames the world and its relationships within that world as a rectangle of varying sizes. The frame size affects composition. Guidelines for composition are put forth in terms of following the rules: the rule of thirds (dividing the frame into thirds horizontally and vertically to place points of interest in the composition), rules of symmetry, rules of allowing look space in front of characters and walkspace and headroom for openness or closure and rules for creating depth and perspective through lighting, camera angles, and use of multiple planes of action. Guidelines also advocate the widescreen projection in theaters of feature films in 35mm and 70mm as more suitable for presenting open spaces, for example, than the more intimate 4:3 aspect ratio of 16mm film and television. Film and TV composition also depend on movement; movement of the camera and of the elements within the frame. There are also rules for the use of this movement for its conventionally agreed upon effects:

> The illusion of depth can be enhanced by the movement of a camera or of objects within the frame. Objects that move toward or away from the camera naturally create greater sense of depth than those that move laterally with respect to the camera. Diagonal lines of movement, like diagonal lines within a static frame, add dynamism and force to the composition. (Kindem, 1987, p. 114)

Camera Shots

The director also learns the "correct" use of shots for the desired effects. A director must learn to select a variety of shots in terms of the distance from the camera to the subject, camera angle, and shot duration. In texts each of these is often defined in terms first of visual look on the screen and then in terms of impact on, or probable reception by, the audience. Camera distance to subject is broken down into long shot, medium shot and close up (Figure 5), with a corresponding increase in dramatic emphasis and focus on the subject matter.

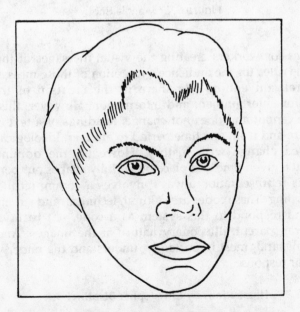

Figure 5. Close-up Example.

Camera angles include point of view shots, reverse angle shots, low-angle (Figure 6) and high-angle shots, and how they establish a specific viewpoint or perspective: "The high-angle shot places the camera high above the subject and tends to reduce its size and importance" (Kindem, 1987, p. 108). Thus, the practitioners of film and video can learn the rules by which to encode their messages because there are agreed upon standards and results.

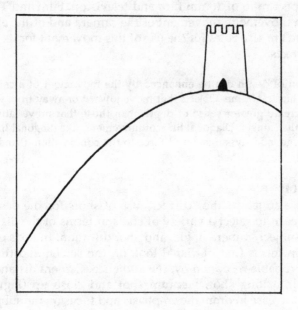

Figure 6. Low-angle Shot.

Both the rules for workers creating the visual messages of the mass media industry and the rules for the audience's reception of those messages have their basis in cultural convention. We share in the creation of this system of representation for entertainment and information. However, this is not to say that the system cannot and does not change. Readings of a text can vary from culture to culture and from one time period to another. Ideological codes which are incorporated change with history. However, the dominant mode of representation at a given time and place powerfully shapes our perception of the world. And this representation always involves a communication process of coding and decoding. These codes are cultural, technical, and structural. We need to recognize and respond to this system as a code, not reality. We need to recognize the transparent, illusionary nature of the images. And we need to uncover, examine, and, most importantly, understand the underlying elements that structure our responses.

Illustrations by Christopher Bisplinghoff.

References

Allen, R. (1992). *Channels of discourse, reassembled*. Chapel Hill, NC: University of North Carolina Press.

Becker, S., & Roberts, C. (1992). *Discovering mass communication*. New York: Harper Collins.

Bordwell, D., & Thompson, K. (1990). *Film art*. New York: McGraw-Hill.

Edmonds, R. (1982). *The sights and sounds of cinema and television*. New York: Teachers College Press.

Heim, C. (1988, September 4). Tuning up music videos. *Chicago Tribune*, 13–14.

Holbert, G. (1992, September 22). Kennedy leap makes history on *Quantum*. *Chicago Sun-Times*, 2: 37.

Kawin, B. (1987). *How movies work*. New York: Macmillan Publishing Co.

Kindem, G. (1987). *The moving image*. Glenview, IL: Scott Foresman.

Lesage, J. (1974). Feminist film criticism: Theory and practice. *Women & Film, 1* (5-6), 12–19.

Lesage, J. (1976). S/Z and rules of the game. *Jump Cut* (12–13), 45–51.

Mayne, J. (1976). S/Z and film criticism. *Jump Cut* (12–13), 41–44.

McGarry, E. (1975). Documentary realism and women's cinema. *Women & Film, 2* (7), 50–59.

Pelfrey, R. (1985). *Art and mass media*. New York: Harper & Row.

Wead, G. (1981). *Film: Form and function*. Boston, MA: Houghton Mifflin.

SECTION VII

Ethical Considerations

Any examination of visual media can reveal that there may be purposeful distortion or manipulation, particularly, if there is a point or profit to be made in supporting a particular view. In today's society, we get correct or incorrect perceptions from the media we view. Stereotypes are formed. Are there things we should not see? Who determines this?

Ann DeVaney provides methods for the acquisition of non stereotypic images of people of color for use in the classroom. Structural analysis is applied to recent Hollywood films of African-American directors to locate and describe credible representations of black characters. In this chapter, the critical model for analysis of images is flipped to consider non stereotypic, rather than stereotypic, representations. DeVaney provides valuable information to all educators or trainers who produce, select, employ, and interpret visuals for classrooms of the 1990's.

Randall Nichols asks the reader to examine the relationships that exist among visuals, morals, and self. Nichols begins his discussion with reasons for examining visual-moral issues. He contends that you have obligations not only to understand the issues for yourself, but that you owe this understanding and action to other people as well. Then, after a short section suggesting differences between morals and ethics, he presents some common notions about what makes morally good or bad visuals. He discusses several kinds of pictures and the purposes behind them. The search for morally acceptable visual guidelines is followed by a review of several theories of ethics and the implications of these theories for visuals. Nichols peaks with an argument that something like a universal guide for visual morality is possible, and each of us must reflect on its nature. Nichols concludes with an example of the process one may use to make decisions about the morality of visuals.

Chapter Twenty

Ethical Considerations of Visuals in the Classroom:
African-Americans and Hollywood Film

Ann DeVaney

Objectives

After reading this chapter, you should be able to:

1. *Discuss what is meant by "ethical considerations."*

2. *Define culturally representative images.*

3. *Discuss the school's role in the construction of social knowledge.*

4. *Explain how the camera is involved in the ethical considerations of visuals.*

5. *Explain what is meant by Cornel West's call for attention to long-standing cultural stereotypes.*

Introduction

As educators who produce, promote, and employ visual images for student consumption, what is the most ethical space we can occupy at the close of the 20th century? Certainly, any description of that area must contain renewed attention to issues of diversity. While most U.S. classroom teachers remain white, their student population is dramatically changing in ways we read about daily.

> It is predicted that about 40% of the nation's school-age youth will be students of color by the year 2020. Already students of color comprise about 30% of our public school students, are the majority in 25 of the nation's 50 largest school districts and in some states like New Mexico, Texas, and California. In the 20 largest school districts, students of color comprise over 70% of the total school enrollment. (Zeichner, 1992, p. 6)

It is my contention that ethical production for and use of classroom visuals must incorporate responsible (handling) of images of people of color. To confront the new racism educators must "go out of their way" to create and select credible, non stereotypic visuals in the classroom. Only when all students begin to understand some of the culturally authentic events and faces of the other, will the color gap start to be bridged.

Purpose: Non Stereotypic Images

With attention to shifting demographics, the producers of postmodern images frequently attempt to recreate culturally authentic images today. These images may be appropriated for the classroom to implement goals of diversity and equity. In this chapter, I will provide methods for and examples of the appropriation of non stereotypic, popular media representations of people of color for educational use. More specifically, I will indicate those attempts by recent African-American film directors to portray culturally authentic events and credible black people. The scope of this chapter is limited to African-Americans for two reasons; there has been a recent spate of Hollywood films by African-American writers and directors about life for blacks in the 1990's, and these films are available to me and any classroom teacher on videotape. The selection of images from this arena of popular culture is one of convenience, but the method of identification could be employed with any persons of color and the analysis could be used with any form of popular culture such as television or rap.

Audience

The reader of this chapter could be any educator or educator in training who produces, selects, employs, and interprets visuals for the classroom. The reader could be white or a person of color. White educators need to take time to understand the nature of a non stereotypic representation of a person of color, and the educators who are people of color need to share authentic cultural moments with students. The specific level of analysis in this chapter might best be suited to high school curriculum which aims to prepare students to identify and appreciate ethical, responsible representations of African-Americans in films and on television. It is hoped that if high school students learn to become responsible consumers of African-American film images, that the skill will transfer to the interpretation of representations of other people of color.

Assumptions: Images as Teachers

This chapter is based on certain pedagogical assumptions. I assume that the visual image is a ubiquitous teacher in this post modern age. Children are introduced to their world primarily through images, especially popular culture, images on television, in films and in advertisements. Television, which incorporates most popular images today, whether from music, commercials or Hollywood films, exists as a major transmitter of culture for children of the 1990's. What children learn from exposure to popular culture icons has never been determined, because educators construct the debate as one of popular culture vs. schooling. Yet, popular culture remains as a teacher who competes with the classroom teacher for students from pre-school through college, whether educators care to acknowledge it or not. It has a profound effect on the construction of student knowledge. It has a profound effect on the internal construction of student's perception of the Other. These effects should not be ignored.

In an eloquent plea for new ways to speak of race, Cornel West says,

> ... we confine discussions about race in America to the "problems" black people pose for whites rather than considering what this way of viewing black people reveals about us as a nation. ... To engage in a serious discussion of race in America, we must begin not with the problems of blacks in America but with the flaws of American society—flaws rooted in historic inequalities and long-standing cultural stereotypes. (West, 1992, p. 24)

As an educator, researcher, and writer concerned with students' visual literacy, I can enter West's discourse at the moment his rhetoric turns to "long-standing cultural stereotypes." I am one of many writing in the broad educational field who has been concerned for some time with the production and dissemination of culturally stereotyped images in the classroom. Issues of stereotyping in popular media was brought into sharp focus as a result of the civil rights movement of the 1950's and 1960's, and later became problematized for consumers and producers of educational texts, both written and mediated. Some consider that the consciousness of producers of educational images has been raised and that the issue of diversity is now a moot point. An examination of educational television leads me to conclude otherwise. While the *Children's Television Workshop* is conscientiously producing multicultural sequences for the pre-school viewer, they are unconsciously creating stereotyped Latinos for the 8–12 year old viewer. On *Sesame Street* Whoopi Goldberg is encouraged to talk about the feel of her brown skin and black hair, while on *Square One*, Luisa Lechin is required to exaggerate her Hispanic accent in most of the skits in which she appears. In these skits, Lechin plays Latino women whose cultural characteristics are exaggerated to elicit laughter from student viewers (DeVaney & Elenes, 1990). The fact that this is an age of new racism is reflected, not only by some of the artifacts of popular culture which influence the production of classroom images, but by frequent news reports of racial tension and violence across the nation. Recently, one writer speaking to African-Americans offered advice on *How to Survive the New Racism* (Whitaker, 1991).

Method: Inverting the Critical Model

Visual images from film and television have, heretofore, been critiqued in some classrooms under the aegis of visual or media literacy, but no formal space for such work exists in the U.S. public school curricula today. Efforts to incorporate visual literacy have usually been the pet projects of specific faculty members, usually those in the humanities. (Many other western countries, such as Great Britain, Australia, the Netherlands, and Switzerland, understand the impact of popular media on the learning lives of their students and have incorporated media literacy as part of the official curriculum from pre-school through high school.) Whether here or in foreign countries, the intention of critiquing media images in the classroom has been to empower students in their consumption of these images, to make them critical readers of media. A critical media curriculum provides students with the ability to understand the constructed nature of an image, to reject the notion that a camera is a window on the world, and to reject stereotypic images. Media critiques have usually been employed in the classroom for ethical purposes. Students may be alerted to the manner in which an advertisement may trick them into buying a product. Those who must live in an increasingly diverse world are also alerted to stereotypic representations of people of color. What a critical curriculum has not done to date is to provide students with non stereotypic images and events which may attempt to convey a culturally authentic occurrence, or a credible representation of a person of color. If the critical model for the analysis of media were to be flipped to investigate non stereotypic, rather than stereotypic images, educators would have incorporated that aspect of popular culture to which children should attend. If they were trained to identify attempts at authentic representations, they might incorporate these as part of their social knowledge.

Textual Analysis and African-American Narrative

With a visual literacy curriculum in mind, I will draw my methods for this chapter from two sources. Structural textual analysis, especially semiotics, will be applied to the recent Hollywood films of black directors to empower educators as critical viewers. They will be reminded of the manner in which visual messages are created through lighting, camera angle, distance, and other structural elements and referred to books on the reading of film. The second source to inform the method here will be critiques of African-American narratives, particularly novels. A goal of this chapter is to select non stereotypic black images. Since I and many of my readers are not African-American, I must rely on analysis of black narratives by African-American critics to describe authentic cultural events and representations. I assume here that if I can recognize the styles, images, themes, tones, characterizations, and subjects of African-American literature, I will develop some facility for tracing rhetorical echoes of these narratives in popular culture. The rich expanse of African-American narrative with its unique characteristics has been described by Louis Henry Gates, Jr., Toni Morrison, Nellie McKay, Bell Hooks, Alice Walker, Zora Neale Hurston, and many others. The works of these writers will be culled for clues to authenticity and manners of representation, styles of communication, recurring themes, formats, and motifs. Black film makers often strive for moments of authenticity when portraying African-Americans, and one can see reflected in these moments codes of a larger narrative heritage.

The impetus to develop a new method for this analysis stems in part from Cornel West's plea (West, 1992) for a new language with which to speak of race in the U.S. today, and in part from a dissatisfaction with old critical methods employed in visual literacy curricula. While it is necessary to teach all students to recognize stereotypic representations, it is imperative that a lesson not stop there. One may question if the sole appropriation of stereotypic images for the classroom does not simply reinforce those images. One may also ask if this sole appropriation disenfranchises students of color. (When I used the analytical model I suggest here in a classroom, students of color were enfranchised in a way

I had not experienced before. They were the cognoscenti of the class, sought after for their cultural knowledge. The social order of the class was inverted.)

The Limitations of Popular Culture

While popular culture may be for an educator what found objects are for some modern sculptors, it comes encumbered. While both sculptors and educators may find beauty in what is sometimes a discardable object, popular culture artifacts have a life of their own and are fraught with problems for the educator. Many current Hollywood films, from whatever source, are simply "money makers" aimed at an adolescent audience. To maintain this teen audience which subsists on a daily diet of TV, producers must churn out plots with action and dialogue not found on television. Once this trend is started, they must outdo themselves with each succeeding film, therefore action can become more and more violent or farcical; dialogue can become more bizarre (Roget); and characters can become more stilted. Even though teens watch these throw-away films from white or black directors, I do not recommend their images for inclusion in the classroom. Other representations, however, of people of color in popular media may be deliberately stereotypic even though produced by people of color. For example, the films of black film makers run the gamut from complex to simplistic and their characters can be believable or deliberately stylized. Ice Cube plays the credible character, Doughboy, in *Boyz N The Hood*. But a narrative technique, which dramatists employ when they wish to teach or to evoke laughter, is that of making the character more than s/he is. Stereotypes or archetypes are sometimes produced in melodrama to make viewers laugh or in symbolic plays, such as *Mother Courage*, for polemic reasons. Many black film makers are interested in presenting films which teach audiences about their culture, therefore, choices to be melodramatic and present exaggerated characters are sometimes made. But unlike the modern Brechtian Mother Courage, their postmodern characters are played for irony. Bill Duke, for example, chose to present and even exaggerate stereotypes for his highly stylized *Rage in Harlem*. One can guess that his intent was to employ irony, a distancing technique, so that the viewer might see clearly the tragedy of his morality play. Just as I have not recommended inadvertently stylized images for the classroom, I am not recommending deliberately stereotyped images for the classroom. White children do not need to see more stereotypes and children of color do not need continual disenfranchisement.

African-American Hollywood Films of the 1990's

In 1991, 19 films by black directors were released. Another 20 films starred African-American actors. Although that accomplishment is still only a tiny share of the 400 or more films realized by Hollywood each year, it represents more movies by African-Americans than in the entire decade of the 1980's. About these films, Henry Louis Gates, Jr. commented,

What we haven't had in Hollywood are a group who not only make social statements, but who are also concerned about charting the contours of African-American culture, revealing what black people say to one another in moments of intimacy (quoted in Easton, 1991, p. 1, 2).

As a viewer of these films, I am struck by the difference between adolescent problems delineated in the films of John Hughes and adolescent problems described by black film makers. While many white children are concerned about relations with their parents, many black children are trying to stay alive and unscathed in their neighborhoods. What this particular set of 1991 films from black directors offered me was a glimpse into the lives of this country's most troubled group, African-American adolescent males. (It is true that with the exception of Julie Dash, all the black film directors of 1991 were men.) Because of the availability of those films on video, I have concentrated on that set of 19. Admittedly, the films incorporate male themes and I am not unaware of the charges of sexism that have been leveled against Spike Lee and other black directors. But the issue of gender in African-American films, as in music and literature is broad, and deserves a separate investigation. Euzhan Palcy, Julie Dash, and Debbie Allen are the only three black film directors whose work over three years addresses the social problems of African-American women. In 1991, Roland Jefferson did take a stab at black women's issues in *Perfume*.

Of the 19 films, I recommend appropriating images for the classroom from the following eight.

1991 FILMS BY BLACK DIRECTORS

Film	Director	Studio	Description
The Five Heartbeats	Robert Townsend	20th Century Fox	Charts the lives and loves of five men in a 1960s musical group
Straight Out of Brooklyn	Matty Rich	Samuel Goldwyn Co.	Teen living in New York housing project gets caught up in deadly crime in an effort to better his family's life
Livin' Large	Michael Shultz	Samuel Goldwyn Co.	Ghetto teen sells his soul to get ahead in the course of pursuing his dream to become a TV newscaster

Jungle Fever	Spike Lee	Universal Pictures	Interracial couple tries to keep relationship intact despite attacks from friends, family and neighbors
Hanging' With the Homeboys	Joseph Vasquez	New Line	The all-night adventures of a quartet of Hispanic and black friends
Boyz N The Hood	John Singleton	Columbia Pictures	Teen deals with parents, girls, friends and the violence of the streets as he grows up in South-Central L.A.
Daughters of the Dust	Julie Dash	American Playhouse	Turn-of-the-century story about a family of women who emigrate to the northern United States
Perfume	Roland Jefferson	Independent	Relationships between five women friends who open a cosmetics company

Most of the current African-American films are message films. Just as black writers have sought to describe the plight of African-Americans to whites, so do black film makers. It is my thesis here that many characteristics of black literature can be located in these films and I will specify that similarity later. But generally speaking these films present a picture of people living in extreme circumstances in the United States; people living with poverty and social oppression who are, for the most part, religious with a fine moral sensibility. (This is certainly not a picture painted by some of our conservative politicians.) There is bonding and brotherhood present among these filmic black males and they have the ability to laugh at themselves and their problems. Although these characters are predominantly from a lower socioeconomic group, middle class African-Americans are beginning to make their appearance in films, i.e., *Livin' Large*, *Jungle Fever*, and *The Five Heartbeats*. These appearances come, however, with a moral such as, "money corrupts," or the message that middle class blacks have sold out their brothers. The latter theme is portrayed in Michael Shultz's *Livin' Large*; is the subject of the book, *Black and Popular*; and is the key message in many current rap hits. It appears that African-Americans' climb out of poverty is compounded by problems of perceived betrayal.

Interpreting Film Characters

How can credible black film characters be identified in scenes for use in the classroom? Primarily one must rely on student and teachers' ability to read films, their visual literacy. Although it is not my intention here to detail a process for reading film, I will recommend one process and describe the communicative theory behind it. Some methods of reading film are based on structural theories of language, such as semiotics. Semiotics has been applied to films because the cinema is a communicative system which contains socially constructed signs and symbols, which are employed by a director with intent, and interpreted by viewers who have access to the meanings of those signs and symbols. The system functions much as a language functions and codes are established by means of daily production practices. Audiences become facile at reading codes by interpreting techniques in the audio and visual tracks. Alfred Hitchcock taught viewers that a hand held camera could symbolize a menacing stalker, and film noire directors taught viewers that low key lighting symbolized a somber or mysterious mood. Hollywood cinema even has codes for "realism." Generally, students can interpret and articulate the verbal and musical codes they encounter in films. Although they can read visual codes, they often have no language for describing them. It is important that they have basic visual literacy training to empower them as readers of media. Structural theorists believe that the form of an artifact, such as a film, communicates as much as the content. Students' tacit knowledge about film form could be made apparent to them, if they were trained in some film reading techniques. Monaco (1977) (*How to Read a Film*) and Wollen (1972) (*Signs and Meaning in the Cinema*) are basic books in the structural reading of film. Those film structures which need to be understood are the elements of a frame, a shot, and a scene; these include, but are not limited to border of the frame, angle of the camera, distance of the camera from the focal point, lighting, camera motion (pan, zoom, tilt, dolly), shot transitions (cut, wipe, dissolve, etc.), placement of shots in a scene, and placement of scenes in a reel.

The Camera Lies

Film like other media is artifice, constructed, contrived, and the task of finding believable characters in any film is hard. If student are visually literate, they will already know that the camera always lies. In this chapter, I have been careful to use phrases such as "a director's attempt at representation of a culturally authentic event or a credible character," not to obfuscate, but to qualify my use of "authentic," "believable," and "credible." Nothing is real when one is working with a contrivance, but the task is posed in literature classes for students of novels, and can be posed with cinema as well. Authors have codes for the presentation of realistic characters and so do film makers. Some Hollywood codes of realism that are used in the 1991 black films can be described. When a character is shot on the level, the viewer sees him eye-to-eye, and begins to think he is "on the level." When a character is shot with "natural" lighting, she is placed in a realistic setting. Natural lighting is not natural, but attempts to imitate the light your eye would see in the same live setting. When shot transitions and editing are composed of primarily matched cuts, they are considered "real" in film. When a film calls attention to itself by using jump cuts and montage, it does not invoke "realism." John Singleton used seamless editing in 1991 to create a believable story and Spike Lee did not.

Clues from African-American Literature

Educators and students can identify non stereotypic characters in films by black directors by referencing characteristics of African-American literature. One sign, however, of a non stereotypic character in any literature is that of agency. A character is thought to be human when s/he has agency, in other words, when s/he acts, not only reacts. When a character is instrumental in advancing the plot and her own destiny, she has agency. In simulating reality, writers often display the agency of a character by allowing him to face odds from a protagonist or protagonistic force. The character's humanity is shown by the manner in which he faces and overcomes or does not overcome these odds. In such a display, the audience may be able to see some growth in a character. Growth is another sign of humanity. In Matty Rich's *Straight Out of Brooklyn*, the central character, Dennis, is instrumental in advancing the plot and controlling his own destiny. Facing what he perceives as the insurmountable odds of poverty he plans and executes a robbery which propels the plot. Dennis' girlfriend, Shirley, is instrumental in controlling her own destiny, yet she makes the opposite choice by rejecting Dennis and his plans. The viewer sees some growth in these adolescents. Two of the central players, Tre and Rickie, in John Singleton's *Boyz N the Hood* display agency, because they face and overcome the odds of their childhood. Likewise, the troubled brother of Rickie, Doughboy, is instrumental, because he does not overcome the odds. The viewer, however, sees these three boys thinking and struggling in a most humane way to make sense of their lives. On the other hand, Choir Boy in Robert Townsend's, *The Five Heartbeats*, does not display agency and is not instrumental until the end of the film. During most of the film, he simply reacts to his parents and other boys in the singing group.

African-American writers are the most reliable source for the creation of credible black characters. Louis Henry Gates, Jr., Nellie McKay, Toni Morrison, and others critics of black literature have identified some themes, motifs, and styles of this body of literature. These literary characteristics are reflected in the films of African-American writers and directors and I will elaborate a few here.

Opposition

It should not be surprising that opposition to an oppressing social system is a theme that runs through black literature as well as black films. American classics such as *The Invisible Man, Native Son*, and *Go Tell it From the Mountain* are clear representations of the oppositional novel. As in any literature of the oppressed, this theme is central and continues to be so in current Hollywood films. All of the 19 films of 1991 have oppositional moments, if not oppositional themes. Even the upbeat films, such as *The Five Heartbeats* and *Livin' Large* have oppositional moments. In *The Five Heartbeats*, the quintet is stopped on a Mississippi road and treated in a thoroughly demoralizing fashion by the state police. (If anyone doubts that harassment of blacks by white police takes place, I would like to refer to the common phrase among today's African-American drivers who ask one another, "Did you have a DWB on your trip?" DWB is the code word for being stopped if you are "driving while black.") The opposition in Robert Townsend's film is registered in an ironical moment after the quintet is stopped and allowed to proceed. Eddie, one of the singers, attempts to sing *America the Beautiful* as they ride along the highway. These northern adolescents have just seen the need for opposition.

Opposition takes another form in *Jungle Fever* when a black man and a white woman decide to become a couple. This coupling expresses the opposition of an ethnic white woman as well as that of the black hero. Different forms of opposition are presented in *Boyz N the Hood*. Revenge against a killer is opposition to existing laws while obtaining an education is opposition to existing poverty.

Humor

Mimicry and the giving of dozens are two forms of humor illustrated in African-American literature and Hollywood films by black directors. Examples of mimicry abound in *Perfume, Hangin' With the Homeboys, Livin' Large,* and *The Five Heartbeats*. Gates (1988) suggests that mimicry as a form a humor grew out of the black experience of life in the U.S. Since their roles were devalued, he suggests, African-Americans learned quickly to imitate the Other, for purposes of entertaining whites as well as blacks. Mimicry in these films represents an authentic cultural habit.

"Dozens" is an old form of deprecating humor in which one black friend may "put down" another with a phrase that may begin, "Oh your mother...". It is a sarcastic method of throwing barbs and is particularly masculine. The giving of dozens arose, strangely enough, in African-American oral tradition from the practice of selling handicapped slaves by the dozen. Gates defines an old form of "dirty dozens" in the following manner.

> ... a very elaborate game traditionally played by black boys, in which the participants insult each others relatives, especially their mothers. The object of the game is to test emotional strength. The first person to give into anger is the loser. (Gates, 1988, p. 68)

But the form of dozens which appears in these films corresponds to a newer definition by Gates. More recently he notes that "dozens" is

> ... language behavior that makes direct or indirect implications of baiting or boasting, the essence of which is making fun of another's appearance, relatives, or situation. (Gates, 1988, p. 68)

All of the 19 films of 1991 contain examples of the giving of dozens, but I would like to cite two which portray this type of humor.

Dennis and his friends, Larry and Kevin, the central characters in *Straight Out of Brooklyn*, have dropped out of school and "hang" in the Red Hook section of Brooklyn where they live. The lighting in this low budget film is usually low key without much fill light, therefore, shadows are often cast on walls, and silhouettes are prevalent. The mood is somber. Viewers are startled by the seemingly unending acres of tan apartments. These buildings fill and overflow the screen in long aerial shots suggesting that this project is the whole world of these young men; it looks boundless. Other shots, of people wending their way through the maze of apartments, add an element of entrapment in this project world. In one of those scenes, a car crawls slowly through the project streets and the driver yells, "Dennis, come out. You know we're going to find you." The boys cannot escape. This film, however, contains life affirming humor.

Against this somber background and in contrast to it, there are three scenes in which Larry and Kevin give each other dozens. Here the two of them are lit in high key for a lighter mood. The funniest of the three scenes takes place in a small convenience store and does not serve to advance the plot; the focus is on humor. The repartee is fast and rhythmic in rich Black English. The two boys tease a larger third boy and are confronted by him; the confrontation and speed of this give and take increases, until the third boy's girl friend breaks up an incipient fight, and Kevin and Larry rush out the door. Since this and the other two Larry and Kevin scenes do not advance the plot, I think the director is reveling in an enjoyable part of black culture and sharing it with the audience for their pleasure. He is also depicting the ability of these characters to laugh in the face of adversity.

A similar scene occurs on Ricky and Doughboy's front porch in *Boyz N the Hood*. Doughboy and his friends are "hangin" and giving each other dozens to pass the time of day. This scene is lit "naturally" to portray what the eye would see, as is most of this film. Since it does not serve to advance the plot, one might question its presence. But, the audience learns more about these boys, their humor and musical language.

Dozens is often sexist humor. I assume that black film writers and directors included it in these films, because of their desire for authenticity and their need to present black adolescents as they saw these boys. As such, the giving of dozens, is an integral and appropriate part of these films. The incorporation of these scenes in any classroom, however, should be handled with care. Sexist humor could be problematized in the classroom, if any of these scenes are shown. The charges of sexism leveled against many of these black film makers could be discussed in conjunction with "dozens." The now famous scene in *Jungle Fever* in which black women articulate the problem of black male sexism could be juxtaposed and shown after a "dozens" scene. In that case, African-American women themselves would be describing the problem. Also the appropriation of "dozens" by black women on some recent TV programs could be discussed.

Black English

The rich dialect of black English has been celebrated by African-American authors, such as Zora Neale Hurston, Richard Wright, James Baldwin, Toni Morrison, and many others. It is incorporated in stand-up acts of black comedians, and in Hollywood films by white directors. In the oral and written tradition of African-Americans, it is perhaps the most unique cultural product. The musical nature of this dialect with its rising and falling intonation has been admired by many authors, even Mark Twain. There is new evidence to suggest that Twain patterned Huck Finn's dialogue on the speech of a young African-

American boy whom he knew. The 19 films of 1991 all celebrate black English. If there were any narrative measure of cultural authenticity, this would be it. These films are musical, even without a musical sound tract; the rhythm of youthful repartee is like recitative. The music of black English is most noticeable in humorous scenes, as those described above, with young men "hangin," and, also in the women's scene in *Jungle Fever*. Spike Lee has claimed that this scene, in which women sit in a circle and talk about black men, was ad-libbed.

The Role of the Black Male

In African-American literature, the social construction of the black male in the United States has been described for decades. The work of Richard Wright, James Baldwin, Ralph Ellison, Malcolm X, and many others have repeated the message about intensive, continual oppression which creates disenfranchised, socially impotent black male citizens. If there is any theme that is hammered in these films of 1991, it is this social construction. The unheeded cries of black authors continue. All the serious films and parts of the lighter or comedic films address this issue. The number of ways these films describe black men's lack of social power would amaze any audience.

In *Straight Out of Brooklyn*, there are numerous high-angle shots of one man in a frame. The height and position of the camera allows the viewer to "look down" on the man in the frame. These men are usually slouched and look dejected. One of these shots is set in a gas station; Dennis's father, an attendant, sits on the ground with his head hanging. Several other frames are point-of-view shots from a window on about the 10th floor of a project building from which Dennis is looking. From his point of view, he sees a dejected older black man walking to or from his apartment. One of these high-angle shots is juxtaposed with an extremely low-angle shot of an adolescent boy with a gun; the frame is distorted, so it appears the youth is shooting the viewer. Director, Rich, has portrayed black men in menial jobs as powerless and hopeless.

Few of these films present any adult male role models for the troubled teen boys. *Boyz N the Hood* is the exception. John Singleton, who wrote as well as directed this film, creates Furious Styles as the father of the young hero and role model to Tre and his friends. Singleton gives Mr. Styles a symbolic first name and then allows him to be a reasonable and controlled person in the film. At moments, Mr. Styles becomes larger than his father role dictates, and the voice of John Singleton breaks through in polemic tones. One friend even says to Tre Styles, "Did your father ever think of becoming a preacher." Furious' messages are about the plight of the black male. Singleton and most of the other directors break their narrative form to deliver such dire messages.

To contextualize the roles of black male teens depicted in these films, a teacher might make reference to *Cool Pose: The Dilemmas of Black Manhood in America*, a text from two sociologists, Richard Majors and Janet Mancini Billson (1992). The text is a wonderful accompaniment to the black films mentioned here. Reasons why black males often act detached, calm, fearless, aloof, and tough are suggested. Portraits of the conditions of black males are provided.

If there is an overarching reason for the appropriation of images from these films for the classroom, it is to depict the plight of the African-American adolescent male. Even though these depictions are fraught with issues of violence and some sexism, they reflect the violence and sexism present in the lives of these youths. Their lives as well as their filmic representations are problematic. For improved racial relations, it is important that all citizens understand the struggle these children have in their neighborhoods. It is important for film audiences to see the morality and brotherhood of these children; it is important for film audiences to see these teens celebrating life in the face of enormous odds.

Summary

I have attempted in this chapter to respond to Cornel West's call for attention to "long-standing cultural stereotypes" by describing non stereotypic images of African-American males from black film directors. I suggest, here, that the film language of these directors constitutes part of the "new language" Mr. West proposes we adopt when speaking of race. This chapter used structural methods for the reading of film, and borrowed narrative characteristics from African-American literature and criticism to assist in the reading of these 1991 films. Both structural reading techniques and clues from African-American narrative could be applied in the reading of black television programs and rap music. Educators, in general, but producers of classroom images and teachers, should be aware of the attempts in popular culture to produce credible African-American images. West reminds us that in or out of the classroom

> the presence and predicaments of black people are neither additions to nor defections from American life, but rather constitutive elements of that life. (West, 1992, p. 24)

(Editors' note: This chapter was placed in the ethics section; however, it could also be placed in the section dealing with use of visuals or in the previous section on cultural aspects.)

References

DeVaney, A., & Elenes, A. (1990). *Square One* television and gender. In R. A. Braden, D. G. Beauchamp, & J. C. Clark-Baca (Eds.), *Perceptions of visual literacy*. Conway, AR: International Visual Literacy Association.

Easton, N. (1991, May 3). New black films, new insights. *Los Angeles Times*.

Gates, H. L. Jr. (1988). *The signifying monkey: A theory of African-American literary criticism*. New York: Oxford University Press.

Majors, R., & Mancini Billson, J. (1992). *Cool pose*. New York: Lexington Books: Macmillan Publishing Co.

Monaco, J. (1977). *How to read a film: The art, technology, language, history, and theory of film and media*. New York: Oxford University Press.

West, C. (1992, August, 2). Learning to talk of race. *New York Times Magazine*, pp. 24–26.

Whitaker, C. (1991, October). How to survive the new racism. *Ebony*, pp. 106, 108, 110.

Wollen, P. (1972). *Signs and meaning in the cinema* (3rd ed.). Bloomington, IN: Indiana University Press.

Zeichner, K. (1992). *Educating teachers for cultural diversity* (Report). East Lansing, MI: National Center for Research on Teacher Learning, Michigan State University.

Chapter Twenty-One

Considering Morals and Visuals (Beyond School)

Randall G. Nichols

Objectives

After reading this chapter, you should be able to:

1. *State characterizations of "media," "ethics," and "morals."*

2. *Discuss common understandings of the moral nature of the content and purposes of visuals.*

3. *Identify several common Western normative theories and a postmodern theory of ethics.*

4. *Identify common moral imperatives that can guide examination and action directed at visuals.*

5. *Formulate a way or ways by which to approach specific instances of morally questionable uses of visuals.*

Why Ethics and Visuals

It has been suggested that perhaps as much as 80 percent of what we know we have learned visually (Heinich, Molenda, & Russell, 1989). On this account alone, ethical considerations are revealed. What, for instance, is the moral standing of educators who knowingly resist using most forms of visual production and interpretation (visual literacy) in secondary school curricula if so many secondary students learn this way? What about people who refuse to consider the implications of the knowledge that learners are unwittingly influenced by the visuals around them?

Being aware of ethics and visuals can help you personally to be more aware of and act on the influence pictures have on you. Have you thought about the fact that many advertising pictures intend not for you to think much about a product, but to feel emotionally attached to a group of people you want to be like? You are meant to identify with people you like so you will buy the clothes they wear, and not so you will think much about the quality of the clothes or the salaries of the people who make them or whether producing clothes outside America is ethical behavior. This is not to say the pictures do not inform you of a product at all, or that a product is bad, or that advertising doesn't help the economy—all of which may be the case. If you understand how your sense of wanting to belong to a group is being manipulated, how the pictures are used to do something to you, you may have more freedom to act responsibly for yourself.

Further, you are responsible for understanding visuals because you live with others. You live in society. You affect other people and they affect you. Your considered understanding of visual ethics is important so you won't needlessly, systematically, and perpetually hurt others. For example, isn't it a shallow representation of wealthy people if they are always pictured as confident, in control, and satisfied with life? Even they have fears, failures, and insecurities.

Understanding the moral and ethical influences of pictures on people's lives also means that you can help others to be more aware. Teachers who help learners to interpret and produce visuals are doing just this. Likewise, you may want to help your own children and communities to be more visually knowledgeable.

Some of us may not have or want to think about ethics and visuals. Perhaps we consciously choose to acquiesce to the motives of those who are influential in our lives. However, unless you are somehow unconscious of these issues, you are virtually required to think about and act on the notion that visuals have moral and ethical facets. Otherwise, anyone might use visuals to subject others to terrible conditions and do so without a second thought. To give an extreme example, people could justify using pictures in which children are having sex with adults. You have a moral obligation to think about the morals and ethics of visuals.

Media, Morals, and Ethics

Before directly addressing the question of goodness in visuals, let's make distinctions about media and, then, about the relationship of morals to ethics. "Media" are all those ways by which the visuals are delivered: paper, television, computer monitors, film of all sorts, holograms, chalkboards, etc. Visuals with accompanying sound, smell or feel are included, so even home videos count. Although there are interesting issues about ethics and media, we are focusing on the pictures themselves.

What is the distinction between morals and ethics? The answer is not at all clear. In much of the literature on this topic, the terms appear to be used interchangeably if not synonymously. For our purposes, though, let's adapt Wilson's (1990) conclusions and see "moral" as the most basic dispositions of humans to our desires, emotions, intellect, actions, and the earth's ecology. "Ethics," on the other hand, are the more explicit principles/guides by which humans might live. In many cases, the guides are codes of ethics, that is, statements explaining specifically how people associated with the codes ought to act. For instance, the National Education Association has a code of ethics to help teachers act morally.

Throughout this chapter, it is intended that the moral sense is pervasive. We are thinking about those basic ideas and intuitions that seem to guide many humans.

Content and Purposes of Visuals

There are many ways of approaching the question of the moral goodness of visuals. One of these ways includes studying the visuals themselves (as distinct from studying any ethical or moral guideposts) in terms of commonly held, largely American, notions of right and wrong. More particularly, we can ask about how we react to a visual's content and its purpose.

The "content" of a visual means whatever is produced and viewed, especially as these terms are commonly understood in the West. The "purpose" of a visual is meant to indicate the reason or reasons for a visual's existence, use, or display. Content and purpose aren't the only ways to think about visual ethics and morality, but they are indicative of what many of us seem to believe about visuals.

Visual Content

Morally controversial visuals are the ones we often attend more to vocally and publicly, so let's first examine some kinds of visual content that many Americans find questionable or even completely unacceptable. Many visuals which depict gratuitous, lusty sex are objectionable, especially when they are public, expose genitals, are close-up, are presented for a long duration, or show incest.

Portrayals of human excrement are often opposed. What sort of public display, if any, is appropriate for showing Robert Mapplethorpe's photo of a man urinating on another man? Visuals of our own private lives, visuals made and shown without our permission receive criticism; should a news source publish close-up pictures of your mother after her bloody suicide?

On the other hand, many kinds of visuals appear to have what many of us would consider to be acceptable content. This is to say that almost no one would wonder about any negative moral implications of such pictures as those which show gentle, non-sexual human love, or pastoral landscapes, or our animals/pets. Most religious scenes and educational illustrations are considered acceptable.

Visual Purposes

Regardless of their content, pictures nearly always have some purpose attached to them. Visuals are meant to affect humans intellectually, emotionally, physically, and spiritually. At a glance, these purposes seem mundane. If we extend this line of thinking a little and ask why these purposes are being engaged, we usually find other more specific motives at work.

Some of these other motives are morally questionable. Visuals are sometimes used to create emotional hatred and dominance of cultural groups. Hitler's photographers did just this to Jews with uses of selected and culturally one-dimensional pictures. Political uses of visuals rarely help to inform voters at length about the range of candidates' legislative intellect or positions; these kinds of visuals are intended mostly to make the viewer feel good about the politician. As mentioned earlier, pictures that recklessly aim only at making a profit are often considered unethical. Satellite pictures, for instance, have been used to find and harvest endangered species of fish in the oceans. This use of images threatens the fish, people's food, and the earth's existence and, therefore, is morally questionable.

Likewise, visuals may have what many of us would consider to be positive moral and ethical purposes. Family portraits make us emotional and help us to remember our histories, ourselves. In this way, they are nearly always believed to be moral.

Computer generated images are often felt to be moral when they help to avoid dangerous invasive surgery. Explanatory pictures in academic settings are rarely morally questionable. Some advertising pictures appear to help economies. Satellite pictures can show where to find large schools of fish so that starving people can eat.

This discussion of content and purposes suggests some rough agreements that many of us share about the goodness of visuals, and it introduces a range of pictures we may include in our discussion of morals. To this extent we may have some guidance. Additionally, these rough categorizations of visuals show that moral contentions arise when we too neatly define our moral relations to visuals. For example, the fishing images could be used morally or not, depending on the circumstances in which they are used. So far, then, we have no completely satisfactory ways of helping to determine what we ought to do in relation to morals and visuals.

Ethical Traditions

If studying a visual's content or intention doesn't always help us determine its exact morality, there are several widely accepted ways of thinking about morals and ethics that could help us. This section sketches some of the more organized theories and traditions associated with ethics so that you might gain insight for thinking about and using visuals.

How Ought We Live?

This section draws heavily from a text called *A Companion to Ethics* (Singer, 1991) to give an overview of ethics that might help us to think and act in moral fashions in relation to visuals. Several broad conceptions make up the sections of the *Companion*, and only one of those sections is dealt with here in any detail. That section deals with Western normative theories whose purpose is to guide our conduct; they suggest how we ought to act. They are normative in that they examine ideas of typical and correct behavior.

Western Theoretic Traditions

Western ethical traditions are probably less openly religious, intuitive, culturally bound, or mystical in nature than some of the oldest and most widespread of the ethical traditions, and they rely on rational, conscious means. The Western tradition can be said to be historical, abstract, and characterized by formal theorizing (Bilimoria, 1991). These theories suggest to us how we ought to live, "ought" indicating that we have an imperative to think and act in certain ways.

Brief characterizations of some major features of some of these theories follow. Because no theory is directly connected to implications for visuals, an ongoing example of a questionable picture is used with each theory. The example is of a famous woman—say an astronaut—whose picture is taken without her knowledge and consent. She is nude in the photo, and the photographer took the picture from an alley behind her house, through a window, while she dressed. The picture is sold to a magazine and published worldwide.

Natural law is a general moral view that holds that good or right conduct is pre-determined in nature, including human nature. In one form, it defends unchanging human goods such as life, knowledge, play, practical reason, aesthetic experience, and friendship. Natural law theories are alternatives to the moral view that there are no exact moral answers. Human rationality will uncover the laws so that we may live in right ways (Buckle, 1991). This theory might hold that the ethical goodness of secretly taking photos of the woman and using them to titillate viewers into buying magazines is already decided—we just need to discover the decision by looking to nature and by thinking logically about it.

Kant's ethics seek to posit universal moral principles not dependent on theologies or traditions or particular societies. He argues that these fundamental moral principles must be reached through human free will and rationality. His "Categorical Imperative" says that if a principle cannot be willed freely for and by all, it must be rejected, not because of any harmful effects but because it cannot be willed freely. An important second-order principle of this theory, the "Formula of the End in Itself," demands that we treat people as we would ourselves, as ends in and of themselves. It is moral failure if we use others in such a way that they cannot consent to that use. For example, using titillating photos to make a profit rather than to act for the good of others would be immoral—if all concerned could discuss the use and conclude so (O'Neill, 1991).

Social contract theory says that morality is the fixed agreements humans make to regulate social interaction. Agreement has been taken to be the way to identify requirements for mutual advantage or impartiality. Advantage focuses on physical power making it mutually beneficial for people to protect one another, while impartiality stresses people's equal moral status. Agreements are reached because we have a common concern and equal nature. The idea of mutual advantage suggests we rule out prior, divine, natural duties, actions, and obligations. Impartiality asks that we develop these notions of priority (Kymlicka, 1991). In terms of this theory, the question of the morality of the acquisition and use of her secret photo is to be mediated by mutual social agreement. What, for instance, would Western societies say about taking and using the photo of the celebrity? Apparently our society has not developed a widely accepted rule on this matter.

Egoism theorizes that an individual puts her or his own good, interest, and concern above everyone else's. It is this relationship with others that indicates the moral issues of egoism. Five versions of egoism seem to exist. First, there is a common sense version in which persons attend to themselves in ways beyond those which are morally permissible by others. Psychological egoism is the idea that deep down everyone is an egoist because our beliefs and desires are aimed at our own greatest good. Bringing about our own individual good is best for everyone's good. Third, "good" is based in factual claims. Finally, rational and ethical versions of egoism claim that egoism is self-evident, and we decide simply as we see appropriate (Baier, 1991). For our purposes, we might speculate that egoism urges us secretly to take and use the celebrity photo for our own purposes because in one way or another each of us is moral—even if we appear somehow to hurt someone else.

Deontology indicates duty. Deontologists believe there are certain acts that are wrong in and of themselves; there are moral principles that pertain regardless of consequences for which humans may argue. The world of immoral acts is narrow, specific, and before contexts of human intervention. We have it in our power of reason and sincere effort to avoid wrongdoing, and we must do so. Because moral rules are specific, we are bound to follow them. For example, we must comply with not breaking civil laws (Davis, 1991) such as the right to privacy. In terms of our ongoing incident, the photography constitutes an invasion of privacy. It is immoral and illegal.

An ethic of *prima facie duty* holds that coming to a complete understanding of ethics is not likely. In fact as a theory, it doesn't claim to be much of a coherent argument itself! However, theorists here might argue that some kinds of principles must exist—it just doesn't make sense that the moral tone or claim or outcome in one instance doesn't also apply in another (Dancy, 1991). We cannot appeal to some established theory to decide our case of the secret photo. We must settle the issue in the context of the present, but our previous experiences will in some way shed light on the here and now.

Consequentialist theories propose that right actions are those which maximize goodness and that there are intrinsic values. We might, for instance, determine that good health for all is a fundamental goodness, and most actions that lead to it are moral. One form of this tradition is known as utilitarianism. It holds that we should determine what is good by appealing to the idea of the greatest good for the greatest number of people (Strike & Soltis, 1985). The secret photo case is decided by whether either the taking or the publishing of the picture serves the interests of the largest possible number of people. If public pictorial information about this woman's body is deemed to be a greater good than an individual's objections to such information, public information overrules other views.

A problem with utilitarianism is that it has not convincingly described what it would be like to live the good life. *Virtue theory*, on the other hand, focuses on just that issue. It asks: what is virtuous character? It wonders if character traits are sustainable over time. Some virtue theorists stake a claim for the virtuousness of courage, temperance, wisdom, or justice, for instance. Some want to claim that moral tradition in life narratives, in our own stories, give us guidance (Pence, 1991). In the ongoing case of our celebrity photo, notions of virtue would require that we determine who—the photographed, the photographer, the publisher, the public consumer—is acting virtuously, acting with character or wisdom, in order to decide what is normal.

Theories of *rights* are ideas about human rights like life, health, liberty, or fair political representation. These theories are of particular importance recently because of all the places in which human rights violations seem to be occurring. We hear of rights in terms of claims, powers, liberties or immunities people have in relation to other humans—or even in relation to animals and the earth itself. The relation of morality and rights often is especially appealing when it takes the case for oppressed peoples. Rights also imply that the use of force is justified in pursuit of them. Theories of rights are appealing, too, because they appear to be valid—though not absolute—across most nations and cultures. Ultimately, ideas of rights may be justified because they contribute to the potential for widespread human agreement (Almond, 1991). Privacy is such a right, and in the case of the photo of the nude woman, her rights are being violated.

Additional Views of Good Living, Good Visuals

One other section of essays in *A Companion to Ethics* (Singer, 1991) is worth highlighting for a moment. In "The Great Ethical Traditions," the authors discuss many of the oldest major ethical traditions or theories. These traditions include *Indian ethics, Buddhist ethics, classical Chinese ethics, Jewish ethics, Christian ethics*, and *Islamic ethics*. The ideas in these theories are basically religious, mythical, and mystical. Many of the world's people look to these living traditions for guidance in moral/ethical thinking and actions more than they look to the Western traditions just sketched. Christian ethics, for instance, appear to urge us to be against the photographer, the publisher, and the consumer of the photo of the naked woman in our ongoing example, especially because of the profit motive and prurient nature associated with the photo.

At least one other view of ethics has begun to emerge over the past several decades—morality as seen from *postmodern* eyes. Immediately note the sense in which "postmodern" is often used: it is meant to oppose so-called "modern" notions (of the enlightenment era especially), which claim that humans can apply rationality and technology to discover and control nearly all aspects of our existence. Postmodernists defy this thinking. Knowledge is not the stable, objective, true entity many have sought. The contexts of history and cultural milieu help to shape our understanding of knowledge, including moral and ethical knowledge. As well, many postmodernists propose the emancipation of people from given ways of knowing and doing, especially when the specialized powerful and elite groups found in politics, economic systems, and schools are in control (Aronowitz & Giroux, 1991).

Postmodernists might question the received traditional ethical theories by asking, for instance, how those theories have helped to favor or impose one ethical tradition over those of other cultures. Who suffers under a dominant morality? Further, several people of a postmodern bent are looking at the moral implications of mass media, including films and television. They are asking who is justified and empowered and who is delegitimized and "othered" by mass media such as television (Schwoch, White, & Reilly, 1992). For many postmodernists, the issue of morality and images is ever-present. To ask about visuals is to be moral. In our running example, to the extent that the magazine uses the photo of the nude woman to exploit her and other women, it is morally culpable.

Objections and Irresoluteness

The traditions and theories noted above have not been developed without objections. Postmodernism, for example, is accused of having useless and even dangerous subjectivity and relativity. In addition, a review of the theories just visited reveals less than perfect alignment of their arguments. If we take a wide view, no universal law or immutable code has emerged to tell all people how to decide and act morally with regard to visuals.

A Critical Sense?

Although we can conclude that no universal moral-visual law appears to exist, we also see that formal theories and thoughtful common sense are available to us. This section extends notions of common sense and formal theorizing in relation to morality and visuals.

The idea of "common sense" has appeared occasionally in this chapter. In this section, however, common sense is altered somewhat to become "critical sense." This is to say that a reflective and conscientious stance—as well as a more leisurely, intuitive, and common stance—should help us discuss and act on issues of morality and visuals.

This critical sense means that we reflect broadly and deeply about visuals. This reflection enables us to discover and develop some of the basic, common principles of morality that seem to exist on a widespread, if not totally codified, way in many societies. The formal theories described earlier manifest one form of this reflection. A critical sense also means that we are conscientious about our reflections, "conscientious" suggesting that we care about good and bad, right and wrong. We search out instances where individuals, social groups, and whole cultures are being positively and negatively influenced by visuals.

Perhaps one of the best examples of a critical sense about visuals is expressed in what The United States Supreme Court decided (upon deep reflection) when it declared that it couldn't exactly define pictorial obscenity but that community standards are the ones by which we will judge the decency (an act of conscientiousness) of pictures.

A critical sense has sometimes led to suggestions for several moral principles explicitly related to visuals. Gross, Katz, and Ruby (1988), for instance, have concluded from their studies that there are *common moral imperatives* when making images public, although the imperatives are very general:

1. The image maker should produce images which reflect his/her intention, to the best of his/her ability.
2. The image maker should adhere to the standards of his/her profession and fulfill his/her commitments to the institutions or individuals who have made the production economically possible.
3. The image maker is obligated to his/her subjects.

4. The image maker is responsible to his/her audience.

Given that not all of us are producers of images, but that most of us are viewers, and given discussion earlier in the chapter about visuals and ecology, additional imperatives also seem to apply:

5. Viewers should reflect on and interpret the commitments, responsibilities, intentions, and obligations of the image maker.
6. Viewers should consider the relationships of images and image makers to the ecology of the earth.

What emerges from a critical sense approach to our topic is the understanding that all societies have discernible beliefs about what is good and bad in relation to visuals and we have ways to investigate these issues. Can't we say that an overwhelming majority of people in the world are morally repulsed by the depiction of children having sex with adults? Don't a majority also have high regard for the notion and depiction of a god—even if everyone doesn't share the same god? There is a critical sense about moral uses of visuals, even if that sense is not always explicit.

A Case in Point: Television and Children

By way of example, let me, the author of this chapter, try to come to some decisions about the morality of a pervasive form of television in America—commercial programming for children. This is a personal example of how I deal with the decisions, but its intent is to show you that decisions can be made and to encourage you to deal with the issues in your own ways. Further, although this is an example with morally suspect visuals, please keep in mind that critical examination can lead to the proliferation of positive visuals.

We'll start with the conclusion of the American Pediatrics Association and other groups that most television for children is violent, and viewing of this programming increases violent dispositions in most children (Hickey, 1992). Many, many of America's children watch violent TV and are likely to be more violent themselves because of this viewing. You and I must deal with some of these children because they live and scream next door to us, they cause our taxes to go up when they fill our prisons, and, finally, they are our own relatives!

To deal with TV, children, and violence, I first decide that most physical aggression not used strictly in self-defense is wrong. My entire personal history says so. But further, the content of the programs (cartoons, especially) is violent in and of itself. The focal characters (kids, animals, fantasy things) beat the hell out of one another all the time! Also, I decide (referring to the common moral imperatives from earlier) that the purpose of this programming is almost solely to excite the children and have them associate this feeling with the purchase of commercial products. This purpose does not best serve the children, but adults trying to make money.

At a more theoretic level, I believe that morals and ethics are personal positions we come to best through open, often long-term, and consensual conversations. Referring to an earlier section in this chapter, we could call them "critical" conversations. The conclusion about violence and TV noted above by Hickey (1992) serves as an example of such a conversation. It has taken decades of critical sense to begin to reach this conclusion. So, everything affecting morality has to be discussed and analyzed. Every visual has moral implications that we have an obligation to communicate about. From this point of view, I note that many children who watch TV (and their caregivers) do not partake of any such discussion. To this extent, violent children's programming and those who bring it to us are morally suspect.

In terms of the theories sketched earlier in this chapter, I'm probably best described as predominantly a postmodernist. I believe visuals need to be analyzed to judge the extent to which they are destructive or supportive of democratic, economic, ecological, physical, and moral conditions for individuals and their social groups. Because less powerful groups of children (and their caregivers) are encouraged by it to act in harmful ways, I am mostly opposed to violent children's television.

Altogether then, my personal, critical history about children's TV programming leads me to conclude that most of it is immoral. Further, there are several actions I choose to take in relation to this immorality. Note that I do not advocate banning children's violent programs; this runs contrary to the notion of consensual conversations about tough issues. But I must carry out research and publishing on these issues. Most importantly, I am obligated to carry on conversations which teach my students and which teach me about children and violent TV.

So What Are You Going to Do?

Many instances of morally questionable visuals confront you constantly, and your decisions about them are very difficult to make. Where exactly does your pictorial right to privacy begin and end—in your house or at the edge of your property? If someone imports your original visual to a computer and manipulates the image so you barely recognize it, to whom does it belong? Who gets any profits from the image?

You may believe that, "Decisions about morality and visuals are all too much to handle. I'm not going to deal with it." If you take this position, you may not be wrong in terms of some formal ethical scheme, but in terms of a critical sense, the position may be immoral. Even further, it may be an impossible position to take—not to choose is to choose. By not thinking and acting, you may be exacerbating any of the ill effects of visuals, and you may be limiting the positive effects.

So you have choices to make, and the ideas of this chapter are available to help you. You may be guided by a religious ethical system and its code. The Ten Commandments of Christianity, for instance, can help you decide the morality of visuals. You may choose to rely on one or more of the formal theories noted earlier in the chapter. You may choose to accept the six image makers' imperatives laid down at the end of the last section, especially the imperative to interpret the intentions of the image maker. In addition, your local community standards, perhaps expressed in formal laws, provide ways to examine moral issues.

However you choose to approach the issues discussed here, please act with a critical sense about the relationships of morals and visuals. Acting in this way is in itself a moral act because you are searching for good ways to live with visuals and the people who make and view them.

References

Almond, B. (1991). Rights. In P. Singer (Ed.), *A companion to ethics* (pp. 259–269). Cambridge, MA: Basil Blackwell.

Aronowitz, S., & Giroux, H. (Eds.). (1991). *Postmodern education: Politics, culture, and social criticism*. Minneapolis, MN: University of Minnesota Press.

Baier, K. (1991). Egoism. In P. Singer (Ed.), *A companion to ethics* (pp. 197–204). Cambridge, MA: Basil Blackwell.

Bilimoria, P. (1991). Indian ethics. In P. Singer (Ed.), *A companion to ethics* (pp. 43–57). Cambridge, MA: Basil Blackwell.

Buckle, S. (1991). Natural law. In P. Singer (Ed.), *A companion to ethics* (pp. 161–174). Cambridge, MA: Basil Blackwell.

Dancy, J. (1991). An ethic of prima facie duties. In P. Singer (Ed.), *A companion to ethics* (pp. 219–229). Cambridge, MA: Basil Blackwell.

Davis, N. A. (1991). Contemporary deontology. In P. Singer (Ed.), *A companion to ethics* (pp. 205–218). Cambridge, MA: Basil Blackwell.

Gross, L., Katz, J. S., & Ruby, J. (1988). *Image ethics*. New York: Oxford University Press.

Heinich, R., Molenda, M., & Russell, J. (1989). *Instructional media* (3rd ed.). New York: Macmillan Publishing Co.

Hickey, N. (1992, August 22–28). How much violence? *TV guide* (pp. 10–11). Radnor, PA: News America Publications.

Kymlicka, W. (1991). The social contract tradition. In P. Singer (Ed.), *A companion to ethics* (pp. 186–196). Cambridge, MA: Basil Blackwell.

O'Neill, O. (1991). Kantian ethics. In P. Singer (Ed.), *A companion to ethics* (pp. 175–185). Cambridge, MA: Basil Blackwell.

Pence, G. (1991). Virtue theory. In P. Singer (Ed.), *A companion to ethics* (pp. 249–258). Cambridge, MA: Basil Blackwell.

Schwoch, J., White, M., & Reilly, S. (1992). *Media knowledge*. Albany, NY: SUNY Press.

Singer, P. (Ed.). (1991). *A companion to ethics*. Cambridge, MA: Basil Blackwell.

Strike, K. A., & Soltis, J. F. (1985). *The ethics of teaching*. New York: Teachers College Press.

Wilson, J. (1990). *A new introduction to moral education*. London: Cassell Education Limited.

SECTION VIII

Use of Visuals and
Research Implications

We live in a visually oriented society; consequently visualization has become an integral part of our communication process. However, very little research is available to provide guidelines for the effective design and use of visualization in the teaching-learning process. Francis Dwyer identifies most criticisms associated with prior research that have contributed to the lack of useful guidelines. He provides a rationale for experimental research, along with systematic procedures for implementation. He identifies the instructional consistency/ congruency matrix as an integral part of this paradigm. The assumptions underlying the Program of Systematic Evaluation (PSE), its orientation, and an overview of some of the basic research findings obtained in Phases 1, 2, 3 of PSE are provided. Dwyer concludes with a list of recommendations for further research.

Chapter Twenty-Two

One Dimension of Visual Research: A Paradigm and Its Implementation

Francis M. Dwyer

Objectives

After reading this chapter, you should be able to:

1. *Explain why with all the existing research there are so few guidelines for using visualization in the teaching-learning process.*

2. *Discuss the function of visualization in information processing.*

3. *Explain and construct an example explaining what is meant by instructional consistency and instructional congruency.*

4. *Discuss the importance of visual testing.*

5. *Outline strategies which could be used in the development of a model for visual research.*

6. *List several of the generic conclusions resulting from the Program of Systematic Evaluation.*

Introduction

Visualization is an ever-present variable in the teaching-learning process. Educators at all levels have been incorporating visualization into their instructional strategies in an information acquisition and retention on the part of the learner. Visualization can allegedly be used to impart information in almost any subject area, compress information, illustrate salient parts of an instructional presentation, and stimulate information processing. Similarly, visualization has been characterized as being able to stimulate learner interest and motivation, span linguistic barriers, summarize important points in a lesson, provide important instructional feedback, foster generalizations of responses to new situations, facilitate discrimination and identification of relevant cues, etc. (Dwyer, 1978).

The traditional media along with the implementation of the new emerging electronic technologies have all functioned to increase the use of the visual medium. However, the primary justification for the use of visual materials regardless of presentation medium must be to facilitate student information acquisition.

Visualization as Rehearsal

Rehearsal may be considered to be any activity which causes the learner to hold information in short term memory (STM). Rehearsal strategies are generally used by learners to facilitate cognitive processing of new information. Without such processing there is no storage. Weinstein and Mayer (1986) have indicated that rehearsal strategies are designed to repeat information while it is in short term memory to compensate for the time and storage limitations of short term memory. Murray and Mosberg (1982) have indicated that the longer an individual can be involved in rehearsal activities (taking notes, inspecting, interacting with visuals, etc.), in which he/she is actively processing information, the greater the possibility that this information will be moved from short term memory into long term memory (LTM), and the greater the possibility that increase in learning will occur and be retained. Using visualization to complement oral and/or verbal instruction has been found to be an effective rehearsal strategy in facilitating learners' achievement (Dwyer, 1978, 1987). Visualization may be considered to be a rehearsal strategy in that it provides the learner with the opportunity to observe the structure of the objects being illustrated and their relationship (positioning) to other objects within the illustration. In this sense, it may be that the effectiveness inherent in visual rehearsal is that it allows the learner to process information simultaneously on several levels. For example, when using visualization to complement instruction on the human heart the student can quickly see the structure of the mitral valve, where it is positioned relative to the tricuspid valve, and also, by further inspection, its location between the left auricle and the left ventricle. Additionally, this type of visual representation of information has a tendency to reduce (short-circuit) learner dependence on oral/verbal comprehension skills. This is probably the basic reason why visualization has been found to be such a powerful variable in facilitating the achievement of students identified as possessing "low" verbal and/or oral comprehension skills (Dwyer, 1978, 1987).

It is also important to recognize that different rehearsal strategies differ in the intensity of learner involvement that they provide and, thus, may have differential effects on specific learning outcomes. Since different levels of visualization can portray different levels of realism, the type of visualization used to complement instruction can instigate different levels of rehearsal activity and thereby function differently in facilitating student achievement of different types of educational objectives.

Popularity of Visualization

Despite the widespread acceptance and use of visual materials for instructional purposes, surprisingly little is known relative to the instructional effectiveness of different types of visual materials, both from the standpoint of how learners react to variations in the amount and kinds of stimulation contained within the various types of visual delivery systems. How learners react to variations in the amount and kinds of stimulation contained within the various types of visual delivery systems and how visuals differing in amounts of realistic detail influence learner achievement of different educational objectives are questions which still remain to be answered.

Answers to these questions are critical because it seems reasonable to assume that for instructional purposes visualization is not multi-purposed in character—some types may be more or less effective than others in facilitating student achievement of different types of educational objectives. For example, if a visual does not provide sufficient rehearsal stimuli it will not facilitate learning, and it may also be that a visual that contains realistic detail (stimuli) beyond a certain point adds very little or actually may impede rather than facilitate the acquisition of intended information. For this reason, difficulty has been experienced in designing visualization that functions effectively in increasing learner information acquisition of designated educational objectives.

An explanation for the current widespread use of visualization can be traced back to the 1940's and 1950's when a number of theoretical orientations were identified—specifically, the iconicity theory identified by Morris (1946), Dale's (1946) cone of experience, and the sign similarity orientation developed by Carpenter (1953). Collectively these theories have been referred to as the realism theories. The basic assumption from each theory is that learning will be more complete as the number of cues in the learning situation increases. The writings of several other authors appear to substantiate this basic concept (Gibson, 1954; Osgood, 1953; Knowlton, 1964).

An Experimental Rationale for Visual Research

Theorizing and philosophizing about the advantages of visualized instruction and how learners interact, process, store, and retrieve information acquired visually are useful in establishing general structures which can be used to provide a focus for explanation; however, it is only through experimental research that actual cause and effect relationships can be established among variables. Acknowledging that characteristics of stimuli inherent in and presented by different types of visuals differ in kind, amount, and degree of realism, ideally, the goal to be achieved through research is one which would provide guidelines for the effective use of different types of visuals, which in turn would enable educators to design and/or select specific kinds of visualization. To facilitate student achievement of specific types of educational objectives, these guidelines would possess the highest degree of predictability for the design and use of visualization, to ensure that a majority of the learners, for whom the instruction was designed, would receive the intended message. This goal, however, is not easily attainable, since there are many different kinds of visual illustrations, i.e., line drawings, detailed, shaded line drawings, drawings of models, realistic photographs (both in black and white and color). Presumably all these different types of visuals are not equally effective in facilitating student achievement of different kinds of educational objectives. Consequently, visuals designed to complement oral and/or verbal instruction not only need to have a high correlation with the message they are attempting to support, but specific types of visuals may need to be designed to provide the learning environment with the prerequisite types of stimuli needed by particular types of students to achieve specific kinds of educational objectives.

Why then is there a lack of guidelines related to the design and use of visualization to optimize student learning since there is certainly no scarcity of experimental research associated with visualized instruction? An inspection of the experimental research relating to visualized instruction reveals that much of the research, in addition to suffering from many of the threats to internal validity identified by Campbell and Stanley (1966), has additional problems. These problems tend to further complicate data interpretation and frustrate any attempt to derive broad generalizations useful to practitioners in the classroom. Following is a sampling of the types of complications found in many of the experimental studies examining the effectiveness of visualized instruction (Dwyer, 1978, pp. 39–41):

- Many studies have obvious weaknesses in experimental design.
- Studies have been conducted without any hypotheses or predictions based on theory or prior research.
- Content being employed in studies (nonsense syllables, digits, letters, etc.) has been for removed from the type of subject content which is currently being taught in the schools.
- Instructional treatments lack congruency among levels of objectives, strategy of instructional presentation, and criterion measures.
- The meaningfulness and difficulty levels of the content have not been defined.
- The relationship that exists between the printed content and the visualization had not been defined.
- The type, number, and rationale for visual placement in the printed instruction has not been described precisely.
- The type of realistic detail (line drawings, realistic photographs, etc.) in the visualization and whether the visualization is black and white or color has not been stated in many studies.
- The method by which the visualization (self-paced or externally paced) was presented to students has not been described precisely.
- Validity and reliability of the tests have not been reported.

Visual Testing

The concept of visual testing is one which complicates the interpretation of research dealing with visual literacy/visual learning. Instructional environments are purposely designed to facilitate student acquisition, storage, and retrieval of designated information. Even though visualization is commonly used to facilitate student information acquisition, most evaluation strategies currently used are of the verbal pencil-and-paper type. Paivio, Rogers, and Smythe (1968) and Dwyer

(1987) have suggested the possible existence of dual encoding and retrieval systems; one having the capability of processing verbal symbols and the other having the capability of processing visual information. Support for the use of test items that employ visuals of the same type as those employed in the instruction has surfaced regularly in the research literature in the form of hypotheses and theories, for example, the sign-similarity hypotheses (Carpenter, 1953), stimulus generalization theory (Hartman, 1961), cue summation theory (Tulving & Thomson, 1973), and the transfer-appropriate processing principle (Morris, Bransford, & Franks, 1977). Lindsay and Norman (1977) have stated that in the teaching-learning environment, "the problem in learning new information is not getting the information into memory; it is making sure that it will be found later when it is needed"(p. 337).

At the practical level this position seems to imply that in a teaching-learning environment where visualization is used in the presentation phase and is not used in the evaluation phase, student performance measures will yield gross underestimates, if not distortions, with respect to what and how much information was originally acquired (Dwyer & DeMelo, 1983). This conceptualization suggests that information retrieval is a very sensitive process, easily disrupted. Since the features of the original learning cues are processed during a test, any reduction in the individual distinctiveness of the cues themselves should produce concomitant reductions in recall (Nelson, 1979).

The strategy of attempting to use the same type of visualization both in the presentation and evaluation phases of instruction is an attempt to implement the stimulus generalization theory which contends that the amount of information that will be acquired by students increases as the testing situation becomes more similar to the situation in which the students receive their instruction (Hartman, 1961; Severin, 1967). In general, these theories contend that student achievement will be maximized to the degree that the evaluation conditions reflect the conditions in which the initial information was encoded. In summarizing the visual testing issue Dwyer and DeMelo (1983, p. 12) have stated: "probably, the oldest and least controversial fact that can be derived from the research on human learning is that any change in the retrieval (evaluation) environment from that which occurred in the original learning environment produces marked decrements in learner performance" (Battig, 1979; Nitsch, 1977).

Another generic problem associated with the interpretation of media-related research is that researchers often do not consistently state the type of learning the students are expected to achieve. This in turn prevents researchers from generalizing results obtained from individual studies and probably explains why some studies using visualization achieve significant results while others obtain insignificant results. It is generally agreed that if students are to achieve at the different levels of learning, they need to interact and participate in different levels of information processing. This being the case, one of the most important steps in any research study focusing on cognitive information acquisition is the development of an instructional unit which contains several different levels of learning (facts, concepts, rule/procedures, problem-solving) and the appropriate types of tests to measure the objectives at each level.

The unit needs to be sufficiently complex so that the students who are interacting with the control treatment (the non-visualized oral or print version) do not achieve optimally. For example, if such an instructional unit were developed without the use of visualization and piloted with students, and they achieved a mean score on the test of 75 out of a possible 80 points, there would be little possibility that embedded visualization of any type would impact positively on the mean score. Obviously, it is not useful or economically justifiable to add visualization to an instructional unit in which the students are already successfully acquiring information being presented. Ideally the complexity of the control treatment would be such that optimum achievement would not be realized so that the embedded visualization would have the opportunity to facilitate increased achievement. Once you have piloted your control treatment and it has been determined that the control treatment, in and of itself, is not optimizing student achievement, the next task is to identify where to position visualization to maximally improve achievement.

Instructional Consistency/Congruency

The instructional consistency/congruency paradigm (Canelos, 1983) presents a useful conceptual rationale for the development of a useful instructional module for research purposes. The paradigm assumes a hierarchy of learning objectives. For example, students will not achieve at the rule/principle level if they do not possess the prerequisite conceptual base for such learning to occur. However, even if students do possess the conceptual base and the instructional environment does not bring together the relevant concepts in a manner which facilitates rule/principle level integration, learning will not occur.

Figure 1 presents the hierarchical learning paradigm which illustrates the different levels of learning. For example, it assumes that when students are introduced to unfamiliar content, they first have to learn the basic terminology and facts which make up the basic components of the language of the discipline. The more terms, facts, and definitions (◯), etc. that a student is familiar within a content area, the better prepared they will be to relate and combine these units of information to form concepts (◊) (Figure 1). The more concepts students possess, the easier it is for them to form rules and/or procedures (☐). In addition the more rules and/or procedures that students possess the easier it will be for them to be successful at problem solving (Δ). Based on this kind of orientation to learning, ease of subsequent learning is directly related to the quality and quantity of the prerequisite learning.

The Instructional Consistency Congruency Matrix (Figure 2) requires, for example, that if your final objective is to have learners engage in problem-solving, that you inspect the instructional unit to make sure that the content contains the appropriate facts, concepts, rules/principles, etc. which are a prerequisite for the intended learners to engage in successful problem-solving. The instructional consistency concept functions to verify that the prerequisite kinds of learning are present; it also requires that the objectives for each category be stated specifically. This step of the unit development is critical because it alerts the researcher to the fact that the learners are going to be processing information

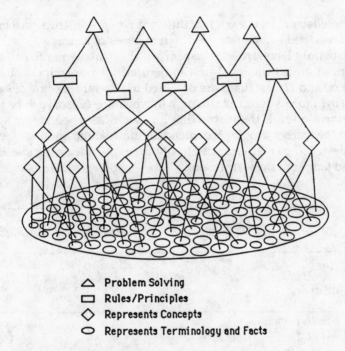

△ Problem Solving
▭ Rules/Principles
◇ Represents Concepts
◯ Represents Terminology and Facts

Figure 1. Phases in a Learning Hierarchy.

	Objectives	Instruction	Testing
Problem Solving			
Rule/Principle Using			
Concepts			
Facts			

Instructional Congruency

(left side vertical label) Instructional Consistency

Figure 2. Instructional Consistency/Congruency Matrix.

at different intellectual levels and that different types of instructional experiences need to be developed to facilitate the different levels of learning.

The instructional congruency aspect of the matrix requires that in the development of an instructional unit to be used for research (1) objectives are clearly defined and (2) test items are designed to measure specific objectives. The series of X's in Figure 3 depicts a situation in which the objective to be taught is at the rule/principle level, the instruction has been designed at the appropriate level to help the learner acquire the intended information, and that the test items have been designed to measure specifically the type of learning specified in the objective and taught in the instruction.

			Objectives	Instruction	Testing
I n s t r u c t i o n a l	C o n s i s t e n c y	Problem Solving			
		Rule/Principle Using	(X) (B)	(X) (B)	(X) (A)
		Concepts	(A)	(A)	(B)
		Facts			

Instructional Congruency

Figure 3. Instructional Consistency/Congruency Matrix.

The A's in Figure 3 illustrate the situation in which the objective has been written at the concept level and the instructional experiences were designed to facilitate concept information acquisition. However, the testing was implemented at the rule/principle level. The level of "congruency" identified in this scenario usually results in poor academic performance and frustrated students. The B's in Figure 3 present a different kind of mismatch. Here the objective is stated at the rule/principle level and the instruction was also designed to facilitate information processing at this level; however, the testing was designed and implemented at the concept level. Testing performance resulting from this paradigm is usually good but excessively costly in terms of time and money. It generally costs more to design instructional experiences which instigate the higher levels of information processing—and in this case in which the testing occurred at the concept level, we have no way of knowing for sure whether the rule/principle objective has been achieved.

Developing an instructional sequence based on the instructional consistency/congruency paradigm ensures that the hierarchy of learning levels are present in an instructional sequence and that test items are designed and constructed to measure specific levels of learning. The use of the matrix, along with item analysis, permits the researcher to precisely locate the area in the instruction where the students are experiencing difficulty in acquiring the intended information so that appropriate instructional strategies including visualization may be embedded in the instruction. The procedure of identifying precisely where students are experiencing difficulty in learning from an instructional unit is critical since it is possible to incorporate visualization (or some other type of rehearsal strategy) into an instructional unit where it is not needed, thereby failing to improve student information acquisition. Once difficult areas in the instructional unit have been identified, visuals (and/or other rehearsed strategies) can be designed specifically to illustrate the same information in the instruction that students are having difficulty acquiring. The justification for using redundant information in both print/oral and visual channels is to provide the learner with the opportunity to receive information alternatively from either channel and to help them short-circuit their dependence on printed and/or oral instruction.

The Program of Systematic Evaluation (PSE)

The Program of Systematic Evaluation (PSE) was initiated in 1965 by the author at Penn State University. Its basic purpose was to identify the types of visual materials which would be most effective in facilitating student achievement of different educational objectives when the content material is presented via different instructional formats. To achieve the program's basic objective, appropriate measures were implemented to reduce and control, as much as possible, many of the criticisms and/or deficiencies identified in prior visual research. By controlling many of the variables which were normally allowed to vary in prior experiments, it is more credible that the independent variables influenced achievement on the different dependent measures. Continuity throughout the studies has been maintained by utilizing the same 2,000-word instructional unit on the human heart. This unit was developed in compliance with the principles associated with the instructional consistency/congruency paradigm. The heart content was selected because of its motivational value and because it permitted the evaluation of different types of educational objectives. Specifically, the terminology test measured students' knowledge of specific facts; the identification test measured students' ability to identify facts or positions of the parts within the heart; the drawing test evaluated students' ability to construct and/or reproduce the parts of the heart in their appropriate context, and the comprehension test measured the students' total understanding of the heart functions and positions of the parts during the diastolic and systolic phases. The items contained in the four individual criterion tests were combined into an 80-item total criterion test which was a measure of the students' total understanding of all of the content material presented in the instructional unit. Test formats exist in both the verbal and visual versions. Average Kuder-Richardson-20 reliability coefficients for each criterion test has been computed from a random sampling of the studies; they are .83 terminology test, .81 identification test, .83 drawing test, .77 comprehension test, and .92 total criterion test (Dwyer, 1978, p. 47).

Once the instructional script and the criterion tests were developed they were piloted with students at different age and grade levels. Item analysis was conducted on performance scores achieved on the different criterion tests to identify the areas in the instruction where students were experiencing difficulty in acquiring the designated information. Eight complete visual sequences were designed and developed for the original studies (simple line drawings presentation, black and white and color; detailed line drawing presentation, black and white and color; heart model presentation, black and white and color; realistic photographic presentation, black and white and color). Each instructional sequence contained thirty-nine illustrations. Recommended experimental procedures were followed in all studies.

In order to provide a general orientation to guide the Program of Systematic Evaluation, a number of initial questions were developed. A sampling of these questions follow (Dwyer, 1972, pp. 3–10; 1978, pp. 37–39).

1. How do you use visualization in instruction?

2. What do you visualize?

3. What kinds of visualization do you use?

4. When do you use visualization?

5. Are all types of visual materials equally effective in facilitating student achievement of all types of educational objectives?

6. Are identical types of visual illustrations equally effective in complementing both oral and printed instruction?

7. What is the relationship between verbal and visual testing?

8. What kinds of independent variables used in conjunction with different types of visualization significantly improve the instructional effectiveness of visualized instruction?

9. Is color in visuals an important instructional variable in facilitating student achievement of specific objectives?

10. Will the use of visuals to complement oral/print instruction affect delayed retention of the content material?

11. Are student perceptions of the value of different types of visual illustrations a valid assessment of the instructional effectiveness of the visuals?

12. Does the method in which visuals are presented to students, e.g., slides/audiotape, television, programmed instruction, etc., affect the ability of the visuals to facilitate achievement of different educational objectives?

13. Does the amount of time students are permitted to interact with visualized instruction affect their level of achievement of different educational objectives?

14. Are identical types of visual illustrations equally effective for all education levels, or do the different types of visual illustrations possess differing degrees of instructional effectiveness for students at different educational levels and for different educational objectives?

15. Are different cueing techniques (motion, inserted questions, knowledge of specific learning objectives, etc.) equally effective in complementing visualized instruction?

16. Can oral and printed questions be used to improve the instructional effectiveness of visualized instruction?

17. Do boys and girls in the same grade level (high school) learn equally well from the same types of visual illustrations on tests designed to measure achievement of different educational objectives?

18. Is there only one visual learning continuum representing instructional effectiveness of visuals for complementing both oral and printed instruction?

19. Will the use of visual illustrations that are specifically designed to complement oral and printed instruction automatically improve student achievement?

20. What effect does specific individual difference variables (intelligence, reading comprehension, prior knowledge, etc.) have on students' ability to profit from different types of visualization?

21. What kinds of visual illustrations—in what patterns, combinations, and sequences—provide the best stimulus conditions for maximum achievement of specific kinds of educational objectives?

22. How does the type of reinforcement (printed versus visual) that students receive in progressing through a visualized instructional module affect their level of achievement of different kinds of educational objectives?

To date more than 50,000 high school, college, and adult learners have participated in over 200 research studies conducted in the PSE (Dwyer, 1972, 1978, 1987). A significant number of these studies were conducted by students in master and doctoral degree candidates at Penn State University, Ohio State University, Texas A&M University, Virginia Tech, etc. The instructional unit and tests have been translated into Spanish, Chinese, Arabic, and Korean, and research has been conducted in Puerto Rico, Korea, Taiwan, and Qatar. The experimental results accumulated in the PSE are considered to represent a departure from the fragmented research which in the past has failed to contribute to a cumulative analysis of the role of visualization in the instructional process. The data analyzed from studies conducted in this program substantiates the fact that the human being is a very complex organism and that the variables which influence learning are likewise extremely complex. However, specific effectiveness of a visual learning environment is primarily dependent on the following factors (Dwyer, 1985, pp. 10–15):

1. The amount of realistic detail contained in the type of visualization used;

2. The method by which the visualized instruction is presented to students (externally paced vs. self-paced);

3. Student characteristics, i.e., intelligence, prior knowledge in the content area, reading and/or oral comprehension level, etc.;

4. The type or level of educational objective to be achieved by the students;

5. The technique used to focus student attention on the essential learning characteristics in the visualized materials, e.g., cues such as questions, arrows, motion, verbal/visual feedback, overt/covert responses, etc.;

6. The type of test format employed to assess student information acquisition (verbal/visual, etc.).

Program of Systematic Evaluation—Phase 1

The evaluation of the PSE can be envisioned as having progressed through three phases. During Phase 1 the basic conceptual rationale for the program was developed. The specific types of objectives to be used were identified; a specific instructional unit which facilitated meaningful learning to occur was constructed; four individual criterion tests were constructed which measured student achievement of different types of instructional objectives; and eight complete visualized experiment treatments ranging from line drawings to realistic photographs (black and white and color) were assembled; and a stable experimental procedure was identified. Following is a list of general conclusions derived from the research conducted in Phase 1 of the Program of Systematic Evaluation (Dwyer, 1972, pp. 89–90).

1. The use of visuals specifically designed to complement oral and printed instruction does not automatically improve student achievement. For certain types of educational objectives, oral and printed instruction without visualization is as effective as visually complemented instruction. For other types of educational objectives the use of visuals designed to complement a particular instructional method and to facilitate achievement of a specific educational objective will increase student achievement of that objective.

2. All types of visuals are not equally effective in facilitating student achievement of different educational objectives. The type of visual illustration most effective in transmitting information is dependent upon the type of information to be transmitted.

3. The method by which students receive their visualized instruction (television, slides, programmed instruction) determines the type of visual that will be most efficient in facilitating student achievement of specific educational objectives. Identical visual illustrations are not equally effective when used for externally-paced and self-paced instruction.

4. The effectiveness of a particular type of visual in promoting student achievement of a specific educational objective depends on the amount of time students are permitted to interact with the visualized instruction.

5. For students in different grade levels, the same visuals are not equally effective in increasing achievement of identical educational objectives.

6. For specific students and for specific educational objectives, the use of color in certain types of visuals appears to be an important instructional variable in improving student achievement. For other educational objectives, however, the added cost of color may not be justified.

7. In general, for high school students for whom slides are used to complement oral instructions, differential effects attributed to various visualized treatments on immediate retention tests disappear on delayed retention tests.

8. Student perceptions of the value of different types of visual illustrations are not valid assessments; that is, aesthetically pleasing visuals may deceive students about their instructional value.

9. The realism continuum for visual illustrations is not an effective predictor of learning efficiency for all types of educational objectives when the visualized instruction is presented via television, slides, programmed instruction, and textbook formats. An increase in the

amount of realistic detail contained in an illustration will not produce a corresponding increase in the amount of information a student will assimilate from it.

10. The use of questions to focus student attention on the relevant visual learning cues in the more realistic illustrations used to complement externally-paced and self-paced instruction is not an effective technique for improving the instructional potential of the illustrations.

11. Boys and girls in the same grade level (high school) learn equally well from identical types of visual illustrations when they are used to complement oral instruction.

12. Identical visual illustrations are not equally effective in facilitating the achievement of students possessing different levels of entering behavior (prior knowledge in a content area).

13. Merely increasing the size of instructional illustrations by projecting them on larger viewing areas does not automatically improve their effectiveness in facilitating student achievement.

Program of Systematic Evaluation—Phase 2

Strategies for Improving Visual Learning (Dwyer, 1978) summarized the research findings generated in the PSE from 1972 to 1978. The research findings emphasize the importance of the interrelatedness of variables (e.g., degree of realism, cueing techniques, level of educational objectives, individual differences, method of presentation, and testing format) associated with the effective use of visual materials. Trends are drawn from prior research relative to the effective design and use of visual media. In this respect, the test presents the concept of visual instruction, not as an isolated phenomenon, but as an interrelated constituent process operating at varying levels of complexity—the elements of which acquire significance only in the context in which they are used. The following list provides a sampling of the generalizations which were derived from the studies (Dwyer, 1978, pp. 96–97).

1. The realism continuum for visual illustrations applied to externally paced instruction is not an effective predictor of learning efficiency for all types of educational objectives. An increase in the amount of realistic detail contained in an illustration will not produce a corresponding increase in the amount of information a student will acquire from it.

2. The use of specific types of visual illustrations to facilitate specific types of educational objectives significantly improves student achievement of externally-paced instruction.

3. All types of visuals are not equally effective in facilitating student achievement of different educational objectives when instruction is

externally-paced. The type of visual illustration most effective in transmitting information is dependent upon the type of information to be transmitted.

4. The use of visuals specifically designed to complement oral instruction does not automatically improve student achievement. However, for certain types of educational objectives the use of visuals designed to complement a particular instructional method and to facilitate achievement of a specific objective will increase student achievement of the objective.

5. For specific students and for specific educational objectives, the use of color in certain types of visuals presented via the slide/audiotape format appears to be an important instructional variable in improving student achievement. For other educational objectives, however, the added cost of color may not be justified from the instructional effectiveness standpoint.

6. For certain types of educational objectives, externally-paced (oral) instruction without visualization is as effective as visualized instruction for certain types of students.

7. All types of cueing techniques do not equally facilitate the instructional effectiveness of different types of visual illustrations; some types of cueing techniques are significantly more effective than others in externally-paced instruction.

8. The effectiveness of a particular type of visual in facilitating student achievement of a specific educational objective depends, in part, on the amount of time students are permitted to interact with the visualized instruction.

Program of Systematic Evaluation—Phase 3

Merely integrating visualization into an instructional sequence is not always a sufficient condition for maximizing student achievement of all types of objectives. In many cases, visualization must be used in conjunction with one or more additional independent variables to significantly increase student achievement from visualized instruction. The main topic of the research in this phase focused on how different independent variables may be manipulated and combined to facilitate increased student learning from visualized instruction. Following is a sampling of some of the types of variables utilized in Phase 3 (Dwyer, 1987):

Cognitive trace compatibility	Cognitive strategies
Color coding	Computer based instruction
Cue summation	Cued recall
Dogmatism	Elaborate/reduced step cueing

Encoding specificity	Eye movement
Field independence/dependence	Free recall
Imagery learning strategies	Instructional congruency
Intelligence	Interactive/interruptive TV
Levels of self-pacing	Locus of control
Mode of instruction	Motion
Networking	Note-taking
Order of testing	Organizational chunking
Overt/covert practice	Post questions
Prior knowledge	Programmed instruction
Rate modified speech	Reading comprehension
Realism	Rehearsal
Rote learning strategies	Short term/long term retention
Visual testing	

In general studies investigating the above cited variables have found that:

- Achievement is enhanced when embedded cueing strategies are integrated into computer based instruction;
- Learners with higher I.Q.'s learn more from complex visual displays;
- The more elaborate visual cues tend to be most effective;
- Visuals possessing varied degrees of realistic detail can be used to reduce differences in the performance of learners possessing different levels of prior knowledge;
- Combining visualized instruction and visualized testing improves student achievement;
- Learners with higher I.Q. fixate more on complex instructional visuals, and learners with lower I.Q. have fewer fixations as visual complexity increases;
- Pre-program question cueing is more effective than motion and arrows in facilitating student achievement of specific educational objectives;
- Color coding improves attention, learner motivation, and the formation of structure in memory;
- Chunking of information can be a beneficial variable in facilitating student achievement when using imagery learning strategies;
- Learners possessing different levels of field-dependence/independence learn quantitatively different amounts of information from visuals which vary significantly in terms of visual complexity;
- Imagery strategies involving networking or information chunking are effective in assisting learners to process new information;
- Externally-Paced methods of pacing computer based instruction were more effective in promoting learner achievement than were self-paced methods;
- Different rehearsal strategies impact differentially in facilitating student achievement of different educational objectives;
- Visual testing is a valid strategy for assessing students' learning from visualized instruction;

- Learners who are given quality interaction opportunities spend more time learning and achieve significantly more on tests measuring specific educational objectives;
- Amount of rehearsal activity provided to students significantly influence the performance of students identified as external locus of control;
- The addition of audio redundancy to an instructional sequence has a significant negative effect on the achievement of learners identified as being in the low I.Q. level.

Future Research Recommendations

The scope of the PSE is constantly expanding to take advantage of the new research opportunities provided by the new emerging technologies and the "new" cognitive constructs such as structural knowledge, generative and constructionist learning, etc. Research currently in progress is utilizing the microcomputer's capabilities to assist in examining the effects of varied internal and external environmental conditions in learning.

The fact that the basic instructional treatments and criterion tests are available for use and that the treatments have been translated into several languages is stimulating the international scope of the PSE. Increasingly the materials are being used at the public school level and the business/corporate level in an attempt to identify effective design and utilization strategies for learners in specific settings. At the college level it appears that research interests will be multi-focused and will continue to explore the instructional effect of intervening variables used singly and in combination—to assess their influence in improving student information acquisition. It is anticipated that this research will become more comprehensive in nature and continue to employ the most sophisticated techniques available.

It is hoped that through the efforts expended in the PSE, prescriptive guidelines will eventually be developed which will identify those generic conditions which must be attended to by designers of instructional materials to maximize student information acquisition. For this goal to be achieved it will be necessary to expand the content of the present instructional unit to permit the assessment of different levels of learning, and that additional instructional units be developed which can be used to evaluate similar educational objectives in other content areas.

In essence, the PSE*, as extensive as it is, has only begun to scratch the surface of what is yet to be explored. Different types of visuals, tests (both print and visual), different cueing, individual difference variables, interaction strategies, etc., are all variables which need to be explored more comprehensively and extensively if the ultimate goal of the PSE is to be realized.

*Information related to the availability and use of experimental materials used in the PSE can be obtained by writing to Learning Services, Box 784, State College, PA 16804.

References

Battig, W. F. (1979). The flexibility of human memory. In L. S. Cermak & F. I. M. Craik (Eds.), *Levels of processing in human memory*. Hillsdale, NJ: Lawrence Erlbaum Associates.

Canelos, J. (1983). Instructional congruency as an educational tool for engineering education. *Proceedings: Frontiers in education conference* (pp. 47–52). American Society for Engineering Education.

Campbell, D. T., & Stanley, J. C. (1966). *Experimental and quasi-experimental design for research*. Chicago: Rand McNally.

Carpenter, C. (1953). A theoretical orientation for instructional film research, *AV Communication Review, 1*, 38–52.

Dale, E. (1946). *Audio-visual methods in teaching*. New York: Dryden Press.

Dwyer, F. M. (1972). *A guide for improving visualized instruction*. State College, PA: Learning Services.

Dwyer, F. M. (1978). *Strategies for improving visual learning*. State College, PA: Learning Services.

Dwyer, F. M. (1985). Visual literacy's first dimension: Cognitive information acquisition. *Journal of Visual/Verbal Languaging, 5*, 7–15.

Dwyer, F. M. (1987). *Enhancing visualized instruction-recommendations for practitioners*. State College, PA: Learning Services.

Dwyer, F. M., & DeMelo, H. (1983). The effect of visual testing in assessing the instructional potential of variables associated with visualized instruction. *Journal of Instructional Psychology, 10*, 126–140.

Gibson, J. J. (1954). A theory of pictorial perceptions. *AV Communication Review, 2*, 2–23.

Hartman, F. R. (1961). Recognition learning under multiple channel presentation and testing conditions. *AV Communication Review, 9*, 24–43.

Knowlton, J. Q. (1964). *A conceptual scheme for the audiovisual field*. Bloomington, IN: Indiana University, Bulletin of the School of Education.

Lindsay, P. H., & Norman, D. A. (1977). *Human information processing*. New York: Academic Press.

Morris, C. D. (1946). *Signs, languages, and behavior*. New York: Prentice-Hall.

Morris, C. D., Bransford, J. D., & Franks, J. J. (1977). Levels of processing versus transfer appropriate processing. *Journal of Verbal Learning and Verbal Behavior, 16*, 519–533.

Murray, F. B., & Mosberg, L. (1982). Cognition and memory. In H. E. Mitzel (Ed.), *Encyclopedia of educational research* (5th ed.). New York: The Free Press.

Nelson, D. A. (1979). Remembering pictures and words: Appearance, significance, and name. In L. S. Cermak & F. I. M. Craik (Eds.), *Levels of processing in human memory*. Hillsdale, NJ: Lawrence Erlbaum Associates.

Nitsch, K. E. (1977). *Structuring decontextualized forms of knowledge*. Unpublished doctoral dissertation, Vanderbilt University.

Osgood, C. (1953). *Method and theory in experimental psychology*. New York: Oxford University Press.

Paivio, A., Rogers, T. W., & Smythe, P. C. (1968). Why are pictures easier to recall than words? *Psychonomic Science, 11*, 137–138.

Severin, W. J. (1967). Another look at cue summation. *AV Communication Review, 15*, 233–245.

Tulving, E., & Thomson, D. M. (1973). Encoding specificity and retrieval processes in episodic memory. *Psychological Review, 80*, 352–373.

Weinstein, C. E., & Mayer, R. R. (1986). The teaching of learning strategies. In M. C. Wittrock (Ed.), *Handbook of research on teachers* (3rd ed.). New York: Macmillan Publishing Co.

EPILOGUE

Visual literacy as a concept has many interpretations. The authors of the chapters in this text have brought together under one cover a variety of perspectives on an evolving field. They have examined such constructs as: visual language, perceptional and cultural coding, creativity, visual and verbal relationships, deconstructionism, the historical, social, theoretical foundations, and research.

Since the 1960's the growth of and acceptability of the visual literacy concept has been phenomenal. The charisma and potential associated with the use of visuals in instruction, business, and other fields have provided considerable interdisciplinary appeal. Consequently, there have been numerous attempts to define visual literacy. Unfortunately, a universal definition of the visual literacy concept has yet to be agreed upon even though the basic concept is gaining credibility from the steady flow of research, theory, and technology from many areas.

In one sense visual literacy is becoming less complex as the basic notion of learning with visuals becomes more universally accepted. However, as a field of study, it is becoming more complicated because new theories, technologies, and knowledge are being brought forward to explain and to expand the concept. New questions concerning the foundations of the visual literacy concept will continue to surface and their resolution will continue to define the field. We feel that this book goes a long way in providing an initial perspective to the field of visual literacy, explaining the concept, illustrating its uses, and responding to some of the evolving questions.

ABOUT THE CONTRIBUTORS

Editors

Francis M. Dwyer is Professor and Head of the Department of Adult Education, Instructional Systems, and Vocational and Industrial Education at The Pennsylvania State University. He has served as President of the Association for Educational Communications and Technology and the International Visual Literacy Association. He has conducted more than 200 research studies related to visual learning, which have resulted in the publication of three texts directly related to the design and use of visualization in the instructional process. In 1991, he received the IVLA's Research Award for 25 years of sustained research contributions to the field of visual learning.

David M. (Mike) Moore is Professor of Education, Virginia Polytechnic Institute and State University (Virginia Tech). He has published more than 80 articles in professional journals primarily in the area of visual research. He is Past-President of the International Visual Literacy Association.

Contributors

Ann Marie Seward Barry is Associate Professor of Communication at Boston College. Author of *The Advertising Portfolio* and a variety of interdisciplinary articles in literature and communication, she holds Masters degrees in American Literature and Mass Communication, in addition to an interdisciplinary Ph.D. in Perceptual Psychology, Literature, and Film from Boston University, where she was a University Scholar.

Gretchen Bisplinghoff is currently Assistant Professor of Media Studies at Northern Illinois University. She received her Ph.D. in Film from Northwestern University. At Northwestern she co-edited *Film Reader 5* and was a founding member of the Feminist Film Seminar, which organized the first national feminist film criticism conference. Her publications include the co-authorship of two books, on film directors Robert Altman and Roman Polanski. Her other publications and professional activities reflect an ongoing interest in the image of women in the media and feminist film theory.

Roberts A. Braden is Professor of Communication Studies at California State University–Chico. He is Past-President of the International Visual Literacy Association and a Board Member of the Association for Educational Communications and Technology. He the author of many professional journal articles and is the Book Review Editor for *Educational Technology Research and Development Journal* as well as a long-time contributor to *Educational Technology* Magazine.

John K. Burton is Professor of Educational Psychology at Virginia Tech, where he has been a faculty member since he completed his Ph.D. at the University of Nebraska–Lincoln in 1977. Dr. Burton has published widely in educational psychology and instructional technology. His current interests include the use of hypermedia to prototype and modify learner interfaces.

Edward J. Caropreso is currently Assistant Professor of Education in the Department of Education at Clarion University of Pennsylvania. His teaching responsibilities include undergraduate courses in Educational Psychology and Educational Evaluation and Measurement. His research interests include the teaching and learning of critical and creative thinking skills, the development of planning and problem solving, and the relationship between intrinsic and extrinsic motivation and their effects on learning.

Richard A. Couch is Assistant Professor of Education at Clarion University of Pennsylvania. He teaches a variety of classes including Microcomputer Applications, methods courses, and educational foundations courses. His research interests include creativity, critical thinking, imagery, authentic assessment, microcomputers, school reform, and any combination of all of the above.

Ann DeVaney is Professor of Education and Associate Dean of the College of Education at the University of Wisconsin–Madison. She is Past-Editor of *The Journal of Visual Literacy*. Her research interests include the study of film in instructional situations.

Barbara W. Fredette is Associate Professor in Education at the University of Pittsburgh. Her research deals with the role of visual literacy in art and education and the role of drawing in developing young writers. Her resent publications include "From stereotype to prototype" and "To see or not to see."

Robert E. Griffin is Instructional Specialist for the College of Business Administration at the University Park Campus of The Pennsylvania State University. Additionally, he has produced over fifty television programs and multimedia programs and has developed the Center for Business Graphics for the College of Business Administration. Mr. Griffin has extensive professional experience in advising management with respect to media utilization, computer graphics and presentation speaking. He is the author of *Harvard Graphics: Creating Effective Visual Presentations*.

John A. Hortin is Professor of Education at Kansas State University. He is Past Vice-President of the International Visual Literacy Association. His expertise is in visual learning. He is the Past-Editor of two journals: the *Journal of Visual/Verbal Languaging* and the *Media and Adult Learning Journal.*

Nancy Nelson Knupfer earned her doctorate in Educational Technology at the University of Wisconsin–Madison. Dr. Knupfer has been involved with design, production, implementation, and evaluation of interactive, technology-based instructional materials within industry, government, and educational settings. Formerly at Arizona State University, Dr. Knupfer is now a faculty member at Kansas State University. She has an active interest in visual messages as they impact learning through technology-driven materials, in both local and distance delivery modes.

Nikos Metallinos is Professor of Communication Studies at Concordia University, Montreal, Quebec, Canada. His teaching areas are Television Production, Visual Literacy and Television Aesthetics, and Research Methodologies in Visual Communication Media. His research works, which center on the aesthetic principles governing the visual communication media, are based on his studies and research in the fields of perceptual psychology, neurophysiology, cognitive psychology, and art composition.

Helen B. Miller is a senior human factors engineer with *NCR* Corporation in Atlanta, GA. Her main responsibility is consulting with *NCR* customers on redesigning work processes and training programs. She also has responsibility for providing human interface design support for retail peripherals and terminal systems. Prior to joining *NCR*, Dr. Miller was an Assistant Professor at Clemson University.

Robert Muffoletto is Associate Professor of Education at the University of Northern Iowa. His writings on the analysis of representations, culture, and education have appeared in publications such as *The Journal of Thought, Journal of Visual Literacy,* and *Paradigms Regained.*

Randall G. Nichols is Associate Professor of Education at the University of Cincinnati. He is in the Department of Curriculum and Instruction, where, in part, he examines and uses various aspects of instructional design and technology with undergraduates and graduates. His writing often focuses on the cultural, moral, and ethical aspects of educational technology.

Rhonda S. Robinson is Professor of Education at Northern Illinois University (NIU), where she directs the Masters degree program and teaches courses in instructional technology research, design, and development. She has her Ph.D. from the University of Wisconsin. She has been teaching at NIU for 13 years and has five years of secondary school experience as well. Her research interests are in using interpretive and qualitative methods to look at technology applications in education and business.

Ann C. Saunders is Associate Professor of Design in the School of Art and Design at Southern Illinois University at Carbondale. She has worked as a designer for Johnson Publishing Co. and The National Clearinghouse for Criminal Justice Planning and Architecture. She was the senior development designer for The Division of Public Broadcasting at the University of Illinois (WILL-AM/FM and TV) in 1978–80 and served as art director for *Sunbelt Magazine* in 1980. Her research interests include documenting the significance and function of graphic forms used in network television news, visual literacy, and the use of the design process and design activities in general education.

Barbara A. Seels is Associate Professor and Program Director for Instructional Design and Technology at the University of Pittsburgh. She has published extensively in the area of instructional technology and visual learning. She is the author of *Exercises in Instructional Design.*

Edward H. Sewell, Jr. is Associate Professor of Communications Studies at Virginia Tech University. His primary research areas are visual communications, especially political cartoons, and human-computer communication.

Richard C. Stern is currently Assistant Professor of Holistics at St. Meinrad School of Theology in St. Meinrad, Indiana. He was formerly on the faculty of Northern Illinois University, the Department of Communication Studies. He has also been an Instructor in the financial service and motorcycle safety industries. His current consulting activity includes communication programs for parishes, synods, and dioceses. He has degrees from St. Olaf College, Luther Theological Seminary, and Northern Illinois University (Ed.D.).

Merton E. Thompson is Associate Professor in Education and the Director for the Center for Information Media at St. Cloud State University, Minnesota. His research areas include the design of instruction and field articulation and the design of information for microcomputers.

Forrest G. Wisely is Associate Professor of Communication at Illinois State University. He teaches training and development and visual communication courses. He received a B.A. in mathematics and philosophy and an M.S. Ed. from Southern Illinois University at Carbondale and an Ed.D. from the University of Southern California.

Andrew R. J. Yeaman consults nationally on information design and human-computer interaction and from his office in Denver, Colorado. His scholarship emphasizes critical theory and cultural anthropology. Before emigrating to the United States, he was educated at Hampton in England. Among his contemporary publications are: "Media Resources: From the Rosetta Stone to the Rolling Stones" and "An Anthropological View of Educational Communications and Technology: Beliefs and Behaviors in Research and Theory."

Author Index

A

Adams, H., 312, 314
Adler, R., 44
Allen, D., 360
Allen, R., 347
Almond, B., 375
Amabile, T., 281, 288
Amey, L. J., 12, 13, 14
Anderson, J. R., 68, 69, 72, 73, 74, 75
Anderson, L., 320
Anderson, R. C., 68
Anderson, R. H., 239, 248, 250
Anglin, G. J., 241
Aristotle, 66, 86, 115
Arnheim, R., 5, 8, 10, 14, 22, 99, 101, 102, 104, 115, 116, 253
Aronowitz, S., 313, 323, 327, 330, 375
Atkinson, F. D., 239, 248
Atkinson, P., 296, 306
Atkinson, R. C., 75
Austin, G. A., 68

B

Bach, K. T., 107
Baddely, A. D., 72
Baggett, P., 240
Baier, K., 374
Baldwin, J., 365, 366
Ball, J., 11, 108
Ball, T. M., 72
Barley, S. D., 6, 8, 10, 21, 24
Barthelme, R., 325
Barthes, R., 314, 315
Bartlett, F. C., 66
Bate, W. J., 95, 117, 131

Battig, W. F., 387
Baudrillard, J., 314
Beach, D. R., 76
Beauchamp, D. G., 195, 197
Beauchamp, G. A., 102
Becker, S. L., 102, 340
Beitchman, P., 328
Belland, J. C., 313
Belmont, J. M., 71
Belsey, C., 296, 297, 298
Benjamin, A., 314, 315, 325
Berelson, B., 86
Berger, B., 296, 300
Berger, J., 296, 298, 299, 300
Berger, P. L., 296, 299, 300, 305, 306
Berlo, D., 91, 92
Bernard, E., 127
Bernstein, B., 300
Bertoline, G. R., 199
Bilimoria, P., 373
Binkley, T., 9
Blackwood, R. E., 141
Blevins, T. H., 141
Blomberg, S., 296
Bloom, F. E., 58
Bloomer, C. M., 222
Boddy, J., 57, 58
Bordwell, D., 347
Bostdorff, D. M., 141
Boswell, S. L., 76
Bower, G. H., 73
Boyle, M. W., 214
Bradbury, R., 327
Braden, R. A., 101, 102, 103, 104, 109, 193, 195, 197, 201, 204
Brainard, H. L., 11, 14
Brannigan, C., 150
Bransford, J. D., 77, 387

Briggs, L., 239
Broadbent, D. E., 66, 71
Bronowski, J., 300
Brooks, C., 141, 143
Broudy, H. S., 11, 251
Brown, B. B., 22
Brown, R. M., 75
Bruner, J. S., 68, 100
Brunette, P., 315
Brush, L. R., 76
Brusic, S. A., 318, 319
Buber, M., 13, 22
Buckle, S., 373
Buettner, S., 9
Burgoon, J. K., 146, 148, 150,
    155, 156
Burton, T. L., 199
Busic-Snyder, C., 191
Byrnes, F. C., 11, 108

C

Calvert, S. L., 75
Campbell, D. T., 386
Canelos, J., 388
Cannizzo, S. R., 76
Carney, R. N., 241
Carpenter, C., 385, 387
Case, R., 71
Cassidy, M. F., 99
Cassirer, E., 8, 10, 136
Cezanne, P., 123, 126, 127
Chantadisai, R., 211
Cherryholmes, C. H., 297, 299,
    313, 314
Chi, M. T. H., 71, 72
Chinsky, J. M., 76
Chomsky, N., 7, 22, 99
Cixous, H., 314
Clarke, J. H., 246
Cleveland, W. S., 68
Cochran, L. M., 68, 323
Comenius, 240
Comley, N. R., 328, 330
Comstock, G., 100
Conrad, J., 131
Cooke, C., 325
Cowan, N., 70
Coward, R., 299
Cramer, P., 75
Curtiss, D. C., 99, 104, 107

D

Dale, E., 72, 86, 98, 385
Dancy, J., 374
Dash, J., 360, 361
Davis, B. J., 9
Davis, N. A., 374
Dayton, D., 211, 213, 216
Debes, J. L., 5, 6, 9, 20, 21, 24, 99, 100,
    101, 102, 103, 146, 188, 194
Deetz, S., 43
Deleuze, G., 313, 319, 328, 330
de Man, P., 313, 328
DeMelo, H., 387
Derrida, J., 311, 312, 314, 315, 316, 317,
    323, 328, 329
de Saussure, F., 314
Descartes, R., 66, 113
DeSousa, M. A., 98
Deutsch, K. W., 87, 88
DeVaney, A., 357
Dibb, M., 296
Dondis, D. A., 6, 98, 100, 101, 102, 103
Donlan, D., 214
Dornfreid, B., 143
Dos Passos, J., 127
Douglas, M., 136
Doyle, A., 71
Duchastel, P., 197, 199
Dworkin, M. S., 26
Dwyer, F. M., 72, 107, 195, 196, 215, 240,
    244, 249, 384, 386, 387, 392, 394,
    396, 397

E

Eagleton, T., 300, 306, 313
Easton, N., 360
Edmonds, R., 344
Edwards, B., 10
Egan, D. E., 77
Eimas, P. D., 71
Einstein, A., 10
Eisenstein, S., 129–130
Ekman, P., 149
Elenes, A., 357
Eliot, T. S., 117, 118, 121, 123, 130
Ellis, J., 299
Ellis, W. D., 123, 124, 125
Ellison, R., 366
Ellsworth, E., 296, 299, 303, 313

Erickson, R. P., 61
Evers, J. L., 16, 17, 24

F

Faieta, F., 39
Fales, J. F., 318, 319
Farnham-Diggory, S., 71
Fast, J., 156
Fearing, F., 13, 22
Feenberg, A., 299
Feldman, E. B., 7, 17, 21, 25
Ferris, T., 125
Fillion, B., 14
Finkle, D. L., 70, 71
Firth, R., 137
Fischer, R. A., 141
Fish, S., 300, 304
Flavell, J. H., 69, 76
Fleming, M., 37, 107, 182, 236, 249
Flory, J., 14, 20, 24
Foote, J., 187
Fork, D. J., 6, 8, 107
Foucault, M., 313, 314
Fox, C., 296
Franks, J. J., 387
Fransecky, R. B., 6, 20, 24, 102, 103, 146, 188
Freund, E., 300, 304
Fries, C. C., 6, 21, 22
Friesen, W. V., 149
Frisby, J. P., 60, 61

G

Gagné, R. M., 14, 211, 239
Gardner, H., 66, 98, 253, 317
Garrison, J. W., 320
Gates, H. L., Jr., 358, 359, 363, 364
Gazzaniga, M., 125
Geertz, C., 320
Geffen, G., 71
Gibbs, W. J., 273, 274
Gibson, J. J., 11, 12, 13, 22, 31, 33, 48, 385
Gibson, R., 211, 213, 215, 221, 312, 313
Giroux, H. A., 313, 323, 327, 330, 375
Glasgow, Z., 239
Goffman, E., 299, 302, 303, 305
Goodman, N., 251

Goodnow, J. J., 68
Gozemba, P. A., 7, 22
Grant, S., 72
Greeno, J. G., 68
Gregory, R. L., 55
Griffin, R. E., 258, 261, 266, 271, 272
Gropper, G. L., 203
Gross, L., 376
Gross, P. H., 326
Gross, T. F., 70, 71
Guattari, F., 313, 319, 328, 330
Guilford, J. P., 281, 283

H

Haber, L. R., 204
Haber, R. N., 33, 204
Hadamard, J. S., 10
Hagen, M. A., 33, 48
Hall, E. T., 146, 155
Hall, N., 98
Hall, S., 304
Hanhardt, J. G., 8
Hanna, M., 44
Hannafin, M., 215, 218, 219
Hansen, J., 114
Harpole, C. H., 8
Hartley, J., 211
Hartman, F. R., 387
Hartman, G. H., 313
Hathaway, M. D., 211
Hawkes, T., 301
Hayes, D. S., 75
Hefzallah, I. M., 289
Heim, C., 345
Heines, J., 220
Heinich, R., 103, 107, 279, 369
Hemingway, E., 119, 126, 127, 128
Herring, R. D., 103
Hewes, G., 99
Hickey, N., 377
Hightower, C., 186–187
Hill, J. E., 11
Hiscock, M., 71
Hlynka, D., 313, 320, 321, 323
Hoagland, R. C., 323
Hobson, D., 304
Hocking, F. O., 9
Hofstader, L., 58
Holbert, G., 338
Holdaway, D., 98

Hollis, R., 296
Holub, R. C., 300, 304
Hooks, B., 358
Hortin, J. A., 6, 101, 103, 104, 109
Houghton, H. A., 203
Howard, V., 317
Humphries, D., 150
Hurston, Z. N., 358, 365
Hurt, J. A., 248
Huston, A. C., 75
Hutton, D. W., 14

J

Jacklin, C. N., 77
James, H., 128
Jamison, W., 77
Jefferson, R., 360, 361
Jencks, C., 313
Johnson, B. D., 10, 19, 25, 98
Johnson, M. K., 77
Jonassen, D. H., 6, 8, 107, 203
Joyce, J., 312, 328, 329
Jung, C. G., 136

K

Kaelin, E. F., 98
Kail, R., 70
Kant, I., 115, 124, 373
Katz, J. S., 376
Kawin, B., 340
Keeney, T. J., 76
Kees, W., 9, 20, 146, 147, 149, 150, 151,
    154, 155, 156, 157, 158
Kellner, H., 296, 300
Kemp, J., 211, 213, 216, 221
Kepler, J., 113
Ketchum, A., 141
Kindem, G., 347, 349, 350
Kinsbourne, M., 71
Klahr, D., 70
Klatzky, R. L., 67, 68, 73, 74
Kline, P. J., 68
Knowlton, J. Q., 99, 195, 385
Koffka, K., 116, 117, 118, 120, 122, 127
Kohler, W., 116, 117, 118, 124
Koroscik, J. S., 251
Kosslyn, S. M., 72, 73, 75, 76
Kozma, R., 240

Kreitler, H., 251
Kreitler, S., 251
Kristeva, J., 314
Kuetemeyer, V. F., 318, 319
Kymlicka, W., 373

L

LaConte, R. T., 98, 100
Lakshmanan, R., 211
Lane, D. M., 71
Langer, S. K., 301
Larkin, J. H., 69
Lasky, S. M., 70
Laswell, H. D., 88
Lazerson, A., 58
Leathers, D. G., 147, 159
Lee, S., 360, 361, 363, 366
Lentz, R., 195, 220
Lesage, J., 338, 339, 345, 346
Levie, W. H., 37, 72, 75, 107, 182, 187,
    195, 236, 240, 244, 249
Levin, J. R., 241, 240, 242
Levi-Strauss, C., 314
Lewin, B. D., 9
Liben, L. S., 71
Lilienthal, E. T., 141
Lindsay, D. T., 71
Lindsay, P. H., 387
Linton, D., 326
Locatis, C. N., 239, 248
Lowe, A., 304
Luckman, T., 299, 300, 305, 306
Lyotard, J., 313

M

Maccoby, E. E., 77
Macintyre, A., 304
Mackey, K., 220
Magliaro, S., 68
Majors, R., 366
Malcolm X, 366
Mancini Billson, J., 366
Mandler, G., 71
Mandler, J. M., 77
Marx, M., 102, 103
Matlin, M. W., 247, 248
Matthews, R. T., 141
Mayer, R. E., 68

Mayer, R. R., 384
Mayne, J., 345
Mayta, M., 211, 213, 215, 221
McBride, S., 141, 142
McCardle, E. S., 155
McFee, J. K., 108
McGarry, E., 343
McGee, L. M., 99, 102
McGill, R., 68
McKay, N., 358, 363
McKendrick, J. E., 273, 274
McKim, R. H., 5, 10, 106, 253
Mead, G., 13, 22
Medhurst, M. J., 98
Mehrabian, A., 155
Meinig, D. W., 107
Mellini, P., 141
Merlau-Ponty, M., 114, 118
Metzler, J., 77
Meyer, P. A., 70
Miller, G. A., 66, 67, 74
Miller, J. L., 71
Miller, M., 108
Minsky, M., 319
Misanchuk, E. R., 203
Molenda, M., 103, 107, 279, 369
Monaco, J., 300, 301, 362
Moore, D. M., 320
Morlek, R., 68
Morris, C. D., 136, 385, 387
Morris, D., 146, 147, 148, 150
Morrison, G. R., 211, 220
Morrison, T., 358, 363
Morse, P. A., 70
Mosberg, L., 384
Mourant, S. J., 211
Moyers, B., 108
Muffoletto, R., 297, 298, 300, 301, 304
Mullens, S., 156
Murch, G. M., 55, 58, 60, 61
Murray, F. B., 384
Myers, P. J., 107

N

Nash, H., 9
Neely, J. H., 77
Negroponte, N. P., 320

Neisser, U., 66, 113, 114
Nelsen, R., 9
Nelson, C., 313
Nelson, D. A., 387
Nelson, T. O., 77
Neves, D. M., 68
Newell, J. M., 14
Newhall, B., 298
Newhouse, J. J., 8
Nichols, B., 296, 298, 299, 301
Nichols, R., 329, 330
Nitsch, K. E., 387
Norman, D. A., 68, 387
Norris, C., 314, 315
Nygard, K. E., 214

O

O'Dell, J. K., 211
Olson, D., 253, 254
O'Neill, O., 373
Ornstein, R., 114
Osgood, C. E., 90, 385

P

Paivio, A., 73, 74, 99, 386
Palcy, E., 360
Papadakis, A., 325
Parker, R. C., 217
Parker, R. E., 77
Parsons, M. J., 9
Patterson, M. L., 147, 156
Peck, K., 215, 218, 219
Peeck, J., 240
Pelfrey, R., 342
Penley, C., 320
Perkins, D., 253, 317
Peters, J. M. L., 101
Peterson, C. R., 71
Peterson, M. J., 71
Pettersson, R., 182, 194, 195, 201, 203
Phillips, J. L., 70
Piaget, J., 11, 14, 70, 71
Piak, H.-J., 100
Pierce, C. S., 137
Platt, J., 98, 101, 103
Poe, E. A., 123, 124, 125
Pomerantz, J. R., 73, 76

Popkewitz, T. S., 296, 298, 299, 300
Posner, M. I., 66, 72, 77
Postman, N., 24, 296, 318
Pressley, M., 74, 240
Presson, D. A., 71
Provenzo, E. F., Jr., 98
Pryluck, C., 101, 102
Pylyshyn, Z., 73
Pynchon, T., 319, 325, 328

R

Randhawa, B. S., 104, 107
Ranganathan, B., 214
Rankin, R. T., 85
Reed, D. A., 77
Reese, H. W., 76
Reilly, S., 375
Reinjing, D., 214
Reiser, B. J., 72
Renais, A., 128–129
Rich, M., 360, 363
Richgels, D. J., 99, 102
Ricoeur, P., 136
Roberts, C., 340
Rodman, G., 44
Rogers, E. M., 317
Rogers, T. W., 386
Roget, P., 340
Rohwer, W. D., Jr., 76
Romano, J., 156
Ronell, A., 317, 319
Rorty, R., 320
Rosner, S. R., 71, 75, 76
Ross, L., 126
Ross, S. D., 130
Ross, S. M., 211, 220
Roth, C., 98
Ruben, B. D., 85, 86, 147, 149, 156, 158
Rubin, E., 120
Ruby, J., 376
Ruch, F. L., 106
Ruesch, J., 9, 20, 146, 147, 149, 150, 151, 154, 155, 156, 157, 158
Russell, J. D., 103, 107, 279, 369

S

Saint Augustine, 66
Salomon, G., 98, 238

Samples, B., 107
Samuels, M., 107
Samuels, N., 107
Sapir, E., 10
Saunders, A., 187
Scholes, R., 328, 330
Schramm, W., 90, 91
Schwartz, B. J., 77
Schwoch, J., 375
Scott, J. C., 320
Searle, L., 312, 314
Seaton, J., 223
Seels, B., 101, 239
Severin, W. J., 387
Sexton, M. A., 71
Shannon, C. E., 88, 89, 317, 318
Sheingold, K., 70
Shepard, R. N., 73, 75
Shiffrin, R. M., 75
Shultz, M., 360, 361
Simon, H. A., 69
Simpson, H., 220
Sinatra, R., 188
Singer, H., 214
Singer, P., 372, 375
Singleton, J., 361, 363, 366
Slesnick, T., 220
Sless, D., 99
Smith, W., 119
Smythe, P. C., 386
Snyder, C. R. R., 77
Sollers, P., 314
Soltis, J. F., 374
Sorflaten, J., 68
Soulier, J. S., 211, 213, 214, 215, 216, 221
Soumi, K., 70
Spiro, D., 70
Stafford, K. R., 123
Stanley, J. C., 386
Stansfield, S. S., 123
Stantis, S., 143
Steel, L., 77
Stein, A. H., 76
Stein, G., 119
Steiner, G. A., 86
Stevenson, S., 43
Stocking, S. H., 326
Strike, K. A., 374
Szarkowski, J., 306

T

Taylor, I. A., 11, 13, 152, 154
Taylor, M., 141
Theall, D. F., 9
Theodorson, A. G., 86
Theodorson, S. A., 86
Therborn, G., 297, 298
Thomas, H., 77
Thompson, K., 347
Thomson, D. M., 387
Thomson, N., 72
Torrance, E. P., 281, 284, 285, 286, 288
Townsend, R., 360, 363, 364
Treichler, P. A., 320
Tuchman, G., 326
Tufte, E. R., 203, 222
Tulving, E., 387
Tuman, M. C., 98
Turbayne, C. M., 5, 6, 14, 15, 16, 17, 18, 19, 20, 24
Turkle, S., 326
Twain, M., 365
Tzara, T., 328

U

Ulmer, G., 312, 313, 315, 320, 328, 330

V

Van Gundy, A. B., 288
Vasquez, J., 361
Vernon, M. D., 12
von Ehrenfels, C., 123
von Hornbostel, E., 123

W

Wadley, N., 123, 127
Wager, W. W., 211, 239
Wakefield, B., 41
Walker, A. D., 102, 103, 358
Waller, R., 199

Wallschlaeger, C., 191
Watkins, B. A., 75
Wead, G., 340
Weaver, W., 88, 89, 317, 318
Weedon, C., 296, 299, 301, 304
Weinstein, C. E., 384
Welsandt, R. F., 70
Welsh, G. S., 284
Wendt, P. R., 6
Wertheimer, M., 116, 123, 125
West, C., 357, 358
Whatley, M. H., 296, 299, 303, 313
Whitaker, C., 357
White, E., 72
White, M. A., 238, 375
White, R., 135
Whyte, L., 9
Wileman, R. E., 103, 104, 108, 109, 137, 195, 197, 198, 200, 201, 203
Wiley, S. E., 199
Williams, C. W., 5, 6, 24, 101, 102
Willis, P., 304
Willows, D. M., 203
Wills, D., 315
Wilson, G., 44
Wilson, J., 370
Winn, W., 37, 75
Winner, E., 244, 247
Wise, L. L., 77
Wolfgang, A., 146
Wollen, P., 301, 362
Woods, D., 251
Wright, J. C., 75
Wright, R., 365, 366

Y

Yeaman, A. R. J., 320, 321, 323
Younghouse, P., 68

Z

Zeichner, K., 355
Zettl, H., 184
Zimbardo, P. G., 106

Subject Index

A

Action codes, 345

Action language, 146–156

  See also Nonverbal language

  conventional signals, 148

  cues in, 147–156

  cues provided by use of space, 155–156

  determining existence of groups, 151–155

  gestures as, 149–151

  in groups, 151–155

  personal appearance as, 148–149

  physical attributes providing cues, 149

  reflexive actions, 147–148

  roles of sender and observer in, 151

  supplementing verbal language, 147

Aesthetic literacy, need for, 98

Aesthetics

  See also Perceptual aesthetics

  defined, 114, 115

  implying judgment, 115

African-American film makers, using stereotypic images, 359

African-American Hollywood films of the 1990's, 359–362

  See also Film

  adolescent problems delineated in, 360

  black English used in, 365–366

  charges of sexism against, 360, 365

  codes of realism used in, 362–363

  finding credible black characters for classroom use in, 362

  humor used in, 364–365

  images for classroom use from, 360–361

  opposition as a theme or incident in, 363–364

  reasons for using in classroom, 366–367

  role of black male depicted in, 366–367

  showing African-American lives, 360, 361

  showing problems of adolescent males, 366

African-American literature

  finding clues to non stereotypic images in, 363–365

  opposition as a theme in, 363–364

  reasons for using in classroom, 366–367

African-American narrative, and textual analysis, 358–359

Analog communication, 33–34

Analytic graphics, 270–271

Analytic seeing, 253

Animation of computer images, 216

Appearance, providing nonverbal cues, 148–149

Aqueous humor, 55

Arbitrary symbols, 136–137. *See also* Symbols

Art

  composition judged by simplicity, regularity, and symmetry, 118

  contributing to concept of visual literacy, 8–11, 22

  creative and critical interpretation of, 253–254

  defined by Aristotle, 115

  dense meaning structures of, 251

  description and analysis of form in, 252–253

Art *(continued)*
    extracting symbolic connotations from,
        253–254
    importance of, in schools, 9, 11
    judged by simplicity, regularity, and
        symmetry, 118
    multileveledness of, 251
    one-point perspective in looking at,
        299
    and perceptual aesthetics, 126–128
    reading, 250–254
    theories useful to visual literacy
        theory, 8–10
Artist, catalytic role of, 117
Attention role of visuals, 197
Attitudes
    affected by culture, 42
    derived from beliefs and values, 43
Audio-verbal language, 195
Audio-visual language, 195
Auditory nerve, 56, 58
Auditory perception, 4
    See also Hearing; Perception
    as stimulus-response process, 60
Auditory stimulation, 61
    threefold process of, 62
Auditory strategies, development of, 71

B

Balance
    in design of visuals, 174–175
    formal and informal, 175
Bar graphs, 263
Beliefs
    affected by culture, 42
    defined, 43
Black americans. *See under*
    African-American
Black english, 365–366. *See also under*
    African-American
Body language. *See* Action language
Brain
    basic anatomy of visual and auditory
        centers in, 58–59
    receiving most information from the
        eyes, 114
    role in vision, 114
Brain stem, 58
Business visuals, 258–274
    See also Visuals

computer generated business
    graphics, 270–273
document visuals, 261
electronic visuals, 260
flip charts, 260
graphs, 261, 263–266. *See also* Graphs
importance of, 258–260
inadequate training in creating,
    273–274
increasing use of, 258
learning to use, 273–274
linking visuals, 267, 270
maps, 266
overhead transparencies, 258, 260
purpose of, 267, 270
supporting visuals, 267, 270
2 x 2 slides, 260
types of, 260–266

C

Capital letters, harder to read, 178
Categorical imperative, 373
Cerebral cortex, 58
Children
    capacity to recognize objects, 247
    cognitive development in, 70
    development of mental imagery in, 12
    development of selective auditory
        attention in, 71
    immorality of most television
        programming for, 377–378
    lacking scanning strategies, 247
    learning to read pictures, 247
    maintenance rehearsal by, 76
    mediational deficiency in, 76
    preferences for visuals, 248–249
    not processing information as quickly
        as adults, 70–71
    production deficiency in, 76
    readiness for visual literacy training,
        14–15
    sex stereotyping by, 76–77
    teaching to read pictures, 248
    and television violence, 377–378
    visual environment of, 236–238
    visual learning preceding verbal
        learning, 9–10
    visual literacy allied with middle stage
        of development, 12
Chunking, 76

Clarity, in design of visuals, 174
Closure and good form, used to
     organize stimuli, 40–41
Cochlea, 56, 57, 58
Coding
  action codes, 345
  creating context for signs, 302
  cultural coding levels in mass media,
     345–346
  enigmatic codes, 345
  historical reference codes, 346
  positioning reader in relation to text,
     345
  of reality, 343
  semic and symbolic codes, 346
  socially produced codes, 303
  structural coding, 346–348
  technical coding, 348–350
Cognition. *See* Human cognition
Cognitive development, 69–72
Color
  cautions for use of, 215–216
  emotional appeal of, 284–285
  for graphic images, 215–216
  interaction between age and color
     preference, 248
  and student preferences for visuals,
     248
  in visuals, 171–172
Column graphs, 263
Communication
  See also Human communication;
     Language; Nonverbal
     communication
  as a circular process, 90–91
  analog and digital, 33–34
  analogic nature of human
     communication, 34
  areas of research in, 88
  basic to learning, 36–37
  controlling factors important in, 91–92
  deconstructing, 317–320
  defined, 85–86
  definition criticized, 318–319
  elements of, 92
  factors making definition difficult, 86
  graphics as tools for, 186
  inanimate objects not capable of, 319
  learning process as, 108
  media communication model, 338–339
  models of, 88–92

  noise in, 89
  nonverbal actions used in, 147
  as one-way process, 89
  presented as a telephone
     conversation, 317
  process of, 88
  role of self-concept in, 45, 50
  semiotics as a model for
     understanding, 301–303
  successful only when experience of
     sender and receiver overlap, 90
  symbols as, 137–138
  visual. *See* Visual communication
Communication models
  Berlo's model, 91–92
  heuristic function of, 88
  Laswell's model, 88, 89
  media communication model, 338–339
  mensurative function of, 88
  organizing function of, 87
  predictive function of, 88
  Schramm's models, 89, 90–91
  Shannon and Weaver's model, 88–89
Communication studies, development
     of, 86–87
Communicative function of language, 18
Composite graphics, 186
Composition, for filming, 348–349
Computer-controlled multimedia
     presentations, 210
Computer-displayed images, 210
Computer generated business graphics,
     270–273
  analytic graphics, 270–271
  forms of output for, 272–273
  not all suitable for presentations, 270
  presentation visuals, 271–272
  software packages, 272–273
Computer-generated displays, 222–227
Computer-generated virtual
     environments, 228–229
Computer graphs
  correct information essential in,
     223–224, 227
  guidelines for design of, 222–227
  using appropriate displays, 224–227
Computer images
  See also Images
  animation in, 216
  cautions for use of color, 215–216
  clarity important to, 214

Computer images *(continued)*
    computer creation of data displays,
        222–227
    design aiding discovery of meaning,
        222
    graphics in, 213–215
    graphics in, guidelines for using,
        214–215
    graphs in, 213–214
    learning from, 222
    meaning of the image, 222–227
    in multimedia presentations, 216
    power of the image, 228–229
    principles for layout of, 222
    realistic data display, 228
    screen design considerations, 216–221
    structure of the image, 211–221
    text considerations for, 211–213
    virtual reality, 228–229
Computers, providing visual
        communication, 210
Cone of Experience theory, 72
Cones, 55–56
Consequential theories, 374–375
Constructed self, 296
    and ideology, 299
Constructivism, historical concept of, 66
Continuity, learning, 348
Continuity of space, 347
Contrast, affecting legibility, 177
Control, symbols as, 137, 140–141
Conventional signals, as nonverbal cues,
        148
Conventional symbols, 136–137. *See also*
        Symbols
Cooperative learning, 245
Creative process, linked with perceptual
        process, 126–127
Creative thinking
    connection with visual literacy,
        280–281
    defined in relationship to visual
        learning, 287
    enhancing, 288–289
    factors suppressing, 288
    inhibited by overemphasis on verbal
        language, 10–11
    integrating into daily life as a goal, 290
    intrinsic motivation needed for, 288
    models of, 281–287
    need for, 289–290

    possibility of teaching, 287–288
    recognizing need for, 288–289
    restricted choices diminishing, 288
    visual thinking essential to, 99
Creative thinking skills, 284–286
    in interpretation of visuals, 280–281
Creativity
    associated with alternative visual
        perspectives, 285
    characteristics associated with, 281
    continuum of, 281
    defined as proficiency in fluency,
        flexibility, originality, and
        elaboration, 281–284
    developing, 281
    domain specific nature of, 281
    rich, colorful imagery associated with,
        284–285
    visual literacy essential to, 99
Critical sense, applied to moral uses of
        visuals, 376–377
Critical theory, and deconstruction,
        312–313
Critical thinking, 313
Cultural bias
    design elements affected by, 191
    in mass media, 344
Cultural coding levels in mass media
    action codes, 345
    enigmatic codes, 345
    historical reference codes, 346
    semic and symbolic codes, 346
Cultural conditioning
    affecting perception, 341–343
    cultural pre-existence, 343
    Western way of seeing the world, 342
Cultural conventions
    rules for creators and audiences
        based in, 350
    symbols deriving meaning from, 42
Cultural stereotypes
    See also Stereotyping
    in the classroom, 357
    creating, 357
    learning to reject, 357–358
    and new racism, 357
    perpetuating, 357
Culture
    affecting beliefs, values, and attitudes,
        42
    popular culture, 356–357, 359

D

Data displays
  computer graphs, 222–227
  data visualization, 227
  design guidelines for computer
    creation of, 222–227
  realistic, 228
Data graphs, compared with data
    visualization, 227
Data visualization, compared with data
    graphs, 227
Decoding, differentiation critical
    component of, 279
Deconstruction
  as a mode of experiencing ideas, 316
  applied to communication, 317–320
  applied to visuals, 316
  creation of a deconstructive visual
    document, 320–323
  and critical theory, 312–313
  deconstructing the dominant
    narrative, 327–328
  literary interpretation and analytic
    philosophy affected by, 314
  in perspective, 312
  Post Post News illustrating, 323–327
  resistance as an activity of, 320, 330
  theory of, 314–316
Decoration, as a function of visuals, 241
Deontology, 374
Design elements
  affected by cultural bias and semiotics,
    191
  color as, 171–172
  form as, 169
  in graphics, 191
  light as, 170–171
  line as, 167–168
  motion as, 172
  point as, 166
  shape as, 168
  space as, 169
  texture as, 170
Design principles, 173–181
  balance, 174–175
  clarity, 174
  emphasis, 177
  framing, 181
  harmony, 176
  legibility, 177–179

  organization, 176
  perspective, 179–180
  point of view, 180–181
  simplicity, 173
  unity, 179
Diagrams
  in business, 261
  defined, 185
  representing and identifying parts of a
    whole, 185
  training in use needed, 69
Differentiation, as analytical component
    of decoding, 279
Digital communication, 33–34
Discourse
  controlling, 298–299
  relationship with ideology, 297
Distal stimuli, 62
Document visuals, 261. *See also* Visuals
Dual coding model, 73–75
Dynamic verbal elements, 195
Dynamic visuals, 195. *See also* Visuals

E

Ear
  See also Hearing
  basic anatomy of, 56–58
Eardrum, 56, 57
Effective stimuli, 60, 62
Egoism, 372–373
Elaboration
  as an aspect of creativity, 283
  use of, 284
Electronic visuals, 260
Emphasis in design of visuals, 177
Enigmatic codes, 345
Ethical considerations, educators'
    responsibilities, 355–356, 369–370
Ethical traditions
  categorical imperative, 373
  consequential theories, 374–375
  deontology, 374
  egoism, 372–373
  Formula of the End in Itself, 373
  to help determine morality, 372–375
  Kant's ethics, 373
  natural law, 373
  non-Western, 375
  postmoderist approach to, 375–376
  prima facie duty, 374

Ethical traditions *(continued)*
   social contract theory, 373
   theories of rights, 375
   utilitarianism, 274
   virtue theory, 374–375
   Western normative theories guiding
     conduct, 372–375
Ethics
   distinguished from morals, 370–371
Eustachian tube, 56, 57
Expectations, affecting interpretation of
     stimuli, 44
Experience
   affecting beliefs, values and attitudes,
     43
   affecting perception, 38–39
   and recency/primacy effect, 43
Explicative role of visuals, 197
Expression, symbols as, 137, 139–140
External auditory meatus, 56, 57
Eyes
   See also Vision
   basic anatomy of, 55–56

F

Feelings
   affecting interpretation of stimuli, 43–44
   affecting perception, 39
Figure and background, used to
     organize stimuli, 40
Film
   See also African-American Hollywood
     films of the 1990's; Mass media
   codes of realism used in, 362–363
   omission used in, 128–129
   and perceptual aesthetics, 128–130
   persistence of vision and phi factor
     allowing perception of motion,
     340–341
   principle of perceptual closure
     used in, 129
   seeing motion in, 340–341
   training students to read, 362
Flexibility
   as an aspect of creativity, 283
   use of, 284
Flip charts, 260
Fluency
   as an aspect of creativity, 282
   use of, 284

Forebrain, 58
Form
   in graphics, 191
   in visuals, 169
Formula of the End in Itself, 373
Fovea, 55, 56
Frames of reference
   affecting selection, organization, and
     interpretation of stimuli, 36
   assessing, 36–37
   factors affecting, 35
   importance in visual learning, 36
Framing, in design of visuals, 181
Functional symbols, 137. *See also*
     Symbols

G

Gestalt
   as basis for literary aesthetic, 125
   compared with a sum, 117–118
Gestalt isomorphism, 117–118
Gestalt principles
   perceptual regularity, 120–122
   perceptual simplicity, 118–120
   perceptual symmetry, 122–123
Gestalt psychology, perceptual
     aesthetics based on, 116
Gestures
   context important for, 150–151
   culturally specific, 150
   defined, 149
   practice needed in reading, 150–151
   providing nonverbal cues, 149–151
   uses of, 149–150
Graphic devices, 186
Graphics
   See also Pictures; Visuals
   as a form of visual communication,
     184, 186–188
   as a language, 187–188
   attributes of, 191
   communicating, 187
   communication process illustrated,
     190
   composite, 186
   in computer images, 213–215
   defined, 184
   design elements in, 191
   diagrams, 69, 185, 261
   easy delivery of, 186–187

Graphics *(continued)*
  elements, forms, and attributes
    necessary for creation of, 189, 191
  emotional and intellectual appeal of,
    187
  form in, 191
  forms of, 184–186
  functioning as communication tools,
    186
  graphic devices, 186
  graphs. *See* Graphs
  guidelines for computerized graphics,
    214–215
  icon-digital continuum of, 200, 201
  illustrations, 185
  important in mass-communications,
    184
  knowledge and components needed
    to develop, 188–189
  maps, 185, 266
  as one way communication, 183–184,
    188
  outline graphics, 205
  perceptual and organizational
    principles and techniques for
    creating, 191
  pervasiveness of, 186–187
  political use of, 187
  presented through mass media, 188
  process of communication through,
    188–191
  symbols. *See* Symbols
  3-D models, 185–186
  training needed to derive information
    from, 187–188
  verbally dominated, 201–202
  visual literacy essential to allow parity
    in response, 188
  visually dominated, 200
  as visual metaphors, 213
Graphic symbols, 137. *See also* Symbols
Graphs
  bar graphs, 263
  in business, 261, 263–266
  column graphs, 263
  compared with data visualization,
    227
  computer-generated, 222–227
  in computer images, 213–214
  defined, 185
  line graphs, 263

pie graphs, 263, 266
presenting changes in things, 185
representing relationships, 185
Groups
  common movement suggesting
    membership, 154–155
  identifying members of, 151–154
  losing identity in, 152
  nonverbal cues in, 151–155
  proximity indicating membership,
    152, 154
  similarity indicating membership,
    153–154
  ways of grouping, 153–155

H

Halo effect, 42
  affecting interpretation of stimuli,
    42, 44
Harmony, in design of visuals, 176
Hearing
  auditory stimulation, 61
  basic anatomy of the ear, 56–58
  development of selective auditory
    strategies, 71
  intricacy and sensitivity of, 56
  neurophysiological factors, 54–55
  perception of auditory space, 61
  primary auditory area in the brain,
    58–59
  sound localization important to, 61
  temporal lobe in the brain, 58
  time frequency and temporal order of
    stimuli, 61
Hindbrain, 58
Historical reference codes, 346
Human cognition
  complexity of, 69–70
  defined, 53, 69
  development of, 69–72
  development of, explained, 70
  graphic representation more effective
    than text representation, 69
  information processing approach to,
    66–69
  models of, compared, 70
  overview, 66–69
  traditional and contemporary views
    compared, 69
  visual cognition, 72–75

Human communication
  See also Communication
  analogic nature of, 34
  causes of misunderstanding in, 34
  requiring interpretation, 34
Human information processing
  attention crucial to, 68
  criteria for models, 68
Human information system
  anatomy of, 54–60
  basic anatomy of the brain's visual
    and auditory centers, 58–59
  basic anatomy of the ears, 56–58
  basic anatomy of the eyes, 55–56
  importance of duplication,
    polarization, and interconnection of
    eyes, ears, and brain, 54–55
  reception/cognition model of process,
    62–63
  stimuli and the perceptual process,
    59–60
  threefold process of stimulation in, 62

I

Iconic signs, 137, 301
  compared with indexual signs and
    symbols, 137
Ideology
  and constructed self, 299
  forming relationships to
    representations, 299
  relationships with variety of texts, 303
  relationship with discourse, 297
  resisting by offering other
    interpretations, 303
  role of images in maintaining,
    299–300
Illustrations, defined, 185. *See also*
    Images; Photographs; Pictures;
    Representations; Visuals
Image makers, common moral
    imperatives for, 376–377
Imagery, 4
  aiding memory, 76
  historical concept of, 66
  sources of, 107
Imagery theory
  controversy over imaginal storage,
    72–73
  dual coding model, 73–75

Images
  See also Computer images;
    Photographs; Pictures;
    Representations; Visuals
  to aid learning and recall, 65–66
  assumptions of pro-image storage
    theory, 73
  captured by photographs, 185
  computer-displayed, 210
  controversy over storage of, 72–73
  cultural stereotypes in, 357
  effectiveness of, in learning, 78
  found images, 246–247
  importance of, 5
  moral imperatives for viewers of,
    376–377
  perceived differently by different
    viewers, 77–78
  realist, 297–298
  relationship to, and meaning of,
    298–299
  remembered better than words, 75
  role in maintaining ideologies, 299–300
  structure, meaning, and power of,
    209–210
  as teachers, 356–357
  understanding the constructed nature
    of, 358
Indexual signs, 137, 301
  compared with iconic signs and
    symbols, 137
Ineffective stimuli, 60
Infography, 201
Information. *See* Visual information
Information processing model of human
    cognition, 66–69
Inner ear, 56, 58
Instructional consistency/congruency
    paradigm, 388–391
Interpretation
  as a function of visuals, 241, 242
  involving creative thinking skills, 280
  of visual messages, 279–281
Intertextuality, 303
Invisibility, 347
Iris, 55

J

Jargon, reflecting specialized perception,
    39

K

Knowledge, symbols as, 137, 138–139

L

Language
  See also Action language
    (body language); Object language;
    Verbal language; Visual language
  as a closed system, 297
  as a coded system, 339–340
  communicative function of, 18
  defined, 146
  functions of, 18
  graphics as, 187–188
  ideological basis of, 297
  jargon, 39
  nonverbal codes as, 147
  nonverbal language, 9–10, 146–147
  pragmatic function of, 18
  setting meaning for signs, 301
  shaping visual perception, 38–39
  symbolic basis of, 339–340
  verbal/visual language analogy, 19–21
  visible language, 203–205
Law of good continuation, 123
Learning
  See also Visual learning
  accurate perceptions required for,
    36–37
  affected by self-concept filters, 47–48
  communication basic to, 36–37, 108
  making a conscious activity, 37
  perception critical to, 31–32
  and principles of perception, 37
  from print and images, 238
  and self-concept, 45
Legibility
  capital letters harder to read, 178
  on computer screens, 211, 213
  contrast affecting, 177
  in design of visuals, 177–179
  guidelines for, in projected images,
    250
  letter style affecting, 177–178
  limited number of words important
    for television, 179
Lens, 55
Letter size, affecting legibility, 177
Letter styles, affecting legibility, 177–178

Lexi-visual language, 195
Light, in visuals, 170–171
Line graphs, 263
Lines, in visuals, 167–168
Linguistics
  approach used in study of visual
    language, 6–8
  contribution to visual literacy, 21–22
  impact on other fields, 8
  relationship to visual literacy, 6–8
Literacy
  See also Visual literacy
  changing meanings of, 98
  encompassing verbal and visual
    literacy, 98
  evolution of concept, 98
  evolution of term, 24–26
Long-term memory, 66, 67, 68–69
  activating knowledge from, 68
  encoding in, 68
  information restructured in, 68
  method of presentation determining
    storage and retrieval, 68–69
  as permanent storehouse, 67

M

Maintenance rehearsal. *See* Rehearsal
Maps
  in business, 266
  defined, 185
  showing relative position and size of
    places, 185
Mass communications, graphics
    important in, 184
Mass media
  See also Communication
  action codes in, 345
  affecting experience of events, 344
  choosing elements on which to focus,
    344
  classroom critiques of, 357–358
  consistency in, 345
  cultural bias in emphasis and
    exclusion, 344
  cultural coding levels in, 345–346
  and cultural conditioning, 341–343
  encoding and decoding, 339–340
  enigmatic codes in, 345
  historical reference codes for, 346
  iconic properties of, 340

Mass media *(continued)*
  illusions of reality hiding construction,
    339
  images not really existing, 340
  impact of, 357
  investigating non-stereotypic images
    needed, 358
  media as metaphor, 16–17
  media communication model, 338–339
  moral implications of, 375–376
  need for critical media curriculum,
    357–358
  perceptions, of affected by cultural
    and technological structures, 338–339
  pervasiveness of, 337–338
  presenting illusion of reality, 338
  production/distribution/consu mption
    system, 338–339
  rules for creators and audiences based
    in cultural conventions, 350
  selection of images by, 338
  selectivity of, 344–345
  semic codes for, 346
  social context for, 344–345
  structural coding for, 346–348
  symbolic codes for, 346
  technical coding for, 348–350
Meaning
  combining, to form message, 302
  context affecting, 301
  in poststructuralism, 304–306
  reader experience affecting, 306
  social and power relationships
    affecting, 300
Media
  See also Mass media
  making students critical readers of,
    357–358
  as metaphor, 16–17
Media communication model, 338–339
Mediational deficiency, 76
Memory. *See* Long-term memory;
    Short-term memory
Memory use, improving with age, 70
Mental imagery, in development of
    children, 12
Mental representations, 74–75
Menus, on computer screens, 220
Metaphor
  distinguishing from reality, 15–16
  media as, 16–17

as myths, 15–18
  nonverbal, 16
  uses of, 15
Midbrain, 58
Middle ear, 56, 57
Mind
  as a gestalt, 125
  importance in perception, 13–14, 22
  as seeing organ, 66
Mind research, 22
Moral imperatives, for makers and
    viewers of images, 376–377
Morality
  common moral imperatives for image
    makers, 376–377
  critical sense suggesting principles for,
    376–377
  ethical traditions to help determine,
    372–375
  moral implications of mass media,
    375–376
Morally controversial visuals, 371–372
Morals
  applied to content and purposes of
    visuals, 371–372
  distinguished from ethics, 370–371
Motion, in visuals, 172
Multimedia presentations
  computer-controlled, 210
  using computer images, 216

N

Natural law, 373
Natural symbols, 136. *See also* Symbols
Non-stereotypic images, 356
  finding, in African-American films, 363
  finding, in African-American
    literature, 363–365
Nonverbal communication, and
    self-concept, 49–50
Nonverbal language
  See also Action language (body
    language); Language;
    Communication; Object language
  ambiguity a problem with, 146
  functions of, 147
  importance of, 146
  type of information conveyed by, 146
  and visual growth of children, 9–10
  and visual literacy, 9

O

Object language, 146, 156–159
  and concept of utility, 157
  defined, 156
  information provided by, 156–158
  objects as symbols, 158–159
  setting tone for activities, 157–158
  used by archaeologists, 156–157
  used to command, 157–158
Occipital lobe, 58
Optic chiasm, 56
Optic nerve, 55, 56
Oral-visual language, 195
Oral window, 56, 57
Organization
  as a function of visuals, 241
  in design of visuals, 176
Organs of Corti, 56, 58
Originality
  as an aspect of creativity, 283
  use of, 284
Ossicles, 56, 57
Outline graphics, 205
Overhead transparencies, 258, 260
Overscan and underscan, 221

P

Past experience. See Experience
Pattern recognition
  importance in human information
    processing, 68
  integrating information, 68
  by sensory registers, 66–67
People of color. See under
  African-American
Perceived stimuli, 62
Perception
  adding missing information, 118–120
  as an analogic process, 33–34
  auditory perception, 4, 60
  closure, good continuation, and unity
    in, 122–123
  cohesion, segregation, and figure and
    ground in, 120–122
  as a component of visual literacy, 3, 22
  critical to learning, 31–32
  cultural conditioning affecting,
    341–343
  defined, 32–33, 114

differences in, 33–35
as a dynamic process, 3–4
experience needed to develop skills,
  12
frames of reference for, 35–37
gestalt approach to, 116
importance of mind in, 13–14, 22
individual differences affecting, 35
interaction of stages, 44, 45
jargon reflecting specialized
  perception, 39
limited by experiences, 34
of motion, 340–341
past experience affecting, 38–39
and perceptual constancy, 42–42
perceptual regularity, 120–122
perceptual simplicity, 118–120
perceptual symmetry, 122–123
personal and contextual nature of, 48
physiological factors affecting, 38
present feelings affecting, 39
principles of, and learning, 37
process of, 59–60, 126–127
psychological factors affecting, 38
and recency/primacy effect, 43
role of perceiver, 33
selection, organization, and
  interpretation of stimuli, 36
selection process in, 37–39
self-concept influencing, 3, 44–45, 46
and sensation, 32–33
shape, omission, and closure in, 118–120
stages of, 35–44
as a system of organization, 340
training improving, 38
as transaction, 13
visual perception, 4, 38–39, 60
Perceptions, defined, 53
Perceptual aesthetics, 115–117
  and analysis, 123–126
  as an approach to art, 115–116
  based on Gestalt psychology, 116
  and film, 128–130
  and visual art, 126–128
Perceptual constancy, used to organize
  stimuli, 41–42
Perceptual process
  law of causality applied to, 60
  linked with creative process, 126–127
  role of stimuli in, 59–60
  as stimulus-response process, 60

Perceptual regularity, 120–122
Perceptual simplicity, 118–120
Perceptual symmetry, 122–123
Persistence of vision, 340–341
Personal appearance
  power dressing, 148
  providing nonverbal cues, 148–149
Personal space
  coping with crowding, 156
  cultural differences in need for, 155
  destroyed by crowding, 156
  distancing zones indicating familiarity,
    155–156
Personal visuals, 195. *See also* Visuals
Perspective
  in design of visuals, 179–180
  learning to perceive, 342
Phi factor, 340–341
Philosophy, contributing to visual
    literacy theory, 15–21, 24
Photographs
  See also Pictures
  allowing society to record itself, 299
  as ideological representations, 297–300
  locating time and capturing image,
    185
  offering realism, 297–298
  one-point perspective in looking at,
    299
  providing social message, 298
  way to look at derived from other
    forms of representations, 299
  working on a technical-pictorial level,
    297–298
Physical attributes, providing nonverbal
    cues, 149
Physiological factors affecting
    perception, 38
Pictorial superiority effect, 75
Pictorial symbols, 137. *See also* Symbols
Pictures
  See also Images; Photographs; Visuals
  as a collections of signs, 302–303
  as constructed "texts," 296
  creative and critical interpretation
    levels of reading, 253–254
  description and analysis of form levels
    of reading, 252–253
  developing skill of analytic seeing, 253
  elaborating on text, 185
  explaining text, 185

levels of information to be addressed
    in reading, 252
  levels of learning to read, 252–254
  meaning of, 298
  representing objects accurately, 185
  systematic approach to reading,
    250–254
Pie graphs, 263, 266
Point of view, in design of visuals,
    180–181
Points, in construction of visuals, 166
Political campaigns, use of visuals in,
    187, 372
Political cartoons, symbols in, 141–143
Popular culture
  generating stereotypic images, 359
  television as transmitter of, 356–357
Postmodernism, distinguished from
    poststructuralism, 313
Postpedagogy, 328–329
Postsemiotics, 303–304
Poststructuralism,
  distinguished from postmodernism,
    313–314
  meaning not fixed in, 304–305
  placing image in a changing and
    conflicting world, 305–306
  seeing reader as partner in creation of
    meaning, 304
Potential stimuli, 60, 62
Pragmatic function of language, 18
Presentation visuals, 271–272
Present feelings
  affecting interpretation of stimuli,
    43–44
  affecting perception, 39
Prima facie duty, 374
Primary auditory area, 58–59
Primary visual area, 58
Printed words, 203–204
Printing conventions, 203–204
Production deficiency, 76
Program of Systematic Evaluation (PSE)
  development of conceptual rationale
    for, 394–396
  findings, 398–399
  generalizations derived from,
    396–397
  to identify effective types of visual
    materials, 391–399
  pilot testing, 392

PSE *(continued)*
 questions for orientation guide,
  392–393
 recommendations for further research,
  399
 reliability coefficients for criterion
  tests, 391–392
 variables used, 397–398
Proximal stimuli, 62
Proximity
 used to organize stimuli, 40
PSE. *See* Program of Systematic
 Evaluation
Psychological factors affecting
 perception, 38
Psychology, contribution to visual
 literacy, 11–15, 22
Pupil, 55

R

Racism, 357. *See also* Cultural
 stereotypes; Stereotyping
Reading
 art, 250–254
 film, 362
 gestures, 150–151
 media, 357–358
 visuals, 247, 248, 250–254, 317
Realism theories, 385
Realistic data display, 228
Realist images, 297–298
 power of, 298
Reality
 coding of, 343
 critical theorist approach to, 312–313
 humanistic explanation proposed, 18
 mass media presenting illusion of, 338
 mechanistic explanation of criticized,
  17–18
 representations of, as metaphor,
  16–17
 thinking about, 297
Recency/primacy effect, affecting
 perception, 43
Reception/cognition model, 62–63
Reflexive actions, as nonverbal cues,
 147–148
Rehearsal
 importance in storage in short-term
  memory, 67, 76, 384

strategies affecting learner
  involvement, 384
 visualization as a strategy for, 384
Representation, as a function of visuals,
 241
Representations
 See also Images; Pictures; Visuals
 codes and meanings in, 300
 context affecting meaning, 301
 as metaphors, 16
 moral imperatives for makers and
  viewers of, 376–377
 not neutral objects, 300
 placing in a social landscape, 295
 producer, text, and reader
  relationships, 300
 producers of, exerting control, 303
 realistic, 297–298
 referring to something other than
  themselves, 300–301
 relationships to, formed by ideology,
  299
 relationships with, 296
 reproducing dominant ideologies, 299
 as socially constructed objects, 296
Resistance, as an activity of
 deconstruction, 320, 330
Retention role of visuals, 197
Retina, 55
Rights
 relation to morality, 375
 theories of, 375
Rods, 55
Roles
 providing nonverbal cues, 151
 and self-concept, 46–47

S

Schools
 See also Visuals in schools
 visual environment of, 236–238
Screen design, 216–221
 characteristics of good screen design,
  220–221
 for copy frames, 219
 elements of good design, 220–221
 empty spaces important in, 217
 grouping information, 220
 improving text display, 220–221
 information flow, 217

Screen design *(continued)*
    for instructional frames, 218–219
    for interlaced frames, 219
    keeping menu screens clear, 220
    menus, 220
    not like printed page layout, 217
    overscan and underscan
      considerations, 221
    partitions and borders, 217
    for prompt frames, 219
    for question frames, 219
    screen layout, 216–220
    tips from video production, 221
    for transitional frames, 218
    use of status lines, 220
Seeing
    See also Vision
    as a complex process, 20
Selection of stimuli, 36, 37–39
    past experience affecting, 38–39
    physiological factors, 38
    present feelings affecting, 39
    psychological factors, 38
Self, constructed, 296, 299
Self-appraisal, 45–46
Self-concept
    and communication, 50
    as filter of perceptions, 47–48
    formation of, 45–47
    functions of, 47–50
    as influence on style, 49–50
    influencing perceptions, 3, 44–45, 46
    in interaction with others, 46–50
    and learning, 45
    and nonverbal communication, 49–50
    overcoming effect of filters, 48
    as predictor of behavior, 48–49
    reactions and responses of others in
      formation of, 46
    role of, in communication, 45
    roles as a function of, 46–47
    self-appraisal in formation of, 45–46
    as self-fulfilling prophecy, 49
    terms used to define self, 45–46
Self-concept filters, 47–48
Self-fulfilling prophecy, 49
Semic codes, 346
Semicircular canals, 56, 57
Semiotics
    See also Signs
    as model for understanding
      communication, 301–303

Sensation, and perception, 32–33
Sensory registers, 66, 67, 68
    holding information only briefly, 66
    pattern recognition by, 66–67
Sex stereotyping, by children, 76–77
Shape, in visuals, 168
Short-term memory, 66, 67, 68
    chunking maximizing capacity of, 76
    difference between children and
      adults, 71
    explanations for differences with age,
      75
    information presented in variety of
      modalities, 75
    information rehearsed in, 67, 76
    limited capacity of, 67
    processing limitation for visuals, 75
    receiving information from long-term
      memory, 68
Signs
    codes for, 302
    collections of, forming pictures,
      302–303
    context determining meaning, 302–303
    iconic, 301
    indexual, iconic, and symbols, 137
    language setting meaning for, 301
    meaningfulness essential to, 301
    symbols functioning as, 137
Similarity, used to organize stimuli, 40
Simplicity, in design of visuals, 173
Simplicity and pattern, to organize
    stimuli, 39–40
Social context, for mass media, 344–345
Social contract theory, 373
Social institutions, functions of, 296
Sound localization, 61
Space
    See also Personal space
    in visuals, 169
Spoken verbal elements, 195
Stages of perception, 35–44
    data organization, 39–42
    frames of reference for, 35–37
    interacting, 44, 45
    interpreting information, 42–44
    selection factors, 37–39
Static verbal elements, 195
Static visuals, 195. *See also* Visuals
Stereotypes. *See* Cultural stereotypes
Stereotyping
    affecting interpretation of stimuli, 44

Stereotyping *(continued)*
  of people of color, 358
  sex stereotyping by children, 76–77
  unconscious, 357
Stimuli
  See also Perception
  distal, 62
  effective, 60, 62
  factors affecting interpretation of, 42–44
  figure and background used to
    organize, 40
  ineffective, 60
  interpreting, 36, 42–44
  perceived, 62
  potential, 60, 62
  principles used to organize, 39–42
  proximal, 62
  proximity used to organize, 40
  selecting, organizing, and
    interpreting, 36
  selection of, 37–39
  similarity used to organize, 40
  simplicity and pattern used to
    organize, 39–40
Structural coding
  convention of invisibility, 347
  expectation of continuity of space, 347
  verisimilitude, 348
  visual time cues, 347–348
Students. *See* Children
Symbolic codes, 346
Symbolic communication, 138
Symbols
  additions changing meaning, 138
  approaches to study of, 136–137
  arbitrary symbols, 136–137
  as communication, 137–138
  compared with indexual and iconic
    signs, 137
  concrete to abstract continuum of, 137
  as control, 137, 140–141
  deriving meaning from cultural
    convention, 137
  emotional power of, 140–141
  expressive function of, 136, 137,
    139–140
  functional symbols, 137
  functioning as signs, 137
  graphic, 137
  graphics as, 185
  Greek meaning of symbol, 36
  as instruments of thought, 301–302
  intuitive function of, 136
  as knowledge, 137, 138–139
  levels of use of, 137–141
  natural, arbitrary, and functional
    origins of, 136–137
  natural symbols, 136
  objects as, 158–159
  pictorial, 137
  in political cartoons, 141–143
  as power, 137
  taking on emotional meaning, 140
  verbal, 137

T

Technical coding, 348–350
  camera shots, 349–350
  composition, 348–349
  composition rules, 348–349
Technology
  achievement of, implied as being
    desirable, 318
  seen as social technology, 317
Television
  See also Mass media
  children's programming not serving
    children, 377
  commercials, 11
  immorality of most programming for
    children, 377–378
  limited number of words important in
    visuals, 179
  persistence of vision and phi factor
    allowing perception of motion,
    340–341
  as transmitter of popular culture,
    356–357
  violence in, and children, 377–378
Temporal lobe, 58
Text, 203–204
  for computer images, 211–213
  improving text display, 220–221
  legibility of, 177–179, 211, 213, 250
Texture, in visuals, 170
3-D models, 185–186
Transaction theory, 13
Transformation, as a function of visuals,
  241, 242
2 x 2 slides, 260
Typographical cuing, 203
Typography, 203

U

Unity, in design of visuals, 179, 179
Universal grammar, 7, 22
Utilitarianism, 274

V

Values
  affected by culture, 42
  defined, 43
Verbal, as a noun, 194
Verbal elements
  matrix of support relationships with
    visual elements, 196
  spoken (dynamic), 195
  written (static), 195
Verbal information
  coded differently from visual
    information, 73–75
  not remembered as well as visual
    information, 74
Verbal language
  See also Language
  analogy with visual language, 19–22
  characteristics compared with visual
    language, 101–102
  context for, 101–102
  linguistics providing connection with
    visual language, 8
  overemphasis on, inhibiting creative
    thinking, 10–11
  sequential nature of, 101
  supplemented by body language, 147
  verbal/visual language continuum,
    19–21
  visual language promoting learning
    of, 10
Verbal learning, following visual
    learning, 9–10
Verbally dominated graphics, 201–202
Verbal symbols, 137. *See also* Symbols
Verbo-audio-visual language, 195
Verbo-visual language, 195
Verisimilitude, 348
Vestibular systems, 56, 57
Virtual reality, 228–229
Virtue theory, 374–375
Visible language
  defined, 203
  outline graphics as, 205
  printing conventions, 203–204

typographical cuing, 203
typography, 203
Vision
  as a cognitive activity, 247
  basic anatomy of the eye, 55–56
  basic principles of theory of, 18–19
  neurophysiological factors, 54–55
  occipital lobe in the brain, 58
  persistence of vision and phi factor
    allowing perception of motion,
    340–341
  primary visual area in the brain, 58
  seeing as a complex process, 20
  spatial organization of stimuli, 61
  using eye and brain, 114
Visual
  as a noun, 194
  defined, 194
Visual cognition, 72–75
  See also Human cognition
  controversy over imaginal storage,
    72–73
  dual coding model, 73–75
  limits on visual processing, 75
Visual communication, 108
  See also Communication; Human
    communication
  graphics as a form of, 184, 186–188,
    190
  innate grammar of images of, 7–8
  process of, 4
  provided by computers, 210
Visual content, morally controversial,
    371
Visual cues, personal appearance
    providing, 148–149
Visual detail
  meaningful organization aiding recall,
    77
  not important for recognition, 77
Visual elements, matrix of support
    relationships with verbal elements,
    196
Visual environment of schools, 236–238
  encouraging individual expression,
    237
Visual images, 72. *See also* Images
Visual information
  coded differently from verbal
    information, 73–75
  importance of knowledge about,
    289–290

Visual information *(continued)*
  interpreting creatively, 289–290
  meaningful interpretation essential,
    278
  remembered better than verbal
    information, 74
Visualization
  popularity of, 385
  as rehearsal, 384
  uses of, 383–384
  where to use to maximize student
    achievement, 388
Visualization skills, 284–286
  visualizing from new perspectives, 285
  visualizing richly and colorfully,
    284–285
  visualizing the inside, 286
Visual language
  See also Language; Verbal language
  analogy with verbal language, 19–22
  analyzed like verbal language, 6–8
  characteristics compared with verbal
    language, 101–102
  concept of, 194
  context for, 101–102
  innate grammar of images of, 7–8
  linguistics providing connection with
    verbal language, 8
  promoting learning of verbal
    language, 10
  simultaneous nature of, 101
  spoken form of, 20
  verbal/visual language analogy, 19–21
  written form of, 20, 203–205
Visual learning, 107
  See also Learning
  creative thinking defined in relation
    to, 287
  creativity applied to, 278–279
  differentiation stage of, 279
  factors affecting effectiveness of
    environment for, 394
  frames of reference important to, 36
  interpretation stage of, 279–281
  preceding verbal learning, 9–10
  sound localization important to, 61
  two meanings of, 107
Visual literacy
  allied with middle stage of children's
    development, 12
  analogy with verbal language, 6–8
  art studies as, 17

basis of, 5
as a concept, 6–21, 97–100
concept derived from perceptionists,
  12–13, 22
concept ill-defined, 103–104
concepts supporting rationale for, 14
conferences, 100–101
connection with creative thinking,
  280–281
as a construct, 100–103
contribution of art to, 8–11, 22
contribution of linguistics to, 6–8,
  21–22
contribution of philosophy to, 15–21,
  24
contribution of psychology to, 11–15,
  22
defining parameters for, 11–12
definition of, 25
essential in achieving two way
  communication, 188
as an essential skill, 17
evolution of definition of, 103–104
importance of, 21, 99, 108
importance of duplication,
  polarization, and interconnection of
  eyes, ears, and brain, 54–55
incorporating into classroom, 357
increasing need for, 21
innate abilities for, 99
interpretations of, 3
and judging images, 108
metaphor in relation to, 15–18, 24
and mind research, 22
needed for deriving information from
  graphics, 187–188
need for, 99–100
neither concept nor construct, 102–103
and nonverbal languages, 9
operational definitions difficult to
  construct, 104
operationalized in terms of visual
  learning, thinking, and
  communication, 104, 105–106
perception as a component of, 3, 22.
  See also Perception
research needs, 11, 103
roots of, 3
and television commercials, 11
terms defined, 20
terms not well defined, 103
theoretical foundations, 21–24

Visual literacy (continued)
  as thinking process, 25
  training needed for, 14–15, 17, 21–22
  visual thinking an important aspect
    of, 25–26
  visual thinking as internal reaction
    stage of, 104, 106–107
  and visual thinking concept, 10, 22
Visual literacy movement, 24
Visual literacy training
  importance of, 14–15
  need for, 17
  rationale for, 21–22
  readiness for, 14–15
Visually dominated graphics, 200
Visual media
  options for, 239
  pervasiveness of, 277–278
Visual messages
  differentiation stage of learning from,
    279
  interpretation stage of learning from,
    279–281
  morally controversial content of, 371
  thinking creatively about, 289
Visual noise, 237
Visual perception, 4
  See also Perception
  shaped by language, 38–39
  as stimulus-response process, 60
Visual perspective, creativity associated
    with alternatives in, 285
Visual processing, limits on, 75
Visual research
  experimental rationale for, 385–386
  instructional consistency/congruency
    paradigm as conceptual rationale
    for, 388–391
  problems with, 386
  Program of Systematic Evaluation
    (PSE) to identify effective types of
    visual materials, 391–399
  visual testing as a topic for, 386–388
  visual testing complicating
    interpretation of, 386–387
Visuals
  See also Business visuals; Graphics;
    Images; Pictures; Representations;
    Visuals in schools
  active reading of, 317
  analytic graphics, 270–271
  attention role of, 197

decoding, 279–281
deconstructing, 316
decoration function of, 241
degree of realism in, 196
design elements for, 166–172
design principles for, 173–181
details not important for recognition,
  77
displaying in print, 203
document visuals, 261
dynamic, 195
ease of creating, 165–166
effect of, on reader or learner, 199
electronic, 260
ethical importance of understanding,
  370
expertise impacting memory for, 77
explicative role, 197
eye movements necessary when
  studying, 247–248
factors determining ability to learn
  from, 236
guidelines for using to illustrate text,
  199–200
importance of, 72
interpretation function of, 241, 242
linking visuals, 267, 270
meaningful organization of details
  aiding recall, 77
morally controversial, 371
morally questionable, dealing with,
  378
morally questionable uses of, 371–372
morals and ethics applied to, 370
need for analysis of, 378
organization function of, 241
personal, 195
political uses of, 141–143, 187, 372
positive moral and ethical purposes
  of, 372
presentation visuals, 271–272
Program of Systematic Evaluation
  (PSE) to identify effective types of
  visual materials, 391–399
reading, 247, 248, 317
representation function of, 241
retention role, 197
roles in text, 197–200
static, 195
supporting visuals, 267, 270
as teachers, 356–357
in teaching, 72, 73

Visuals *(continued)*
  in testing, 386–388
  transformation function of, 241
  types of, 195–196
  used to influence and manipulate, 370
  used to organize incoming
    information, 77
  viewers constructed for, 302
  visual content of, 371
  visual purposes of, 371–372
Visual schema and "priming," 77
Visuals in schools, 238–248
  checklist for uses of, 244
  in cooperative learning, 245
  educators' ethical responsibilities,
    355–356, 369–370
  found images, 246–247
  guidelines for legibility, 250
  illustrating and adding to text,
    240–241
  for induction activities, 245
  for learning tasks involving memory,
    240
  media options, 239
  motivational use of, 244
  multiple uses of, 246
  simplicity important, 247–248
  for specific purposes, 246
  student preferences for, 248–249
  types to use, 239
  visuals as objects vs. visuals as tools,
    250
  ways to use, 244–247
  when to use, 240–242
  where to use, 249–250
  who will use, 247–248
  why to use, 242–244
Visual stimulation
  process of, 60–61
  threefold process of, 62

Visual stimuli
  as nonverbal metaphors, 16
  as pieces of an object, 60, 61
Visual symbols. *See* Symbols
Visual testing, 386–388
  arguments for, 387
Visual thinking
  defined, 104, 106
  essential to creativity and
    problem-solving, 99
  importance of, 25–26
  as internal reaction stage of visual
    literacy, 104, 106–107
  sources of imagery for, 107
  as visualization through images, 106
  visual literacy as a means of, 22
Visual thinking concept, 10
Visual time cues, 347–348
Visual-verbal discontinuity, 193–194
Visual/verbal relationships
  categorizations of, 197
  degree of visualization vs. degree of
    verbalization, 196–197
  matrix of support relationships, 196
  printed words, 203–204
  verbally dominated graphics,
    201–202
  visually dominated graphics, 200
  Wileman's typology of, 197
Visual-verbal symbiosis, 193
Vitreous humor, 55

W

Western theoretic traditions, 372–375
Whorf-Sapir Hypothesis, 38–39
Wileman's typology of visual/verbal
  relationships, 197
Written verbal elements, 195